Michigan Government, Politics, and Policy

◆ Michigan Government, Politics, and Policy

Edited by
JOHN S. KLEMANSKI
and
DAVID A. DULIO

UNIVERSITY OF MICHIGAN PRESS
ANN ARBOR

Copyright © 2017 by John S. Klemanski and David A. Dulio
All rights reserved

This book may not be reproduced, in whole or in part, including illustrations, in any form (beyond that copying permitted by Sections 107 and 108 of the U.S. Copyright Law and except by reviewers for the public press), without written permission from the publisher.

Published in the United States of America by the
University of Michigan Press
Manufactured in the United States of America
♾ Printed on acid-free paper

2020 2019 2018 2017   4 3 2 1

A CIP catalog record for this book is available from the British Library.

Library of Congress Cataloging-in-Publication Data

Names: Klemanski, John S., editor. | Dulio, David A., editor.
Title: Michigan government, politics, and policy / edited by John S. Klemanski and David A. Dulio.
Description: Ann Arbor : University of Michigan Press, 2017. | Includes bibliographical references and index.
Identifiers: LCCN 2017012500| ISBN 9780472037001 (paperback) | ISBN 9780472123261 (e-book)
Subjects: LCSH: Michigan—Politics and government. | Local government—Michigan. | BISAC: POLITICAL SCIENCE / Government / State & Provincial.
Classification: LCC JK5816 .M53 2017 | DDC 320.4774—dc23
LC record available at https://lccn.loc.gov/2017012500

For
Sheryl
J.S.K.

and

Adrianne
D.A.D.

✦ Contents

Preface and Acknowledgments ix

1 Introduction to Michigan Government, Politics, and Policy 1
   John S. Klemanski and David A. Dulio

FOUNDATIONAL ELEMENTS

2 Michigan's Constitution 29
   Joyce Baugh

3 Federalism and Intergovernmental Relations in Michigan 52
   Dale Thomson

4 Local Governments in Michigan I: Urban Governments
   and Detroit 78
   Lyke Thompson and Robert J. Mahu

5 Local Governments in Michigan II: Michigan's Rural Areas
   and Small Towns 100
   Thomas J. Greitens and J. Cherie Strachan

POLITICAL INSTITUTIONS

6 Michigan's Governor and Executive Branch 123
   Mitchel A. Sollenberger

7 Michigan's Legislature 148
   Kevin G. Lorentz II and Timothy Bledsoe

8 Michigan's Court System 170
   Mark R. Beougher and Mark S. Hurwitz

POLITICAL ACTORS AND PROCESSES

9 Political Parties and Interest Groups in Michigan 197
   James M. Strickland and Logan T. Woods

| 10 | Elections and Political Participation in Michigan
John A. Clark | 221 |
| 11 | Ballot Proposals in Michigan
John S. Klemanski and David A. Dulio | 246 |

PUBLIC POLICY CASE STUDIES

12	Education Policy in Michigan *Douglas Carr*	269
13	Budget and Fiscal Policy in Michigan *Mitch Bean*	293
14	Economic Development Policy in Michigan *Richard Jelier*	316
15	Flint's Water Crisis: A Case Study in Historical Context, Decline, Responses to Challenges, and State-Local Government Relations *Paul Rozycki*	343
16	Conclusion *John S. Klemanski and David A. Dulio*	364

| *List of Contributors* | 377 |
| *Index* | 383 |

✦ Preface and Acknowledgments

When we began this project, Michigan was squarely between two of the most important and significant events in the state's history—Detroit's bankruptcy had ended and the city was transitioning back to local control; and details of the Flint water crisis were just beginning to become known more widely. While these two events were certainly well chronicled in the national and international press, the decades of difficulties experienced by the state of Michigan, which contributed to both events, run much deeper. Indeed, the state has faced a general and far-reaching economic downturn. Included here is the most recent economic decline that saw Michigan suffer as the hardest-hit state in the "Great Recession" that struck the nation at the end of the first decade of the 2000s. Among the sectors of the economy hit the hardest were automobile manufacturers, as evidenced by declared bankruptcies of both General Motors and Chrysler LLC (which later became Chrysler Group LLC, and Fiat US LLC, and then Fiat Chrysler Automobile (FCA)).

The economic decline experienced by the state was only the tip of the iceberg, as political and economic leaders faced many additional challenges in the state. In many instances the state has seen declines in areas related to the economy or which sprang from economic decline. For instance, Michigan was the only state in the United States to experience a net population loss between 2000 and 2010. Residents left the state looking for jobs elsewhere in response to the troubling economic times. In addition, Michigan saw some of the highest unemployment rates during the "lost decade" of the Great Recession.

The challenges experienced by the state have, as one would expect, also led to policy responses by the government. Detroit entered into bankruptcy and struggled with the austerity budget that its emergency manager imposed. Emergency managers served in several other Michigan cities as well, including Ecorse, Flint, Benton Harbor, and Pontiac. Given this recent history of decline and subsequent policy responses, two of the underlying themes of this volume are *decline* and *responses to challenges*. As readers will discover in the chapters that follow, some responses to these challenges have been more successful than others. The book also includes two other themes that are critical to understanding the context surrounding the first two. Both Michigan's *historical context* and *state-local government relations* are key factors in both the decline that has been seen and the responses to the challenges faced.

This volume brings together scholars from across the state of Michigan and provides a comprehensive analysis of the foundational aspects of government (e.g., the Michigan Constitution, intergovernmental relations), the state's political institutions (i.e., the state Legislature, governor, and court system), politics (e.g., political parties and elections), and areas of public policy critical to the state (i.e., education, the budget, and economic development). We have included a separate case study chapter on the Flint water crisis that uses our book's themes to help describe and explain how that city's history of decline and attempts to stop that decline contributed to the crisis and its aftermath.

We believe the early portion of the 21st century is an important time for the state, which drives the need for a scholarly examination of many of the issues the state has faced and continues to confront. We view this volume not only as a valuable tool for students who are studying issues related to state politics, state-local relations, and Michigan politics specifically, but also for members of the general public who are interested in how the state has come through the difficult times it unquestionably has faced. As political scientists in Michigan, we see it as part of our duty to help people in Michigan understand issues of government, politics, and policy in our state to not only understand what has happened in the past but to be able to look to the future for what are hopefully better and more prosperous times.

We would like to thank the Department of Political Science at Oakland University for providing support and encouragement of our scholarly work over time and of this volume in particular. We also would like to thank the University of Michigan Press and its editorial and production staff, especially Production Editor Kevin M. Rennells, and Acquiring Editor Scott Ham who not only guided us in our work but who showed tremendous belief in our ideas. Finally, we would like to thank the University of Michigan; both of us are undergraduate alums from the University. Our time in Ann Arbor started us on our own career paths and is a big reason why we are able to work on a project like this. We are grateful for that and are delighted to represent Michigan with this volume.

John S. Klemanski *and* David A. Dulio
Rochester, Michigan
March 2017

1 ✦ Introduction to Michigan Government, Politics, and Policy

JOHN S. KLEMANSKI AND DAVID A. DULIO

The state of Michigan is known for many characteristics and qualities—automobile manufacturing; the Great Lakes and miles of shoreline; extensive forests and inland rivers for hunting, fishing, and recreation; its two peninsulas and abundant natural resources; Mackinac Island; and popular music from Motown to Madonna, from Glenn Frey to Eminem, and from Kid Rock to Jack White. Early on, the natural beauty and resources of the state first brought many people from the U.S. northeast for the fur and timber trade. Later, immigrants primarily from southern and eastern Europe, and newcomers from the U.S. south came to work in Michigan's factories. In particular, the city of Detroit grew substantially as it became the automobile capital of the world in the first half of the 20th century, increasing from 465,766 residents in 1910 to its peak of 1,849,568 in 1950.[1] News stories at the beginning of this growth period reported on the thousands of people who flocked to Michigan for high-paying jobs in the auto industry.[2] According to census figures for both 1950 and 1960, the city of Detroit was the wealthiest (per capita) large city in the United States.

The second half of the 20th century was more a story of decline, especially for industrialized Michigan cities such as Detroit, Flint, and Pontiac. The history of this decline and the governmental attempts to deal with this decline comprise the heuristic themes of this book. In order to better understand Michigan government, politics, and policy, each chapter will present the state through the following analytical framework:

- historical context
- decline

- responses to challenges
- state-local government relations

While more detail about the book's themes are provided later in this chapter, two major stories involving Michigan reveal the importance of these themes—and how connected the themes are to each other. As readers will see throughout all of the chapters of this book, these four themes are a useful way of analyzing and understanding the fortunes of Michigan, and they help explain why certain government actions were taken.

These themes are illustrated in two recent and historic events in Michigan—the Flint water crisis and the City of Detroit's bankruptcy. These two events captured the attention of the national and international media, and caused state and local policymakers to respond to the challenges that each crisis brought to the state. Each of these stories involves a history of decline in a major Michigan city, attempts to respond to the challenges posed by this decline, and investigates state-local government relations. In many instances, we note how new government policies intending to fix a problem ultimately created a new set of problems. There also is a more specific connection between these two events because at the time they occurred both Detroit and Flint were operating under a controversial emergency manager (EM) law, which gave state-appointed individuals extensive powers to run financially troubled cities in Michigan.

Flint Water Crisis

In its March 2016 Final Report, the Flint Water Advisory Task Force transmitted its findings to Governor Rick Snyder. The Task Force began its report by noting that "[t]he Flint water crisis is a story of government failure, intransigence, unpreparedness, delay, inaction, and environmental injustice."[3] This story is particularly important to students of Michigan government and politics, because it touches directly on numerous political and policy decisions made by state elected officials and civil servants. The Flint water crisis also reveals the challenges facing a declining city with an aging infrastructure, tensions between state and local officials, and the relationship between state government and its citizens.

Since 1967, the City of Flint had been a customer of the Detroit Water and Sewerage Department (on January 1, 2016, a regional body called the Great Lakes Water Authority began to operate the water system as part of the city's reorganization of assets and responsibilities after bankruptcy). In 2013, in an effort to save money (under the advice of a consultant and urging by Flint's emergency manager), the Flint City Council decided to join a separate water system called the Karegnondi Water Authority, which was composed of mid-Michigan communities located in Michigan's Thumb area. Construction of a new pipeline would take over two years, so Flint intended to remain with the Detroit water system until 2016, when it could connect to the new system. However, in 2013, shortly after receiving notice of Flint's intent to leave its system, the Detroit water system informed Flint that it would terminate water services in 2014. This meant that Flint would need a water source for about two years, until the Karegnondi water system was operational.

In a separate decision, Flint's emergency manager decided to use water from the Flint River (the city's water source in its early years) prior to connecting to the new water system. However, shortly after switching, residents began complaining of discolored and murky water, water with a bad odor and taste, and rashes on children as well as other health problems. Federal, state, and local officials initially dismissed these complaints and claimed that such problems were temporary due to seasonal differences or other temporary causes. However, within a few months, city officials issued "boil water" advisories after *E coli* bacteria were found in samples of city tap water. The Michigan Department of Environmental Quality (MDEQ) continued to publicly dismiss the complaints and blamed weather, old pipes, and the city's declining population for problems with the water.

After months of complaints, Detroit offered to reconnect Flint to its system in January 2015 (and to waive the reconnection fee). However, the Flint EM at the time declined the offer. Advisors to the governor continued to downplay problems and claim no imminent public health risks existed. However, in early 2015, unsafe levels of lead were found in Flint's drinking water. A federal Environmental Protection Agency official voiced some concern, but his concerns were ignored by the MDEQ. In subsequent months, more samples of Flint River water found high levels of lead, and medical professionals in the city began finding high levels of lead in the blood samples of the city's children. By late September 2015, Governor Snyder, in a joint phone call with federal and state regulators, was officially briefed on the lead problems in Flint's water.

Shortly after that, the governor ordered the distribution of water filters to residents, testing of drinking water in Flint schools, and an increase in blood testing of residents. By October 16, 2015—about 18 months after Flint began using the Flint River as its water source—the city was reconnected to Detroit's water system. Residents were warned to continue the ban on using unfiltered tap water for drinking, cooking, or bathing (as the water system still needed to flush completely). About this same time, the director of the MDEQ, Dan Wyant, reported that his department had misapplied federal protocols for corrosion control. The caustic nature of the Flint River, without sufficient corrosion controls, caused the water pipes to leach lead into Flint's water. Moreover, between 2014 and 2015, almost 100 cases of Legionnaires' disease occurred in the Flint area, which ultimately led to 12 deaths.[4] The connection between Legionnaires and Flint's switch to the Flint River as a water source had not been fully established, but several investigations were mounted.

The Flint water crisis became a national and international news story by 2016, and came to involve hearings in the U.S. Congress, a variety of lawsuits, recall petitions being circulated against Governor Snyder, and a presentation to the United Nations by a group of activists. The Flint water crisis brings together each of this book's four themes in a powerful way. Understanding the current water crisis requires an appreciation of the city's history. Flint's history is about early growth but also a long economic decline—intimately tied to the fortunes of the General Motors Corporation, which had established a major presence in the city beginning in the 1930s. The city grew in the 1940s and 1950s, but beginning in the 1970s, General Motors began to leave the city (leading to Michael Moore's 1989 film, *Roger and Me*, which chronicled the downsizing of GM facilities in the Flint area and its effects on the city). In 1987, *Money* magazine had placed Flint last out of 300 metropolitan areas to live in America. In more recent years, Flint has often made the list of the "worst places to live" in the United States, largely due to high crime rates, a poor school system, high levels of unemployment, high poverty rates, and deteriorating housing values.[5] The city's population was 193,317 in 1970, but that declined to 98,310 in 2015, according to the U.S. Census Bureau.[6]

As part of Flint's decline, the city government faced an all-too-common story in older industrial cities in the United States. The city government's many financial challenges ultimately led to appointment of an EM by Governor Jennifer Granholm (a Democrat) in 2002, and several others by Governor Snyder (a Republican) between 2011 and 2015. The issue of a state-appointed EM with extensive decision-making powers has been a controversial one. In effect, an EM renders local elected officials essentially powerless; critics claim that this destroys the democratically elected governments in the areas where EMs are placed.

Partisans on both sides tried to blame the other side for the problems surrounding Flint's water crisis. Republicans blamed the federal Environmental Protection Agency and local Flint officials, while Democrats blamed

Governor Snyder for his appointments to the Michigan Departments of Environmental Quality and Health and Human Services. Democrats also blamed the governor for the decisions made by appointed emergency managers (in both Flint and Detroit, which was partly to blame for Flint's split from Detroit's water system in the first place), and for failing to act quickly enough and in a more transparent way. In the meantime, a number of class action lawsuits were being considered and filed throughout 2016, and petitions to recall Governor Snyder were circulated.

But Flint's story is useful also because it underscores a common occurrence related to one theme of this book. Several discussions related to the *responses to challenges* theme involved a story in which the policy response to a challenge itself became a problem. The history of Michigan's public policies includes many examples of attempts to fix a problem, only to have that policy fix become a problem later on. For example, the appointment of an emergency manager for Flint was a response to the budget challenges Flint faced. In attempting to respond to the city's many budget challenges, the emergency manager and city officials sought a cheaper alternative to increasing costs of participating in the Detroit water system. The Flint Water Advisory Task Force was commissioned by Governor Snyder to investigate the causes of Flint's water problems. In the end, the task force placed most of the blame on the MDEQ. However, it also noted that all levels of government failed, and summarized its findings in a March 2016 report: "The conclusion we made in December 2015 that primary responsibility for causing the Flint water crisis rests with the MDEQ has only been substantiated by our subsequent interviews and research. This final report, however, documents the failings, shortcomings and problems in other agencies and entities as well, such as MDHHS [Michigan Department of Health and Human Services], GCHD [Genesee County Health Department], the local water treatment plant, the Emergency Manager structure, the Governor's office, and the U.S. EPA [Environmental Protection Agency]."[7]

Detroit's Bankruptcy

As with the Flint water crisis, the story of Detroit's bankruptcy is first about history—Detroit saw massive economic and population growth in the first half of the 20th century—but also about economic decline in the second half of the 20th century. As with Flint, again, much of Detroit's decline came once automobile manufacturers began to leave the city. Both cities lost population and local tax revenue, while being forced to deal with higher rates of crime, unemployment, and poverty.

The city of Detroit declared Chapter 9 bankruptcy in July 2013, with over $18 billion in debt. The city's government was faced with high legacy costs owed to retirees, a declining population and tax base, poor city services, a major problem with nonfunctioning streetlights, and other problems. Under bankruptcy, about $7 billion of the $18 billion of debt was forgiven, but the city still needed cooperation from a variety of actors—including the governor and Legislature, nonprofit foundations, the city's retirees, financial creditors, and a federal bankruptcy court—to create a path for the city out of bankruptcy but also with a plan that would keep the city from becoming bankrupt again.

A delicate negotiation among the major players occurred in the early months of the city's bankruptcy. Two major items were at stake that became the centerpiece of what became known as the "grand bargain." Those items were needed to provide some level of protection from substantial benefit cuts to the city's retirees, and protection from creditors of the valuable art collection held by the city's Detroit Institute of Arts. The bargain that was struck required that foundations, the State of Michigan, and the Detroit Institute of Arts raise $816 million in order to save the art collection and to minimize cuts to the city's over 30,000 retirees.[8] The negotiations were particularly tricky because the nonprofit foundations had never dispersed so much money (the Ford Foundation had pledged $125 million; the Knight Foundation pledged $30 million; and the Kresge Foundation pledged $100 million). In addition, the leaders of the Detroit Institute of Arts pledged to raise $100 million from its donors. With these pledges, the Michigan Legislature (which originally was not inclined to support the bankrupt city) provided $350 million over a 20-year period, along with a provision for state financial oversight of the city once it had exited from bankruptcy.[9]

While Detroit's financial troubles culminated in the largest municipal bankruptcy ever at the time, the city was able to successfully emerge from bankruptcy on December 10, 2014, less than two years after first declaring it. On that day, Michigan's governor, Rick Snyder, and Detroit's mayor, Mike Duggan, met with the press to discuss Detroit's exit from bankruptcy. Detroit was able to leave bankruptcy much more quickly than many had predicted, and it allowed the city to shed almost half of its debt, restructure nearly $3 billion more, and invest about $1.7 billion into badly needed city services such as police and fire, as well as public transportation.[10]

The story of Detroit's bankruptcy fits well within the framework of this book's four themes. The historical context of the city's growth and decline helps us understand the city's reliance on the automobile industry.

For example, the high legacy costs (in the general retirement fund, but especially for police officers and firefighters) grew in part because city leaders assumed they would be able to pay these obligations well into the future because the high-paying automobile industry jobs would be around forever and the City would continue to enjoy a large tax base. That turned out to be a poor assumption.

Decline for Detroit (and for Michigan generally) came as the automobile industry left the city and the state. Detroit's population grew as the auto industry grew, but the city suffered first as people began to move to the suburbs in the 1950s, then later as the auto companies began to build smaller factories in the South or in other countries. Automation and improved production technologies also reduced the labor force in the auto industry during the second half of the 20th century.

The declaration of bankruptcy and the subsequent negotiations that sought to bring Detroit out of bankruptcy were responses to one of the most dire challenges that can face a city or a state. While the grand bargain has been received positively by many, some observers remained concerned about the long-term sustainability of the city's finances.[11]

This story also reveals a number of important state and local government interactions necessary for the successful emergence of the city from bankruptcy. Governor Snyder helped broker a number of agreements among the major actors involved, and the Michigan Legislature approved over $300 million in aid to Detroit. The governor also had appointed Kevyn Orr as EM to the city, who helped shepherd the local government through the bankruptcy process.

Of course, the appointment of an EM was controversial in Detroit as it was in Flint and other cities where EMs were in place. The appointment of Orr was vigorously questioned early on after the state law that allowed for emergency managers (Public Act 4) was repealed by voters in a statewide proposal on the 2012 ballot. A mere 13 days later, the Michigan Legislature passed and the governor signed a new emergency manager law (Public Act 436, the Local Fiscal Stability and Choice Act) that replaced the previous law and paved the way for Governor Snyder to appoint an EM in Detroit. The purpose of the original EM law was to put fiscally distressed cities on the path to recovery and prevent municipal bankruptcies. While other states also allow for EMs, Michigan's laws have been considered more extreme, in that the EM had greater powers compared to other states.[12] Many criticized the new law as a strike against local democracy as it meant that duly elected local officials were stripped of their financial decision-making authority. Such powers were then placed into the hands of individuals who were not elected and who did not answer to the public. Many also saw partisan and racial components to this move, noting that the Republican governor and Republican-controlled Legislature imposed the EM on a city with a population over 80 percent African American.[13] The controversy continued through the bankruptcy negotiations as many individuals and groups needed to make concessions that many considered too deep. For instance, in the final agreement, roughly 32,000 city retirees saw their pensions and health care coverage cut, some by up to 4.5 percent, with additional cuts to previously agreed upon yearly cost-of-living adjustments.[14]

The driving force behind Detroit's bankruptcy was the city's declining fiscal health. At the time Detroit declared bankruptcy, unemployment in the city was 18.6 percent.[15] The national unemployment rate at the time was 7.3 percent,[16] while Michigan's unemployment at the time was the highest in the nation at 10.6 percent.[17] We have already noted the city's declining population, but its remaining residents tended to be much poorer than in previous decades. For example, the per capita income in the city at the time was only roughly $15,000.[18]

While the focus of this book centers on the state of Michigan, a brief set of comparisons to the nation as a whole and to other states can provide a useful context. The section below provides comparisons between Michigan and other states, especially regarding economic indicators. By doing so, the themes of historical context and decline are reinforced and offer a framework for understanding Michigan government, politics, and policy.

Michigan in Comparison

When considering the 50 U.S. states, one great lesson learned quite early is that states vary. This variation can be seen in some obvious ways, including climate, topography, and population. But states vary considerably within the context of government and politics as well. The U.S. system of federalism allows states to determine their own policy paths on many issues, subject to protections granted by the U.S. Constitution and the establishment of federal minimum standards (see chapter 3). Therefore, it should not be surprising that Michigan has both similarities and differences with other states in its range of policies and approaches to its residents, its economy, and what the state considers the proper role of government in society. Moreover, Michigan can be placed in context relative to the rest of the nation; this also highlights important factors that have to be accounted for in Michigan government, politics, and policy.

Michigan vs. the Nation

We begin by comparing some of Michigan's economic indicators with U.S. averages. This comparison allows us to identify measures where Michigan may fall below the overall national average, but also any areas where Michigan can be considered above average. Not surprisingly, many of the economic struggles faced by Detroit over the past 25 years also occurred across the entire state. Whether it is high unemployment, low per capita income, population loss, or negative gross domestic product growth, Michigan has tended to suffer in both social and economic terms compared to the rest of the United States.

Certainly the entire nation felt the dramatic economic difficulties during the Great Recession of the late 2000s. Across the nation, unemployment was up while incomes and gross domestic product were down. However, on nearly every measure these indicators were worse in Michigan. As seen in figure 1.1, at the height of the recession—2008—when the entire U.S. economy was slowing down and getting smaller, Michigan's was contracting even more severely. As illustrated in figure 1.1, the state saw negative growth in gross domestic product (GDP) of nearly 5.5 percent while the U.S. economy shrank at a rate of just over 2 percent. In addition, throughout the late 1990s and into the 2010s, Michigan's GDP performed worse than the nation's, with only a few exceptions.

On multiple conventional measures between the late 1990s and 2010s, Michigan experienced a decline that was, in many instances, more extreme than one felt by the nation as a whole. Much of Michigan's decline can be attributed to the disappearance of manufacturing jobs or the movement of those jobs elsewhere. As is well known, Michigan has historically been a center of automobile manufacturing. As shown in figure 1.2, the number of manufacturing jobs in the state dropped after reaching a high of nearly 900,000 jobs in 1999 to almost half that number in 2009. This exodus of jobs has had an impact on a number of state and local government dynamics including the tax base—fewer jobs means fewer tax dollars for the state and local governments.

Prior to the 2000s, Republican governor John Engler had sought to address the state's decline by promoting a personal income tax reduction and a reform of the state's business tax. During his tenure, the state government also invested in infrastructure projects and promoted a "Life Sciences Corridor" to encourage research in biotechnology that could lead to economic development benefits for the state. A more recent effort began in the early 2000s under Democratic governor Jennifer Granholm to further diversify

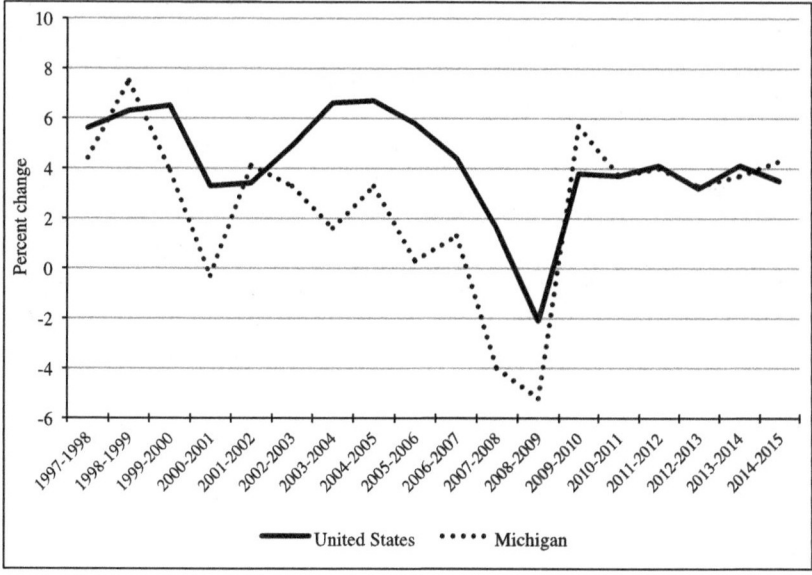

Fig. 1.1. Percent Change from Preceding Period in Gross Domestic Product for Michigan and the United States, 1997–2015
Source: "Regional Data: GDP in Current Dollars," U.S. Bureau of Economic Analysis, accessed October 28, 2016, http://www.bea.gov/itable/iTable.cfm?ReqID=70&step=1#reqid=70&step=10&isuri=1&7003=200&7035=-1&7004=naics&7005=-1&7006=00000,26000&7036=-1&7001=1200&7002=1&7090=70&7007=-1&7093=levels

the state's economy. Some of these policies—which included tax incentives and subsidies to encourage business investment by alternative energy companies, and those in the life sciences, tourism, and the film industry—were more successful than others.

Michigan's experience with economic indicators lagging behind the nation's is also found on two other key measures—unemployment and per capita income—that can both be tied, at least in part, to the disappearance of manufacturing jobs. Figure 1.3 shows the unemployment rate in Michigan and the United States from the mid-1970s through 2014. At least two important facts can be drawn from this figure. First, around the height of the recession, Michigan's unemployment spiked to nearly 14 percent; we noted above that the unemployment rate in Detroit at the time was over 18 percent, but other localities found themselves in a similar situation. According to the State of Michigan's Department of Technology, Management and Budget, 15 Michigan cities had an unemployment rate in 2008 of over 10 percent with Detroit, Flint, Pontiac, and Highland Park all hav-

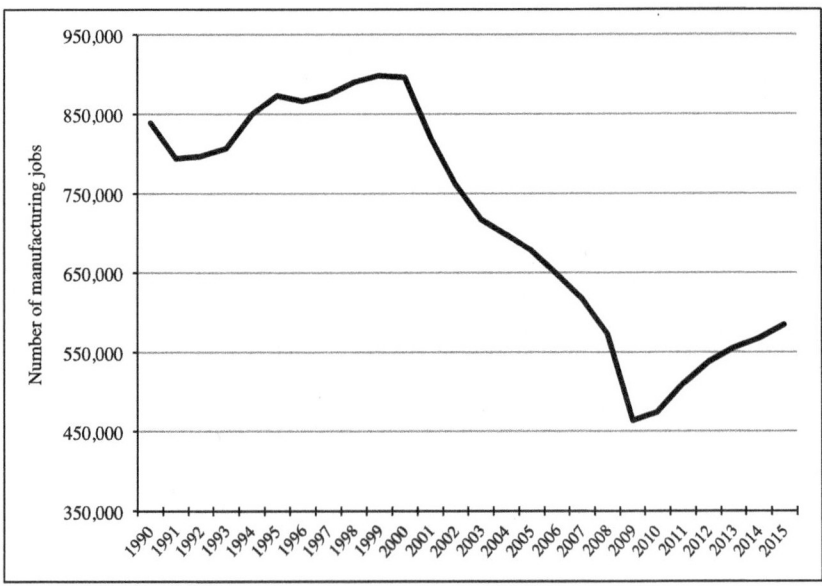

Fig. 1.2. Number of Manufacturing Jobs in Michigan, 1990–2015
Source: Michigan Department of Technology, Management and Budget; accessed March 30, 2015, http://milmi.org/cgi/dataanalysis/AreaSelection.asp?tableName=Ces

ing rates above 15 percent. Responding to this challenge, the state made a number of cuts in the fiscal year 2011, including reducing funding for the state police, reducing aid to state universities, and cutting $42 million from prisons. These were critical times across the state and many were looking to government for solutions to the economic and budgetary distress.

With the exception of a short time period between the mid-1990s and early 2000s, the unemployment rate in Michigan was higher than across the United States. In addition, when a spike in unemployment occurred nationally (i.e., 1982, 1991, 2003, and 2008), a larger spike was seen in Michigan. This trend mirrors that of state versus national GDP found in figure 1.1. In addition to high unemployment rates, Michigan suffered from reduced income levels. Income in Michigan saw a similar dramatic decline around the time of the Great Recession and was worse than the national trends. Figure 1.4 shows that prior to 2003, median household income in Michigan was actually higher than the national average, dating back to the mid-1980s.

These figures that paint a partial picture of Michigan's economic health clearly show the economic stress found in the state for quite a number of

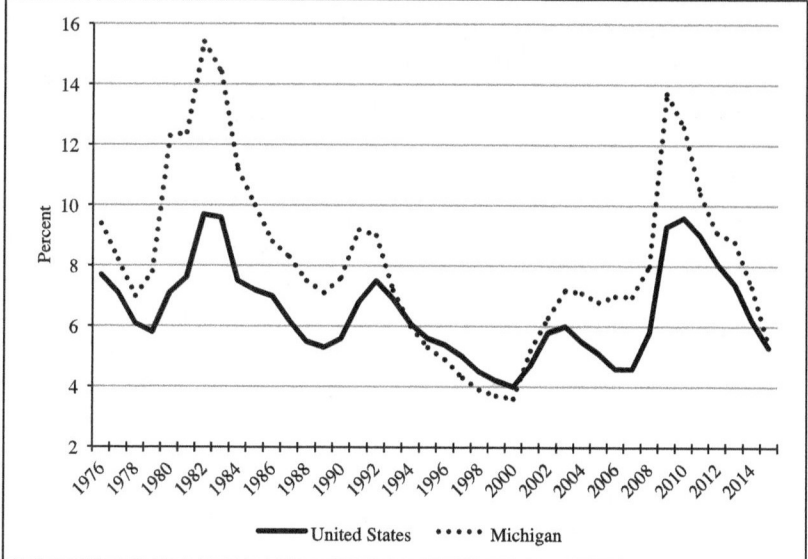

Fig. 1.3. Percent Unemployed in Michigan and the United States, 1976–2015
Source: "Unemployment Rate in Michigan [MIURN]," U.S. Bureau of Labor Statistics, retrieved from FRED, Federal Reserve Bank of St. Louis, accessed October 30, 2016, https://fred.stlouisfed.org/series/MIURN

years. The figures, however, also collectively demonstrate another important dynamic in Michigan—resurgence. Indeed, after the difficult times of the Great Recession, Michigan made a comeback with lower unemployment, a growing economy (i.e., GDP), and slightly higher incomes; even the number of manufacturing jobs has rebounded. Whether economic turnarounds like those in figures 1.1–1.4 are driven by the natural flow of the economy or the specific actions of government is debatable in many circles, especially political ones. But what cannot be denied is that government usually tries to have an impact on the economy in tough economic times. Elected officials typically want to see their constituents' lives improve and citizens often demand action toward that goal. There is usually widespread disagreement about how exactly to do this. These types of debates are outside of the scope of this book. For our purposes, the focus is that the rebound in Michigan did occur. There was at least somewhat of a resurgence in the state as Michigan tried to respond to the challenging times nearly every citizen experienced.

The comparisons provide a framework for understanding the extent of economic decline in Michigan. For a government, politics, and policy

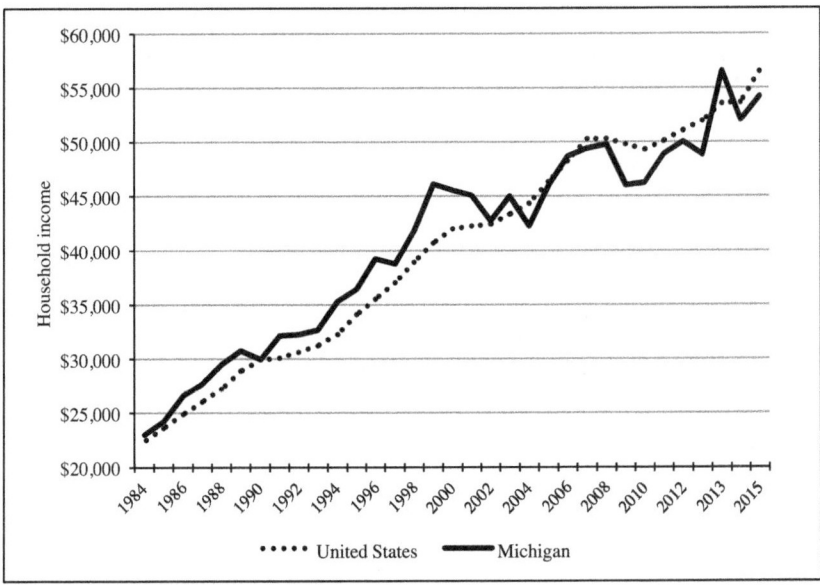

Fig. 1.4. Median Household Income in Michigan and the United States, 1984–2015
Source: "Median Household Income by State," U.S. Census Bureau, accessed October 30, 2016, http://www.census.gov/data/tables/time-series/demo/income-poverty/historical-income-households.html
Note: Income in current and 2015 CPI-U-RS adjusted dollars.

book, it also would be helpful to provide some state-level comparisons on government and policy dimensions. In terms of politics, Michigan has term limits for its state legislators, along with 18 other states, but also is only one of nine states that has a full-time legislature (see chapter 7). A large number of states have enacted election reforms such as voting by mail, no-excuse absentee voting, early in-person voting, or Election Day registration. Michigan has enacted none of those, but the state was a pioneer in the 1970s in registering voters at the Secretary of State's driver's license offices—20 years before Congress passed the National Voter Registration Act (also called "motor voter") for all states (see chapter 10). Michigan is one of 24 states that allow citizens to place issues on a statewide ballot, and only one of nine states to allow all three forms of direct democracy—initiatives, referendums, and recalls (see chapter 11).

Michigan has also followed a general trend in electoral politics since 2010. Republican elected officials have come to form majorities in both chambers of state legislatures, often along with a Republican governor. Indeed, by 2017, 25 states had elected enough Republicans for the party to control both the state Legislature and governor's office. Michigan was one of those states, but had gone ever further in that Republicans were elected to majorities in both houses of the Legislature, all of the major positions in state government (governor, lieutenant governor, secretary of state, and attorney general) as well the state Supreme Court.

Another way to compare states is to use various social, economic, and political indicators to determine a state's overall quality of life. This approach can be useful because it uses a wide variety of measures to rank states against each other. One comparison examines states from the period between 1992 and 2012.[19] This study uses 19 indicators (e.g., personal income per capita, unemployment rate, poverty rate, environment for business), assigns weights to each, calculates totals for each state, and places each state in a ranking from best to worst. In the period covering 1992–2012, Michigan ranked 32nd (with New Hampshire ranked 1st and Mississippi ranked 50th). However, most telling about these results is that Michigan also suffered the biggest decline when comparing state rankings in the 1992–2001 period to the 2002–2012 period. The state lost almost 16 spots in the second half of the study's time frame. Other states with large drops included Illinois, Indiana, and Connecticut.[20] This significant drop in quality of life rankings underscores the challenges that Michigan faced in the first decade of the 2000s, which, as we noted above, has been referred to as the "lost decade" in Michigan.

It also can be useful to compare Michigan with other states by identifying ways in which the state is unique. In at least two ways, Michigan is clearly unique among the states. A quick glance at a map of the United States reveals Michigan's two prominent peninsulas with extensive shorelines. The Great Lakes always has been an important part of Michigan's economy—in shipping raw materials and manufactured goods as well as for recreational boating and fishing. As sources of freshwater dwindle around the world, and as other states face water shortages, Michigan has the potential to exploit its position in the "blue economy," which we discuss below.

Michigan also has had a long history of significant labor union activity, stemming in part from the organization of the United Automobile Workers (UAW) beginning in the 1930s. While other states have experienced influential labor unions, Michigan's experience has been a prominent feature of its political landscape over the years. Labor unions grew and became active politically in the state. Unions endorsed political candidates and were able to elect a number of union-friendly legislators to office in the post–World War II years. However, that political influence has waned, as we describe next.

Loss of Labor Union Influence

As we noted at the beginning of the chapter, decline is a major theme of the book—most notably seen in the decline of population in the state's larger cities and in the economy generally. But decline can take many forms. For example, as the automobile industry grew in the early part of the 20th century, it gave rise to labor unions by the 1930s and 1940s. As the UAW and labor unions such as the Teamsters negotiated higher wages and benefits for their members, unions also became involved in state politics. By the 1960s, public employee unions in Michigan and around the United States began to grow as well. Organizations of police officers, firefighters, nurses, and public school teachers grew both in membership and in political influence. The Michigan Education Association and later the Service Employees International Union became active in state politics, in addition to their collective bargaining efforts.

However, changes in the economy and decisions by automakers led to a decline in union membership over time. Restructuring of automobile production meant that many production facilities moved to the southern states, where states often had right-to-work laws that made union organizing difficult or impossible. Later, automobile companies also began moving overseas or to countries such as Mexico, due to lower production costs and low import fees thanks in part to free trade agreements such as the North American Free Trade Agreement. There also were differences evident in what the labor union leadership had advocated or endorsed and what the union's rank-and-file members wanted. These differences became obvious during the 1980s and President Ronald Reagan's election. Many union members voted for Reagan and his more conservative views on social policy. In fact, with this, Michigan became known as the birthplace of an entirely new political category of voter—the Reagan Democrat. Macomb County, in southeast Michigan, was where the term was coined and where many union workers were persuaded to vote for Reagan over the Democratic candidate, Walter Mondale. Some would argue that this phenomenon was repeated nearly 40 years later as Macomb County was a major center of Donald Trump supporters in 2016 and key to him winning Michigan's Electoral College votes (see chapter 10).

In the period after the 1990s, a more conservative mood became more popular among voters. In Michigan, voters supported term limits for state elected officials, and increasing numbers of Republicans were elected to office. The newer state legislators were less inclined to support the interests of labor union members, and indeed, in many cases, felt that unions were responsible for the fiscal problems facing state and local governments at the time. Although the UAW has had some more recent gains in national membership by 2015 compared to 2008, overall UAW membership in the United States was only about 400,000 in 2015. This represented a drop from about 650,000 in 2006, and a steep decline from its peak in 1979 at 1.5 million members.[21] Union membership generally has also declined nationally from its peak in 1954, when roughly 28.3 percent of wage and salary workers were members of a union, to 2016, when that number shrank to only 10.7 percent.[22]

In an attempt to sidestep the state Legislature, union advocates proposed a few ballot proposals in the early 2000s, all of which were defeated by voters (see chapter 11). In 2002, a proposed constitutional amendment (Proposal 3) would have given public and private sector workers a constitutional right to collectively bargain, but this was defeated by voters 54.4 percent to 45.6 percent. In 2012, two proposals sought to give home health care workers limited rights to collectively bargain (Proposal 4) and public and private sector workers the right to collectively bargain (Proposal 2). Proposal 4 was defeated 56.2 percent to 43.8 percent and Proposal 2 was defeated 57.4 percent to 42.6 percent. In the face of a declining economy, enough Michigan voters were convinced that extending or continuing collective bargaining rights would prevent the state from economic recovery. After 2010, the state of Michigan was not as union-friendly as it had been in the 1930s and 1940s.

State policy after 2010 began to limit the power of public employee unions as well. The expansion of charter schools reduced the Michigan Education Association's membership size and its political clout. Once a powerful lobbying group in the state, the Michigan Education Association also was faced with a more hostile Legislature, frustration with the quality and performance of some public school districts—especially the Detroit Public Schools and some other large city school districts in the state. In March 2013, the state Legislature passed a "right-to-work" bill (see chapter 7), which some observers linked directly to a subsequent double-digit drop in statewide MEA membership by 2015.[23] These policy changes and the economic decline in Michigan has resulted in union membership declining from nearly 45 percent of workers in 1964 to only about 14 percent in 2016.[24]

Michigan, Water, and the "Blue Economy"

Despite its many challenges, Michigan has a coveted natural resource readily available that many states do not—fresh surface water from the surrounding Great Lakes. The state touches four out of the five Great Lakes: Michigan, Superior, Huron, and Erie. As news reports from California and Arizona describe water shortages and conservation efforts, Michigan remains at the center of a valuable resource for the state's and the region's economy—for agriculture, manufacturing, and recreational opportunities, to name just a few industries and activities that rely on freshwater. Some Michigan counties have taken on various blue economy initiatives (such as Macomb and Ottawa Counties), and the University Research Corridor (comprising researchers from the University of Michigan, Michigan State University, and Wayne State University) received about $300 million in research grants between 2009 and 2013 to explore innovations in water usage and preservation of water quantity and quality into the future.[25]

Michigan also is a member of the Great Lakes Compact (formally, the Great Lakes—St. Lawrence River Basin Water Resources Council), composed (with approval from the U.S. Congress) of the eight states that border one or more of the Great Lakes: Michigan, Illinois, Indiana, Ohio, Pennsylvania, New York, Wisconsin, and Minnesota. The Compact seeks to manage and protect the Great Lakes through cooperation among its members. Michigan also has recognized the importance of the blue economy in its "Pure Michigan" advertising campaign, which emphasizes the Great Lakes as an area of outstanding natural beauty and a tourist attraction for a variety of recreational activities.

Themes of the Book

We introduced the book's four themes above and offered two compelling stories of government, politics, and policy in Michigan that can better be understood through the lens of those four themes. We now examine each of the book's themes in more detail by providing some broader context for the state of Michigan in each area as well as offering selected examples of how the themes help us understand Michigan politics.

By design, each chapter provides examples of how the book's four themes touch on events and policies relevant to the chapter's topics. Some of the book's chapters will play out certain themes more than the others, but each chapter includes some discussion on the following—*historical context, decline, responses to challenges,* and *state-local government relations.* The themes cut across a wide variety of experiences in Michigan and involve governmental institutions and nongovernmental actors, and are found in the areas of policy discussed in the chapters that follow.

Historical Context

In addition to Michigan's early years as a fur trading and timber center, the area grew in population and importance with completion of the Erie Canal in 1825, and expansion of the canal's capacity that occurred into the 1860s. The canal opened up an important transportation link between the Great Lakes and the Atlantic Ocean.[26] This greatly increased the economic importance of cities on the Great Lakes such as Buffalo, Cleveland, Chicago, and Detroit.

The economic decline that would come to Michigan stands in stark contrast to the state's growth up through World War II. In earlier times, Michigan was a center of economic and population growth. When Michigan became a state in 1837, its population had grown somewhat, as the state became a center of the timber industry. Moreover, copper and iron ore mining in the state's Upper Peninsula served the emerging industrial era for the state and the United States. Furniture making in Grand Rapids and breakfast cereal production in Battle Creek also became major economic activities in the state. Michigan has been a center of agricultural and dairy production and it continues to be a leader in the production of apples, corn for grain, sugar beets, and soybeans. In 2011, Michigan was the leading producer among all U.S. states of tart cherries, cucumbers, blueberries, and squash, and was second in navy beans, celery, and carrots.[27] Tourism has been and remains important to the state, as there are many recreational opportunities associated with the Great Lakes, as well as the many inland lakes and rivers in the state. The Pure Michigan advertising campaign that began in 2006 has brought in many out-of-state visitors, such that in 2011, those from outside of Michigan spent more in the state for leisure travel than state residents spent.[28]

The 20th-century economic history of Michigan was dominated by automobile production. The "Big Three" car companies (General Motors, Ford, and Chrysler) all had a major presence in the state—not only in the metropolitan Detroit area, but also in other Michigan cities such as Flint, Pontiac, and Lansing. Detroit grew to the fourth largest U.S. city by 1920—and remained fourth until 1950, when Los Angeles moved past Detroit.[29]

While a complete history of the state is beyond the scope of this volume, some attention to the historical components to the institutions, actors, and policy areas is needed for a full understanding of government, politics, and policy today. The chapters typically offer a brief *historical context* of a topic or policy that will serve as an important lead-in to a discussion of more recent events. The context could include social, political, economic, or cultural factors—or some combination thereof. A brief examination of relevant historical considerations in each chapter sets the stage for an analysis of the modern elements of the particular chapter topic. This historical examination includes addressing contextual factors important for the chapter's focus. For instance, the chapter on Michigan's Constitution (chapter 2) examines each of Michigan's four constitutions as well as the evolution of constitutional principles and the organization of governmental structures in the state from the period in which statehood was granted.

Decline in Michigan

Earlier, we presented a broad framework summarizing the economic decline that industrialized cities in Michigan such as Flint and Detroit suffered in the post–World War II period. However, the economy in the state overall did not suffer as much during the decades immediately after 1950. In fact, the entire state of Michigan gained almost 1 million jobs between 1950 and 1970, with over 15 percent of that total in durable goods manufacturing.[30] The postwar period was a boom period for the state in some ways. Michigan's population, as a share of the overall U.S. population, increased from 4 percent in 1940, to 4.2 percent in 1950, to 4.3 percent in 1960, and finally to 4.4 percent in 1970 (before declining since then, to 3.3 percent in 2010).[31]

In addition to the decline that began as early as the 1950s, the period after 1970 saw a spike in decline for Michigan industrialized cities. The U.S. economy had been changing from an industrial- to a service-based economy, and the days of plentiful low-skill, high-wage jobs that were the hallmark of the automobile production process were gone. Changes in the automobile manufacturing industry in response to the 1973 energy crisis included a restructuring of the auto industry. This included the dispersion of manufacturing plants around the United States and the world. Some cities in Michigan grew as automobile factories moved out of Detroit and into suburban and formerly rural areas, but the state ultimately lost many automobile manufacturing jobs. Even before the Great Recession, in which both General Motors and Chrysler declared bankruptcy, Michigan lost 211,000 automobile jobs between 2000 and 2007.[32]

There have been declines in other areas in the state's economy. For example, as noted above, Detroit saw its population shrink from a high of almost 2 million in the 1950s to only about 700,000 according to the 2010 Census. However, Michigan as a whole also saw important population shifts in the latter part of the 20th century and in the early years of the 21st century. From 2000 to 2010, Michigan was the only state in the nation to actually have a net population *loss*. Table 1.1 shows the state's population between 1840 and 2010. In particular, Michigan's population of 9,883,640 in 2010 was down 0.6 percent from the 2000 population of 9,938,444.[33] In his 2017 State of the State address, Governor Snyder said "Our goal should be to reach 10 million people again. We were there once. We're at 9,928,000. We need 71 thousand people. Let's get 'em over the next three years. Let's put 'em to work in Michigan."[34] To put this goal in context and picking up on the aforementioned comparisons of Michigan and other states, Michigan's shrinking population and the governor's goal to add about 71,000 people is striking in contrast to states like Nevada, which saw its population increase by over 35 percent between the 2000 and 2010 censuses, and Texas, Arizona, Utah, and Idaho, all of which saw population growth of more than 20 percent in the same time frame.[35]

These population figures have a great impact on government in the state. The most dramatic area is arguably the state's influence in the U.S. House of Representatives, which uses a state's population total to allocate seats in the chamber. While Michigan has retained a number of senior members of the U.S. House (John Dingell, now retired; John Conyers; Sander Levin), the state's number of congressional seats has consistently declined. This is illustrated in table 1.1, which shows that since the 1970s, Michigan has lost a total of five congressional seats. This decrease in rep-

TABLE 1.1. Michigan's Population and Number of U.S. House Seats, 1840–2010

Year	Population	Number of U.S. House Seats
1840	212,267	3
1850	397,654	4
1860	749,113	6
1870	1,184,059	9
1880	1,636,937	11
1890	2,093,890	12
1900	2,420,982	12
1910	2,810,173	13
1920	3,668,412	13
1930	4,842,325	17
1940	5,258,106	17
1950	6,371,766	18
1960	7,823,194	19
1970	8,881,826	19
1980	9,262,044	18
1990	9,295,297	16
2000	9,938,444	15
2010	9,883,640	14

Source: "Resident Population and Apportionment of the US House of Representatives," U.S. Census Bureau, accessed March 29, 2015, https://www.census.gov/dmd/www/resapport/states/michigan.pdf

resentational allowance decreased Michigan's power at the federal level. Moreover, since a state's membership in the U.S. House is part of the formula for determining a state's number of electoral votes in the Electoral College for presidential elections, this means that Michigan has also seen a decline in voting power for the nation's chief executive. In the 1976 presidential election Michigan had 21 electoral votes while 40 years later that was down to 16. Projections are for Michigan to lose another seat in Congress and, therefore, another electoral vote after the 2020 census.[36]

Decline has been felt or has been a major aspect of governmental and political action in nearly all areas of government, politics, and policy in Michigan. The chapters that follow cover many of these areas in greater detail.

Responses to Challenges

As we also noted above, in the wake of the difficult economic time endured by many in Michigan, the state has responded to the challenges. To be sure, not every attempt to respond to challenges in the state has been successful. However, the long-term decline that the state has suffered has required decision makers to face these challenges directly. Much of what policy making centers on are the debates about what program or degree of government involvement will most effectively lead the state on a path to ongoing recovery. The discussions in the chapters on the governor's office (chapter 6) and the Legislature (chapter 7) briefly address some of the ways in which those institutions pursued solutions to the state's economic problems. In addition, the policy chapters trace the varying levels of success that past policies have had on the state's economic recovery. Voters elect political leaders to help solve problems—whether those leaders solve those problems or not can be an important criterion for their reelection. Leaders can be well intentioned, but still not successfully address a state's problems. They also could make matters worse—the economy could get worse, for instance, with no apparent policy fix in sight. In a Michigan gubernatorial debate during the campaign of 2014, Governor Snyder, who was running for reelection, noted the economic decline that occurred under a Democratic governor and said, "Let's not go back to the lost decade. Let's not let professional politicians mess up Michigan again."[37] The reference to the "lost decade" referred to the period when the state was headed by Governor Granholm (who served from January 2003 to January 2011).

State-Local Government Relations

While this volume is about state government and politics in Michigan, one cannot forget the importance of local governments in the state's set of intergovernmental relations. The fourth and final theme of this book acknowledges this important dynamic in Michigan; and indeed, it is one that is present in all states. The nature of state-local relations and the implications of those relations remains a major feature of how states operate, how politics is waged, and how services are delivered to citizens. For example, the legal relationship between the state and local governments can create political tensions between the different levels of government. Even under home rule, cities are often limited in what they can do on their own given the power the state has. As we noted above, the economic decline that plagued Michigan resulted in many struggles, one of which was the loss of revenue sharing from the state to local governments (see chapter 13). Some of the struggles between the state and its localities are debated by candidates for office and elected officials; some may be resolved through ballot proposals; still others are played out in the courts. But state-local relations are crucial elements of public policy as well, as the policy chapters in this volume illustrate.

The ongoing dynamic of state-local relations, therefore, touches on much of what government does and how it operates. Some of the broader questions of policy responsibility have been answered over time, but there continues to be considerable discussion and debate about which level of government has the proper responsibilities in making and executing public policies (as can be seen in the case of the Flint water crisis). Running through those questions is the matter of how programs and services will be funded—and by which government or combination of governments. Funding programs necessarily raises questions about government revenues, taxes, and fees, as well as Michigan-specific policies such as the Headlee Amendment[38] (named after anti-tax activist Richard Headlee) and the state government's decisions on issues such as the allocation of revenue sharing dollars to local governments.

Organization of Book

This book is organized into four major sections. The first section (chapters 2–5) on *foundational elements* covers the state Constitution and formal powers of Michigan's state government and its various local governments. This section also summarizes the different types of local governments that operate within the state, as well as the legal relations between the state and local governments. The second section (chapters 6–8) focuses on the state's *political institutions*, including the governor and the executive branch, the state Legislature, and the state's court system. The next section (chapters 9–11) investigates the major *political actors and processes* in Michigan. In particular, this section includes discussions of political parties and interest groups in the state, as well as elections and political participation. Finally, Michigan's recent experience with citizen-initiated ballot proposals is explored.

The final section (chapters 12–15) includes *public policy case studies* of selected policy areas important to Michigan—and to most states for that matter. In the United States' federated system, state governments traditionally have been responsible for public health and safety, public education, economic development, transportation and infrastructure, and law enforcement and corrections. More recent controversies include the politics and policies surrounding same-sex marriage, immigration, and homeland security. While we could not cover all policies important to state government and politics, we chose three issue areas that are both important and are illustrative of the state experience with policy making. As such, we selected the policy areas of public education, budget and finance, and economic development.

Public education is a top spending area in most states, as it is in Michigan. It is a constitutional responsibility of the state to provide public education. Economic development is an important policy as well, since it is crucial to a state's economy and quality of life. Business investment in a state increases jobs and state and local revenues. Jobs, especially those with higher wages and benefits, help create or maintain a vibrant middle class. State and local governments must coordinate efforts in order to attract businesses. A number of state and local incentives are often provided to qualifying businesses in an effort to reduce the cost of locating or relocating to a particular jurisdiction, which reinforces the theme of state-local relations. We also include a chapter on the state's budget and finance policy. For a state such as Michigan—with all of its funding challenges in the past 30 years—a chapter on how well the state brings in revenues and how well it can fund its programs is key to understanding both the process and the outcome of government and politics in the state. Moreover, a major theme of this book is the economic decline that Michigan has suffered over the years. Indeed, this decline has likely framed many of the policy debates in the past 30 years, as well as proposals for a rebirth in Michigan. Understanding budget and fiscal policy will help readers understand those frames and the policies themselves.

We end the section on policy case studies with a chapter on the city of Flint and the Flint water crisis. No current book on Michigan government, politics, and policy could ignore this tragic and compelling story. Interestingly, we believe the Flint water crisis illustrates the book's themes quite well. Readers will better understand the Flint story through the lens of our four themes—*historical context, decline, responses to challenges,* and *state-*

local government relations. This is a story that has touched the entire United States, but it remains a reality for those who live in the city and in our state.

NOTES

1. "Table 23: Race and Hispanic Origin for Selected Large Places and Other Cities, Earliest Census to 1990," U.S. Census Bureau, accessed May 20, 2016, http://www.census.gov/population/www/documentation/twps0076/MItab.pdf

2. "'Gold Rush' Is Started by Ford's $5 Offer: Thousands of Men Seek Employment in Factory," *Times-Star Special Dispatch*, accessed May 20, 2016, https://www.thehenryford.org/collections-and-research/digital-collections/artifact/99336#slide=gs-188124

3. "Flint Water Advisory Task Force—Final Report," commissioned by the Office of Governor Rick Snyder, March 2016, p. 1, accessed October 30, 2016, https://www.michigan.gov/documents/snyder/FWATF_FINAL_REPORT_21March2016_517805_7.pdf

4. Elisha Anderson, "Why Were Officials Silent on Legionnaires' in Flint?," *Detroit Free Press*, April 10, 2016; accessed May 22, 2016, http://www.freep.com/story/news/local/michigan/flint-water-crisis/2016/04/09/flint-water-crisis-legionnaires/82397428/

5. "Top 10 Worst Cities, Worst Places to Live 2013," *Area Vibes*, accessed January 21, 2016, http://www.areavibes.com/library/top-10-worst-cities-to-live-2013/

6. "Table 20: Population of the 100 Largest Urban Places, 1970," U.S. Bureau of Census, accessed January 21, 2016, https://www.census.gov/population/www/documentation/twps0027/tab20.txt; see also, "Quick Facts, Flint, MI, 2014 Population Estimate," accessed January 21, 2016, http://quickfacts.census.gov/qfd/states/26/2629000.html; and Christine MacDonald, "Detroit Population Rank Is Lowest since 1850," *Detroit News*, May 19, 2016, accessed May 22, 2016, http://www.detroitnews.com/story/news/local/detroit-city/2016/05/19/detroit-population-rank-lowest-since/84574198/

7. Flint Water Advisory Task Force—Final Report, 62.

8. Monica Davey, "Finding $816 Million, and Fast, to Save Detroit," *New York Times*, November 7, 2014, accessed June 1, 2016, http://www.nytimes.com/2014/11/08/us/finding-816-million-and-fast-to-save-detroit.html?_r=0

9. Jonathan Oosting, "State Money for Detroit? New Michigan Panel to Consider 'Grand Bargain' Legislation, Oversight," *Mlive.com*, May 6, 2014; accessed June 1, 2016, http://www.mlive.com/lansing-news/index.ssf/2014/05/state_money_for_detroit_new_mi.html

10. Christine Ferretti, "Detroit Emerges from Bankruptcy Today," *Detroit News*, December 10, 2014; accessed April 3, 2015, http://www.detroitnews.com/story/news/local/wayne-county/2014/12/10/detroit-bankruptcy/20192957/

11. Matthew Dolan, Susan Tompor, and John Gallagher, "Detroit Rising: Life after Bankruptcy," *Detroit Free Press*, November 8, 2015, accessed June 1, 2016, http://www.freep.com/story/news/local/detroit-reborn/2015/11/08/detroit-rising-life-after-bankruptcy/75085252/

12. Ryan Holywell, "Emergency Financial Managers: Michigan's Unwelcome Savior," *Governing.com*, May 2012; accessed April 3, 2015, http://www.governing.com/topics/mgmt/gov-emergency-financial-managers-michigan-municipalities-unwelcome-savior.html

13. Monica Davey, "Detroit Is Out of Bankruptcy, but Not Out of the Woods," *New York Times*, December 10, 2014, accessed March 30, 2015, http://www.nytimes.com/2014/12/11/us/detroit-bankruptcy-ending.html?_r=0

14. Christine Ferretti, "For Detroit Retirees, Pension Cuts Become Reality," *Detroit News*, February 27, 2015; accessed March 30, 2015, http://www.detroitnews.com/story/news/local/wayne-county/2015/02/27/detroit-retirees-pension-cuts-become-reality/24156301/

15. Brian Plumer, "Detroit Just Filed for Bankruptcy: Here's How It Got There," *Washington Post*, July 18, 2013; accessed March 30, 2015, http://www.washingtonpost.com/blogs/wonkblog/wp/2013/07/18/detroit-just-filed-for-bankruptcy-heres-how-it-got-there/

16. "Labor Force Statistics from the Current Population Survey," U.S. Bureau of Labor Statistics, accessed March 30, 2015, http://data.bls.gov/timeseries/LNS14000000

17. Authors' calculations based on data from the U.S. Bureau of Labor Statistics, nonseasonally adjusted unemployment figures, accessed March 30, 2015, http://data.bls.gov/map/MapToolServlet

18. Plumer, "Detroit Just Filed for Bankruptcy."

19. Geoff Pallay, "State Quality of Life Index," *Who Runs the States? Part 2*, accessed June 1, 2016, https://ballotpedia.org/Ballotpedia:Who_Runs_the_States

20. Geoff Pallay, "Dramatic Changes from 1st Half to 2nd Half," *Who Runs the States? Part 2*, State Quality of Life Index, 9; accessed June 1, 2016, https://www.heartland.org/sites/default/files/whorunsthestates_part2_sqli.pdf

21. Brent Snavely, "UAW Membership Tops 400,000 for First Time since '08," *USA Today*, March 31, 2015; accessed May 19, 2016, http://www.usatoday.com/story/money/cars/2015/03/31/uaw-membership-tops-first-time-since/70753012/

22. Data from 1954 are taken from Gerald Mayer, "Union Membership Trends in the United States, Congressional Research Service, report RL32553, August 31, 2004, accessed February 1, 2017, http://digitalcommons.ilr.cornell.edu/cgi/viewcontent.cgi?article=1176&context=key_workplace; 2016 data are taken from "Union Members Summary," U.S. Bureau of Labor Statistics, accessed February 1, 2017, https://www.bls.gov/news.release/union2.nr0.htm

23. Brent Snavely, "Michigan Union Membership Falls to 14.5%," *Detroit Free Press*, January 23, 2015; accessed May 19, 2016, http://www.freep.com/story/money/business/columnists/2015/01/23/union-membership-michigan-right-work-fall-state/22219305/

24. Data for 1964 are taken from Barry T. Hirsch, David A. Macpherson, and Wayne G. Vroman, "Union Density Estimates by State, 1964–2015, accessed February 1, 2017; data for 2016 is from Keith Laing, "Michigan Union Membership Dipped in 2016," *Detroit News*, January 26, 2017, accessed February 1, 2017, http://www.detroitnews.com/story/business/autos/2017/01/26/michigan-union-membership-dipped/97108546/

25. Alex L. Rosaen, "Innovating for the Blue Economy," Anderson Economic Group, May 29, 2014; accessed May 19, 2016, http://urcmich.org/wp-content/uploads/2015/03/URC_Water-Industry-Sector.pdf

26. "Erie Canal," NY Canals, accessed March 29, 2015, http://www.nycanals.com/Erie_Canal

27. "Michigan Agricultural Statistics: 2010-2011," State of Michigan, Department of Agriculture and Rural Development, accessed March 30, 2015, http://www.nass.usda.gov/Statistics_by_State/Michigan/Publications/Annual_Statistical_Bulletin/stats11/agstat11.pdf

28. Jeff Alexander, "The Pure Michigan Effect: 3.2 Million Out-of-State Visitors, $1 Billion Economic Impact," *The Bridge*, February 19, 2013; accessed March 30, 2015, http://www.mlive.com/business/index.ssf/2013/02/1_billion_economic_impact_that.html

29. "Population of the 100 Largest Cities and Other Urban Places in the United States: 1790 to 1990," U.S. Census Bureau, June 1998; accessed March 30, 2015, https://www.census.gov/population/www/documentation/twps0027/twps0027.html

30. Reynolds Farley, "Michigan's Demographic Outlook," Population Studies Center Research Report 10-699, Institute for Social Research, University of Michigan, April 2010; accessed April 6, 2015, http://www.psc.isr.umich.edu/pubs/pdf/rr10-699.pdf

31. Ibid.

32. Randall W. Eberts, and George A. Erickcek, "Where Have All the Michigan Auto Jobs Gone?," *Employment Research* 16, no. 4 (October 2009); accessed April 6, 2015, http://research.upjohn.org/cgi/viewcontent.cgi?article=1003&context=empl_research

33. Paul Mackun and Steve Wilson, "Population Distribution and Change: 2000 to 2010," U.S. Census Bureau, accessed March 30, 2015, http://www.census.gov/prod/cen2010/briefs/c2010br-01.pdf

34. As quoted in Rick Pluta, "Snyder Says 10 Million People Should Live in Michigan by 2020," Michigan Radio, accessed February 1, 2017, http://michiganradio.org/post/snyder-says-10-million-people-should-live-michigan-2020

35. "2010 Census Data," U.S. Bureau of Census.

36. "States Gaining/Losing Seats based upon 2020 Projections," Polidata.org, accessed February 1, 2017, http://www.polidata.org/census/ST016NCA.pdf

37. "Michigan Debate: Governor Rick Snyder, Mark Schauer Spar over Tax and Education Spending," *Mlive.com*, October 13, 2014, accessed March 4, 2015, http://www.mlive.com/lansing-news/index.ssf/2014/10/snyder_schauer_debate_recap_mi.html

38. The Headlee Amendment was a tax limitation constitutional amendment approved by voters in 1978, which established an overall limitation on total state spending each year. It also required a local unit of government to reduce its millage when annual growth on existing property is greater than the rate of inflation; see "Headlee Rollback and Headlee Override," Michigan Municipal League, accessed April 3, 2015, https://www.mml.org/resources/publications/one_pagers/opp_headlee_override.pdf

Foundational Elements

2 ✦ Michigan's Constitution

JOYCE BAUGH

Like any constitution, Michigan's four constitutions are products of the state's unique history and the political, economic, and social context in which they were written. The first was created in 1835, two years before Michigan achieved statehood, and the second emerged 15 years later in 1850. It took nearly 60 more years, until 1908, before the third one was written. The fourth and last overhaul was completed more than a half century later in 1963. Each of these documents reflects the political movements, ideology, and important events that dominated each time period within the state, region, and nation. As such, the four state constitutions created and approved over time reveal one of this book's themes—the importance of history. That historical context illustrates how the state, its government, and its citizens have changed since the 1830s.

In addition to discussing the importance of the historical context of the state constitutions, this chapter also frequently shows how state government officials—and citizens, through state ballot initiatives—have attempted to respond to social, economic, governmental, and political challenges that Michigan has faced over the years. Finally, the chapter addresses the place of local government in the state's governmental system as detailed by the Constitution. The functions and powers of local government (including the limits of local power) are contained in several articles of the Constitution and in a number of important amendments. The discussion begins with the history of Michigan's constitutions by investigating events and processes that led to the creation of Michigan's first Constitution.

Toward the 1835 Constitution and the Battle for Statehood

The road to statehood in Michigan and the creation of its first Constitution were the result of several somewhat unusual events. Although Michigan did not become a state until 1837, a constitutional convention actually was called in 1835 and the Constitution was written that year. To understand why this path was taken, one has to look back to the Northwest Ordinance of 1787, a land dispute between Michigan and Ohio, and controversies over the expansion of slavery. The normal pattern for achieving statehood was for a territory to request an enabling act from Congress before writing a constitution, which would then be submitted to Congress for approval. Michigan was a part of the Northwest Territory that was guaranteed statehood once the population of the territory surpassed 60,000 residents. In 1833, with support from the voters, Michigan formally submitted its request for an enabling act to Congress. Despite the fact that census data indicated that the Michigan territory included more than 85,000 people, well above the 60,000 minimum requirement, Congress denied the petition. In January 1835, frustrated by the Congress, Stevens T. Mason, the acting territorial governor, requested that the legislative council (which was the precursor to the Michigan Legislature) call a convention to write a constitution. With the council's agreement, delegate selection was scheduled for April, and the delegates were to assemble in Detroit in May 1835.[1]

Michigan's decision to call the convention exacerbated the tensions the territory had with the state of Ohio over a portion of land around the Toledo community called the "Toledo Strip." This land was a crucial part of the region's economy because it had access to the Great Lakes, the Erie Canal, and therefore, the Atlantic Ocean. The dispute began in the early 19th century, with both Michigan and Ohio claiming ownership based on various land surveys. Ohio officials were particularly concerned about losing the land if Michigan were to achieve statehood. As a state rather than a territory, Michigan could request the U.S. Supreme Court to resolve the boundary dispute. Consequently, after Michigan called its convention, Ohio reasserted its claims of ownership and hostilities between the two escalated, leading to dueling pieces of legislation and eventually to the Toledo War, which saw shots fired but no one killed. President Andrew Jackson dispatched representatives to try to help resolve the conflict.[2]

While the conflict over the Toledo Strip continued, the convention delegates met in Detroit in May 1835 to begin writing a constitution. It took 38 days. A majority of the delegates were Jacksonian Democrats, although one member of the Whig Party was elected as president and two Whigs were elected as secretaries.[3] The Jacksonian Era had begun after Andrew Jackson was elected president in the election of 1828. While the Framers believed in a republican form of government in which the "best person" governed, the Jacksonians viewed this as elitist and undemocratic.[4]

Many Jacksonian Democrats favored ending property and taxpaying requirements for voting. By contrast, members of the Whig Party generally favored these voting qualifications. Thus the subject of most controversy at the Michigan convention involved voting, specifically the age of voters. Governor Mason "was credited with suggesting that voting rights be given to every white male citizen above the age of 21 years old who had lived in Michigan for six months, and to every white male who lived in Michigan at the time of the signing of the constitution."[5]

It is no surprise that the convention also produced a document explaining Michigan's position regarding the boundary dispute with Ohio ("The Appeal of the Convention of Michigan to the people of the United States"). This was seen as necessary given that while the convention was meeting, hostilities over the disputed territory worsened, and Ohio passed additional legislation aimed at protecting its legal claim over it.

Although Michigan still had not yet achieved statehood, in October 1835 the state's voters approved the Constitution by a vote of 6,752 to 1,374; at the same time they elected a governor and lieutenant governor, as well as members of the state Legislature and the U.S. House of Representatives. Subsequently, the new Legislature elected two U.S. senators in preparation for statehood, assuming this would happen by its next meeting in February 1836.[6] They were to be disappointed, however, as a long debate in Congress ensued.

A major breakthrough came in June 1836, when Congress passed a compromise bill to resolve the boundary conflict. Under the bill, Ohio was granted the Toledo Strip and Michigan was offered the western Upper Peninsula and immediate statehood. An additional requirement in the bill stipulated that a Michigan convention be called to approve this compromise. Many Michigan residents recoiled at the loss of the Toledo Strip and they viewed the Upper Peninsula as a wilderness that would never be suitable for habitation. It is perhaps prescient that Lucius Lyon, one of the newly elected senators, saw great potential for this "wilderness":

> A considerable tract of country between Lake Michigan and Lake Superior is known to be fertile and this with the fisheries on Lake Superior and the copper mines supposed to exist there may here-

after be worth to us millions of dollars. At any rate, it can do us no harm and I am in favor of getting it while we can, for at best, if we are cut down in the south, as we certainly shall be, our State will be quite poor and small enough.[7]

Lyon and Governor Mason became convinced that there was no alternative but to accept the compromise, but at the September 1836 convention called by the Michigan Legislature, the delegates rejected it by a 28 to 21 vote.[8]

The convention's rejection of the compromise was disconcerting to some Michiganders who were concerned about the disadvantages of remaining as a territory, especially losing out on potential revenues from the federal government. Their efforts at overturning the decision with a new convention were assisted by advocates who wanted to admit Michigan into the Union as a free state to reestablish the balance of free and slave states that was lost when Arkansas, a slave state, was admitted with passage of the Northern Ohio Boundary Bill. A second convention was held on December 14, 1836, where the delegates approved the compromise, and President Jackson sent the results of both conventions to the Congress nearly two weeks later. Despite continued controversy, statehood for Michigan was approved by both the U.S. House and Senate in January 1837, and President Jackson signed the bill to officially admit Michigan into the Union on January 26, 1837.[9]

The Michigan Constitution of 1835

The 1835 Constitution drew greatly upon the Northwest Ordinance of 1787 and the constitutions of New York and Connecticut, and various provisions of the Northwest Ordinance have become important parts not only of the 1835 document but also of its successors.[10] The use of the New York and Connecticut constitutions is not very surprising, given that many Michigan residents had come from New York and New England more generally.[11] The completion of the Erie Canal in 1825 became a critical factor in the development of Michigan, as it provided a more accessible means of transportation for people on the East Coast.

Key Provisions of the Constitution of 1835

There are several key provisions contained in the Constitution of 1835, including some that focus on religious rights, due process protections, voting rights, and the separation and shared powers of the three branches of state government. A key provision related to the path to statehood is contained in the Preamble, which indirectly defined state boundaries based on the compromise over the Toledo Strip and indicated that qualifications for statehood were met.

In Article I, a Declaration of Rights proclaimed that "All political power is inherent in the people" and affirmed that people have the right to alter, reform, or abolish a form of government when the public good requires it. The list of rights included principles from the Northwest Ordinance—provisions protecting religious liberty but also preventing public monies from being used for religious purposes; due process guarantees including protections against unreasonable searches and seizures, the right to jury trial, the right to a speedy and public trial, prohibitions against double jeopardy and cruel and unjust punishment, the right to counsel, and others; and freedoms of speech, press, assembly, and petition. Susan Fino writes, "Although the framers of the 1835 Constitution had available to them the federal Bill of Rights as a model, they chose to write a unique Michigan Bill of Rights with greater and more specific protections for the liberty of the people."[12]

Article II covered voting rights, procedures, and qualifications. This article permitted white males over 21 years of age who had lived in the state for six months to vote. No property qualifications were required for eligible voters, but it did exclude women and blacks from voting.

Articles III through VI dealt with the structure of state government. In Article III, the Constitution described the division of powers among the "three departments"—the legislative, executive, and judicial branches. Article III also prohibited members of each department from exercising the powers of the other two departments unless called for by the Constitution itself.

Articles IV, V, and VI dealt with the establishment of the legislative, executive, and judicial branches, and defined their terms of office, selection methods, powers and responsibilities, and procedures for operating. A bicameral legislature was established, with between 48 and 100 members of the House of Representatives and a Senate consisting of one-third as many members as the House (see also chapter 7). House and Senate members were to serve one- and two-year terms, respectively. Article V provided for a governor and lieutenant governor, to be elected for two-year terms, and other state officers to be appointed by the governor and Legislature. A judiciary was created with a Supreme Court to be appointed by the governor with the consent of the state Senate, with judges who would serve seven-year terms. Judges in probate, county, and circuit courts were to be elected by the people to four-year terms. The Legislature also was authorized to create additional courts as needed.

Article VII covered several aspects of state and county government. State officers included in this article are the secretary of state, state treasurer, and attorney general. Unlike the current selection process for these positions, the Constitution of 1835 provided for the appointment of these positions rather than election by voters. This article also provided for the election of county officers. Among these elected positions were sheriff, treasurer, register of deeds, and county surveyor.

Article X addressed public education in the state. It required the state Legislature to maintain a system of common schools and earmarked funding for this purpose, called for the creation of public libraries in townships and for the Legislature to "encourage, by all suitable means, the promotion of Intellectual, Scientific [sic] and Agricultural improvement." This later led to the creation of what became referred to as a land-grant university (Michigan State University). It is contended, nonetheless, that earmarking funding for education proved to be somewhat of a defect in the document. In later constitutions, funding was earmarked for additional purposes, which often restricted the state's ability to deal with future fiscal emergencies.

In Article XII, the Constitution dealt with "Miscellaneous Provisions." For example, it established Detroit as the state capital "or at such other place or places as may be prescribed by law, until 1847, when it shall be permanently located by the legislature."[13] Another important provision in Article XII directed the Legislature to (1) engage in internal improvements, that is, the building of roads and canals, and (2) to appropriate funds for this purpose. These sections proved to be problematic, however, as the Legislature authorized numerous construction projects, including railroads, that were not completed and that severely strained the state's resources, nearly to the point of bankruptcy.[14] Furthermore, this constitution did little to regulate corporations, simply noting that an act of incorporation required the consent of at least two-thirds of each chamber of the Legislature. For example, railroads and banks received charters from the state with no personal liability clauses included, "so that when these businesses failed, investors had no recourse."[15] George Fuller argues, "It would be difficult to assert whether the people of the State suffered more from the internal improvement scheme than from the flood of banks let loose."[16] Willis Dunbar and George May note that this document, nonetheless, "has been lauded by political scientists, and it has been claimed by some that it was the best constitution Michigan has ever had."[17]

The Constitution of 1850

The first major overhaul of the original Michigan Constitution occurred in 1850. In the 15 years since the 1835 document was written, three amendments had been added, the most significant being a requirement that voters must approve every law that authorized the borrowing of state money or the issuance of state stocks. This idea of a popular referendum eventually became one of the major reforms advocated by Populists in the early 20th century.[18] The impetus for a new constitution centered on the defects of the initial one, as perceived by some, as well as the continuing push for popular control of government exemplified in the principles of Jacksonian democracy. This democratic spirit was widespread, and many states sought to write new constitutions or amend existing ones.[19]

The constitutional convention met in Lansing in June 1850. Like the 1835 convention, the majority of delegates in attendance were Democrats—80 of 100. Nearly half were farmers; and there were nearly two dozen lawyers, while other delegates included merchants, doctors, millers, printers, mechanics, as well as a teacher, clergyman, and county judge.[20]

Key Provisions of the 1850 Constitution

This constitution was written with much greater detail than that of 1835, in large part because it created numerous elected offices, and the delegates wanted to create mechanisms to achieve both accountability and consistency. As Fino notes, this resulted in language that was "more appropriate to a simple statute than a state constitution,"[21] and a document that was more than double the length of the previous one. A particularly puzzling feature was that the original Bill of Rights article "disappeared" and its provisions were scattered throughout the document, including in the legislative and judicial articles and a "miscellaneous" category. A quite significant issue that appeared as a miscellaneous provision was the following: "Neither slavery nor involuntary servitude, unless for the punishment of crime, shall ever be tolerated in this state."[22]

Other key provisions of the 1850 Constitution maintained or revised elements from that of 1835. For example, the state capital was changed from Detroit to Lansing, but the system of separation of powers among the legislative, executive, and judicial branches of government continued. With respect to the legislative branch, Article IV provided for two-year terms for members of both the Senate and House of Representatives, the numbers to be elected, qualifications for legislative service, and rules of apportionment.

It also specified in great detail the powers of the Legislature and rules of legislative procedure.

The executive branch was addressed in Article V. Just like the 1835 Constitution, under the 1850 version a governor and lieutenant governor were to be elected to serve two-year terms, but other executive officers who had previously been appointed by the governor, legislature, or both, were now to be chosen by the voters. These included the secretary of state, attorney general, auditor general, state treasurer, and superintendent of public instruction.[23] This requirement for election of these additional executive branch positions reflects the Jacksonian Era sentiment for greater participation by citizens in choosing their public officials.

Article VI dealt with the structure and powers of the judicial branch. The original Constitution said that the judicial power was to be vested in one Supreme Court, gave the Legislature the authority to create other courts, and recognized probate, county, and circuit courts as they existed. The 1850 document vested the judicial power in one Supreme Court, circuit courts, probate courts, and justices of the peace. In addition, it permitted the Legislature to establish municipal courts in cities. Under the 1835 charter, the Supreme Court was to consist of one chief justice and associate justices, appointed by the governor to seven-year terms with approval by the state Senate. Again, reflecting the democratic spirit of the times, the 1850 Constitution switched from appointing members of the Supreme Court to election by the citizenry. The framers in 1850 also made an interesting decision that resulted in the state being without a supreme court for a significant period of time. They decided that the judges of the circuit courts were to serve as Supreme Court justices for six years, after which the Legislature was to establish a Supreme Court consisting of one chief justice and three associate justices who would serve eight-year terms. These judges would be elected by the voters, just as the 1835 Constitution had specified for their counterparts in county courts, circuit courts, and probate courts. Article VI also spelled out the jurisdiction and rules and procedures for the courts.[24]

The subject of most debate and controversy at the convention was the qualifications of voters, which would become part of Article VII. Part of this concerned whether suffrage would be extended to free African Americans, a question that also was controversial in other states. Ultimately because of fears of social equality between blacks and whites and the specter of interracial marriage, the issue threatened to jeopardize the ratification of the document, so it was abandoned. When a separate amendment on the subject was later introduced, it was defeated overwhelmingly by the voters by an almost two to one margin. By contrast, members of the convention sought to encourage the arrival of German and Scandinavian immigrants, so the qualifications for residency were not made too stringent in the document. Eventually the delegates agreed to a provision extending suffrage to white male citizens over 21 and "civilized male inhabitants of Indian descent also meeting the same age qualifications."[25] The Framers also refused to extend the vote to women.

An important shortcoming of the original Constitution was the lack of attention to important issues of state finances and taxation, which had resulted in dire financial consequences. The 1850 version included a section focused on these matters, including the goal of ending the state's debt and balancing its budget. Other notable provisions concerned improvements in the criminal justice system, an article on exemptions that protected the property rights of married women, and calls for creating institutions to serve persons with certain disabilities, a free public primary school system, and a land-grant institution. One of the most important provisions with future significance established a system for a possible general revision of the Constitution to occur every 16 years. An election would be held and a majority affirmative vote would require the Legislature to organize a convention.

Important National and State Developments after 1850

Dunbar and May contend that the 1850 document "has to rank as Michigan's worst state constitution."[26] Consequently, there were several attempts at creating a new constitution to remedy its defects, but these efforts were unsuccessful. For example, after the Civil War, citizens called for a convention in 1866; although it was held in 1867, the document created was defeated soundly. While there were several objectionable provisions, once again the issue of suffrage for African Americans played a significant role. The delegates had deleted the word "white" from the list of qualifications for voting. Scholars have noted the irony of Michigan's members of Congress voting to require suffrage for blacks in the South while denying it to those in their own state. It is interesting that blacks in Mississippi received the franchise before those in Michigan, and it took a state constitutional amendment to get this done in Michigan in 1869, one year before the Fifteenth Amendment to the U.S. Constitution was ratified.[27] That Amendment reads, "The right of citizens of the United States to vote shall not be denied or abridged by the United States or by any State on account of race, color, or previous condition of servitude."

In 1873, as a result of a special action taken by the Legislature, a constitutional commission was called by the governor. This commission drafted a new constitution, but it also was rejected by the voters. Once again, the issue of suffrage was a major factor, but this time a stumbling block was extending the franchise to women. The question of female suffrage was submitted in a separate amendment along with the proposed constitution, but the voters refused to approve either one. Two more attempts by citizens to use the 16-year interval allowed by the 1850 Constitution failed—in 1866 and 1882—before the third Constitution finally was created in 1908. The Legislature had not fared any better in its attempts in 1890 and 1892. Any changes that were made before 1908 came through the amendment process.[28]

The Constitution of 1908

As the nation and state moved into the 20th century, a new push was made for an overhaul of the Michigan Constitution. By 1906, Michigan voters became convinced that the mid-19th-century document was not suitable for governing a state that was in the midst of rapid change. After the voters approved a convention to write a new constitution, 96 delegates began this task in Lansing in October 1907. Unlike the two previous conventions, this one was dominated by Republicans, with only eight delegates elected as Democrats. Moreover, farmers (only seven) were vastly outnumbered by lawyers (60) and businesspeople (20), with a few other occupations sprinkled in—publishers, professors, a clergyman, and a carpenter.[29] They completed their work in February 1908 and the voters approved the new Constitution in November of that year.

The document drafted by this convention has been described as "basically a re-writing of the 1850 Constitution,"[30] with major improvements being a reorganization of the material, the return of the Bill of Rights to a single article, and each article representing a specific subject.[31] The 1908 Constitution was about as long as its predecessor, as it both eliminated or consolidated some sections and added new ones. Important changes included provisions that increased the power of local governments, specifically revising home rule requirements for villages and cities (see chapter 5). In addition, the governor was given the line-item veto for appropriations bills, the process for legislative action was made somewhat more transparent, and provision was made for the judiciary to be expanded by a two-thirds vote of each house of the Legislature.[32] Limited progress was made on women's suffrage, as women taxpayers were permitted to vote on bond issues, and the Legislature was authorized to pass labor laws aimed at protecting women and children. Fino concludes, "The new twentieth-century constitution . . . was firmly rooted in the antebellum world."[33]

Slow Movement toward the 1963 Constitution

The defects of the 1908 document led to numerous amendments—nearly 70 were approved between then and the next convention in 1961. The 1908 Constitution permitted voters to petition for amendments, not just the state Legislature. The first set, adopted in 1913, concerned initiative, referendum, and recall elections—mechanisms to promote direct democracy advocated by Progressives but that had been rejected by the Republican-dominated convention in 1907–08 (see chapter 11). Democrats were able to capitalize on the division that developed between the more conservative Taft Republicans and the Progressive wing of the party led by Theodore Roosevelt. A new alliance between Democrats and Progressive Republicans led to the pro-direct democracy amendments that Fino describes as "[p]erhaps the most important single development in Michigan constitutional history."[34] Additional amendments in the 1940s and 1950s were designed to improve the structure and efficiency of government, including changes to home rule for cities and villages; the creation of a civil service system for government employees; a nonpartisan primary and general election of Supreme Court justices, circuit court and probate judges, and county judicial officers; specifying the line of succession after the governor; and the election of board members for Michigan State University and Wayne State University. Provisions that created, defined, and punished the crime of subversion were added in 1950 amid the anti-Communist hysteria that was sweeping the nation, and severe limits were placed on the Legislature's taxing and spending powers.[35]

The effect of all these amendments was that the 1908 Constitution became "a document full of anachronisms and inconsistencies,"[36] and it also became clear that a new constitution was necessary to resolve serious problems of governance in a polity that had changed from a largely agricultural society to an industrial, urban state. In 1900, 60 percent of the population lived in rural communities, but by 1960 that number had dropped to 25 percent, and the apportionment of the state Legislature in the Constitution did not reflect this shift.[37] Thus the existing apportionment "discriminated against urban areas, the Democratic Party, working-class people, and [African Americans]" and "favored the Republican Party, rural interests, and sparsely populated areas."[38] This malapportionment also helped produce political stalemates between the executive and legislative branches as a Democratic governor often clashed with the Republican-dominated Legislature. One significant impact of the impasse was that it became impossible for the state to balance its budget and to respond to serious fiscal crises as its revenues decreased with the decline of the automobile industry, which had become the driver of Michigan's economy.[39] Furthermore, constitutional limits on raising revenue and the earlier practice of earmarking taxes for specific purposes exacerbated the situation.

Despite the increasing recognition that a new constitution was needed to resolve these and other issues, yet another constitutional restriction made it difficult to do so. Prior to the 1908 Constitution, a majority of those voting on the question of general constitutional revision had been sufficient for a convention to be called. Under the 1908 document, however, this was changed to a majority of those voting in the election at which the issue was submitted. But because of the phenomenon termed "ballot roll-off" or "ballot fall-off," attempts at calling a constitutional convention failed in 1942 and 1958. Fino offers this description of the problem:

> Voters most often vote for the high-profile offices at the beginning of a ballot but often tend to ignore the low-salience offices and questions placed towards the end. Given the placement of the constitutional convention question at the end of the ballot and ballot fall-off, the majority-voting-in-the-election requirement proved to be an insurmountable barrier to the call for a new constitution.[40]

The problem eventually was resolved in 1960 due to the efforts of a coalition led by the League of Women Voters and the Michigan Junior Chamber of Commerce. This coalition led a petition to enact an amendment that would authorize a convention to be called based on majority approval of those voting on the issue. This "Gateway Amendment" was approved in the November 1960 election and, under another of its provisions, the question of constitutional revision was scheduled to be put to the voters at the April 1961 election and every 16 years after that. In addition, the amendment changed the way that delegates to the convention were to be chosen. Rather than having three delegates from each state Senate district, which the 1908 Constitution required and which would intensify the power advantage already enjoyed by areas of the state outside of Detroit, a compromise solution was to have one delegate from each state Senate district and one from each state House district.[41]

Voter turnout at the November 1960 election, which approved the

Gateway Amendment, was significant. Over 1.31 million voters supported the Amendment, with 959,927 voters opposing it.[42] By contrast, turnout was much lower in the April 1961 election, when voters decided whether to support constitutional revision, and it passed by a much smaller margin—23,421 votes out of the 1,169,445 that were cast.[43] In general, voters in the Detroit area supported revision while those in the outstate counties, especially rural areas, opposed it. Support and opposition "reflected the potential winners and losers under a new constitution."[44] Those in rural communities wanted to maintain the advantages they held under the 1908 document, while urban interests thought that legislative malapportionment would be addressed in the convention in ways that would allow for more equitable representation in the Legislature and would shift the balance of power in state politics in their direction.

The 1963 Constitution

A number of issues had emerged in Michigan that prompted calls for a constitutional convention. By the late 1950s and early 1960s, the limits of the governor's powers (e.g., few appointment powers, a two-year-only term of office), legislative malapportionment, and problems of taxation and finance highlighted the inability of the 1908 Constitution to address a modern society that was much more complex than 50 years before. After the April 1961 election that approved constitutional revision, voters went to the polls to choose delegates to participate in the convention, first in a primary in June and then a general election in September. Neither election generated much turnout, and the September turnout was the lowest since 1945, but there was greater turnout among Republicans compared to Democrats. Consequently, Republicans received a significant advantage—99 out of 144 delegates.[45] The delegates to this convention differed from those in earlier ones in that this was the first to include women (11), African Americans (13), and a majority of Michigan natives. As in 1908, lawyers constituted the largest occupational group, but the convention also included prominent businesspeople (e.g., George Romney of American Motors and Dan E. Karn, board member and president of Consumers Power), two leaders in higher education (Charles L. Anspach, former president of Central Michigan University, and John Hannah, president of Michigan State University), a prominent University of Michigan political scientist (James K. Pollock), journalists, labor leaders, farm group leaders, public officials, and leaders of civic organizations.[46]

The "ConCon" (short for Constitutional Convention) began in early

October 1961 in Lansing. Prior to this, the governor had appointed a commission to do preparatory work, paid for through a grant from the Kellogg Foundation because the Legislature would not appropriate the necessary funding. Stephen S. Nisbet, a Republican and former Gerber Products executive and State Board of Education member, was elected president of the convention. The delegates completed their work by May 1962, and on August 1, after making a few minor changes, they voted 96–48 to approve the final draft of the document.[47]

Following the convention, proponents and opponents of the new constitution initiated a vigorous campaign. Support for approval came primarily from the Republican Party, while the Democratic Party spoke largely against it, although there were some in each party who took the opposite view. Subsequently, when the document was submitted to the voters, it was passed on April 1, 1963, "by the very narrow margin of 7,424 votes, a bare 0.5 of 1 percent of the 1,614,296 cast."[48] Voters in Detroit and "outstate Republican strongholds" generally disapproved, while those in suburban areas outside of Detroit and large western counties such as Kalamazoo and Kent were in favor.[49] The new Constitution took effect on January 1, 1964. The most controversial and hotly contested subjects at the ConCon appear to have been legislative apportionment and taxation issues (see below).

Key Provisions of the 1963 Constitution

As was the case with prior iterations of Michigan's four constitutions, the current Constitution of 1963 built upon many provisions contained in the state's earlier constitutions. Many of the core principles found in the 1963 Constitution also can be found in the original 1835 Constitution. The historical evolution of the constitutions and the common threads that connect them all are an important part of understanding the current Constitution and its provisions. Many of each Constitution's provisions were attempts to respond to the major challenges that Michigan has faced in the 19th and 20th centuries. In addition, there are a number of articles and sections of the Michigan Constitution that directly and indirectly affect local governments, local school districts, and state-local government relations. The discussion below identifies selected key provisions of the 1963 Michigan Constitution, along with comparisons to the earlier versions of the state Constitution.

Preamble

The document begins with the following statement: "We, the people of the State of Michigan, grateful to Almighty God for the blessings of freedom, and earnestly desiring to secure these blessings undiminished to ourselves and our posterity, do ordain and establish this constitution."

Article I: Declaration of Rights

This article generally maintained the rights included in 1908 (and 1835 and 1850). There are sections protecting freedom of expression and religion, the right to keep and bear arms, due process in civil and criminal matters, as well as prohibiting slavery. The article reflects some broadening of rights and changes in phrasing. A more important change was the addition of an equal protection clause, similar to the clause in the federal Constitution. Also, the amendment regarding subversion was deleted.

Article II: Elections

This article retains the qualifications for voting to include United States citizenship, the age requirement of 21, six months' residence in the state (with residence determined by the Legislature), and local residence as provided by law. It excludes persons from voting who are mentally incompetent or incarcerated in jail or prison. Section 5 abolished biennial spring elections except for special elections to fill vacancies, requiring that "all elections for national, state, county and township offices shall be held on the first Tuesday after the first Monday in November in each even-numbered year." A significant change allows for acts that were adopted by the people through initiative or referendum to be amended or repealed by the Legislature by a three-fourths vote.[50] Elections are more fully covered in chapter 10 of this book.

Article III: General Government

This article generally maintains the provisions from 1908 with a few changes, most notably the addition of a section regarding "advisory opinions." Here the Legislature (either chamber) or the governor may request the opinion of the Supreme Court on the constitutionality of legislation after passage but before its effective date. In 2016, Governor Snyder invoked this section in requesting the Court to weigh in on the question of whether private schools can receive state funding. The new budget authorized the state to reimburse private schools for costs associated with mandated requirements, including employee background checks, immunizations, and compliance with health and safety codes. Critics contended that this was a violation of the state Constitution, but the justices denied Snyder's request, concluding "we are not persuaded that granting the request would be an appropriate exercise of the court's discretion."[51]

Article IV: Legislative Branch

This is an extensive article that includes numerous sections concerning the organization, rules, and powers of the House and Senate, the terms of office for representatives (two years) and senators (four years), and the matter of apportionment, which had been heavily contested in the ConCon. Section 2 set the size of the Senate at 38 members and addressed the problem of malapportionment by distributing seats "on the basis of 'apportionment factors' consisting (for each county) of an eighty per cent county population plus twenty per cent county area blend."[52] This formula, by combining the factors of population and land area, still favored rural areas over urban communities. Under Section 3, the number of representatives was to remain at 110, "reapportioned on a population basis by the 'equal proportions' formula similar to that used by the United States House of Representatives."[53] Section 6 created a bipartisan reapportionment commission to supervise the apportionment process after each federal census. The wide variety of topics is further revealed later in Article IV. For example, the article includes a substantive addition concerning criminal law—the prohibition against the death penalty found in Section 46. Specific information about the organization and structure of the Legislature and its powers and responsibilities is found in chapter 7 of this book.

Article V: Executive Branch

Some of the most important changes in the new Constitution concerned the executive branch. For example, executive offices and agencies were consolidated such that there could be no more than 20 principal departments, to be under the supervision of the governor. As a result, approximately 130 agencies, bureaus, and commissions were eliminated.[54] The number of elective offices was reduced from eight to four: the governor, lieutenant governor, secretary of state, and attorney general. The state treasurer and auditor general are to be appointed by the governor and Legislature, respectively, while bipartisan boards are to select the head of the highway department and superintendent of public instruction. This article also established a bipartisan civil rights commission with the duty "to investigate alleged discrimination against any person because of religion, race, color or national origin in the enjoyment of the civil rights" (Section 29). This provision appears to be connected to the new equal protection clause that is included in Article II. A more substantial discussion of the governor and executive branch is found in chapter 6.

Article VI: Judicial Branch

Section 1 in this article vests the judicial power "in one court of justice which shall be divided into one supreme court, one court of appeals, one trial court of general jurisdiction known as the circuit court, one probate court, and courts of limited jurisdiction that the legislature may establish by a two-thirds vote of the members elected to and serving in each house." The court of appeals, an intermediate appellate court, with judges elected to six-year terms on nonpartisan ballots, was newly created in this constitution. Another change involved the elimination of justice of the peace courts and authorization for the Legislature to establish courts of limited jurisdiction in their place. The number of Supreme Court justices was reduced from eight to seven, with the previous eight-year statutory term now being constitutionally required. Incumbent justices and judges of the court of appeals, circuit courts, and probate courts were given permission to renominate themselves by filing an affidavit of candidacy. See chapter 8 for more information about Michigan's court system.

Article VII: Local Government

This article concerns the organization, powers, and responsibilities of counties, cities, villages, and townships, and the terms and roles of officers in those communities. The major change here was the provision authorizing home rule for county governments with permission from the state. Cities had been given home rule authority by a provision in the 1908 document. Section 27 changed the terms for county officials from two to four years, and the Legislature is authorized to establish "additional forms of government" in metropolitan areas "designed to perform multipurpose functions rather than a single function." This provision is meant to encourage cooperation among metropolitan communities on issues of common concern. See chapters 4 and 5 for more information about local governments in Michigan.

Article VIII: Education

This article deletes earlier provisions that had earmarked funds for education from certain types of land sales. It requires the Legislature to maintain a system of "free public elementary and secondary schools as defined by law" but appears to leave it to the Legislature to determine the meaning of "free."[55] School districts are prohibited from discriminating against students on the basis of religion, creed, race, color, or national origin. Another important provision alluded to earlier involves the prohibition of public funding for private schools. The relevant language reads "No public monies or other property shall be appropriated or paid . . . directly or indirectly to aid or maintain any private, denominational, or other nonpublic, pre-elementary, elementary, or secondary school" (Section 2). Provision also was made in this article for the superintendent of public instruction to be appointed by the State Board of Education rather than be elected by the voters.

Article VIII also designates 10 institutions of higher learning and directs the Legislature to appropriate funding for their maintenance: the University of Michigan, Michigan State University, Wayne State University, Eastern Michigan University, Michigan College of Science and Technology, Central Michigan University, Northern Michigan University, Western Michigan University, Ferris Institute, and Grand Valley State College. It also provides for boards to govern these institutions, with those at the University of Michigan, Michigan State, and Wayne State to be chosen through election by voters and the others to be appointed by the governor with the approval of the Senate. The creation of community and junior colleges is also provided for in this article. Finally, the state is required to continue to provide programs and services for physically and mentally disabled persons and to support public libraries. Education policy is the subject of chapter 12.

Article IX: Finance and Taxation

This is an extensive and complex article and has been the subject of a number of constitutional amendments, including the Headlee Amendment (1978) and Proposal A (1994), which are discussed in several chapters that follow. Among many provisions, this article broadened the borrowing authority of the state, placed strict limits on the use of property taxes to raise revenue, exempted religious or educational nonprofit organizations from property taxes, prohibited a graduated income tax, modified rules regarding the sales tax and set it originally at 4 percent, continued the earmarking of gas and motor vehicle taxes for transportation purposes, established a state school aid fund to replace an earlier primary school interest fund, and provided revenue sharing to local governments from sales taxes. Many of these provisions are explained in detail in chapter 13. It should be noted that the constitutional restrictions on taxation, coupled with increasing responsibilities and the antitax sentiments of many legislators and governors, continue to make it difficult for the state to respond adequately to fiscal crises.

The Headlee Amendment in 1978 was part of a national antitax movement during the late 1970s. It sought to limit state revenue, impose property tax limits, and provide for payments to local governments that needed to comply with state mandates. Proposal A in 1994 shifted how the state would pay for public school operations, by reducing the contribution formerly paid through local property taxes and increasing the contribution made by the state sales tax; the sales tax was increased from 4 percent to 6 percent. The intent of Proposal A was to equalize public education funding across the state's school districts (see chapter 3).

Article X: Property

This article deals with issues such as the property rights of married women, the state's power of eminent domain, and the homestead and personal property exemption. Under ancient common law, a husband gained control over his wife's property, whether acquired before or after the marriage. In addition, a married woman's property could be used to pay the debts and obligations of her husband. These legal disabilities were ended by Section 1. Section 2 streamlines earlier language regarding the power of eminent domain. It reads in part, "Private property shall not be taken for public use without just compensation . . . in a manner prescribed by law," and it requires compensation to be determined through proceedings in a court of record. The homestead and personal property exemption in Section 3 sets minimum amounts that are exempt from forced sales for the payment of debts.

Article XI: Public Officers and Employment

This article includes miscellaneous provisions concerning public officers and employees. These include the oath requirement for legislative, executive, and judicial officers; the terms of office of state and county officers; classification of state civil service positions; the structure and role of the state civil service commission; rules regarding merit systems for local government employees; and the process for impeachment of civil officers.

Article XII: Amendment and Revision

Two methods for amending the Constitution begin this article: one initiated by the Legislature and the other by the voters. Amendments may be proposed in either chamber and may be submitted to the voters after being passed by a two-thirds vote in each chamber. After being put to the voters, a majority vote to approve the amendment is sufficient for it to become law. Amendments also may be introduced by registered voters through a petition process, whereby the full text of the proposed amendment is included in the petition along with a requisite number of signatures. The specific processes for both methods are included in this article. Since 1963, the two articles with the most amendments attempted and approved have been Article IV (Legislature) and Article IX (Finance and Taxation).

This article also calls for the question of general constitutional revision to be put to the voters every 16 years, beginning in 1978. If the vote is in the affirmative, a constitutional convention must be called. The article then prescribes the rules and procedures to be followed in convening and conducting the convention.

Conclusion

This book began by suggesting that several themes can help provide an analytical framework for understanding Michigan government, politics, and policy. In this chapter, those themes have been amply demonstrated. For example, the importance of the state's historical context is seen through the evolution of the four Michigan Constitutions from 1835 to 1963—and from the amendments over time that have sought to keep pace with the changing times. In addition, much of any constitution seeks to address and respond to real and potential challenges that a state may face (whether those challenges are economic, social, political, or governmental). Finally, the importance of state-local government relations is revealed in many different articles and sections of the Michigan Constitution.

A number of articles and sections have been altered as a result of constitutional amendments over the years. For example, Article I, Section 26 was changed by Proposal 2 in 2006, which prohibited the use of affirmative action programs in public education, public employment, and public contracts. This directly affected employment in local government and school districts. It also prevented local governments from entering into "minority set-aside" contracts with vendors who qualified as minority-owned businesses. Article II deals with ballot initiatives, referendums, and recall elections. Local governments must deal with referendums when they want to raise taxes. Moreover, local recall elections have been common in Michigan over the years, as the state has been a leader in the number of local officials who have undergone a recall election.[56]

As detailed above, Article VII specifically deals with local governments. This article covers the powers and functions of local governments and the election processes for local officials. Other important issues such as home rule provisions for eligible local governments are included in this article as well. Article VIII deals with a different kind of local government—public school districts and various public education issues, with details provided earlier in this chapter. This article includes provisions for both K-12 public education and the local school districts that administer public education, as well as the state university system in Michigan.

Article IX deals with taxation and finance. Not surprisingly, a number of taxation and finance issues related to local government have emerged as Michigan local governments have struggled to deal with the Great Recession and its effects. But voters have addressed local taxation and finance issues for many years. In 1978, voters approved the Headlee Amendment, which placed limits on taxes imposed by the Legislature and units of local government. In an effort to respond to increasing problems with funding public schools (and to do so in a more equitable fashion), Proposal A in 1994 raised the state sales and use tax rate from 4 percent to 6 percent while placing limits on local property tax increases, and changed how public schools were funded in Michigan.

As another response to a challenge, voters approved a ballot proposal (Proposal 2) in 2010, which arose in reaction to federal indictments and conviction of former Detroit mayor Kwame Kilpatrick on mail fraud, racketeering, and obstruction of justice charges. Now contained in Article XI of the Constitution, the so-called Kwame Amendment ruled ineligible for public office anyone convicted of a felony involving "dishonesty, deceit, or a breach of the public trust" related to their duties while in public office or employment. Still other proposals approved by voters put limits on local government use of eminent domain powers (2006) and established a new law that would allow up to three casinos specifically in the city of Detroit (1996). Those articles and sections noted above all address one or more of the book's themes. These themes also will be played out in each of the book's chapters that follow.

WEB RESOURCES

The *Citizens Research Council of Michigan* (CRC) conducts regular research on the Michigan Constitution, including analysis of proposed constitutional amendments. Constitution archives can be found at http://crcmich.org/category/constitution/; or go to the CRC home page, at http://crcmich.org/, and click on the "Publications" drop down menu, and find "ballot proposals."

The *Michigan Legislature* home page offers access to each of the state's four Constitutions. They can be accessed at the Legislature's home page (www.legislature.mi.gov), and by clicking on the "Laws" section, and then "Michigan Constitution."

The *University of Michigan's Bentley Historical Library* provides access to a brief bibliography for each of the Michigan Constitutional Conventions. See http://bentley.umich.edu/legacy-support/politics/conventions.php

NOTES

1. Willis F. Dunbar and George S. May, *Michigan: A History of the Wolverine State*, rev. ed. (Grand Rapids, MI: William B. Eerdmans Publishing, 1980), 244–45; Susan Fino, *The Michigan State Constitution: A Reference Guide* (Westport, CT: Greenwood Press, 1996), 4–5; George N. Fuller, *Michigan: A Centennial History of the State and Its People* (Chicago: Lewis Publishing, 1939), 245–46; and Roger L. Rosentreter, *Michigan: A History of Explorers, Entrepreneurs, and Everyday People* (Ann Arbor: University of Michigan Press, 2014), 88–91.
2. Rosentreter, *History of Explorers*, 91–93.
3. Ibid., 95.
4. Howard Gillman, Mark A. Graber, and Keith E. Whittington, *American Constitutionalism: Volume I: Structures of Government* (New York: Oxford University Press, 2013), 186.
5. Rosentreter, *History of Explorers*, 95.
6. Dunbar and May, *Wolverine State*, 249–50.
7. Rosentreter, *History of Explorers*, 99–100.
8. Ibid., 101.
9. Ibid., 100–103.
10. Fino, *Michigan State Constitution*, 5–8.
11. Dunbar and May, *Wolverine State*, 245; Fino, *Michigan State Constitution*, 5; Fuller, *Centennial History*, 245; and Rosentreter, *History of Explorers*, 78.
12. Fino, *Michigan State Constitution*, 6.
13. Citizens Research Council of Michigan, *A Comparative Analysis of the Michigan Constitution* (Detroit: Citizens Research Council, 1961), 4.
14. F. Clever Bald, *Michigan in Four Centuries* (New York: Harper and Row, 1954), 198; James V. Campbell, *Outlines of the Political History of Michigan* (Detroit, MI: Schober & Co., 1876), 538; Fino, *Michigan State Constitution*, 8; and Fuller, *Centennial History*, 250.
15. Fino, *Michigan State Constitution*, 8.
16. Fuller, *Centennial History*, 250.
17. Dunbar and May, *Wolverine State*, 247.
18. Fino, *Michigan State Constitution*, 8.
19. Dunbar and May, *Wolverine State*, 366.
20. Fuller, *Centennial History*, 327.
21. Fino, *Michigan State Constitution*, 9.
22. Citizens Research Council, *Comparative Analysis*, chap. II, p. 17.
23. Ibid., chap. VI, p. 1.
24. Ibid., chap. VII, p. 29.
25. Fino, *Michigan State Constitution*, 11.
26. Dunbar and May, *Wolverine State*, 368.

27. Fino, *Michigan State Constitution*, 10–11.
28. Ibid., 12–13, and Fuller, *Centennial History*, 410.
29. John A. Fairlie, "The Michigan Constitutional Convention," *Michigan Law Review Association* 6 (1908): 533–38.
30. Dunbar and May, *Wolverine State*, 518.
31. Fuller, *Centennial History*, 412.
32. Fairlie, *Constitutional Convention*, 539–47.
33. Fino, *Michigan State Constitution*, 14.
34. Ibid.
35. Ibid., 17–18.
36. Dunbar and May, *Wolverine State*, 648.
37. David A. Booth, "Michigan's New Constitution," *Southwestern Social Science Quarterly* 44 (1963): 268–69.
38. Ibid., 269.
39. Albert L. Sturm, *Constitution Making in Michigan 1961–62* (Ann Arbor: University of Michigan Institution of Public Administration, 1963), 20.
40. Fino, *Michigan State Constitution*, 18.
41. Dunbar and May, *Wolverine State*, 648, and Fino, *Michigan State Constitution*, 19–20.
42. Citizens Research Council of Michigan, "Michigan's Constitutional Issues," Report No. 313-2 (1994): 4.
43. Dunbar and May, *Wolverine State*, 649.
44. Fino, *Michigan Constitution*, 19.
45. Dunbar and May, *Wolverine State*, 650, and Fino, *Michigan State Constitution*, 21.
46. Dunbar and May, *Wolverine State*, 651 and Fino, *Michigan State Constitution*, 21.
47. Dunbar and May, *Wolverine State*, 650–51.
48. Booth, *New Constitution*, 273.
49. Dunbar and May, *Wolverine State*, 657.
50. Melvin Nord, "The Michigan Constitution of 1963," *Wayne Law Review* 10 (1964): 320; see also chapter 11 in this volume.
51. Lori Higgins, "Public Funds for Private Schools? Michigan High Court Won't Weigh In," *Detroit Free Press*, October 5, 2016; accessed November 3, 2016, http://www.freep.com/story/news/education/2016/10/05/snyder-supreme-court-private-school-funding/91601552/
52. Nord, "Michigan Constitution," 329.
53. Ibid., 330.
54. Dunbar and May, *Wolverine State*, 653.
55. Nord, "Michigan Constitution," 351–52.
56. David Eggert, "Michigan Law Could Lead to Fewer Recall Elections, *Detroit Free Press*, July 27, 2013, http://archive.freep.com/article/20130727/NEWS15/307270043/Michigan-law-could-lead-to-fewer-recall-elections

3 ✦ Federalism and Intergovernmental Relations in Michigan

DALE THOMSON

State government relies upon a complex web of governmental and nongovernmental entities for the authority and resources to implement public policies. The relationships among the governmental entities in that network are known as intergovernmental relations (IGR), which often vary by location, time, and policy area. This chapter examines IGR in Michigan during the late 20th and early 21st centuries. This period saw increasing strain on relationships spawned by economic downturn, anti-federal government sentiment, a growing influence of political ideology on policy decisions, reduced revenue-generation capacity, and diminished regard for the needs and challenges of local government among the state's elected leaders. These strained relationships have important implications for the nature of government in Michigan.

IGR has vertical and horizontal dimensions. The vertical dimension encompasses a variety of relationships among superior and subordinate levels of government. For state government, this entails how the state interacts with the federal (i.e., superior) and local (i.e., subordinate) governments. The superior/subordinate distinction is useful, but an oversimplification because, while the state holds supreme power over local government, the federated system of government in the United States embodies the principle of dual sovereignty, which reserves certain powers for the federal government and others for the states through clauses of the U.S. Constitution and the 10th Amendment. In some policy areas, state governments have primary responsibilities; in others, the reverse is true. The horizontal dimension, from the state's perspective, examines the relationship among the 50 states.

State-Federal Relations

Federalism is the starting point for examining the state's role in IGR. It considers the distribution and sharing of authority between state and federal government; the extent to which governmental actors attempt to exert, expand, or contract authority; and the relationships that are engendered by or affect such efforts. The proper division of power between federal and state governments has been a source of tension within the United States since the writing of the Constitution, and we have experienced considerable changes in state-federal relations throughout history.

Since the early 1990s, federal policies have generally continued the devolution of authority that began with President Richard Nixon's "New Federalism," accelerated with the retrenchment of the federal government from many activities under President Ronald Reagan, and was reinforced by subsequent presidents. Yet dramatic counterexamples, such as the expansion of intelligence activity in the wake of the 2001 World Trade Center terrorist attack, the bank bailouts and economic stimulus package in the wake of Great Recession, increased federal intervention in K-12 education, and federal mandates for health care coverage passed under Presidents George W. Bush and Barack Obama complicate characterizations of our recent pattern of federalism. The following sections examine federalism and Michigan government from two perspectives—funding provided from and to the federal government (using a fiscal lens) and the state government's use of the courts to alter federal policy (legal lens).

Federalism through a Fiscal Lens

Federal funding of state and local government is an obvious aspect of state-federal relations. Yet federal funding for individuals (e.g., Social Security), businesses (e.g., defense contracts), and nonprofit organizations (e.g., program grants) is also critical and accounts for the largest share of federal funds spent in Michigan. From fiscal year 2000 (FY00) through FY14, the federal government spent an average of $68.7 billion per year in Michigan (see table 3.1).[1] This accounted for 15 percent of Michigan's annual Gross Domestic Product, on average.[2]

Clearly, the federal government has played an important role in the state. Funding through contracts, grants, loans, insurance, and other assistance ranged from $59 billion in FY00 to almost $93 billion in FY09. Funding increased by an average of 4 percent annually, but fluctuated significantly from year to year. It rose steadily from FY00 to an early peak in

FY03 then decreased slightly but remained in the $70 to $75 billion range for the next three years. After dropping to $62.5 billion in FY08, it grew by 48 percent in FY09 due, primarily, to increased aid in response to the Great Recession through the American Recovery and Reinvestment Act (ARRA) of 2009. It dropped by 25 percent the next year and fluctuated between $64 billion and $70 billion between FY11 and FY14.

A declining economy moved Michigan from a donor state to a subsidized state over the period. From FY00 to FY02, Michigan was a net donor to the federal government, providing between about $1 billion and $37 billion more in tax revenue than it received in federal contracts or assistance.[3] For the rest of the period, Michigan was a net recipient. It received as much as $44 billion more than it provided during the peak year of ARRA funding (FY09) and averaged $10.2 billion in net receipts in the remaining years. Although Michigan was typically a net recipient of federal funds from FY00 to FY14, its annual share of federal funding (2.4 percent) was lower than the share of tax revenue it provided to the federal government (2.7 percent).

In an average year, about 8 percent of federal funding came through

TABLE 3.1. Federal Funding to Individuals, Nonprofits, Businesses, and Governments in Michigan

Fiscal Year	Total Contracts and Assistance	Percent from Contracts	Year-to-Year Change in Dollars
2000	$58.848 billion	5%	
2001	$63.520 billion	7%	8%
2002	$65.805 billion	6%	4%
2003	$75.347 billion	6%	15%
2004	$71.283 billion	6%	-5%
2005	$72.048 billion	9%	1%
2006	$74.113 billion	9%	3%
2007[a]	NA	NA	NA
2008	$62.506 billion	14%	NA
2009	$92.694 billion	9%	48%
2010	$69.107 billion	10%	-25%
2011	$63.808 billion	11%	-8%
2012	$68.769 billion	10%	8%
2013	$64.825 billion	8%	-6%
2014	$69.796 billion	7%	8%
Total	**$972.470 billion**	8%	
Average	*$69.462 billion*	*8%*	*4%*

Source: USASpending.gov (as of November 2015) adjusted to 2015 dollar values using the CPI inflation factor derived from the CPI Inflation Calculator available at http://data.bls.gov/cgi-bin/cpicalc.pl
[a] 2007 omitted due to missing data.

contracts, mostly with businesses. Of the remaining 92 percent, about two-thirds went to individuals through Social Security, Medicare, and Medicaid assistance.[4] In most years—years without significant ARRA funding—individuals' share of the federal funding was higher. Government received 28 percent of funds, on average, and 25 percent of funds after subtracting the years with significant ARRA funding.

Federal Funding to the State of Michigan Government

Federal funding was critical to the State of Michigan government's response to economic downturn. From FY00 to FY14, federal funding to state government ranged from $13.3 to $21.8 billion and accounted for one-third of state government revenues, on average (table 3.2).[5] It accounted for about 25 percent of state revenue in FY00, grew rapidly to around 30 percent, and held at this rate until FY09 when Michigan began receiving substantial ARRA funding. The share of state revenue grew to 38 percent in FY09 and

TABLE 3.2. Federal Funding to State of Michigan Government, 2000–2014

Fiscal Year	State Government Revenue	Federal Funding to State Government		
		Dollars	Percent of Total State Revenue	Year-to-Year Change in Dollars
2000	$50.979 billion	$13.291 billion	26%	
2001	$51.864 billion	$14.367 billion	28%	8%
2002	$52.004 billion	$14.931 billion	29%	4%
2003	$51.069 billion	$15.152 billion	30%	1%
2004	$50.761 billion	$15.478 billion	30%	2%
2005	$50.375 billion	$15.179 billion	30%	-2%
2006	$49.898 billion	$14.459 billion	29%	-5%
2007	$49.711 billion	$14.672 billion	30%	1%
2008	$49.297 billion	$15.039 billion	31%	2%
2009	$50.746 billion	$19.440 billion	38%	29%
2010	$51.994 billion	$21.752 billion	42%	12%
2011	$50.473 billion	$20.275 billion	40%	-7%
2012	$47.697 billion	$17.471 billion	37%	-14%
2013	$47.039 billion	$17.067 billion	36%	-2%
2014	$47.417 billion	$17.568 billion	37%	3%
Total	$751.324 billion	$246.141 billion	37%	
Average	*$50.088 billion*	*$16.409 billion*	*33%*	*2%*

Source: State of Michigan Comprehensive Annual Financial Report Combined Schedule of Revenue and Other Financing Sources General and Special Revenue Funds.

Note: Figures adjusted for inflation; figures adjusted to 2015 dollar values using the CPI inflation factor derived from the CPI Inflation Calculator available at http://data.bls.gov/cgi-bin/cpicalc.pl

42 percent in FY10. As ARRA funds diminished, so did the proportion of state revenue supplied by the federal government, but federal funding still accounted for 37 percent of state revenue in FY14.

Federal funding grew at an average rate of 2 percent annually over the period, though increases were as high as 29 percent when ARRA funds began arriving, and declines were as large as 14 percent as ARRA funding expired. Federal funding increased in nine of 14 years, and, even after ARRA funds diminished, it remained about $2 billion higher than it was prior to ARRA. In contrast, total state revenue decreased from year to year in real terms in nine of 14 years. Federal funding as a share of total and general revenue of state government was somewhat less in Michigan than the national average for states until the Great Recession, when Michigan state government became as dependent—or slightly more dependent—on federal revenue than the average state. These findings demonstrate the importance of federal funding in easing the state's budgetary constraints.

Because federal funding was provided through specific programs targeting federal priorities, the state government had limited discretion regarding how to spend the money. The U.S. Department of Health and Human Services provided the most funding, an average of 64 percent of all federal funding for the state government annually. Most of its funding was dedicated to Medicaid. Medicare, Temporary Assistance to Needy Families, and the Children's Health Insurance Program were also major recipients of this funding. Thus, the state had to spend the vast majority of federal funding on health needs of seniors and the poor, and income support for indigent families. The next largest providers were the Department of Agriculture (16 percent), Department of Education (10 percent), and Department of Transportation (6 percent). These sources led to increased support for the state's agricultural industry, school districts, and highways. So, while the federal government provided much-needed funding to address critical needs, the state government could not necessarily allocate the funding to what it viewed as its most pressing needs.

Federal Funding for the Auto Industry

A discussion of federal funding in Michigan in the early 2000s must include a unique form of federal financial assistance—the "Auto Bailout." Michigan's Big Three auto companies—Chrysler, Ford, and General Motors—and their suppliers were pivotal to the state's economy and received significant federal funding through the years, often in the form of contracts. In 2008, the nation's economic and financial turmoil compounded the automakers' negative profit trends and left no one to provide financing needed for Chrysler and GM to survive the immediate crisis. Bankruptcy and liquidation would have threatened the survival of the automobile supplier network and, potentially, Ford Motor Company, but Ford was the only member of the Big Three that was able to avoid bankruptcy. Such outcomes would have devastated Michigan's economy and extended far beyond the state's boundaries; it was estimated that the industry accounted for more than one million jobs nationwide. The automakers, Governor Jennifer Granholm, state legislators, and Michigan's congressional delegation lobbied the White House and Congress to provide federal support—mainly in the form of loans or loan guarantees—to Chrysler and GM to ensure their survival.

The precedent for federal aid to the auto industry was established when the federal government provided assistance to Chrysler in the late 1970s, and Congress and President Bush had just approved the $700 billion bailout of the financial industry through the Troubled Asset Relief Program (TARP). Despite the precedents and the industry's impact on the nation's economy, the fight for approval was daunting. The U.S. Senate rejected legislation passed by the House of Representatives in late 2008. With heavy lobbying, awareness of the economic impact of the auto industry, and knowledge of the incoming Obama administration's support for aid to the auto companies, President George W. Bush authorized $17.4 billion in loans from the TARP fund, using a very generous interpretation of the legislative language. Following Barack Obama's inauguration, intensive negotiations for additional assistance conditioned upon specific requirements, including continuing government oversight, ensued with leaders from GM and Chrysler. Following his predecessor's lead, President Obama authorized further assistance through TARP. Approximately $85 billion in assistance was provided to GM, Chrysler, and their suppliers. Although both GM and Chrysler went through a managed bankruptcy, both emerged from the crisis and much of the assistance was repaid.

It is difficult to overestimate the uniqueness of this intervention. The amount and form of assistance—a large portion of the loans were converted to stock, meaning the federal government owned a large share of both companies—and the role of the federal government in overseeing the companies during its ownership were unprecedented. So was the means by which the assistance was secured—unilateral presidential action with funds originally approved for a different purpose. While the aid was provided to industry, not government, the federal intervention has several implications for state-federal relations. It shows the significant interplay between economy and government and the potential for blurring the boundary between them. It also shows the importance of Michigan's main industry to the nation's economy during this period of decline. Yet it also shows that the appreciation for this role, the credibility of the industry, and the ability of Michigan's congressional delegation to sway their counterparts had all diminished. Finally, it shows that state-federal relations are not always most evident in the actions of the legislative branch. In the case of the Auto Bailout, action came from the White House. The national economic impact seemed paramount to garnering support from Presidents Bush and Obama. Yet Governor Granholm also actively lobbied President Obama and his top appointees for the increased assistance in 2009. Moreover, labor unions, which supported Obama's presidential campaign, would have been devastated if Chrysler and GM failed. Although the United Auto Workers viewed some provisions of the federal assistance negatively, it backed the effort to provide aid, and helping this important constituency likely factored into Obama's decision.

Summarizing Federalism Viewed through the Fiscal Lens

Federal funding to individuals, companies, nonprofits, and government in Michigan was critical from 2000 to 2015. Support grew over time and became increasingly important as economic decline accelerated. Most of the funding went to individuals for Social Security retirement benefits or disability assistance or as payments to those providing services to elderly individuals through Medicare. Still, funding to state government was vital, especially for helping the state balance its budget during the peak of the crisis. Federal funding supported highway development and maintenance, the state's agricultural industry, and education. Yet the overwhelming target of federal spending was to enable the state to provide medical care to low-income households through the Medicaid program. The federal government also played a critical role in limiting economic crisis by providing financial assistance to prevent the collapse of Chrysler and GM. When viewed through the funding lens, state-federal relations were positive throughout the period. The federal government significantly aided the state in weathering the economic crisis of the 2000s.

Federalism through the Legal Lens

State-federal relations are also affected through nonfinancial channels. One that became especially important beginning in the mid-2000s was the courts.

Michigan's attorneys general—the state's lead attorney who is part of the executive branch and elected in a statewide election—used the courts to try to alter federal intervention in the state. Pursued under the banner of ensuring states' rights, preserving individual liberties, or protecting businesses from unwarranted regulation by the federal government, these efforts were contemporary manifestations of the tensions over state vs. federal authority that have existed since the crafting of the U.S. Constitution.

Most notable among the efforts of attorneys general are legal challenges to the Patient Protection and Affordable Care Act of 2010 (ACA, or "Obamacare"), legal briefs in defense of highly restrictive immigration laws passed in Arizona, opposition to President Obama's executive orders to ease access to work permits for illegal immigrants and protect their children from deportation, and lawsuits challenging the enforcement of clean air regulations by the Environmental Protection Agency (EPA). These were efforts to obstruct federal action, but Michigan's attorneys general have sometimes called for a greater federal role. For example, using lawsuits and lobbying for new federal laws, Michigan attorneys general aggressively called for the federal government to take greater action to protect the Great Lakes from Asian carp and other invasive species.

These legal strategies had mixed effects on federal policy. While unsuccessful in their primary goal of crippling the ACA by having a core component—the individual mandate to purchase health insurance—declared unconstitutional,[6] the opposition to mandates for employers to provide coverage for contraception and abortion-inducing drugs was successful.[7] Some components of Arizona's immigration law were preserved, but the more prominent elements were not. The attorneys general succeeded in blocking the EPA's implementation of more rigorous air quality standards, but had less success forcing action to regulate invasive species.[8] While court actions forced the EPA to regulate the ballast water of international ships,[9] they were unable to make the federal government force the State of Illinois to close the Chicago-area locks to prevent Asian carp from entering the Great Lakes.[10] Advocacy for federal legislation to achieve this goal also had little effect. Regardless, these cases increased tensions between the state and federal government and complicated the federal government's ability to implement its programs.

As the state government's top lawyer, the attorney general defends the state's laws in state and federal courts and initiates or intervenes in lawsuits when it considers the interests of state government or its citizens to be at stake. Such cases commonly relate to consumer protection, citizens' rights, the state's economic interests, the state's authority to exercise its constitutional powers, or keeping the federal government from overstepping its constitutional powers. The multifaceted nature of the attorney general's responsibilities and the complexity of most public policies mean that the attorney general often has considerable discretion in deciding whether or not to pursue legal action. These traits also make unequivocal interpretations of motivations for attorneys' general actions difficult. Some of the actions noted above, such as the efforts to keep invasive species out of the Great Lakes, clearly focused on preserving the economic, cultural, and recreational interests of state residents. Yet some of the actions were clearly motivated by political ideology. The attorneys' general challenges to federal authority emerged under the successive terms of two Republican attorneys general—Mike Cox and Bill Schuette—that began in 2003, and became increasingly aggressive after the election of President Obama, reflecting the growing nationwide antagonism within the Republican Party toward the federal government and President Obama. In most cases, these challenges were consistent with positions of Michigan's governor or Legislature, or both. At other times, most notably during the tenure of Governor Granholm (2003–11), a Democrat, they ran directly counter to her positions. Although Michigan's Constitution gives the governor supervisory authority over the attorney general (see chapter 2), Granholm, who supported many of the Obama administration's policies that Attorney General Cox was challenging, was unable to stop him. This is primarily because the attorney general is separately elected in a statewide election, rather than appointed by the governor. This demonstrates the potential fissures within Michigan's executive branch that result from the attorney general's independence, as well as the difficulty of fully understanding complex state-federal relations.

State-State Relations

Attorneys' general challenges to federal authority often occurred through collaborations of attorneys general from multiple states. As instigators and active participants in these collaborations, Michigan's attorneys general have facilitated interstate collaboration. In the recent challenges, such as those against the ACA, collaboration was often aided by ideological and party affiliation among the attorneys general or the governors in the participating states, or both. Yet several collaborations were fostered by shared interests in protecting citizens from actions by national or multinational corporations and potential efficiency and success when forces were combined. Those collaborations challenged deceptive and fraudulent practices by firms in the tobacco, pharmaceutical, telecommunications, petroleum, and financial industries, and demonstrated cooperative horizontal intergovernmental relationships among the states to protect consumers, local governments, nonprofits, and states' pension systems. The collaborations demonstrate the relatively easy path for collaboration that can emerge through the states' attorneys, versus the governors' offices or legislatures.

In various policy areas, the pursuit of shared interests has been formalized in enduring partnerships known as multistate compacts, contractual agreements among the states binding them to jointly implement programs, adhere to specified standards, or otherwise coordinate actions in a specific policy area. For example, the Great Lakes Basin Compact created the Great Lakes Commission, composed of eight states and two Canadian provinces, in 1955 to coordinate the use and conservation of water and related resources in the Great Lakes Basin and St. Lawrence River, mainly through research and policy advocacy.[11] Recognizing the need for a body with more authority to drive state and provincial policies, Great Lakes Commission members signed an agreement in 2005 that established a more authoritative framework for resource management, and the Great Lakes–St. Lawrence River Basin Water Resources Compact was adopted three years later to govern their adherence to the agreement.[12] A new council was established to implement the compact.

The Great Lakes are an obvious target for interstate collaboration, but collaboration has also emerged through compacts to address other policy areas where the need for coordination is clear. For example, compacts have emerged to address supervision and out-of-state placement of juveniles and adults under state supervision; coordination of higher education in the Midwest; interstate passenger rail service; insurance regulation; radioactive waste; and regulation of the oil and natural gas industry. Each compact provides a unique opportunity for policy coordination. Compacts facilitating basic administrative actions, such as those related to placement of children under state supervision, tend to have more ongoing effect on day-to-day operations. Those addressing higher level policy tend to be advisory and their effect on state policy is dependent upon the priorities and inclinations of people in key policy-making positions.

State-Local Relations

As important as federal-state and state-state relations have been to Michigan, state-local government relations account for the majority of intergovernmental activity for state government. As creations of the state, local governments can only do what the state enables them to do (see chapter 5). The state sets the boundaries for local governments' actions and controls much of their funding, either through direct financial assistance or by passing laws that establish the types of revenue government can raise and how. Since the early 2000s state-local relations in Michigan have been dynamic and contentious as the state has filled budgetary shortfalls with resources formerly dedicated to local government, intervened in local government operations to address fiscal problems, and passed laws constraining local sovereignty.

Since the mid-1990s, local finances and state intervention in local governance have been the dominant themes in the story of state-local relations. A new era of relations began when Proposal A was approved in 1994, giving the state a larger role in financing local school districts, reducing cross-district funding disparities while also limiting growth in local property tax revenue. As the state's economy floundered in the 2000s, the state adopted laws and budgets that dramatically reduced funding to municipalities and altered funding to school districts. When the poorest of these local governments found themselves unable to attain solvency in the wake of the Great Recession and state cutbacks, the state intervened further by replacing elected governing bodies with emergency managers and financial oversight boards that dictated policy and spending decisions. Where the state did not directly intervene, it fostered an environment of austerity, leading to the gutting of core services by many local governments. Under the banner of improved service delivery, it fostered the creation of institutions that directly competed with the traditional public entities for revenue. As the state's economy began to rebound, the state stayed the course by keeping state funding to local government at the new, lower levels; failing to provide adequate road funding and then increasing funding, almost certainly at the expense of other state funding to local government; and passing laws that hampered local self-governance.

Relations Framed by Fiscal Stress

Understanding state-local relations in Michigan requires recognizing the extent to which fiscal stress dominated local affairs starting in the 2000s. Michigan's economy began its tailspin long before the rest of the country, and local government revenue dropped dramatically as the recession progressed.[13] By FY12, 78 percent of municipalities had less general revenue to spend on city services than they did in FY05.[14] In total, municipalities had 28 percent less revenue ($1.4 billion), enough money to pay for almost 16,250 police officers or more than 17,260 firefighters. The biggest impact was felt in the City of Detroit, which lost $822 million. Excluding Detroit, Michigan municipalities had 18 percent less general revenue ($559 million) in FY12 than in FY05.

Declines were substantial in many cities and experienced statewide. At least three-quarters of municipalities that lost revenue had at least 10 percent less revenue in FY12 compared to FY05. At least one-quarter of municipalities had at least 24 percent less revenue. In 91 percent of Michigan's metropolitan areas and 91 percent of Michigan's counties, at least half of the municipalities lost general revenue.[15] In 61 percent of metro areas, at least 75 percent of municipalities lost revenue. There was no clear geographic variation in the scale of loss either. Even extreme losses were widespread. All but three metropolitan areas contained a municipality whose rate of loss was among the 50 largest in the state.

Municipalities responded to revenue loss by making tough decisions. Most emphasized cutting compensation, personnel, and services. Municipalities tried to preserve their most critical services by spreading cuts across an array of activities classified as general government, which accounted for 29 percent of spending cuts.[16] Yet core services could not be spared. Public safety absorbed 20 percent of the cuts, public works accounted for 12 percent, and 12 percent of cuts came from recreation and culture.

Personnel were the dominant focus of cost-cutting. From April 2000 through May 2013, local government employment in Michigan dropped 16.6 percent, 3.4 percent more than the decrease in private sector jobs over the same period.[17] Excluding K-12 schools, local government employment declined 8.4 percent from March 2001 through March 2013. Counter to trends after prior national recessions, declines continued after the Great Recession, despite growth in private sector and state government jobs. Michigan led all other states in loss of local government jobs. From July 2008 to May 2013, Michigan's rate of loss in local government employment, excluding education, was nearly three times the rate for local governments nationwide.[18] These employment cuts hit core service areas. Public safety jobs accounted for 31 percent of all jobs lost in local government in Michigan, excluding K-12 education, from 2000 to 2011. There were 3,650 fewer police officers in Michigan by 2012.[19] Between 2001 and 2013 1,800 union firefighter positions were eliminated.[20]

Fiscal Stress Leads to State Intervention

Revenue declines instilled an era of austerity and an era of state intervention in local government through state-appointed financial overseers that either held ratification authority over policy decisions of local elected officials or replaced local elected officials in the decision-making process. In 1990, as part of its responsibility for ensuring the financial solvency of local governments, the State of Michigan passed the Local Government Fiscal Responsibility Act (Public Act 72). Under Public Act (PA) 72 the state could compel local governments to enter consent agreements with the state dictating how they would resolve serious financial problems or, when a financial emergency existed, appoint an emergency manager (EM) to control the local government's finances. EMs could overrule the financial decisions of local elected governing bodies and were unaccountable to those bodies. Little attention was paid to PA 72 until the economic downturn of the 2000s. From 2000 to 2010, the state declared financial emergencies for seven municipalities. By October 2015, under legislation that replaced PA 72, EMs with more power were put in charge of three new cities, including Detroit, and three school districts.[21] Consent agreements, contracts negotiated between the state and local governments as binding plans for resolving local fiscal stress and avoiding imposition of an EM, were in place in two cities, two school districts, one township, and the state's largest county, Wayne. Generally, these agreements gave local leaders considerable latitude in altering bargaining agreements and other contractual obligations but limited discretion in other areas and subjected decisions of these officials to authorization by financial review boards or the state treasurer.

State intervention under PA 72 was grounded in the reality that local governments are creations of state government, subject to the authority of state government, and they had the potential to impact state finances if they became insolvent. Yet those subjected to consent agreements or EMs often objected to state control. The most vocal opponents tended to be local elected officials, public-sector unions, and citizen advocates for self-governance. Battles over state intervention became heated. As the state's experience with local financial emergencies grew, it realized the limitations of the existing law, so the Legislature replaced PA 72 with the Local Government and School District Fiscal Accountability Act of 2011 (PA 4). Public Act 4 enabled the state to intervene earlier in local finances and increased the authority of EMs, who would now control virtually all decisions of local government, not just financial matters. They could reorganize government, terminate collective bargaining agreements, and unilaterally impose employment and compensation practices for government employees. Legal challenges to PA 72 helped prompt the state's push for PA 4, but opponents did not sit idly once PA 4 passed. A coalition, backed primarily by public-sector unions, mounted a successful ballot campaign to repeal PA 4 through a ballot proposal (see chapter 11). Governor Snyder quickly reacted by mobilizing legislative forces to craft a replacement law, the Local Financial Stability and Choice Act of 2012 (PA 436), which retained several aspects of the repealed law while providing for somewhat greater input from local officials.

The state's intervention put some local governments on more sound financial and managerial footing, at least in the short term. Yet the state's predominant emphasis was cutting or privatizing services, or both, and reducing compensation. Addressing fundamental dynamics affecting the long-term sustainability of the older cities and inner-ring suburbs where most of the state intervention occurred was not. Where revenue generation was addressed, it was usually done through higher taxes on residents. The typical outcome was a significantly altered local government in the communities where the state intervened, one with fewer services that could very well face financial crisis in the near future. These results, combined with the disregard for local elected officials embodied in the state interventions and the concentration of state interventions in predominantly African-American communities, created significant animosity between state and local government.

In Detroit, the story is more complex. The historical animosity between the city and the state; the recent state takeover of the city's schools without demonstrable improvements; the historical disenfranchisement of African Americans, who comprise the overwhelming majority of Detroit residents; and the fact that intervention was being led by a wealthy, white, Republican governor, led to vocal and intense hostility toward the state from many stakeholders. Yet there was also support among many Detroiters, who hoped that city services and finances could be improved.[22] The EM led the city to file for bankruptcy, some services were cut, employee compensation dropped, and city pensioners lost a considerable share of their retirement benefits. Yet the intervention also led to a variety of new service and financing arrangements and the elimination of debt that would have eclipsed any hope for the city's long-term recovery. Some services, such as public lighting, were notably improved, and the state committed $350 million to an $816 million "grand bargain" to reduce cuts to city retiree pensions and protect the Detroit Institute of Arts' collection from being liquidated. Postbankruptcy, the city government was in a much better financial position than prior to the appointment of the EM.

By some measures, the state's appointment of an EM for Detroit and the commitments to the city that emerged through the bankruptcy settlement were the most positive interactions between the city and state in many years—an example of productive relations that could emerge through crisis. For Detroit, the wounds of those who suffered from decisions made by the EM were deep, and even the state's $350 million commitment did nothing to address the underlying revenue challenges of the city, including those brought on by state decisions. In fact, shortly after the city emerged from bankruptcy, it discovered that the actuaries had grossly underestimated the city's future pension obligations during the bankruptcy settlement and the city would be facing a tremendous unfunded liability without dramatic action. Moreover, the state's funding commitment emerged only through the prodding of the federal bankruptcy judge and the commitment of $366 million by private foundations. Skepticism and mistrust of the state remained.

Yet nowhere was the distrust of state intervention in local government more evident than in Flint (see chapter 15). The story of Flint made international news—decisions made relative to the city's water supply under management by an EM led to more than 10,000 children in the city being tragically exposed to lead from water pipes, causing lead poisoning. Moreover, the failure of governmental leaders to respond once they became aware of the crisis greatly escalated the scale of the problem.[23] The city's elected leaders chose to switch its water supply from the Detroit Water and Sewerage Department to the regional Karegnondi Water Authority. Trouble emerged when, to save money, the city's EM decided to switch the city's water source from the Detroit Water and Sewerage Department to the Flint River while connections to the Karegnondi Water Authority pipeline, which would supply water from Lake Huron, were being completed. Flint River water was highly corrosive and required substantial chemical treatment. The required treatment did not occur; lead and other contaminants from old water pipes leached into the water at high levels. Officials ignored clear evidence of the problems that emerged and tens of thousands of people were exposed to lead and *legionella* bacteria, creating substantial developmental and health risks.

Governor Snyder characterized Flint's crisis as a "failure of government at all levels."[24] While technically accurate, this characterization deemphasizes the state's role in creating, and responding poorly to, the crisis. As documented by the Flint Water Advisory Task Force, the crisis did result from failure of individuals and institutions in local, state, and federal government.[25] The Flint Utilities Department relied on undertrained, inexperienced staff and consultants with insufficient expertise and failed to provide adequate treatment and testing of Flint River water. The Genesee

County Health Department conducted inadequate follow-up with children with elevated lead levels and failed to adequately notify the public of health risks associated with Flint's water. The U.S. Environmental Protection Agency's enforcement of federal regulations pertaining to water quality was delayed and inadequate, despite clear evidence of problems. However, the state played the primary role in creating the crisis and failing to adequately respond to it, once it was discovered. The Michigan Department of Environmental Quality was identified as bearing primary responsibility for the water contamination.[26] It misinterpreted and misapplied federal regulatory requirements; provided inaccurate guidance to Flint Public Works Department personnel regarding water treatment and testing; failed to require the city to provide corrosion treatment for the Flint River water, even after tests showed unacceptably high lead levels; provided misleading test results to the EPA; ignored offers of assistance from EPA experts; and dismissed or discredited concerns shared by residents, elected officials, and others. The Michigan Department of Environmental Quality was characterized as having a culture that prevented it from adequately protecting the health of Michigan's residents. Obstinance and slow action by the Michigan Department of Health and Human Services significantly delayed the state's response to lead exposure and *legionella* bacteria once they were discovered, and the department failed to play an appropriate leadership role in coordinating the on-the-ground response to lead exposure. What is, perhaps, most notable is that the bipartisan Flint Water Advisory Task Force, which was appointed by Governor Snyder, also identified the Governor's Office and state-appointed EMs as playing a significant role in the crisis. The Governor's Office ignored key indicators of a problem in Flint, as well as specific suggestions regarding actions to address it. The EMs overemphasized financial considerations at the expense of public health. Indeed, the EM approach to resolving local fiscal stress created an environment that was prone to cost-driven decisions without regard for other important criteria, and decision-making processes that were prone to excluding important voices.

State's Role in Creating Fiscal Stress

The state itself has played a role in creating fiscal stress. One way it has contributed to this has been by reducing funding to local government. Locally generated taxes accounted for the largest share of general revenue lost by municipalities from FY05 to FY12, but diminished state funding was also significant, accounting for 30 percent of the general revenue loss. State funding was more significant when considering what happened in individual municipalities. In 45 percent of Michigan's municipalities, declining state revenue accounted for at least 50 percent of the lost revenue. On average, declining state funding accounted for 79 percent of the total revenue loss in individual municipalities. As the state decreased funding, local residents bore a greater share of the burden for financing local government. By FY12, state funding accounted for 3 percent less of municipal revenue while locally generated revenue accounted for 3 percent more.[27]

The state's struggling economy made funding cuts inevitable, but local governments bore a considerable share of those cuts. General revenue sharing, real and personal property taxes, and road funding have been dramatically affected by state-level policy decisions and, while local leaders occasionally affected those decisions, their voices were largely ignored in a state Legislature seemingly focused on cutting taxes, shrinking government, diluting the influence of organized labor, and reducing business costs and regulations.

Cuts in Revenue Sharing

Since the 1930s, the state has had an unrestricted revenue sharing program for local governments (see chapter 13). This program was designed to have the state "serve in a revenue raising capacity to capitalize on revenue raising efficiencies and share state-collected revenue with local governments, usually because the finances of local governments were negatively affected by statutory changes that exempted parts of the property tax base from taxation."[28] Funding from the program was dramatically altered during the state's fiscal crisis. Revenue sharing generally entailed allocating a specific portion of a state revenue source to local governments to spend on a wide range of general purposes. In the 1970s, the state began providing unrestricted revenue sharing funds through a constitutionally mandated and a statutorily driven program. Payments under these programs peaked in FY01 at $1.56 billion, then decreased in eight of the next 13 years.[29] By FY14, revenue sharing totaled $1.1 billion, 30 percent less than the FY01 peak.[30] The Legislature had discretion regarding how much of the statutory revenue sharing funding it distributed to local government, and from FY02 through FY14, it used about $6.9 billion of statutory revenue sharing to fund shortfalls in other parts of the budget.[31] The FY14 statutory revenue sharing funding to local government was only about 25 percent of the funding generated under the program. Statutory revenue sharing payments to more than 900 of the state's 1,773 units of local government were eliminated, and the state changed the program to a competitive one that required local governments to undertake certain actions, including privatizing services or altering employee compensation and benefits, to qualify for funding.

In sum, the unrestricted revenue sharing program that was adopted primarily to compensate local governments for revenue lost from state limits or prohibitions on local taxes was cannibalized by the state to fill its own budget gaps at a time when local governments' ability to generate funding was drastically reduced. A significant portion of the funding that remained would be provided only to local governments that adopted policies that the state favored.

Eliminating the Personal Property Tax

As local governments were grappling with impacts from the Great Recession and reductions in revenue sharing, the state Legislature began efforts to eliminate another source of local government revenue, the personal property tax (PPT). The PPT was a tax paid by businesses to local government for personal property—not buildings or land—located in a community. While many stakeholders accepted the need to reform the PPT, local leaders whose communities benefited from the tax were desperately trying to avoid losing yet another revenue source. Concerns were so great that municipalities and school districts formed a campaign to lobby state officials to replace any revenue lost from eliminating the PPT with funding from some other source. The battle was long and hard, and the bills that passed were far from what local advocates envisioned. Ultimately, the coalition was able to engender some changes at the state level and approval by voters of a proposal enabling the creation of a replacement revenue stream for 100 percent of the lost PPT revenue. The PPT fight was a partial victory for local governments—partial because this solution did not guarantee full replacement of revenue. They fought a long, resource-consuming campaign that resulted not in increased revenue, but merely in retaining the revenue that they were already generating.

Road Funding

The fiscal stress of local governments greatly hampered their ability to perform core services, including road construction and maintenance, and the state's approach to road funding made matters worse. In 2014, 38 percent of Michigan's roads were in poor condition, and 45 percent were in only fair condition.[32] Absent major policy changes, the percentage of miles in poor condition was forecast to climb to 57 percent by 2025. The cost for improving roads was high, an estimated $14.1 billion in 2015.[33] More than three-quarters of local leaders surveyed in late 2014 estimated they would need at least 50 percent more state road funding just to adequately maintain their roads.[34] Clearly, Michigan had a serious problem with road conditions, a problem that frustrated drivers, hampered economic growth, and posed considerable problems for local governments attempting to maintain and improve roads and quality of life. Despite calls from local leaders, businesses, and citizens to fix the road-funding problem, it took the Legislature five attempts from 2014 through 2015 before it finally approved new funding. In between legislative proposals, a constitutional amendment placed on the May 2015 ballot to fund the state's roads failed miserably, with roughly 80 percent of voters rejecting it (see chapter 11). Only then was a proposal finally passed and signed into law later in 2015. The delay in approving new funding and the nature of the funding scheme that was approved fueled frustration and further demonstrated the modest influence that local government leaders had with the Legislature. While the legislation was expected to increase road funding by $1.2 billion per year by FY21, half of the funds would come from the state's General Fund, a major source of state funding for local government (see chapter 13). Other provisions of the legislation would decrease the General Fund by an additional $206 million in FY21 and more thereafter.[35] Therefore, a good portion of the increased road funding was likely to come from sources otherwise allocated to local government.

Additional State Constraints on Local Revenue

Local governments' ability to increase revenue since the Great Recession was further constrained by two state constitutional provisions governing property taxes—the Headlee Amendment and Proposal A (see chapter 13). The 1978 Headlee Amendment limited the growth in property tax revenue from existing properties to the rate of inflation. The only way to increase property tax revenue at a rate beyond inflation was to add property to the tax rolls through development or have voters approve an increase in the tax rate or a "Headlee Override," which allows the local government to avoid a rollback in the tax rate that would otherwise occur. In 1994, voters approved Proposal A as part of a major reform in public school finance that shifted the primary source of revenue from local property taxes to a state

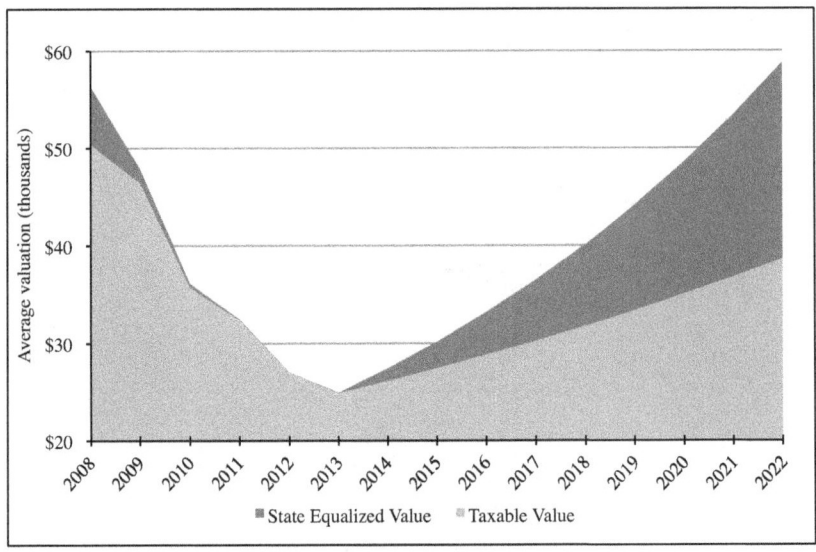

Fig. 3.1. Impact of the Recession and Property Tax Limits on Revenue in Eastpointe, Michigan, 2008–2022
Source: Base figures and estimates provided by the City of Eastpointe, based on historical tax data.

sales tax. Proposal A limited property tax increases by capping growth in the taxable value of individual properties at the rate of inflation, unless the property was sold or substantially improved.

While these constitutional provisions limited increases in total taxes collected (Headlee) or total tax base (Proposal A), neither limited reductions. When taxable values plummeted due to the Great Recession, dramatic reductions in taxable value and, consequently, total property taxes collected ensued. The immediate effect of these reductions was significant, but the lasting effect was greater. The city of Eastpointe in Macomb County illustrates the extent of the problem in some of the hardest-hit communities (see fig. 3.1). The average taxable value for a home in Eastpointe bottomed out in 2013 at about 50 percent of its 2008 value, meaning the city was receiving about 50 percent less in property tax revenue from residential properties. Due to state limits on the annual growth of property taxes, even with overly optimistic assumptions about the growth in property values (10 percent growth in state equalized value per year),[36] by 2022 the city would be collecting only about 75 percent of the revenue that it did from properties that existed in 2008, even though the market value of homes would be greater than it was in 2008.

Proposal A affected local government revenue in additional ways. The

Headlee Amendment also prevented Michigan from decreasing the share of state spending allocated to local government below the FY79 proportion (48.97 percent).[37] While this would seem to ensure that local government funding decreased no more than the decrease in total state spending, the revenue generated by the state through Proposal A's education sales tax vastly increased the total state funding to local government. Much of this funding would have previously been raised by local school districts, via the property tax, but now the state got credit for it. The state could now reduce local government funding from sources other than those associated with Proposal A and still keep the share of state spending devoted to local government above the minimum required under Headlee.

State-Supported Competition for Resources

In the case of school districts, the state further contributed to fiscal stress by creating new institutional competitors for public schools that pulled students and state funding from those schools. This was done through authorization of a large number of charter schools and the creation of the Education Achievement Authority (EAA) (see chapter 12). By FY14, 9 percent of the state's per-pupil school funding went to the state's 370 charter schools, which enrolled more than 140,000 of the state's pupils. State funding for charter schools accounted for almost $1 billion annually.[38] Despite the resources devoted to charters and the Legislature's 2011 decision to remove the cap on the number of charter schools, the state imposed relatively few accountability requirements on them. While high-performing charter schools existed, the overall performance of charter schools that were created to improve performance of the state's schools was no better than the state's traditional public schools. Many fared worse and were allowed to stay open despite inferior performance. The EAA, which was set up in 2011 as the state's turnaround district for poor performing schools, was operating 15 schools in Detroit in 2015. Yet problems with enrollment, staff turnover, executive compensation, and other administrative matters were evident, and early indicators showed students performing no better, and perhaps worse, than their counterparts in the Detroit Public Schools.[39] The EAA was further plagued by an FBI investigation of corruption in contracting. The state-backed EAA was replicating and amplifying the very problems that it was established to eliminate, all at a higher price to taxpayers than if the schools it ran were kept within the Detroit Public Schools. Lawmakers dissolved the EAA as part of the bailout package for the Detroit Public Schools passed in June 2016; in addition, the package shut down the old district—Detroit Public Schools—and created a new one—the Detroit Public Schools Community District.

Uneasy Trends in State-Local Government Relations

It was inevitable that the recession that began in the early 2000s would affect state funding to local government and hamper local governments' capacity to generate revenue internally. Tensions were likely to emerge as local leaders dealt with these mutually debilitating forces. Indeed, in 2012, almost 60 percent of local leaders felt the state's method of funding local government needed to be reformed.[40] The percentage was closer to 80 percent in the state's largest communities. Yet the cumulative effect of specific actions of state government worsened those tensions and extended them beyond matters of finance. By 2014, less than 30 percent of county, city, village, and township officials viewed the Legislature's performance as "good" or "excellent," and almost one-third considered it to be "poor."[41] While local officials' views of Governor Snyder were more favorable, opinions were still split with slightly more than half giving him a positive rating. Dissatisfaction extended to state agencies. Only two out of 14 agencies were considered to have "good" or "excellent" performance by the majority of local officials. Furthermore, less than half of local officials believed that state legislators were "very" or "mostly" ethical, and only slightly more than half considered executive officials to be.[42] Clearly, state-local relations suffered from 2000 to 2015, partly from uncontrollable economic turmoil, but to a significant degree from specific actions from state government that undermined local government and demonstrated a disregard for local governments' concerns.

Conclusion

Intergovernmental relations in Michigan is incredibly complex. How one characterizes IGR depends upon which level of government, time period, and policy area one is focusing. Often, the specific branch or office of government must also be considered. IGR also depends upon the interaction of countless variables internal and external to the government. Factors significantly affecting the state, such as the economy, the political ideology of policymakers, and geography, have spillover effects on other governmental units with which the state interacts. The extent to which those factors affect relations will depend on their scope or scale and the manner in which the state's leaders react to these factors. While these dynamics complicate efforts to characterize IGR for the state in the early 21st century, some factors had prominent effects on IGR and some general patterns emerged.

In Michigan, between 2000 and 2015, the economy had the most evident effect on IGR. It created an extended period of constrained resources and growing needs where competition for resources was intense and the environment for those seeking to minimize government's "burdens" on businesses and individuals was favorable. Specific actions of state policymakers—driven partly by the economy, but also by political ideology—greatly magnified the effects of these forces. State government became increasingly dependent on federal funding, but increasingly hostile toward federal actions. While the state's Republican leaders fended off federal efforts to intervene in what it considered state or individual matters, they were increasingly receptive to interceding in local affairs, often to the detriment of local governments' ability to control their policy decisions or provide basic services. The state's Republican leadership sought to make the state increasingly central in the intergovernmental system by vigilantly pursuing independence from federal intervention where it did not perceive a direct benefit to the state while accepting increased federal funding to support state spending. They limited the discretion of local governments while channeling an increasing share of local government funding to other purposes in the state budget. This approach heightened tensions between the state and its federal and local counterparts and greatly complicated their ability to develop and implement programs.

WEB RESOURCES

The *Citizens Research Council of Michigan* conducts extensive research on state policy issues, including policies affecting the state's relationship with the federal and local governments. They have an extensive selection of reports on state budgets and finance. From their home page (www.crcmich.org) click on "Publications," then select one of the topics that appears in the drop-down menu, or select "Publication Archives" and click on the tag associated with your topic of interest on the right side of the screen.

The *Federal government* maintains a comprehensive database of federal assistance and contracts by state and year that is searchable by several different variables. In the map on their home page (www.usaspending.gov), click on Michigan. For details on assistance, click on "Assistance Awards" under "More Data for Michigan." For contracts, click on "Contracts Awards."

The *Michigan Municipal League* (www.mml.org), *Michigan Townships Association* (www.michigantownships.org), *Michigan Local Government Management Association* (www.mlgma.org), and *Michigan Association of School Boards* (www.masb.org) are trade organizations that represent different types of local governments throughout Michigan. Their websites provide a variety of information about local government, including matters related to state policy and state-local relations.

The *National Center for Interstate Compacts* maintains a comprehensive database of interstate compacts by state. From their home page (www.csg.org/NCIC/default.aspx), click on "Database," then select the state from the map. Click on any of the compact names in the resulting table to get more detail on the compact.

NOTES

1. Figures were derived from USASpending.org in November 2015 and adjusted to 2015 dollar values using the CPI inflation factor derived from the CPI Inflation Calculator available at http://data.bls.gov/cgi-bin/cpicalc.pl. FY07 is excluded from the analysis because of missing data.

2. Gross Domestic Product figures were obtained from the Federal Reserve Bank of St. Louis, https://research.stlouisfed.org/fred2/series/MINGSP#

3. Figures reflect the gross federal tax receipts from Michigan (Table 5: Gross Collections by Type of Tax and State, Fiscal Year, https://www.irs.gov/uac/SOI-Tax-Stats-Gross-Collections,-by-Type-of-Tax-and-State,-Fiscal-Year-IRS-Data-Book-Table-5), less refunds (Table 8: Amount of Refunds Issued, Including Interest, by State and Fiscal Year, https://www.irs.gov/uac/SOI-Tax-Stats-Amount-of-Refunds-Issued,-Including-Interest,-by-State-and-Fiscal-Year-IRS-Data-Book-Table-8). Both figures were obtained from the Internal Revenue Service and adjusted to 2015 dollars.

4. This calculation excludes FY12–FY14, due to discrepancies in coding of the underlying data that prevent an accurate calculation.

5. Figures for federal funding to the State of Michigan government were obtained from the State's Comprehensive Annual Financial Reports, which were retrieved from http://www.michigan.gov/budget/0,4538,7-157-13406_13419---,00.html

6. *National Federation of Independent Business v. Sebelius*, 567 U.S. ___ (2012).

7. *Burwell v. Hobby Lobby*, 573 U.S. ___ (2014).

8. *Utility Air Regulatory Group v. U.S. Environmental Protection Agency*, 573 U.S. ___ (2014).

9. *Northwest Environmental Advocates v. U.S. Environmental Protection Agency*, 537 F.3d 1006 (9th Cir. 2008).

10. *Michigan v. U.S. Army Corps of Engineers*, 667 F. 3d 765 (Court of Appeals, 7th Circuit 2011).

11. Great Lakes Commission, 2015, "About Us," http://glc.org/about/

12. Great Lakes–St. Lawrence River Basin Water Resources Council, 2009, "Great Lakes Agreements," http://www.glslcompactcouncil.org/Agreements.aspx

13. The primary units of local government in Michigan are counties, cities, villages, townships, and school districts. The services of counties and school districts are distinct from those of cities, villages, and townships. Legislative changes have blurred the lines separating cities, villages, and townships to the point where know-

ing the type of jurisdiction does not provide a clear understanding of the type and range of services it provides. The financial data provided in this section applies to cities and villages. The analysis is based on data from FY05 and FY12 Local Unit Audit Reports submitted to the Michigan Department of Treasury by cities and villages that had at least 7,500 residents in 2011. Data were audited to identify obvious errors and corrected using data from municipalities' comprehensive annual financial reports where necessary. After data cleaning, the dataset included 469 municipalities, 88 percent of all municipalities that existed in FY05 or FY12 and 100 percent of municipalities with a population of 7,500 or more.

14. All dollar values have been adjusted to 2012 dollars using a CPI inflation factor of 1.18 derived from the CPI Inflation Calculator available at http://data.bls.gov/cgi-bin/cpicalc.pl

15. These are metropolitan or micropolitan areas, as defined by the U.S. Census Bureau. Michigan's 33 metro areas account for 96 percent of the state's municipal population and 42 percent of the state's entire population. For simplicity, I use "metro areas" to refer to both metropolitan and micropolitan areas. Five counties did not have municipalities with data. They are excluded from this calculation.

16. In this section, data explaining cost cutting by type of activity do not include data for Detroit.

17. Citizens Research Council of Michigan (CRC), *Michigan's Single-State Recession and Its Effects on Public Employment (CRC Memorandum No. 1124)* (Livonia: CRC, 2013), http://www.crcmich.org/PUBLICAT/2010s/2013/memo1124.pdf

18. Craig Thiel, "Public Sector Employment Trends in Michigan and the U.S.," *CRC Column: Citizens' Research Council of Michigan* blog, September 27, 2013, http://crcmich.org/public-sector-employment-trends-in-michigan-and-the-u-s/

19. Michigan Commission on Law Enforcement Standards, *Snapshot of Law Enforcement Officer Positions* (Lansing: Michigan Commission on Law Enforcement Standards, 2013), http://www.michigan.gov/mcoles/0,4607,7-229-41622---,00.html

20. A. J. Jones, "Tax Shift Adds to Fiscal Woes at City Hall," *Bridge Magazine*, April 4, 2013, http://bridgemi.com/2013/04/tax-shift-adds-to-fiscal-woes-at-city-hall/

21. Only one of the cities still had an EM in charge in October 2015, but all still reported to a financial oversight board, which had the authority to veto budgets or legislation that it felt would create financial problems for the city.

22. Khalil AlHajal, "Poll: 41 Percent of Detroit Voters, 67 Percent Statewide Support Emergency Financial Manager," *Mlive*, March 26, 2013, http://www.mlive.com/news/detroit/index.ssf/2013/03/poll_41_percent_of_detroit_vot.html _of_detroit_vot.html; Matt Helms and Joe Guillen, "Free Press/WXYZ-TV Poll: Detroiters Fed Up with Council, Bing, Snyder, Services," *Detroit Free Press*, May 26, 2013, http://archive.freep.com/article/20130526/NEWS01/305260071/

23. Chad Livengood, "High Lead Levels Prompt Appeal to Governor," *Detroit News*, September 29, 2015, A3, http://infoweb.newsbank.com/resources/doc/nb/news/1582971A9E062840?p=AWNB

24. "Gov. Snyder's Staff Responds to Questions about Flint Water Crisis," *MLive*, May 3, 2016, http://www.mlive.com/news/index.ssf/2016/05/gov_snyders_staff_responds_to.html

25. Flint Water Advisory Task Force, "Flint Water Advisory Task Force: Final Report" (Flint: FWATF, 2016).
26. Ibid., 28.
27. These numbers exclude figures for the City of Detroit, which, if included, would skew the results.
28. Citizens Research Council of Michigan, *Reforming Statutory State Revenue Sharing (Report 388)* (Livonia: CRC, 2015), 15.
29. Author's analysis of data from the Michigan House Fiscal Agency and the CRC report on revenue sharing.
30. Michigan House Fiscal Agency, *House Road Package: Preliminary Analysis* (2015), http://www.house.mi.gov/hfa/pdf/summaries/15h4370_house_road_pkg_analysis.pdf
31. Citizens Research Council of Michigan, *Reforming Statutory State Revenue Sharing (Report 388)*.
32. Actual and forecast statewide road condition data retrieved from the Michigan Transportation Asset Management Council, http://www.mcgi.state.mi.us/MITRP/Data/PaserDashboard.aspx
33. TRIP: A National Transportation Research Group, *Michigan's Top Transportation Challenges: Providing a Transportation System to Support and Sustain Michigan's Economic Revival* (Washington, DC: TRIP, 2015).
34. Thomas Ivacko and Sarah Mills, *Local Leaders Say Michigan Road Funding Needs Major Increase, but Lack Consensus on Options That Would Raise the Most Revenue* (Ann Arbor, MI: Center for Local, State, and Urban Policy, 2015).
35. Senate Fiscal Agency, *Senate Fiscal Agency Analysis of Enacted Road Funding Package (11-17-15)* (Lansing, MI: Senate Fiscal Agency, 2015).
36. State equalized value is intended to equal 50 percent of the market value of the property and would serve as the taxable value were it not for the limits imposed by Proposal A.
37. Michigan Legislative Service Bureau, *Michigan Manual 2013-14: Development of the State Budget* (Lansing: Michigan Legislative Service Bureau, 2013), http://www.legislature.mi.gov/(S(ed1ujmbgci5eqlos4xjxxcd5))/mileg.aspx?page=getobject&objectname=2013-MM-P0277-P0280&query=on
38. Jennifer Dixon, "Michigan Spends $1 B on Charter Schools but Fails to Hold Them Accountable," *Detroit Free Press*, June 22, 2014. http://www.freep.com/article/20140622/NEWS06/306220096
39. Ann Zaniewski, "Detroit Schools Brace for Cuts amid EAA 'Fine Tuning,'" *Detroit Free Press*, October 26, 2015, http://www.freep.com/story/news/local/michigan/detroit/2015/10/25/pass-fail-eaa-detroit/72022584/
40. Center for Local, State, and Urban Policy, *Local Leaders Support Reforming Michigan's System of Funding Local Government* (Ann Arbor, MI: Center for Local, State, and Urban Policy, 2013).
41. Deborah Horner and Thomas Ivacko, *Confidence in Michigan's Direction Holds Steady among State's Local Leaders* (Ann Arbor, MI: Center for Local, State, and Urban Policy, 2014).
42. Deborah Horner and Thomas Ivacko, *Michigan Local Leaders See Need for State and Local Ethics Reform* (Ann Arbor, MI: Center for Local, State, and Urban Policy, 2015).

4 ✦ Local Governments in Michigan I
Urban Governments and Detroit

LYKE THOMPSON AND ROBERT J. MAHU

There are many reasons why local governments exist: to provide services that individuals cannot provide on their own, to maintain civil relationships among citizens, and to distribute resources, among other things. Michigan's cities formed for similar reasons, and as the state's economy expanded, these urban centers provided world-class services to their residents. Furthermore, these governments eventually grew to enjoy substantial autonomy through home rule status granted by the state while extending their jurisdictions through annexation and other means. But starting in the mid-20th century, many large cities in Michigan began to suffer from severe and unprecedented challenges for which existing political and economic systems offered few solutions. Given their implications for the state as a whole, recognizing the context, problems, and governance of these cities—particularly Detroit—is an essential part of the bigger picture of Michigan politics.

A Historical Context of Michigan's Urban Areas

In their earliest years under American jurisdiction, Detroit and present-day Michigan were subject to the United States Land Ordinance of 1785. This legislation provided for the division of unorganized land into square mile sections—the building blocks of townships. In these small units, led by volunteer or poorly paid officials, each having their own role and authority, statesmen such as Thomas Jefferson sought a plethora of small republics controlled by the yeoman farmer class. As forests were cleared and wetlands drained, and especially with the opening of the Erie Canal in New

York (1825), large numbers of settlers arrived in Michigan from the American east and northeast. These migrants brought with them resources, place names (e.g., Rochester, Utica, and Troy), mechanisms for public participation, and a "moralistic" political culture, which tends to reprove public corruption and to view government's role as advancing the public interest.[1]

Early Population and Spatial Growth of Michigan Cities

As pioneers dispersed throughout the state, Michigan's major population centers became more well defined. U.S. Census data reveal that four cities—Grand Rapids, Kalamazoo, Jackson, and Port Huron—consistently joined Detroit among the top 10 most populated cities in Michigan from 1850 through 1900. All of these cities were major transportation centers that benefited from the influx of agricultural products and eventually lumber and minerals from peripheral settlements. Detroit, the largest and oldest of these cities, consistently ranked as the primary population center in Michigan. Between 1850 and 1930, Detroit's population grew by an average of 73.5 percent per decade, nearly double the state's average population growth during that period (38.4 percent per decade).[2] The actual population numbers expose the magnitude of this growth; the city's 1850 population of 21,019 increased more than twelvefold to 285,704 by 1900, and with the rise of auto industry this number would more than quintuple to 1,849,568 by 1950.

During this time, Michigan's cities accommodated their expansions through annexation, a sometimes-controversial process by which a city can legally acquire land from an adjacent jurisdiction. Detroit's expansion was particularly dramatic. The city's boundaries relentlessly swallowed the mostly rural sections of surrounding townships, eventually expanding to an area of about 139 square miles by 1926.[3]

Detroit's annexations stopped essentially because its neighbors stopped them. First, nearby communities began to take advantage of Michigan's "home rule" legislation (see chapter 5) when their populations were large enough. These newly incorporated cities developed their own service arrangements and community identities as Detroit's regional dominance began to decline in the 1950s. Second, the Great Depression and World War II facilitated a construction bust throughout Detroit, rendering the city's outermost sections largely undeveloped until the postwar era. Third, state laws made annexation efforts more intricate over time by involving (depending on the circumstances) the State Boundary Commission, carefully designed geographic plans and justifications, legal proceedings, and voter approval from residents of both affected entities.[4] Finally, many tax and service arrangements that once made annexation attractive to outlying areas were provided to townships. Since 1947, for example, Michigan has permitted townships with more than 2,000 residents to become charter townships, with greater taxation powers and specific criteria that enabled these townships to resist annexation. Service agreements such as conditional land use transfers were also made possible by state legislation.[5] In many cases, however, state action was not even necessary; Detroit's massive water and sewerage resources, for example, were eventually made available by contract to nearby cities even if they were not under Detroit's political jurisdiction.

Industrial Growth

In addition to requiring more space for residents, Michigan's urban areas also needed space for industrial activities. Detroit's industrial primacy in the state was established early, thanks to its strategic location on the Great Lakes transportation network. With the 1855 completion of the Sault Ste. Marie (Soo) Canal in Michigan's Upper Peninsula, Detroit became a regional center for iron, limestone, copper, and brass production. Machine and boiler works were established along the Detroit River, along with large foundries, locomotive engine casting, shipbuilding, and pharmaceutical manufacturing. The increasing mechanical capacity of the city's workforce and firms meant that Detroit was poised to emerge as a center of automobile manufacturing.

Other cities benefited from the state's natural resources. Grand Rapids grew substantially in the 19th century, driven by timber distribution networks, and prospering lumber centers such as Saginaw and Muskegon fostered the rebuilding of Chicago after the Great Fire of 1871. Although many lumbering centers declined with the state's dwindling white pine forests, some Michigan cities enjoyed their own automotive booms as supply or foundry centers in the 20th century.[6] The Detroit metropolitan area, meanwhile, became ever more dependent on the metal bending industries, which gradually grew to dominate the overall metropolitan economy. Flint, Lansing, and Saginaw were also peripheral beneficiaries of the automotive industry that characterized much of Michigan's economy in the early 20th century.[7]

Expanding Urban Public Service Provision

Urban growth was propelled not only by the availability of jobs but also by cities' ability to deliver services that were not available, at least as efficiently, in rural areas. Some of these services—such as police and fire protection, libraries, and museums—had been local responsibilities for centuries. Other services developed as the technology for providing them became more sophisticated. Some utilities, such as natural gas and electricity, thus began as small private enterprises in the 19th century.

Larger-scale services such as transportation and water utilities often spurred cities to develop extensive infrastructure and dedicated departments. For example, long before large-scale industry came of age, Detroit had developed an underground sewage system that gradually became one of the largest in the world, and the infrastructure was eventually organized into an executive department accountable to the mayor's office.[8] Later, as the city and its suburbs expanded, this department provided metered water to communities far beyond its borders. Detroit's resulting authority over the water prices for much of southeast Michigan would be a point of contention throughout the region into the 21st century.[9]

Urban Government and Politics in Michigan

In the 19th century, Michigan's urban centers adopted government structures subject to state approval. These structures—often featuring an elected executive and a legislative body—followed the prototypical mayor-council system. Detroit's residents had been accustomed to the presence of a strong authority—the military largely ruled the city for its first century—and it was only with the advent of Jacksonian democracy that the citizens of Michigan's oldest city decided to elect a mayor.[10] It has remained a strong-mayor system ever since.

Michigan's first Constitution (1835) was silent about cities, and the state Legislature would play a key role in the affairs of Michigan's cities throughout the 1800s. The state's strong adherence to Dillon's Rule[11] burdened both the Legislature and municipalities, but Michigan's 1908 constitution permitted the Legislature to enable home rule in the state, which it did the following year.[12] With these laws, Michigan's cities adopted home rule charters and took responsibility for many service demands required by their expanding industrial economies. Cities became, in this era, a powerful force of urbanization, and Jefferson's vision of small governments became less and less relevant to complex urban areas.[13]

Historically, many Michigan cities were Republican strongholds that provided electoral support to Progressive figures such as Theodore Roosevelt and local reform-minded mayors such as Detroit's Hazen Pingree. In the early 20th century, many of these cities implemented some of the urban reforms promoted by national Progressives. One of these reforms was the council-manager form of government, which essentially reduces the mayor to a ceremonial council member and hands the day-to-day administrative responsibilities over to a professional manager. Although Detroit and some of its larger neighbors remained strong-mayor cities, many of Michigan's existing cities adopted the council-manager system over time. The switch to council-manager systems offered voters a response to real or imagined corruption, inaction, or incompetence among elected officials. Some cities, such as Grand Rapids and Monroe, switched early, while other large cities, such as Lansing, Pontiac, Dearborn, and Warren, opted to keep their mayor-council systems.

Detroit's first home-rule charter (1918) maintained the mayor-council system at a time when executive departments and their responsibilities were becoming increasingly expansive. Although many of the city's departments were (and still are) led by nonelected administrators, they remained directly or indirectly accountable to the elected mayor. Acceptance of this situation would persist as Detroit's fortunes declined and its residents perceived hostility from outstate actors. Even in the wake of the scandals of Mayor Kwame Kilpatrick (who served 2002–8), Detroit citizens chose to preserve the mayor's authority over most departments and day-to-day administration in the 2012 charter revision.

Despite an endorsement of a strong mayor, Detroit residents in 1919 chose to abolish its wards in favor of an at-large city council. Urban reformers of that era argued that council members who were elected at-large would be less influenced by the parochial concerns of small constituencies, and more attentive to the greater good of the city. In recent years, however, neighborhood advocates have pushed with limited success for a return to district representation. For example, voters in Saginaw considered (and rejected) such a charter revision in 2007, but Detroit voters approved a hybrid system that combined the at-large and district systems for city council representation—a key feature of the 2012 charter.[14]

Progressive reformers argued that partisan politics had little place in the day-to-day affairs of cities, stressing that "there is no Democratic or Republican way to pave a street," and in 1908 the state Legislature gave Michigan cities the right to conduct nonpartisan elections.[15] The vast majority of Michigan's cites have, in fact, chosen the nonpartisan option.[16] In 2015, city council members in Ann Arbor—one of the few holdouts—rejected a proposal to refer the question of nonpartisan city elections to voters.

Less variation exists among Michigan's county governments. The state

Constitution describes a number of required offices (e.g., sheriff, prosecutor, treasurer, clerk, and registrar of deeds), which in practice are filled through partisan elections. Each county has an elected board of commissioners, but most Michigan counties lack chief executive officers. Some of the state's more populated counties have adopted alternative forms of government permitted by law, and in each case created an elected chief executive office. In the 1970s, for example, voters in Bay and Oakland Counties chose to adopt the "Optional Unified Form," which permits the creation of either an elected chief executive or an appointed county manager.[17] Voters in Wayne (1980) and Macomb (2009) Counties approved new county charters—authorized by the 1963 state Constitution—which also established chief executive offices. In the case of Macomb County, voters hoped that the new executive would give the rapidly growing county a more unified voice in regional discussions with neighboring Oakland and Wayne Counties, as well as Detroit. Despite the presence of these chief executive officers, voters continue to elect a board of commissioners, as well as the constitutionally mandated offices.

Residential Diversity

With the rapid growth of population and industry between 1870 and 1950, Detroit and other Michigan cities became the homes of ethnically diverse residents. Drawn from overseas and the American South by the ample industrial jobs in the state, these individuals often settled in ethnic communities. Larger cities such as Detroit and Grand Rapids had long been the homes of French, Dutch, German, and later, Irish residents. Beginning in the late 1800s, Detroit in particular became the home of predominantly Catholic immigrants from countries in Southern and Eastern Europe. As the political situation in the Middle East deteriorated in the 20th century, new immigrants arrived in Southeast Michigan—including Muslims from the Syria/Lebanon region and Chaldean Christians from Iraq. The large suburb of Dearborn became the home of many Middle Eastern immigrants and their descendants.

Detroit's black community had existed since the age of the Underground Railroad and prior, and in the early 20th century black migrants from the American South joined foreign immigrants in search of coveted manufacturing jobs in the city. As the city expanded, Detroit's black population rose from 5,741 in 1910 to around 120,000 in 1940. African American residents, however, tended to be confined to segregated neighborhoods such as the relatively small Paradise Valley neighborhood on the city's lower east side.

Challenges for Detroit and Michigan's Other Large Cities

Despite their remarkable early growth and prosperity, Michigan's urban areas began to face considerable problems in the last half of the 20th century. Together, these challenges were so severe—particularly in Detroit's case—that they have come to dominate political and economic discussions at the state and national levels.

Deindustrialization and Economic Decline

One of the most visible problems that Michigan's urban areas faced after World War II was the dramatic collapse of the manufacturing sector. Since that time, the automobile industry has followed a cyclical economic pattern characterized by regular downturns, factory closures, and large-scale layoffs. This was particularly difficult for Detroit's workers as the city suffered from no fewer than four recessions between 1949 and 1960.[18] Michigan's heavy industries also lost an increasing share of federal defense contracts as the center of power in the U.S. Congress shifted toward the Sunbelt. Furthermore, the state's factory-reliant cities were impacted by the restructuring of the auto industry itself. The Big Three (i.e., General Motors, Ford and Chrysler) automobile companies embraced decentralization and automation—new approaches to production that reduced work opportunities for lower-skilled laborers and prompted the cancellation of many contracts to outside shops. These reorganizations also required sprawling, single-floor assembly plants that were more amenable to the urban fringe. Older, built-out cities such as Detroit did not have the 400–600 acres of cleared land required by the automobile companies beginning in the 1970s. This spelled decline for the older multistory factories in cities where the land for such expansive new facilities was insufficient, and what little land was available lacked important spatial amenities such as railroad frontage.[19]

The effect of deindustrialization and the subsequent decline of the auto industry on Detroit was especially devastating. Total manufacturing jobs in the city declined from about 338,400 in 1947 to 153,300 in 1977, to a mere 25,700 by 2013.[20] Such a large-scale loss of jobs triggered an urban economic crisis from which many manufacturers would never recover. Despite largely symbolic actions by labor unions and the Urban League to limit the layoffs and arrange job-training programs for those affected, a large underclass of unemployed nonskilled and semiskilled workers emerged throughout the city. In many cases, African Americans, historically relegated to undesirable and dangerous jobs, became marginalized and shut out of those jobs that remained available, especially in Detroit.

A particularly devastating and lasting effect of this decline is evident even in more current poverty statistics of Michigan's former manufacturing centers. The American Community Survey's 2014 five-year estimates reveal, for example, that 39.8 percent of Detroit residents were living below the poverty line. Similarly, more than a third of residents in Flint (41.6 percent), Saginaw (35.5 percent), Pontiac (37.8 percent), Muskegon (35.8 percent), Jackson (36.7 percent), and Kalamazoo (35.0 percent) were living in poverty according to the ACS estimates for the same period.[21]

In addition to the ravages of poverty, economic decline also prompted a series of urban planning disasters. As deindustrialization persisted in the 1950s, city officials often committed to removing what they perceived to be undesirable areas to make room for developments they considered more economically important. These "urban renewal" projects often had dubious or symbolic benefits, while their consequences for neighborhoods and their residents were overwhelmingly negative.[22] In some cases, this took the form of market-based projects such as Detroit's West Side Industrial Project in the 1950s or GM's Poletown plant in the 1980s. In other cases, land clearance accommodated the construction of freeways, which city officials hoped would open the city and its factories to more outside businesses and markets. Unfortunately, the freeways enabled urban residents and businesses to easily leave the cities—often permanently—for new land, jobs, homes, and parks in the suburbs and rural areas. The neighborhoods most adversely affected by freeway construction, such as Detroit's Paradise Valley, tended to be the homes of African Americans, and the displaced residents were forced into a housing market that was both crowded and segregated.

Housing, Neighborhoods, and Race

Urban renewal was largely unsuccessful in stemming the tide of neighborhood decline, partly because it failed to address the severe housing shortages that had grown during the wartime years. During that time, as employment and population increased, the growth of available housing did not keep pace. The situation was especially dire in Detroit. For decades, the city's black residents lived in neighborhoods that were disproportionately affected by unfavorable Home Owners' Loan Corporation ratings, high rents due to overcrowding, advantage-seeking by absentee landlords, and physical deterioration. In these neighborhoods, a generally higher proportion of residents' earnings went to home payments, leaving fewer resources available for other basic amenities such as housing repairs.

The problem was also exacerbated by racial prejudices that afflicted increasingly diverse urban areas. Although the U.S. Supreme Court declared restrictive covenants—clauses in housing deeds that prohibited the sale of the house to certain groups of people—unenforceable in *Shelley v. Kraemer* (1948), residents' attitudes remained largely unchanged.[23] Many racially homogeneous communities throughout Detroit resisted new African American residents with campaigns of intimidation and violence by certain homeowner's associations. Realtors often took advantage of racial tensions through "blockbusting" tactics—convincing existing residents to sell at lower prices while taking advantage of desperate buyers through price markups and land contracts. The new homeowners—usually racial minorities—often faced a disproportionate level of economic hardship due to workplace discrimination and the city's overall deindustrialization.

Often, the end result was the rapid and large-scale abandonment of entire neighborhoods by white, middle-class residents. Such emigrations have been reflected in every decennial census since 1960 and deprived Detroit and other cities of a critical property tax base at a time when the factories were also leaving (see fig. 4.1). By and large, the emigrants stayed in Michigan and moved to the newly incorporated suburbs, where zoning laws had the potential to enforce racial boundaries more effectively.

The resulting demographics are stark. Metro Detroit, in particular, has exhibited very high levels of racial segregation since the postwar era. Among the 100 largest metropolitan areas in the United States, the Detroit-Warren-Livonia region's index of dissimilarity between black and white residents ranked highest in both 1990 (87.6, on a scale of 0 to 100) and 2000 (85.7). Across the state, the Grand Rapids-Wyoming region exhibited the 20th highest index in 1990 (72.7) and 32nd highest in 2000 (66.7). In the 21st century, however, Detroit's inner-ring suburbs in particular have become more racially diverse. As more middle-class African American families left the city in the 2000s, adjacent communities became increasingly diverse, reducing metro Detroit's 2010 index of dissimilarity fell to 75.3—the second-largest 10-year decline among the 100 urban areas studied.[24] Nevertheless, this enduring contrast ensures that race continues to play a role in regional politics.

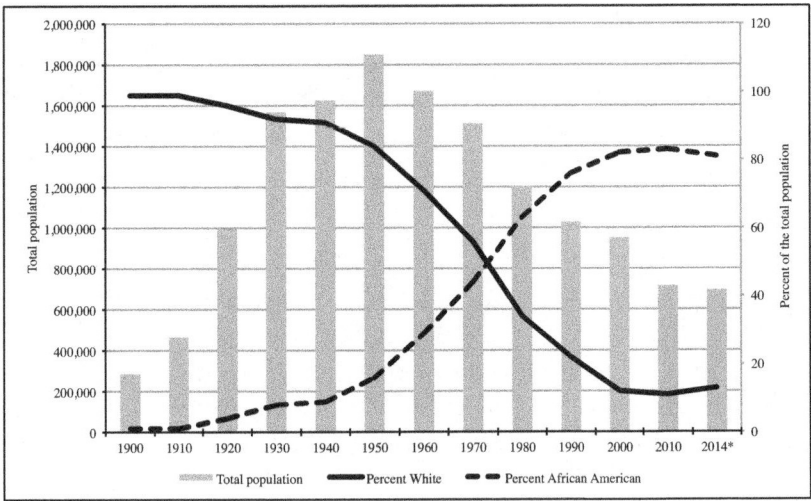

Fig. 4.1. Total Population and Percentage of Whites and African Americans Living in Detroit, 1900–2014

Source: Data are from the U.S. Census Bureau; figures from 1900 through 1990 were compiled from Campbell Gibson and Kay Jung, "Historical Census Statistics on Population Totals by Race, 1790 to 1990, and by Hispanic Origin, 1970 to 1990, for Large Cities And Other Urban Places in the United States," U.S. Census Bureau, Population Division Working Paper No. 76, February 2005; 2010 and 2014 numbers calculated by authors from the U.S. Census Bureau, www.factfinder.census.gov.
Note: Five-year ACS estimate.

Public Safety and Perception

Detroit's national reputation as a dangerous city is evident in FBI Uniform Crime Data. From 1985 to 2002, for example, the city's murder rate averaged 51.5 homicides per 100,000 people.[25] More recent (2015) statistics show that homicide rates in Michigan cities with more than 45,000 residents were highest in Flint (47.9 per 100,000 population), Detroit (43.8), Saginaw (14.2), and Pontiac (11.7). By comparison, large suburbs such as Sterling Heights (3.8), Livonia (1.1), and Troy (1.2) reported much different statistics.[26]

Detroit's crime rates have been especially important to monitor due to the city's relatively large population and its geographic location at the core of a much larger metropolitan area. In addition, as media outlets, beginning in the 1970s, trumpeted the city as the "Murder Capital" of the United States, many associated that distinction with its majority black population.[27] The Detroit riots of 1943 and 1967 were especially destructive not only to lives but also to local, state, and national perceptions of the city.[28] Although the 1967 incident—in which 43 people died—was not a race riot in the strict sense, it sealed the perception of the city's white middle class that Detroit was facing a breakdown of order caused by black residents and ineffectual leadership.

Leadership

Beginning in the 1960s, many of Michigan's urban leaders—especially in Detroit—were confronted and defeated by one crisis after another, although some officials presided over the decline with greater success than others. Some leaders were toppled by the growing attention paid to racial tensions and public order. For example, perceptions of Detroit mayor Jerome Cavanagh's ineffectual handling of the 1967 riot effectively stifled his once promising political fortunes. In the early 1970s, Detroit's paramilitary police unit STRESS (short for Stop the Robberies, Enjoy Safe Streets)—begun under Mayor Roman Gribbs as a response to street crime and the perceived breakdown of order—was regularly accused of using bias and heavy-handed tactics against black suspects.

The city's first black mayor, Coleman Young (1974–94), was an able administrator and one of Detroit's only postwar mayors who made serious efforts to reduce the city's growing structural deficit through department and staff cuts (and tax increases).[29] Young and some of his predecessors had also embarked on affirmative action programs for city departments, with a particular interest in increasing the diversity of the city's police force. In addition, throughout the 1970s, Mayor Young was able to cultivate an amicable relationship with Republican governor William Milliken, which drew the state's attention to Detroit's problems and provided Milliken with surprising electoral success in the city itself.

Yet Mayor Young's tenure coincided with the city's unmistakable decay. The mayor's acerbic rhetoric only confirmed many suburbanites' suspicions that they were considered enemies with whom the city was uninterested in cooperating. For many Detroit residents, Young provided a welcome response to voices such as Mayor Orville Hubbard of Dearborn, who had gained national attention as a supporter of racial segregation. But Young's voice was the one heard throughout the region, and white suburbs remained disaffected. Ultimately, during Coleman Young's tenure as mayor, polarization between Detroit and its suburbs continued for 20 years between the 1970s and 1990s. And although his successor, Dennis Archer (1994–2001), presented a more conciliatory image to the suburbs, little regional progress was made during his tenure, and Detroit's financial crisis continued to grow.

When first elected, Mayor Kwame Kilpatrick (2002–8) promised to address the city's financial problems and reassert the city's role in the region. Unfortunately, Kilpatrick's dramatic 2005 deal to fund the city's pension obligations—over initial resistance from the city council—proved disastrous as the economy tumbled, and accelerated the city's slide into bankruptcy. Kilpatrick's own legal problems, heavily covered by the national media and culminating with his resignation in 2008 and eventual imprisonment for public corruption, distracted state and regional attention away from the city's growing fiscal crisis. The mayor's misdeeds also prompted the creation and approval of a new city charter complete with ethics provisions for elected officials, and seriously tarnished the city's already poor image among its citizens and regional neighbors. Kilpatrick's successors were, in turn, highly limited in their ability to respond to the crises as the city drifted toward bankruptcy.

Other cities had crises of leadership that grew out of frustration with infrastructure deterioration, high taxes, corruption, and perceived ineptitude. For example, Flint residents successfully recalled Mayor Woodrow Stanley after a racially divisive battle in 2002, and unsuccessfully attempted to recall Mayor Don Williamson, who, in early 2009, resigned prior to the vote. Some of Detroit's many suburbs also saw their own scandals and resignations of mayors and council members.[30]

Structural Fiscal Crises

Even cities with the most inspiring and competent leaders would have faced financial problems due to Michigan's economy and a number of constraints imposed by the state. Two amendments to the Michigan Constitution—the Headlee Amendment (1978) and Proposal A (1994)—place a number of limitations on local government finances (see chapter 3). These limits, however, are especially severe for Michigan's older and more developed cities. For example, newly developed land is not included in the Headlee calculations that limit property tax increases—a reality that disadvantages older cities and encourages urban sprawl.[31] Similarly, the property assessment restrictions of Proposal A prohibit most communities from ever recovering tax revenues lost during the Great Recession, even if property values rise to their prerecession levels. Furthermore, these restrictions are lifted when properties are newly built or sold—a mechanism that, again, disadvantages older communities with a smaller volume of new homes and commercial properties.

In Michigan, local sales taxes are prohibited under the state Constitution, and local government income taxing power is limited (see chapter 13).[32] Under the Constitution, however, Michigan shares a portion of its sales tax revenue with municipal governments, as determined by a population-based formula. Local governments may also receive a statutory revenue-sharing payment based on a formula determined by state officials. When the state's economy declined in the 2000s, however, Michigan's statutory revenue-sharing payments stagnated and in some cases disappeared entirely, leaving fewer resources for larger governments to deliver the key services expected by residents. Because much of the revenue-sharing allotments are based on population growth, this decline has adversely affected the payments to cities with dwindling populations, which typically need to serve the often-vulnerable residents who remain. This situation has persisted despite a number of legislative changes to statutory revenue sharing in Michigan during the Snyder administration (see chapters 3 and 13).

Polycentrism

By the 1960s—as large cities like Detroit, Flint, and Saginaw were losing residents—suburban communities' populations were rising sharply. Following the new freeways, residents were lured by open spaces, lower taxes, and even tax-deductible interest on mortgages. As noted above, Detroit and other cities have been unable to expand through annexation, a reality that some have argued is a fatal constraint to local economic growth.[33] In addition, state officials have historically adopted a pro-growth orientation (as opposed to the growth-management orientation of a state like California), and, as a result, low-density urban expansion has been a trend throughout Michigan.[34] Over time, "edge cities"—communities centered around shopping centers, planned subdivisions, or older villages—became regular features of the state landscape.[35] In Southeast Michigan, communities such as Auburn Hills, Novi, and Sterling Heights grew rapidly as Detroit declined—a trend that resulted in a multitude of new local governments by the 1970s. In 2016, the tri-county region of Metropolitan Detroit (i.e., Wayne, Oakland, and Macomb Counties) contained no fewer than 127 municipal governments, not including school and special districts.[36]

Many urban scholars have identified problems associated with fragmented or "polycentric" metropolitan areas, and the fragmentation of Michigan's metropolitan areas has proven difficult to reverse.[37] Polycentrism has led to a decline of central cities such as Detroit and Flint. Efforts to create a "New Flint" out of multiple governments in the late 1950s, for example, were promptly defeated, as were the city of Jackson's efforts in 1961.[38] A number of scholars have also noted that regional fragmentation fosters a competitive public-choice perspective that has considerable difficulty in addressing problems of regional inequity.[39] Fragmentation also militates against some varieties of regional coordination, because regional services require cooperation from jurisdictions with varying household incomes, racial compositions, and desires for exclusivity.

Responses to Challenges

Policymakers in Michigan have used a number of tools to respond to the crises Detroit and other urban areas face. These responses include *development and security strategies*, which are aimed at stemming crime and economic decline; *emergency management*, which seeks to address structural fiscal crises; and *functional regionalism*, which offers a response to the problem of political and racial fragmentation.

Development and Security

In contrast to state or regionally driven responses to local challenges, development and security strategies are driven largely by local officials. In Michigan, local officials have experimented with a number of traditional economic development strategies ranging from building permits and financial incentives to land and infrastructure development. Due to their scope and salience, Detroit's building projects—often the initiatives of private corporations such as GM (Poletown), Chrysler (Jefferson North), or business leaders such as Mike Ilitch and Dan Gilbert—have received considerable attention. Other cities—particularly in Southeast Michigan—have invested in efforts to improve park and recreation services, beautification efforts, marketing through local chambers of commerce, training of economic development staff, and even adopting administrative tools such as geographic information systems.[40]

Cities may also choose redevelopment as an approach to stem decline. In contrast to the disastrous urban renewal efforts of the 1950s, urban planners have considered emerging strategies such as increased use of greenways and parks, "road diets" such as lane reductions and roundabouts, and "daylighting" rivers that were submerged in the 1800s—such as Kalamazoo's Arcadia River, Detroit's Parent's Creek, and the Clinton River in Pontiac.[41] Some cities may also choose to develop a particular industry as a potential tourist attraction, as Detroit did with its casinos. Nevertheless, redevelopment can be costly, and its benefits are not assured.[42] Other cities may reassess their service delivery systems. Detroit's 2012 Strategic Framework Plan, for example, includes a strategy to "right-size" these systems so that their capacity best matches areas with the greatest demand.[43]

Many local governments have also invested in data-driven approaches to fighting crime. For example, in Midtown Detroit, the Wayne State University Police Department began partnering with community leaders, private security personnel, and researchers in an effort to reduce crime in the area. Using CompStat methods, community organizing through AmeriCorps, and biweekly meetings among this wide group of stakeholders, crime in the area dropped more than 50 percent between 2008 and 2015, despite the economic crisis.

Emergency Management

Fragmentation and the very immensity of the problems faced by Michigan's local governments have, in some cases, prompted state-level responses. These, in turn, have affected state-local government relations in a substantial and sometimes-controversial way. One of the more controversial responses to these crises is the state's emergency management law. Michigan's emergency managers are authorized by a series of statutes dating back to the 1980s, culminating in the Local Financial Stability and Choice Act of 2012.[44] An earlier version of this law was rejected by voters in a 2012 referendum, but the Legislature promptly passed a similar version that included appropriations—making it referendum-proof under Michigan's Constitution. This new emergency manager law, which often overrides local elected officials' prerogatives, gained national attention in March 2013 as Governor Snyder appointed bankruptcy attorney Kevyn Orr as Detroit's EM. Michigan's EM law stipulates circumstances or conditions that may warrant state financial review and the eventual appointment of an EM to rectify the financial emergency. To fulfill this charge, EMs are granted considerable administrative and appointment powers, as Detroit mayor Dave Bing (2009–13) learned upon Orr's arrival. During his last year in office, Mayor Bing, whose economic and political power was already severely limited by Kwame Kilpatrick's legacy, was effectively relegated to the sidelines on virtually all of the city's financial decisions.

Michigan's EM laws have always been controversial for their assertion of state power over cities that have enjoyed home rule for decades, and the presence of an EM is often a source of resentment to residents. In Detroit's 2013 mayoral campaign, Wayne County sheriff Benny Napoleon signaled that, if elected mayor, he would not cooperate with Kevyn Orr. Mike Duggan, who eventually won that election, argued that collaboration with the EM was the only realistic way to assure his speedy departure. In fact, Duggan and Orr forged a working relationship that did not impede Orr's timely exit in December 2014.

Michigan's EM strategy came under renewed scrutiny when Flint's emergency manager presided over the city's disastrous transition from Detroit's water system to the corrosive Flint River (see chapter 16). Local officials argued that the temporary switch to river water, prompted by the city's intention to join the new Karegnondi Water Authority, would save money. Instead, the 2014 decision led to a public health emergency. In late 2015, confirmation that residents had been exposed to high levels of lead in their drinking water—despite months of complaints, advisories to boil the water, and no corrosion control—led to national outrage and charges against various state officials. The crisis revealed a lack of empathy for the needs of vulnerable citizens and two former EMs were charged in 2016 with felony false pretenses and misconduct in office. And just as the catastrophe in Flint unfolded in 2016, revelations of the extensive disrepair in many Detroit public school buildings (under the administration of a district EM) came to light—further souring public perception of the state's EM approach.

Finally, some demographic characteristics are evident with respect to EM recipients. At the time Orr was appointed to Detroit, for example, five other communities—Allen Park, Benton Harbor, Ecorse, Flint, and Pontiac—were under emergency management, together accounting for 9.3 percent of the state's population at the time. With the exception of Allen Park, and relative to the respective state averages, these cities tended to have lower rates of homeownership, lower median household incomes, greater numbers of residents below the poverty level, and higher African American populations.[45]

Functional Regionalism

Both through state enabling acts and concerted action across local governments, Southeast Michigan and other metropolitan areas are substantially transforming the governmental landscape. From planning to parks and museums to water, an increasing array of services is being provided through multijurisdictional authorities. This has emerged gradually across the regions' histories, but has accelerated as Detroit and other cities have been forced to shed functions, and many of those have been taken over by regional or at least multicounty entities. Such authorities have become more appealing as many local governments have reduced staff and office hours, consolidated services, renegotiated labor contracts, and even abolished local primary elections to save money. Often, two or more jurisdictions have found it necessary to jointly provide services under the Urban Cooperation Act of 1967. There are hundreds of such arrangements in the Detroit metropolitan area alone, ranging from mutual aid pacts for fire and police to water and sewer contracts to county-level provision of a range of services to townships and cities, especially in Oakland County.[46] Such joint efforts may also take the form of authorities—that is, state-authorized entities established by local voter or legislative approval for the purpose of either raising revenue or jointly administering a particular service or function (see table 4.1).

Michigan governments have not been shy about creating such entities. Perhaps the most visible metropolitan authorities in Michigan are regional planning councils. Fourteen such councils exist in Michigan as of 2015, by far the largest of which is the Southeast Michigan Council of Governments, established in 1968.[47] These planning authorities function less as policy-making entities than as analytical strategists who conduct feasibility studies, demographic forecasts, and regional economic development studies. They can, however, exert substantial influence over regional policy.

A number of large Michigan cities, such as Grand Rapids, Flint, Saginaw, and Lansing, have created regional transportation authorities, designed to extend and fund bus routes over greater distances than those in systems operated by one city alone. For years, the Suburban Mobility Authority for Regional Transportation has operated in Southeast Michigan, although it faced a number of coordination problems. Regional planners hoped that the 2012 creation of the Regional Transit Authority of Southeast Michigan —to be operated at the county level—would eventually address some of these problems, in addition to providing more predictable funding. These hopes were dashed at least temporarily by voters' 2016 rejection of a millage to implement the Regional Transit Authority transportation plan.

Some of the more recently established authorities have targeted specific city services (e.g., Detroit Public Lighting Authority), counties (e.g., Great Lakes Water Authority), and institutions (e.g., Detroit Regional Convention Facility Authority, Detroit Institute of Arts, and the Detroit Zoo). In these cases, the new authorities either replaced existing city departments or provided an extended funding base for historically city-operated infrastructure or institutions that were popular with suburbanites. Detroit's declining influence over regional water service was also evident during the Flint water crisis. For example, Flint decided to leave Detroit's water system (now the Great Lakes Water Authority) in favor of joining the new regional Karegnondi Water Authority.[48]

Once authorized by the state, local officials may seek to create authorities with voter approval, although some authorities such as the Great Lakes Water Authority are the products of executive agreements. Regional fragmentation may, however, make such agreements politically difficult. Less extensive authorities that provide for ambulance service, public safety, and recreation may have a more realistic chance of obtaining voter approval.

TABLE 4.1. Selected Authorities Permitted in Michigan

Service Area	State Authorizing Laws (selected)	Government Level	Example(s)
Parks	PA 147 (1939)	Defined Counties only	Huron-Clinton Metropolitan Authority (HCMA)
Regional Planning	PA 281 (1945), PA 46 (1966), PA 292 (1989)	Counties and Municipalities	Southeast Michigan Council of Governments (SEMCOG), West Michigan Regional Planning Commission (WMRPC)
Waste Management	PA 179 (1947)	Municipalities	Mid Michigan Waste Authority
Water	PA 233 (1955)	Municipalities	Great Lakes Water Authority (GLWA), Karegnondi Water Authority (KWA)
Public Safety	PA 57 (1988)	Municipalities	South Macomb Oakland Safety Authority (SMORSA)
Recreation	PA 321 (2000)	Municipalities and Districts	Rochester Avon Recreation Authority
Zoological Parks	PA 49 (2008)	Counties	Macomb County Zoological Authority (Detroit Zoo)
Convention Center	PA 554 (2008), PA 63 (2009)	Detroit and Defined Counties only	Detroit Regional Convention Facility Authority (DRCFA)
Art Institute	PA 296 (2010)	Counties	Oakland County Art Institute Authority (Detroit Institute of Arts)
Transportation	PA 55 (1963), PA 204 (1967), PA 196 (1986), PA 387 (2012)	Counties and Municipalities	Flint Mass Transit Authority (MTA), Suburban Mobility Authority for Regional Transportation (SMART), Interurban Transit Partnership—The Rapid Regional Transit Authority of Southeast Michigan (RTA)
Lighting	PA 392 (2012)	Detroit only	Detroit Public Lighting Authority (DPLA)

Conclusion

This chapter has discussed the historical context of Michigan's large cities and metropolitan areas, the challenges many of them continue to face, and some of the key responses to those challenges. Michigan's cities, especially older ones with declining populations and little room for new growth, have few options, and are heavily dependent on others to exercise those options. The state of the cities would not surprise many students of urban politics.[49] Nevertheless, in Southeastern Michigan, which has over half of the state's population, decades of crisis are eliciting an increasing range of responses, including an emergent form of regional provision of a diverse set of services by a collection of differentiated entities, each tightly controlled by local governments. It may take decades of trust building to move to more integrated forms of regionalism, and there are major political and institutional obstacles to achieving such integration.[50] Yet there is an increasing range of creative options that governments and political actors are testing. Still greater cooperation among suburbs and inner cities—and especially among private, state, and federal actors—is required if Michigan's regions are to truly reach their economic and political potential. As Michigan's cities continue to suffer from long-term decline and attempt to respond to a wide variety of challenges, state leaders must invest in Michigan's human and physical capital, far more than half of which is in its cities. Drastic cuts in revenue sharing for cities, inaction on infrastructure investment, ignoring environmental challenges, and policies that encourage political fragmentation represent escapism in the face of these responsibilities.

WEB RESOURCES

The *City of Detroit* website (www.detroitmi.gov) provides information about the structure of local government and various government services.

The *Citizens Research Council* (crcmich.org/) conducts research on Detroit and urban areas in Michigan, along with providing a variety of research reports and documents.

Drawing Detroit is a regularly updated collection of maps and data about Detroit and its metropolitan area (www.drawingdetroit.com).

The *Michigan Association of Regions* (MAR) is a portal (www.miregions.com) that contains links to all 14 regional planning councils in Michigan, including the Southeast Michigan Council of Governments. The regional bodies often publish demographic data, reports on economic projects, and planning reports.

The *Michigan Municipal League* (www.mml.org) is one of the primary advocates for local government interests in Michigan and produces a number of informational papers and other data-based publications of interest to students of Michigan government.

NOTES

1. Daniel J. Elazar, *American Federalism: A View from the States*, 3rd ed. (New York: Harper and Row, 1984).

2. This time frame captures the earliest decade in which the Census distinguished Michigan's aggregated municipal populations distinctly from township populations (1850), through the dawn of the Great Depression (1930).

3. U.S. Census Bureau, 2010, http://quickfacts.census.gov/qfd/states/26/262 2000.html. This estimate does not include water area. For a detailed look at each of Detroit's annexations, see http://www.drawingdetroit.com/detroit-annexation-1806-1926/

4. Michigan Municipal League, 2014, *Handbook for Municipal Officials–Local Government*, https://www.mml.org/pdf/hmo/book.pdf

5. For additional information on service agreements in Michigan, including "425 agreements," see the Michigan Economic Development Corporation, 2015, "Conditional Land Use Transfer (PA 425)," http://www.michiganbusiness.org/cm/files/fact-sheets/conditionallandusetransferpa425.pdf

6. An illustration of growth rates based on U.S. Census data from 1850 to 2012 is available at http://www.drawingdetroit.com/few-southeast-michigan-cities-continue-to-grow/

7. Flint's 19th-century carriage building industry is also traceable to the lumber boom.

8. An extensive history of the Detroit Water and Sewerage Department is available online at www.dwsd.org

9. The City of Flint purchased Detroit's water (from Lake Huron) until initiating its own withdrawal from the Flint River in 2013–14. The subsequent discovery of elevated levels of lead in Flint's water supply caused a substantial controversy and the city temporarily reverted to purchasing Detroit's water in 2015 (see chapters 6 and 15).

10. From 1805 to 1824, Detroit's highest executive office was variably the territorial governor, a federal judge, ceremoniously appointed mayors, or appointed chairmen of the Board of Trustees.

11. Dillon's Rule asserts that local governments are creatures of the state and fundamentally subordinate to state actions. It was named after John Dillon, an Iowa judge who rendered an opinion on the matter in the 1860s.

12. The enabling statutes were Acts 278 (for villages) and 279 (for cities) of 1909.

13. In January 2011, the Michigan Municipal League counted 272 home rule cities out of 277 cities (98.2 percent). See Michigan Municipal League, *Organization of City and Village Government in Michigan* (Ann Arbor: Michigan Municipal League, 2011).

14. The Saginaw proposal was a charter revision that contained a number of other proposals, such as the abolition of the council-manager system. Other cities—for example, Flint, Grand Rapids, Lansing, and Ann Arbor—retained their wards, either as the sole electoral method or as part of a hybrid system for electing council or commission members.

15. Carol A. Cassel, "The Non-Partisan Ballot in the United States," in *Electoral Laws and Their Consequences*, ed. Bernard N. Grofman and Arend Lijphart (New York: Algora Publishing, 2003).

16. Michigan townships and counties continue to conduct partisan elections.
17. See PA 139 of 1973.
18. Thomas J. Sugrue, *The Origins of the Urban Crisis: Race and Inequality in Postwar Detroit* (Princeton: Princeton University Press, 1996).
19. Andrew R. Highsmith, "Beyond Corporate Abandonment: General Motors and the Politics of Metropolitan Capitalism in Flint, Michigan," *Journal of Urban History* 40 (2014): 31–47.
20. Data for 1947–77 from Sugrue, *Origins of the Urban Crisis* (144); 2013 data are five-year estimates of the American Community Survey, "2009–2013 ACS 5-Year Data Profiles," https://www.census.gov/programs-surveys/acs/
21. Conversely, some smaller neighboring cities, such as Muskegon Heights (46.5 percent) and East Lansing (41.1 percent), had even higher poverty rates than their larger neighbors.
22. Sugrue, *Origins of the Urban Crisis*.
23. A companion case, *McGhee v. Sipes*, arose from incidents in Detroit.
24. University of Michigan, Population Studies Center, "New Racial Segregation Measures for Large Metropolitan Areas: Analysis of the 1990–2010 Decennial Censuses," http://www.psc.isr.umich.edu/dis/census/segregation2010.html. The largest decline (−12.3) was recorded in Bradenton-Sarasota-Venice, Florida. The index for the Grand Rapids-Wyoming area remained relatively consistent in 2010, falling 2.4 points to 64.3.
25. The data range is not extended beyond 2002 because subsequent changes in reporting methodology prevent comparison to previous years.
26. United States Department of Justice, Federal Bureau of Investigation (September 2015), 2015 Crime in the United States, https://ucr.fbi.gov/crime-in-the-u.s/2015/crime-in-the-u.s.-2015. There are various ways to compare crime rates, and the numbers here are for illustrative purposes only.
27. See Justin T. Pickett, Ted Chiricos, Kristin M. Golden, and Marc Gertz, "Reconsidering the Relationship between Perceived Neighborhood Racial Composition and Whites' Perception of Victimization Risk: Do Racial Stereotypes Matter?," *Criminology* 50 (2012): 145–86; and Robert L. Young, "Perceptions of Crime, Racial Attitudes, and Firearms Ownership," *Social Forces* 64 (1985): 483–86. Detroit became a majority-minority city in the 1970s.
28. A smaller scale incident occurred in Grand Rapids in 1967.
29. For a brief but highly readable *Detroit Free Press* summary of the administrations of Young and other recent Detroit mayors, see http://archive.freep.com/interactive/article/20130915/NEWS01/130801004/Detroit-Bankruptcy-history-1950-debt-pension-revenue
30. For a good discussion of civic participation in suburban communities, see J. Eric Oliver, *Democracy in Suburbia* (Princeton: Princeton University Press, 2001).
31. Charles L. Ballard, *Michigan's Economic Future* (East Lansing: Michigan State University Press, 2006).
32. As interpreted by the Michigan attorney general. Local income taxes in Michigan are authorized by the City Income Tax Act (PA 284) of 1964.
33. David Rusk, *Cities without Suburbs*, 3rd ed. (Washington, DC: Woodrow Wilson Center Press; Baltimore: Johns Hopkins University Press, 2003).
34. Ballard, *Michigan's Economic Future*.

35. See especially Joel Garreau, *Edge City: Life on the New Frontier* (New York: Anchor, 2011); and Dolores Hayden, *Building Suburbia: Green Fields and Urban Growth, 1820–2000* (New York: Pantheon, 2003).

36. The tri-county area includes Wayne, Macomb, and Oakland Counties.

37. See Donald F. Norris, *Metropolitan Governance in America* (New York: Routledge, 2015).

38. Highsmith, "Beyond Corporate Abandonment."

39. Todd Swanstrom. "What We Argue about When We Argue about Regionalism," *Journal of Urban Affairs* 23 (2001): 479–96. The classic public choice through mobility hypothesis is described in Charles M. Tiebout, "A Pure Theory of Public Expenditures," *Journal of Political Economy* 64 (1956): 416–24.

40. Wayne State University, Center for Urban Studies, 2008, "Economic Development in Metropolitan Detroit," http://econdev.cus.wayne.edu/Menu/LocalEd.aspx

41. John Gallagher, *Reimagining Detroit: Opportunities for Redefining an American City* (Detroit: Wayne State University Press, 2010).

42. The scope of redevelopment is often contentious. See Elizabeth Strom, *The Rise of the Creative Class* (New York: Basic, 2002).

43. The plan, called *Detroit Future City*, is available at http://detroitfuturecity.com/wp-content/uploads/2014/02/DFC_ExecutiveSummary_2ndEd.pdf

44. Public Act 436 of 2012.

45. Based on 2011 ACS five-year estimates, which were the most recent available in March 2013.

46. According to the Mackinac Center for Public Policy, there were 494 such agreements in Oakland County, 32 in Wayne County, and 6 in Macomb County as of September 2010, http://www.michigancapitolconfidential.com/depts/policy/ilagreement.aspx?

47. Although Detroit has fallen to roughly 18th place on the list of most populous cities in the United States, the Detroit-Warren-Ann Arbor Metropolitan Statistical Area ranked 14th largest (4,296,250 residents) among Metropolitan Statistical Areas in the 2010 U.S. Census, and has contained 7 of the 10 largest cities in the state since the 1970 Census. The Grand Rapids-Wyoming Metropolitan Statistical Area ranked approximately 52nd largest (988,938) as of the 2010 Census.

48. The fate of Flint's relationship with the Great Lakes Water Authority, with which it reconnected in 2015, and the Karegnondi Water Authority was unknown as of early 2017.

49. See especially Paul E. Peterson, *City Limits* (Chicago: University of Chicago Press, 1981).

50. Norris, *Metropolitan Governance in America*.

5 ✦ Local Governments in Michigan II
Michigan's Rural Areas and Small Towns

THOMAS J. GREITENS AND J. CHERIE STRACHAN

By sheer number, local governments dominate the governance landscape of the state of Michigan. Including cities, townships, and villages, Michigan has over 1,700 local governments in the state. That large number does not include the 83 county governments in the state that provide state-based services to local citizens, or the approximately 1,000 special district forms of local government that provide a single, specialized service (e.g., a school district or a library district).[1] Most local governments exist in rural areas of the state or serve an especially small number of citizens in a rural, urban, or exurban area. For instance, 89 percent of the state's cities, villages, and townships have fewer than 10,000 residents and 57 percent of them have fewer than 5,000 residents.[2] Additionally, the majority of the state's villages have fewer than 1,000 residents and have a small geographic size of one square mile or less (see table 5.1).[3]

The U.S. Census Bureau currently defines rural areas as geographic locations not included in an urbanized area of 50,000 or more individuals, or in an urban cluster of between 2,500 and 50,000 individuals. For all practical purposes, such a definition places rural areas away from the major urban centers of the state (e.g., Detroit, Lansing, Grand Rapids, Kalamazoo), and the suburbanized areas that surround them. Thanks in large part to the significant rural characteristic of the Upper Peninsula, where the largest city, Marquette, has a population of approximately 21,000 individuals, most of the geographic area of the state has a rural aesthetic that is defined by small populations, large areas of undeveloped land, a variety of natural resources, an economy based on summer tourism, and numerous types of local governments. In these types of areas, smaller-sized local governments and counties play an especially vital part in the everyday lives of citizens.

However, these rural areas face a number of challenges in the 21st century. Replicating similar trends across the United States, younger generations of college-educated citizens increasingly reject living in rural areas in favor of living in more urbanized areas.[4] While Michigan as a whole was the only state to lose population between 2000 and 2010, an exodus of young people away from rural areas in the state has occurred since the 1980s. This long-term trend has important consequences for Michigan as a whole as estimates indicate that the state's population in 2040 will be much older than it is currently. In 2040, 23 percent of the state's population is forecast to be over 65 years of age, while 29 percent of the population will be under 25.[5] This is in contrast to the 2010s, which had only 14 percent of the state's population over age 65 and 34 percent younger than 25.[6] These types of demographic changes will dramatically transform local governance in rural Michigan as well as a number of policy areas such as public education. Without a stable population of citizens, rural areas and their local governments will most likely experience declines in economic development, degradations in their governance capacity, and declines in per-capita intergovernmental revenue sharing from the State of Michigan and the federal government. In many ways, such challenges already define the reality of local governance in rural areas and small towns in Michigan.

In the sections that follow, these existential challenges are explored within the rural and small town governance framework in Michigan. To better understand the roots of these challenges, the first section of this chapter explores the history of rural and small town governance in the state and the various political and policy dimensions that have always surrounded rural and small town governance. The second section analyzes the intergovernmental dimensions of rural and small town governance in

TABLE 5.1. Types of Local Government in Michigan

Type of Government	Number in the State	Population Requirement
County Governments	83	None
Township Governments	1,240	Minimum of 2,000 residents for charter townships
Municipal Governments *Villages* *Cities*	533	Minimum of 150 residents for new villages and 750 residents for new cities
Special District Governments	1,019	None or dependent on type of special district (e.g., a school district)

Source: Information compiled by authors from the 2012 Census of Governments from the U.S. Census Bureau (available at http://www.census.gov/govs/).

Michigan with a special emphasis on the importance of centralized state funding to local governments in these areas. Since Michigan as a state has been managing some type of decline, whether it be related to population or economic development, since the 1980s, the third section examines how this type of long-term decline impacts rural and small town areas in the state with a special emphasis on how changes in economic development patterns influence the future of these areas.

Michigan's History of Governance in Rural Areas and Small Towns

Michigan's style of governance in rural areas and small towns is ultimately tied to the addition of the Northwest Territory to the United States after the Revolutionary War. In order to provide for an orderly development of the lands of the Northwest Territory, Congress specifically commissioned land surveys as part of the Northwest Ordinance. These land surveys, also called congressional townships, geographical townships, or survey townships, were areas of 36 square miles and included specific numbered sections of land that could later be sold to settlers and development companies.[7]

The emphasis on these townships in the Northwest Territory originated from Thomas Jefferson. A member of the Continental Congress during this time, Jefferson promoted the value of township governments. Jefferson viewed the township form of government as the primary mechanism for local citizens to govern themselves.[8] Given that county governments were typically administrative subdivisions of the state that provided state-centric services to local citizens, the township government was seen as a way to promulgate more democratic values among local citizens. While the geographical townships formed as a result of the Northwest Ordinance were little more than a way to keep accurate land records, it was hoped that populations of citizens would eventually form around the geographical area of the township and establish local governments of self-determination.

Initial Forms of Local Government

In the area that would become the state of Michigan, the land surveys required by the Northwest Ordinance were completed in a general east-west direction with population growth following survey completion. After a survey was completed in an area, land in the township could be purchased relatively cheaply and the new landowner could be ensured of the validity of the land transaction because of the completed survey.

This resulted in Michigan's population swelling from 4,764 in 1810 to 212,267 in 1840.[9] With the opening of the Erie Canal in 1825, these new citizens primarily came from the northeastern part of the United States.[10] In the Northeast, these citizens were exposed to an active style of local government. Powerful local governments in the state of New York, as well as the New England town meeting form of government where citizens often had a direct vote on all matters, helped to shape the view of the early Michiganders that strong, local governance was a necessity. Consequently, in 1827 the territorial legislature transformed the survey townships (which, as noted, were simply survey divisions for keeping accurate land records) into actual township governments.[11] These township governments were not always congruent with their historical survey township boundaries, but the 1827 territorial act on townships gave these townships names and some limited powers.

The territorial legislature also constructed the legal framework for the governing of counties, cities, and villages. Even though many areas such as Detroit (founded in 1701) and Sault Ste. Marie (founded in 1641) predated the formation of the territory, the legislature designed the governance powers that these areas could possess. However, the real formalization of these local governments and their associated powers started to occur with the state's first Constitution (see chapter 2). Adopted in 1835, the state Constitution briefly mentions townships and counties when discussing matters of local government.[12] This Constitution focused more on establishing the basic processes of state government rather than on dealing with the increasingly complex realities of local government. As a result, its discussion of local government was extremely limited, with very brief discussions on voting in townships, the election of justices of the peace in townships, and removing township officers. What tasks or services township officers were supposed to do (or not do) was not discussed. Presumably, the roles and powers of townships were already realized in the 1827 territorial acts that transformed survey townships into actual townships, and those roles and powers would remain current under the new constitution. Interestingly, discussions on county government were more specific. The 1835 Constitution explained county government in terms of providing state-based services to local citizens. For example, it explained the use of county boundaries for the election of state representatives and senators (i.e., each county should have at least one representative), the administration of the state court system in county government (e.g., judges of circuit courts and probate courts), and the establishment of county clerk offices for record-keeping.[13]

Thus, townships existed in the early history of the state and played a significant role in providing local governance to areas that were primarily rural in nature. But as Michigan formally became a state in 1837, most of the growth in local government was concentrated at the county level. Townships still existed of course, and cities such as Detroit were growing larger in population and political power, but the number of county governments increased during this time. Starting with just Wayne County in the Michigan territory, the area that eventually became the state of Michigan increased its number of counties throughout the mid-1800s. County governments were traditionally viewed as direct subdivisions of the state government. As such, their number increased as the state's population grew in size and the state started to formalize its governance. This created a complex environment for local government whereby county governments, elected by residents of the county, provided state-based services such as keeping records for the state and administering the state's court system, while township governments (as well as cities and villages) elected officers to help manage the everyday affairs of citizens, which could range from keeping the peace to collecting fines.[14]

The state passed its second Constitution in 1850 and its third Constitution in 1908. The 1850 Constitution formalized local governments in the state with direct mentions of the roles and responsibilities of the major offices of county government and township government. For local governments, the 1908 Constitution is especially noteworthy because it and the 1909 Home Rule City Act gave cities and villages the power to amend their original state charter. This often resulted in cities and villages adopting a new style of local government where managers appointed by the local board or council led the executive offices of the local government rather than a politically elected mayor. It also signaled the growing power of local governments in the state. Whereas previously cities and villages were dependent on the state for their charter that allowed them to operate, now they and their citizens could form their own style of government with their own charter.

The Emergence of Modern Local Government

Governance in rural areas and small towns entered the 20th century with a relatively stable mix of local governments and local powers. County governments provided services required by the state such as maintaining records and administering the state court system in local areas. Townships were now located within county governments, with many of them either shrinking from their earlier sizes associated with survey townships due to the formation of cities or enlarging in geographic size by special acts of the Legislature. Townships provided a basic level of service and perhaps most importantly enabled citizens to hold at least one township meeting a year to discuss and deliberate on a variety of community issues. Villages and cities, whose governance operations were traditionally designed by the state in a state-formed charter of operations, now had the power to form their own charter and their own style of governance operations with the power of home rule given to them by the 1908 Constitution and 1909 Home Rule City Act. Additionally, villages and cities were given power to offer more types of services, such as public health services and parks, to meet the growing service demands of a 20th-century population. Especially in rural areas (which can have both villages and cities) and small towns, local governance was relatively static. Counties, townships, and villages provided most of the governmental services in these areas with the occasional small city providing additional services.

This all begin to change in the 1940s. In 1947 the state Legislature passed the Charter Township Act. This act enabled a process where townships could become a "charter township." Under this act, townships wishing to become a charter township had to possess certain characteristics. These included a population size of at least 2,000 residents, the passage of the intent to become a charter township by the township government, and a public vote on the matter by the township's citizens (unless the township had a population of more than 5,000 residents, in which case the vote by the township board became final without a vote by the residents unless challenged by the residents). If a township met these criteria, then it could become a charter township. Compared to the traditional form of township government in Michigan, charter townships possessed greater protections from annexation by neighboring localities and also enjoyed increased powers over taxing property. In that sense, they had more power than a traditional township government (now called a "general law" township with the passage of this act), but less power than a city government with its own locally developed charter.

After passage of the 1947 Charter Township Act, the number of charter townships increased as suburbanization accelerated across the state's urban areas. Suburbanization in Michigan, as well as across the United States in the 1940s to the 1970s, was a highly complex phenomenon driven by increases in automobile ownership, interstate construction, housing shortages (especially after World War II), crime in urban areas, higher taxes in urban areas, and racial politics.[15] As a result, many of the state's urban centers now had corresponding charter townships contiguous or slightly contiguous with an urban city. For example, current charter townships include Flint Charter Township (bordering the city of Flint), Saginaw Charter Township (bordering the city of Saginaw), Ann Arbor Charter Township (bordering the city of Ann Arbor), Royal Oak Charter Township (near the city of Detroit), and Lansing Charter Township (bordering the city of Lansing).

While many townships, whether chartered or general law, existed in urban areas, the strength of township government was most often felt in rural areas. Without an adequate population base to support city government, and perhaps lacking the political will to form a city government due to its increased taxing ability and enhanced governmental operations, many rural areas relied on townships for a type of local service delivery. Townships routinely offered services related to public safety, economic development and zoning, property tax administration, and the regulation of business activities. But, overall, their powers were more limited than city governments because they did not have the power of home rule and faced more limitations by the state on taxation and revenue raising ability.

When the current version of the state Constitution was passed in 1963, the powers of townships (as well as counties, villages, and cities) were mostly left unchanged. The most significant changes involved the solidification of township governance with a supervisor, township clerk, treasurer, and between two and four trustees (note the contrast with charter township governance, which required four trustees, and the governance structure of townships in previous constitutions, which did not mention township trustees), and the added provision of allowing counties to adapt and change their state-formed charter. In this way, counties were granted a degree of home rule previously reserved for villages and cities. But overall, the powers and responsibilities of local government were relatively unchanged. Even though the 1963 Constitution reflected the prevailing trend of the time to simplify the language of state constitutions and modernize state governance operations, the complexities of Michigan's local governments, with direct roots in laws by the Territorial Government in 1827, remained.

Current Realities of Governments in Rural Areas and Small Towns

The historical evolution of local governance in the state reveals five major types of local government that play important roles in rural areas and small towns: counties, townships, charter townships, villages, and cities. It may seem strange to include cities in a list for rural areas and small towns. After all, the notion of a city typically brings up visions of large metropolises with skyscrapers. However, in Michigan a city can be as small as 750 residents and would thus be right at home in the rural areas and small towns that define most of the state's geography. Villages also exhibit the trait of serving small populations of residents with village incorporation only requiring 150 residents with a population density of at least 100 residents per square mile.

Three dominant themes influence the actual structure of local governments in rural areas and small towns. First, as previously discussed, the concept of home rule gives villages and cities in Michigan the power to design their own charter. The charter of the local government is the legal document that codifies into law the roles and responsibilities of the local government's executive branch (e.g., a mayor or city manager), legislative branch (e.g., a city council), and bureaucracy (e.g., police department and fire department). Included in such documentation will be specific information on voting, whether citizens can bring forth ballot initiatives and recall elected officials, as well as at least some documentation on the finances and taxation mechanisms in the city.

The second theme is the idea, starting in the late 1800s, that appointed, professionalized management of a local government's executive branch resulted in better and more ethical governance than management by an elected mayor (or other elected executive). For example, with positions like a city manager or village manager, local government could be led by a professional administrator with expertise in how best to operate a local government. With significant cases of mayoral and executive branch corruption occurring in local governments throughout the 1880s, most notoriously in New York City's Tammany Hall political machine, professionalized management of local government was seen as the better option for effective local governance. The ability to choose this type of government is grounded in the idea of home rule. Emerging as a local government phenomenon in the early 1900s, home rule allows local governments to essentially choose their form of local governance in Michigan. In other words, local governments can choose to either go the way of a professional administrator or a politicized executive (e.g., a mayor). In Michigan, counties, villages, townships, and cities can have professional managers. Generally, research has shown that when these types of governments choose the professional manager route, the operational effectiveness of the local government increases.[16]

Third, townships continue to influence local governance in the state. Especially in rural areas and small towns, townships can exert a tremendous influence on the local governance of the area and provide some ser-

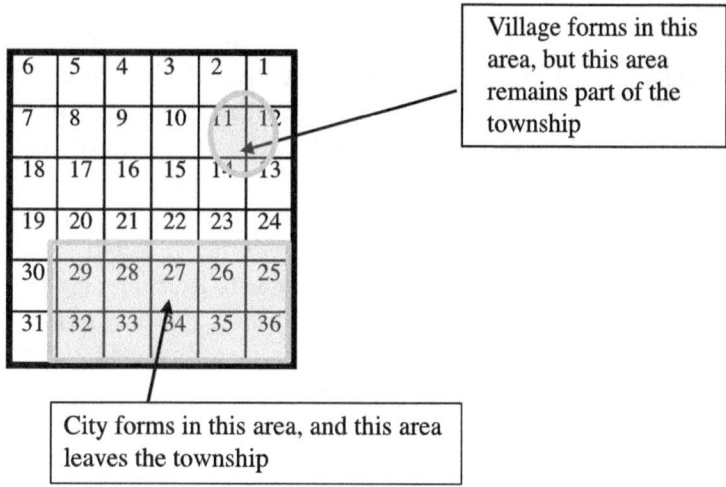

Fig. 5.1. Initial Survey Township (with 36 Sections of Land Six Miles Square) and Subsequent Village and City Formation

vices that are directly provided by other types of local governments. Townships can also breed tension in a governance area due to incorporation and annexation. Remember, townships exist throughout the state of Michigan. They are reflective of the land surveys conducted by the original Northwest Ordinance and then transformed into actual governments in the 1827 Act by the territorial government. Consequently, when cities or villages form they do so on township land. Existing state law mandates that when cities incorporate as their own local government, that geographic land is lost from the township to the city (this is in contrast to the incorporation of a village where the village remains as part of the township) (see fig. 5.1). Additionally, growing cities may need to annex additional lands for development, and that land emerges from the original township. To help empower townships and to give them more protections against such events, charter townships were formed by the state in 1947 as large numbers of citizens fled cities for the suburbs and their consequent townships, but not all townships all charter townships. Many of them retain their original governance structure and are termed general law townships.

Thus, local governance in the state, even in rural areas and small towns, can be exceedingly complex. These complexities and the tensions they often create become magnified by the way the State of Michigan funds local governments and by the history of economic challenges that defines the economic condition of the state. These realities are explored in the next sections of the chapter and include direct implications for the state's rural areas and small towns.

Intergovernmental Challenges in Rural Areas and Small Towns

Although relatively robust in the number of local governments and the various powers they can contain (e.g., home rule), the State of Michigan severely constricts the power of local governments in certain areas. As noted above with respect to home rule, charter townships require a charter crafted by the state government. In addition, the state started giving home rule provisions to cities and villages only in 1908 and then to counties in 1963. Another area in which local governments are constrained is state-local funding mechanisms.

An important fundamental point here is that local governments in Michigan are restricted by the state government in their use of taxation. This restriction is especially significant in rural areas and small towns. Restrictions on taxation emerge in two areas: property taxation and administration of a sales tax. In most states, the state government implements a general sales tax on most items when they are sold. The revenue yield from that rate then goes back to the state government. Counties, towns, cities, and other types of local governments can add to that base state sales tax and then keep that portion of the yield. For instance, if a state charges a sales tax of 5 percent on all goods purchased in the state, then other local governments can add additional sales taxes on top of that amount. In this way, cities and other types of local governments that typically have an influx of nonresidents, such as rural localities with a tourist-based economy, can essentially tax nonresidents to help fund the local government.

In Michigan, such taxation by any local government is forbidden by the state Constitution of 1963. The sales tax is established by the state government and no county or other type of local government can add on to it. Sales taxes are often viewed as regressive taxation since analyses reveal that lower income individuals routinely pay greater shares of their income to sales taxes than higher income individuals.[17] So, the feature of the 1963 Constitution that forbids local governments from adding to the state sales tax can be viewed as a progressive feature of the document. However, the disadvantage of this provision to Michigan's rural areas and small towns is profound. Many of these areas have tourist-based economies that dramatically expand in summer months with nonresident activity and then quickly contract in winter months. If local governments in these areas could charge some type of sales tax, then nonresidents temporarily in the community using community resources and services could be taxed, and the locality could then use that revenue to improve services to citizens or reduce tax levels elsewhere. To compensate for the lack of sales tax, the 1963 Constitution allowed for the administration of a local income tax in cities. The tax rate is 1 percent of income for city residents and 0.5 percent for nonresidents who work within the city's boundaries (additionally, some larger cities in the state, such as Detroit, Highland Park, Grand Rapids, and Saginaw have been allowed to implement greater income tax rates by the state government). Smaller cities in rural areas can also adopt the city income tax. But because of the smaller number of citizens living in these areas, the yield from such a tax never matches the potential of revenue generation with a city sales tax.

In order to adequately fund local government, the State of Michigan redistributes revenue from the state sales tax, state income tax, and associated business taxes to cities, villages, and townships through a mechanism called revenue sharing (see chapter 13). There are two types of revenue sharing: constitutional and statutory. Constitutional revenue sharing contains revenue from the state sales tax and is distributed to cities, villages, and townships on a per-capita basis. Its language is enshrined in the state Constitution. Statutory revenue also originates from the state sales tax (although historically it originated from the state income tax, business tax, and a type of personal property tax).[18] The redistributions from statutory revenue sharing are based on a specific administrative formula designed and routinely updated by the state government.

Since the early 2000s, the state has dramatically reduced statutory revenue sharing to cities, villages, and townships. Since fiscal year 2002, a total of $6.9 billion in funding has been cut from statutory revenue sharing, with fiscal year 2014 amounts 76 percent lower than historical funding levels, and a large number of townships no longer eligible for the funding.[19] Additionally, the state's fiscal year 2012 budget transformed statutory revenue sharing into an incentive-based program where localities had to meet a set of predetermined benchmarks in order to receive statutory revenue sharing dollars.[20] While the state has relaxed the tenets of this transformation in recent years, it still further limited the amount of statutory revenue sharing available to local governments in Michigan.

Local governments can also implement property taxes to generate additional revenue. Because of constraints on the sales tax and limited use of city income taxes in Michigan, most local governments heavily depend on the property tax for most of their revenue.[21] The property tax in Michigan has a long and complicated history. Generally, townships and cities are limited in the rate of their property taxation, but exemptions can and are routinely voted upon by residents. Additionally, reflecting the property tax revolts of the late 1970s that protested the growth in property taxation throughout the 1970s, Michigan limited the growth in property tax revenue with the 1978 Headlee Amendment (see chapter 13). This constitutional amendment prohibited property taxation increasing faster than inflation and made it especially difficult for property tax yields to increase once property values decreased (an especially common result throughout Michigan in the 1980s and again in the 2000s because of economic challenges).[22]

Consequently, with only limited powers to raise revenues, intergovernmental revenue sharing from the state government to local governments becomes especially important. And with statutory revenue sharing declining since the early 2000s, and significant property tax limitations in place, local governments in Michigan find themselves severely constrained in their ability to raise revenue. Local governments can always impose fees, fines, and other specific taxes associated with their operations, but overall their ability to levy major taxes (e.g., sales, property, and income taxes) is limited by the state government. Therefore, while the state promotes the formation of local governments with the power of home rule and specific protections and rules for townships and charter townships, it has a history of constraining their ability to raise revenues and cutting their intergovernmental funding.

Current Realities of Intergovernmental Relations

Because of the limits on imposing taxes faced by local governments, rural areas and small towns are especially dependent on the state. Another factor in this matter is that the state has used the dependence as an opportunity to change local governance. While local governments in the state have some degree of self-determination, especially with home rule provisions that allow for cities and villages to choose their own type of local government, ultimate control of local government always flows back to the state. Under an idea put forth in the late 1800s by Iowa judge John Forrest Dillon, all local governments in the United States are ultimately subservient to state governments.[23] The state government exercises control over the local government and can impose mandates on them. With home rule options, the state has given some of that power away. But overall, the state government exercises a great deal of discretion and power over local governments in Michigan. Dillon's Rule, as the opinion by Judge Dillon came to be known, is now the accepted law of the land and has been cited numerous times to show that state control supersedes local control. Or, as specifically stated by Judge Dillon in the case that first put forth the notion of Dillon's Rule,

> Municipal corporations owe their origin to, and derive their powers and rights wholly from the legislature. It breathes into them the breath of life, without which they cannot exist. As it creates, so may it destroy. If it may destroy, it may abridge and control.[24]

In Michigan, the significance of Dillon's Rule became especially apparent in the 21st century. Due to economic stagnation and decline that began in the early 2000s and then accelerated after the Great Recession of 2008, the state started cutting statutory revenue sharing to local governments. In 2012, the state even tied statutory revenue sharing to incentives for effective governance protocols designed by the state. Termed the Economic Vitality Incentive Program, or EVIP, the changes in the law meant that statutory funding to local governments be tied to certain benchmarks related to privatizing services, reducing health-care costs, and collaborating with other local governments to reduce the cost of local services.[25]

Achieving these benchmarks, while difficult in any type of local area, was especially problematic in rural areas and small towns where service delivery was not as complex and the avenues for privatization and collaboration were generally more limited. Additionally, collaboration between local governments, often termed regionalism, was often more challenging to implement in these rural areas and small towns because of issues associated with geographic distances and administrative capacities. For instance, research on collaborations has revealed that townships, on average, do not collaborate on service delivery as much as other types of local governments in Michigan.[26] Consequently, without additional enhancements to intergovernmental revenue sharing and support from the state, many rural areas and small towns face significant declines in their future revenues and governance prospects. These declines are exacerbated by the economic challenges facing rural areas and small towns.

Economic Challenges of Rural Governments and Small Towns

Of greater concern than the challenges of intergovernmental relations may be the long-term prospects of local governance in rural areas and small towns. Many rural areas of the state have declining or rapidly aging populations. The reasons for this decline are complex and multifaceted. Part of the reason seems to be the long-term declines in numbers of individuals employed in the agricultural and manufacturing sections of the state's economy. Many of the economies in rural areas and small towns were historically built on agriculture, tourism (i.e., a component of the "blue economy"), and some type of manufacturing activity.[27] But by and large, the trend seems to be more systemic and dynamic than that and related to a new type of citizen migratory pattern. In the 21st century, younger generations of citizens, as well as populations of citizens nearer retirement, are choosing to live in urban centers when possible. With better access to medical care, additional avenues of culture, and often better employment prospects, many metropolitan areas are experiencing increases in their population of highly skilled and knowledge-based workers.[28] This pattern has direct consequences for economic development in rural areas and small towns.

Attracting the Creative Class

Part of the challenge is that rural areas face significant barriers in attracting the "creative class." First used by Richard Florida,[29] the term creative class refers to both the professionalized workforce of the 21st century (e.g., doctors, lawyers, educational professionals, engineers, software developers, information technology experts, researchers) as well as artists, musicians, and other early adopters of innovation. Due to their potential to leverage creativity into innovation, these individuals are theorized to be the dominant force in successful economic development (see chapter 14). These types of individuals want their places of residence to possess cultural attractions, outlets for their creativity, green spaces, excellent educational opportunities, and exciting events offered on a routine basis.

In this way, the creative class desires a high quality of life that maximizes the notion of the triple bottom line of sustainability. Consisting of economic prosperity, environmental stewardship, and social responsibility, the triple bottom line of sustainability is routinely achieved by successful local governments in the 21st century (e.g., Austin, Texas; Silicon Valley;

New York City; Portland, Oregon). Unfortunately, many rural areas and small towns fall short of achieving the triple bottom line. These areas can certainly promote green spaces and environmental stewardship, but often lack the ability to sustain economic development and educational opportunities. Especially with declining populations and an uncertain state revenue system, rural areas and small towns face considerable obstacles in achieving the triple bottom line.

In the early 2000s, Governor Jennifer Granholm's administration attempted to implement some principles of the creative class theory through its "Cool Cities" initiative. After reading Florida's book, *The Rise of the Creative Class*, Granholm invited him to consult with the state on economic development strategies. The projects funded through this initiative included projects to improve the walkability of Michigan cities, promote local arts and culture, expand mixed-use development, and improve the downtown areas of many small cities through the "Main Streets" program. Among the smaller Michigan communities that were designated as Cool Cities were Alpena, Boyne City, Calumet, Clare, Adrian, Buchanan, and Saugatuck.

In addition, other rural areas and small towns in the state have been trying to adopt some of the tenets of the creative class ideal. Environmental stewardship and the use of green infrastructure, such as parks, are increasingly promoted as a best practice in local government throughout the state of Michigan.[30] Additionally, rural areas and small towns are increasingly using weekend-based events such as wine tours, festivals, and summer concert series in attempts to place-make their community through the promotion of cultural events.[31] However, given the realities of life in rural areas and small towns, the success of these creative class events remains uncertain.

The Challenge of Citizen Participation

Citizen participation in local government is key to maximizing the triple bottom line. In addition to voting, citizens in local government are often given opportunities to engage in the decision-making process. Indeed, one of the reasons townships were established in Michigan was the opportunity they presented to citizens to participate in town hall meetings. In these types of meetings, citizens could bring forth issues of concern, and at least as initially envisioned, directly vote in the meeting on potential solutions. Special town hall-style meetings are also routinely used by cities and other forms of government to address controversial issues and give citizens a voice in these debates.

An additional avenue of citizen participation is the use of the citizen advisory committee. These committees typically work on planning and zoning decisions, oversight of local governmental departments, and economic development. After deliberating on an issue, they make a recommendation to the elected policymakers of the local government, often a city council, village board, or township board. These policymakers can either choose to accept or not accept the recommendation. But at the very least, these committees allow local citizens to participate in governance decisions and to make their policy preferences known to policymakers. In this way, citizen advisory committees are typically viewed as an effective mechanism that promotes good governance in communities.[32]

Even in the most creative cities, though, participation in government is always uncertain. Indeed, even the New England town meeting form of local government historically suffered from low citizen participation.[33] This reflects a general decline of interest among citizens in collaborating with other citizens to provide services for the public. For instance, communities across the United States have experienced long-term declines in the participation of associations that provide for some type of public benefit.[34] Additionally, surveys reveal that younger generations of Americans have lower levels of civic knowledge and deliberation skills that are vital for citizen participation in government. Rural areas and small towns also have challenges in citizen participation. As younger populations increasingly decline in these areas, participation will most likely become even more problematic in the future.

Conclusion

The future is difficult, if not impossible, to predict. Yet all of the signs point to significant challenges for the future of Michigan's governments in rural areas and small towns. Some of these challenges, like the challenge of funding, are politically based. Yet others, such as the newer trends in economic development, reflect changing lifestyle and demographic patterns in the 21st century. Given these facts, local governments in rural areas and small towns are trying to transform. They are increasingly promoting cultural events to place-make their community among residents of the state. When possible, they are also trying to collaborate on service delivery with other units of local government through the state, even though this is very difficult to do in rural areas.

However, given the state's fiscal realities, which have witnessed significant cuts to revenue sharing to many local governments in rural areas and small towns, the capacity of these governments to provide services and attract economic development remains uncertain. In many ways, the state government of Michigan promotes small, local governance as an ideal. Township government is enshrined in the state's Constitution and most villages and cities in the state have small populations. Yet at the same time, the State of Michigan has dramatically constrained the ability of these governments to raise their own revenue and its own ability to provide for them through intergovernmental revenue sharing. Given migratory patterns that show that citizens are moving away from rural areas and small towns, these areas face the very real possibility of significant decline in the future.

If these trends continue, the state may have to consider ways to transform the governance of these areas through regionalization or, when possible, consolidation. Initial steps in this direction have already been taken by the state with cuts to statutory revenue sharing and incentivized funding. In the future, this may mean that local governance in rural areas and small towns will be significantly altered. If this change does occur, it will most likely reflect the coming demographic and fiscal challenges that the state will confront, rather than the historical emphasis by the state on local self-determination.

WEB RESOURCES

The *Michigan Township Association* (www.michigantownships.org) is a membership association for Michigan townships that advocates for township government and provides numerous resources on the procedures of township government in Michigan.

The *Michigan Department of Agriculture and Rural Development* (www.michigan.gov/mdard) provides numerous reports on the status of the agriculture industry and rural development in the state.

The *Michigan Municipal League* (www.mml.org) is an excellent resource for best practices in all villages, townships, charter townships, counties, and cities in the state.

The *Michigan Local Government Management Association* (www.mlgma.org) is an association that produces resources for professional managers in local governments in the state.

NOTES

1. Citizens Research Council of Michigan, *Michigan Constitutional Issues: System of Local Government, Report 313-09* (Detroit: Citizens Research Council of Michigan, 1994), 2.

2. Citizens Research Council of Michigan, *Lessons from the Proposed Merger of Onekama Village with Onekama Township: Report 381* (Livonia: Citizens Research Council of Michigan, 2013), 4–6.

3. Ibid.

4. Bill Bishop and Robert G. Cushing, *The Big Sort: Why the Clustering of Like-Minded America Is Tearing Us Apart* (Boston: Houghton Mifflin, 2008), 136–40; Daniel T. Lichter and David L. Brown, "Rural America in an Urban Society: Changing Spatial and Social Boundaries," *Annual Review of Sociology* 37 (2011): 572.

5. Donald R. Grimes and George A. Fulton, *The Economic and Demographic Outlook for Michigan through 2040* (Ann Arbor: University of Michigan Institute for Research on Labor, Employment and the Economy, 2012), 9–10.

6. Ibid.

7. James P. Hanley and Paul A. Rozycki, *Politics and Government in Michigan*, 5th Edition (Boston: McGraw Hill, 2007), 135.

8. Philip B. Kurland and Ralph Lerner, eds., *The Founder's Constitution, Volume 1* (Chicago: University of Chicago Press, 2000), chapter 4, document 34, letter to Joseph C. Cabell, 142; Anwar Syed, *The Political Theory of American Local Government* (New York: Random House, 1966), 39–40.

9. Richard A. Santer, *Michigan: Heart of the Great Lakes* (Dubuque, IA: Kendall Hunt, 1977), 166–69.

10. Lois K. Mathews, *The Expansion of New England: The Spread of New England Settlement and Institutions to the Mississippi River, 1620–1865* (Boston: Houghton Mifflin, 1909), 225.

11. Kenneth VerBurg, *Managing the Modern Michigan Township* (East Lansing: Michigan State University and the Michigan Township Association, 1981), 2.

12. Michigan passed its constitution in 1835 and expected to become a state that same year. However, its admittance to the United States was delayed until 1837 because of the dispute with Ohio over the Toledo strip of territory.

13. Information from the 1835, 1850, 1908, and 1963 state constitutions originated from the State of Michigan's historical documents section of the state Legislature's website, http://www.legislature.mi.gov/

14. To ensure cooperation between townships and counties, all of the township supervisors in one county served on the county's board of supervisors. However, this ended with the U.S. Supreme Court's decision in *Baker v. Carr* (1962) that focused on the need for equal representation in state government. The county board of supervisors are now directly elected by county residents.

15. Nathaniel Baum-Snow, "Did Highways Cause Suburbanization?," *Quarterly Journal of Economics* 122 (2007): 775; Juliet F. Gainsborough, *Fenced Off: The Suburbanization of American Politics* (Washington, DC: Georgetown University Press, 2001), 15; Kenneth T. Jackson, *Crabgrass Frontier: The Suburbanization of the United States* (New York: Oxford University Press, 1985), 188; Peter Mieszkowski and Edwin S. Mills, "The Causes of Metropolitan Suburbanization," *Journal of Economic Perspectives* 7 (1993): 136.

16. Jered B. Carr, "What Have We Learned about the Performance of Council-Manager Government? A Review and Synthesis of the Research," *Public Administration Review* 75 (2015): 682–83.

17. John Mikesell, "General Sales, Income, and Other Nonproperty Taxes," in

Management Policies in Local Government Finance, 5th Edition, ed. J. Richard Aronson and Eli Schwartz (Washington, DC: International City/County Management Association, 2004), 302.

18. Citizens Research Council of Michigan, *Reforming Statutory State Revenue Sharing. Report No. 388* (Livonia: Citizens Research Council of Michigan, 2015), vi.

19. Ibid., 16–17.

20. Ibid., 17.

21. Ibid., 6.

22. Naomi E. Feldman, Paul N. Courant, and Douglas C. Drake, "The Property Tax in Michigan," in *Michigan at the Millennium: A Benchmark and Analysis of Its Fiscal and Economic Structure*, ed. Charles L. Ballard, Paul N. Courant, Douglas C. Drake, Ronald C. Fisher, and Elisabeth R. Gerber (East Lansing: Michigan State University Press, 2003), 681–82.

23. Timothy D. Mead, "Federalism and State Law: Legal Factors Constraining and Facilitating Local Initiatives," in *Handbook of Local Government Administration*, ed. John J. Gargan (New York: Marcel Dekker, 1997), 33–34.

24. *Clinton v. Cedar Rapids and the Missouri River Railroad* (24 Iowa 455; 1868).

25. Citizens Research Council of Michigan, *Reforming Statutory State Revenue Sharing. Report No. 388* (Livonia: Citizens Research Council of Michigan, 2015), 23.

26. Jered B. Carr, Elisabeth R. Gerber, and Eric W. Lupher, "Explaining Horizontal and Vertical Cooperation in Michigan," in *Sustaining Michigan: Metropolitan Policies and Strategies*, ed. Richard W. Jelier and Gary Sands (East Lansing: Michigan State University Press, 2009), 220.

27. Angela Lazarean and Katharine Trudeau, "Abating Taxes, Abetting Sprawl: The Geographical Distribution of Tax Abatements in Michigan," in *Sustaining Michigan: Metropolitan Policies and Strategies*, ed. Richard W. Jelier and Gary Sands (East Lansing: Michigan State University Press, 2009), 67; David Murphy, Noelle Schiffer, William Sederburg, and David Verway, "Economic Problems: Issues and Policy," in *Michigan Politics and Government: Facing Change in a Complex State*, ed. William P. Browne and Kenneth VerBurg (Lincoln: University of Nebraska Press, 1995), 260; Beryl A. Radin, Robert Agranoff, Ann O'M. Bowman, C. Gregory Buntz, Steven J. Ott, Barbara S. Romzek, and Robert H. Wilson, *New Governance for Rural America: Creating Intergovernmental Partnerships* (Lawrence: University Press of Kansas, 1996), 62–64.

28. Bruce Katz and Jennifer Bradley, *The Metropolitan Revolution: How Cities and Metros Are Fixing Our Broken Politics and Fragile Economy* (Washington, DC: Brookings Institution Press, 2013), 32–33.

29. Richard L. Florida, *The Rise of the Creative Class: And How It's Transforming Work, Leisure, Community, and Everyday Life* (New York: Basic Books, 2002), 8.

30. Betty Gajewski, "Best Practices in Protecting Green Infrastructure: Benchmarking County Park Systems," in *Sustaining Michigan: Metropolitan Policies and Strategies*, ed. Richard W. Jelier and Gary Sands (East Lansing: Michigan State University Press, 2009), 159.

31. Elizabeth P. Foley, Colleen Layton, and Daniel Gilmartin, *The Economics of Place: The Art of Building Great Communities* (Lansing: Michigan Municipal League, 2014), 173.

32. Richard Box, *Citizen Governance: Leading American Communities into the 21st Century* (Thousand Oaks, CA: Sage Publications, 1998), 49–50.

33. Frank M. Bryan, *Real Democracy: The New England Town Meeting and How It Works* (Chicago: University of Chicago Press, 2004), 45.

34. Robert D. Putnam, *Bowling Alone: The Collapse and Revival of American Community* (New York: Simon and Schuster, 2000), 122–30; Theda Skocpol, *Diminished Democracy: From Membership to Management in American Civic Life* (Norman: University of Oklahoma Press, 2003), 153–56.

◆ Political Institutions

6 ✦ Michigan's Governor and Executive Branch

MITCHEL A. SOLLENBERGER

In July 2013, the City of Detroit entered into the largest municipal bankruptcy in the history of the United States. In nearly every stage of the process, Michigan governor Rick Snyder was a key figure—from the appointment of an emergency manager to the signing of legislation to help Detroit avoid another financial crisis (also known as the "grand bargain"). Standing beside Emergency Manager Kevyn Orr after the city emerged from the bankruptcy process roughly 18 months later, Governor Snyder proclaimed: "This has been an extremely difficult and hard process for many people but people worked together. We've got an outstanding outcome, far better than people's expectation. And now most importantly we have the city poised for a new chapter—a new chapter about the growth of the city of Detroit after decades of decline."[1]

The Detroit bankruptcy and grand bargain (a key agreement designed to protect the city's assets while exiting from bankruptcy) highlight how Governor Snyder and other lawmakers and state officials responded to a serious challenge through extended negotiations with many different and often opposing interests. But these events and decisions also illustrate the powers and standing of the Michigan governor within state politics. The fact is that the chief executive enjoys wide-ranging authority over the budget, bureaucracy, and policy through the use of powers ranging from veto to executive branch restructuring. The legal and constitutional constraints are few with the most significant being the limitation of governors to two terms of office along with qualifications placed on the governor's appointment authority.[2]

Historical Development

The Michigan governorship can trace its origins to the Northwest Ordinance of 1787, which the Continental Congress passed to establish a government for the Northwest Territories that included the current states of Illinois, Indiana, Michigan, Ohio, and parts of Wisconsin and Minnesota. The Northwest territorial governor—chosen by Congress—could appoint magistrates and other civil officers and was the "commander-in-chief of the militia." The governor also had the authority to adopt laws from the "original states" as long as one of three territorial judges on the legislative board agreed.

By the early 1800s the people in the Michigan territory had grown tired of the territory government put in place by Congress. The large territory meant that people in Detroit and other parts of Michigan had to travel great distances (usually to Cincinnati, a home of the territorial legislature) to deal with government business. In addition, the territorial government had little connection to the people in Michigan as Congress selected the governor who, in turn, appointed many of the governing officials.[3] In 1805, Congress corrected for the distance issue by establishing a new territory of Michigan with a similarly structured government that included a governor, secretary, and three judges. That same year William Hull became the first territorial governor of Michigan.

By most accounts, the office of territorial governor was weak even compared to its peers. For example, Territorial Governor Hull exercised no veto authority and even wavered on using the pardon power until 1809 when he received approval from the U.S. attorney general.[4] It was not until 1823, however, that Congress formally granted the Michigan governor the ability to issue pardons.[5] Even Hull's ability to control or influence the laws within the territory proved limiting because he was just one of four officials on the legislative board that also had control over public policy matters. In practice, the real governing power rested with Chief Judge Augustus Woodward who had the unwavering support of fellow Judge John Griffin. That meant that from 1806—when Griffin was appointed—until 1823, Woodward controlled nearly all aspects of the legislative process because he either had the votes to adopt laws or could deadlock the legislative board if he disagreed with the governor.[6]

By the 1830s, the Michigan territory had reached a population level of over 85,000—a threshold under the Northwest Ordinance that was needed for any territory to be considered for statehood. In 1835 a state constitution was drafted and ratified by the voters of the territory. It took another two years, however, before Michigan became a state because it was engaged in a border dispute with Ohio over the "Toledo Strip" (see chapter 2).

Constitutional Evolution of the Governorship

The newly formed state and its Constitution resulted in a vastly different government than what Michigan had experienced as a territory. Under Article III of the 1835 Constitution there were three separate departments—legislative, executive, and judicial—that could "never exercise the powers of another" except in certain constitutionally prescribed situations. The governor—standing for election every two years—continued to be the "commander-in-chief of the militia" and possessed the pardon power. The position also gained significant powers to appoint—with the advice and consent of the Senate—justices of the Michigan Supreme Court, a state superintendent of public information, remove judges of any of the state courts through a joint address of the Legislature, and veto legislation (subject to a two-thirds override vote of the Legislature).

A new Constitution came into existence in 1850 (see chapter 2). Under it the Michigan governor lost significant power. As one scholar noted, the 1850 Constitution "was framed under the continuing influence of Jacksonian democracy," which meant a strong preference for placing government power in the hands of the people through frequent popular elections.[7] The 1850 Constitution maintained the two-year election cycle but placed in the hands of the Legislature the power to select the governor or lieutenant governor if there was a tie between two candidates.[8] More important, the governor was stripped of the power to appoint the justices of the Michigan Supreme Court. Finally, the governor not only lost the power to appoint the superintendent of public information (later renamed "instruction") but the positions of secretary of state, state treasurer, commissioner of the land office, and auditor general—all were to be selected by popular votes for two-year terms.[9] Those changes were perhaps the most damaging to the governor's powers as they created a plural executive system in Michigan where those elected executive officials were no longer beholden to the governor and could claim their own independent power base.

The 1850 Constitution also lacked a provision giving the governor the power to remove public officials (other than judges). The absence of a removal power was in keeping with how other states operated.[10] However, in the early 1860s the Michigan Constitution was amended as a result of an embezzlement scandal and gave the governor the power to remove executive branch officials for "gross neglect," "corrupt conduct," or "misfeasance or malfeasance."[11] In many ways this provision helped restore some of the control and responsibility over the executive branch that the governor had lost under the 1850 Constitution.

However, the inclusion of the removal power did not give the governor absolute authority over the executive branch. By the early 20th century there were over 100 independent departments, commissions, boards, agencies, and other bodies established by the Michigan Legislature. The Michigan governor, like many of his fellow governors throughout the states, functioned more like a coordinator, working alongside other administrative and political actors within the executive branch. In 1920, Governor Alexander Groesbeck led a successful effort to provide some executive branch uniformity by creating the State Administrative Board, which could set administrative policy subject to the veto of the governor. In addition, Groesbeck successfully consolidated 30 separate bureaus into five departments (i.e., agriculture, conservation, labor, public safety, and welfare).[12]

Although Michigan adopted another Constitution in 1908, the only significant change gave the governor the added ability to line-item-veto appropriation bills.[13] In 1913, the voters approved an amendment that permitted the recall of any elective official, except certain judges, upon the petition of 25 percent of the votes cast for governor in the prior election.[14] The addition of the recall power was part of a general push in the Progressive Era to increase the people's ability to affect government.[15] A second amendment, passed in 1940, created the state's first civil service commission and granted the governor the power to appoint its four members.[16] That amendment was born out of general frustration between the political parties as every two years the governorship would change hands and state employees would be tossed out of office. The creation of the Civil Service Commission was seen as a way to ensure a stable, effective state government that would not be tied to changes in elected officials' partisanship.[17]

The final evolution of the governorship through constitutional changes occurred in 1963 when Michigan approved its current Constitution. The powers of the governor largely remained the same as under the previous constitution. The word "chief" before "executive power" was stripped from the executive power clause. That move implies the governor has broader executive powers than the ones expressly outlined in the Constitution but the language is too vague to give it more definite meaning. With some slight modifications, the governor's powers over appointments, removals, vetoes, and other miscellaneous matters remained the same.

In the area of executive branch reorganizational authority the governor's powers greatly increased. Under the 1963 Constitution, Michigan governors can make changes to the organization of the executive branch or in the assignment of functions among its units.[18] As one scholar noted, this power "is regarded as vesting broad legislative power in the governor to effectuate executive reorganization in the interest of efficiency."[19] In part, this grant of new power was born out of a failure of the Legislature to adopt large-scale executive branch reorganization plans. The only restrictions to the governor's reorganization authority is that the executive branch is limited to no more than 20 departments and the Legislature has 60 days to disapprove any reorganization plan.[20]

The Modern Michigan Governorship and Powers

In terms of the formal powers (e.g., budget, veto, and appointment) the Michigan governor has traditionally ranked highly. Written at the end of the 1960s, one study of the formal and informal powers of governors ranked Michigan in the top five of the 39 states sampled.[21] That study was based on a formal power index of governor's first presented in 1965.[22] In recent years the Michigan governor has fallen into the middle of the pack compared to other governors. One should not take away from this fall a sense that the Michigan governor has weakened. Instead, many of the other states have provided their governors with increased formal powers.[23] A 2005 assessment found a 12.5 percent increase to the overall powers of the nation's governors since 1960.[24] By 2011, when combing institutional and personal powers[25] the Michigan governor ranked 35th among all governors.[26]

As the head of the state's executive branch, the Michigan governor benefits from an extensive support system which currently includes 76 staff members.[27] The Michigan Executive Office of the Governor currently includes a chief of staff and offices for legislative affairs, communications, strategic policy, legal, administrative services, appointments, constituent relations, external affairs, and urban initiatives. In terms of relative size, Michigan's governor's office ranks as one of the ten largest in the country.[28] The Michigan governor also benefits from access to state transportation that includes automobile, airplane, and helicopter services. In addition, the governor receives a $54,000 annual expense allowance for travel along with an official residence provided by the state. The annual salary for the governor was $159,300 in 2016.

There are currently 17 departments within the executive branch with the secretary of state and attorney general elected by statewide ballot (see table 6.1). The governor, with the advice and consent of the state Senate, appoints the remaining department heads (see discussion below), except two. In the case of the Education Department, the State Board of Education appoints the superintendent of public instruction. For the Civil Rights Department, the Civil Rights Commission—whose members are appointed by the governor upon the advice and consent of the Senate—selects its director. Under the 1963 Constitution, the governor also can reshape the executive branch through reorganization orders, and they have not been shy to use that power. From 2004 to 2014, there were 118 executive reorganization orders. As recently as 2015, Governor Snyder issued an order creating the Department of Health and Human Services.[29]

TABLE 6.1. Michigan's Principal Executive Departments and Selection Methods of the Chief Executive Officers

Department Name	Current Selection Method
Agriculture and Rural Development	Director appointed by governor with advice and consent of the Senate
Attorney General	Attorney general elected by statewide ballot
Civil Rights	Director appointed by the Civil Rights Commission
Corrections	Director appointed by governor with advice and consent of the Senate
Education	Superintendent of Public Instruction appointed by State Board of Education
Environmental Quality	Director appointed by governor with advice and consent of the Senate
Health and Human Services	Director appointed by governor with advice and consent of the Senate
Insurance and Financial Services	Director appointed by governor with advice and consent of the Senate
Licensing and Regulatory Affairs	Director appointed by governor with advice and consent of the Senate
Military and Veterans Affairs	Director appointed by governor with advice and consent of the Senate
Natural Resources	Director appointed by governor with advice and consent of the Senate
State	Secretary elected by statewide ballot
State Police	Director appointed by governor with advice and consent of the Senate
Talent and Economic Development	Director appointed by governor with advice and consent of the Senate
Technology, Management, and Budget	Director appointed by governor with advice and consent of the Senate
Transportation	Director appointed by governor with advice and consent of the Senate
Treasury	Treasurer appointed by governor with advice and consent of the Senate

Veto Power

Under Article IV, Section 33 of the state Constitution the governor can veto legislation subject to an override of two-thirds of the Legislature. The power of the veto, or even the threat of using it, can help governors in their dealings with the Legislature. Pushed to the limit, governors can veto legislation they believe should not become law. For example, Governor Snyder vetoed relaxed rules on gun ownership twice—once in 2012 and again in 2015. In the most recent case, Snyder noted that the bill could potentially permit people accused of domestic abuse to obtain a concealed gun license.[30] In 2003, Governor Jennifer Granholm vetoed a bill restricting late-term abortions, noting that "federal courts repeatedly declared unconstitutional efforts to end partial-birth abortion."[31]

Vetoes are an important tool of governors; in practice, a veto typically means the end to the legislation being proposed as there have only been three veto overrides in the state's history. The first occurred in 1951 when a Republican-controlled Legislature overrode Democratic governor G. Mennen Williams' veto of a 1.5 cent-per-gallon gasoline tax increase. In 1977, a Democratic-controlled Legislature overrode the veto of Republican governor William Milliken who struck down a bill providing lawmakers with more authority over the administrative rule-making process.[32] The final override came in 2002 when Republican governor John Engler's veto of an $845 million dollar revenue-sharing payment bill was overridden by a Republican-controlled Legislature.[33]

Budgetary Powers

One of the most important powers of the Michigan governor is his or her influence over the state budget. Not only does this power give the governor the ability to control state expenditures but also the ability to set policy priorities for the government. The governor and his staff have the responsibility to propose an executive budget to the Legislature which—by law—must occur within 30 days after that body convenes in January (see chapter 13).

The legislative process includes formal consideration of the governor's budget by the two chambers. It is a formidable process that includes a second sitting of the Revenue Estimating Conference. However, the governor is clearly in the dominant agenda-setting position having formed and proposed the initial budget. Throughout most of Michigan's history the governor and Legislature have worked well together to pass a budget. However, in recent years, when the governor and Legislature (or at least one chamber) are of two different parties, there has been considerable friction. Twice within a two-year period the inability of the two parties to pass a budget resulted in the shutdown of the state government under Governor Granholm (see below). In periods of one-party control of state government there have been few, if any, budget disputes, and none that have resulted in the shutdown of government.

After the Legislature passes the budget, the governor has the additional authority to veto any item or items appropriating money with the remaining parts becoming law. The vetoed items are considered canceled unless the Legislature overrides the governor's decision by a two-thirds vote of each chamber. Governors have different reasons for using the line-item veto. However, they all—to some degree or another—want to cut spending and see a political advantage in doing so.[34] During his tenure Governor Engler used the line-item veto to strategically cut spending by vetoing numerous items after passage of the budget.[35] This is not a new tactic of Michigan governors. Indeed, shortly after receiving the line-item veto authority under the 1908 Constitution, Governor Chase Osborn used his new power to cut spending that added up to nearly a million dollars.[36] Recently Governor Snyder has used the line-item veto but in a more limited fashion. In 2013, Governor Snyder vetoed two spending provisions in the 2014 fiscal year budget.[37] A year later Snyder issued two more line-item vetoes on the 2015 fiscal year budget.[38]

Appointment Powers

Overall the governor has responsibility to make over 4,800 appointments.[39] These appointments have the potential to impact nearly every aspect of government and life in Michigan. The people selected to public office have the responsibility to implement the laws enacted by the Legislature and governor, so possessing the power of appointment provides the governor with the ability to shape the direction of government actions.

Some of the most important appointments a new governor will make are his immediate staff within the executive office of the governor. Those positions include the governor's chief of staff, legislative affairs advisors, director of communications, director of strategy, and others. Historically, the governor's executive office has been organized based on a hierarchical model with advisors and other staff reporting to the chief of staff. This is an organizational structure similar to the one most U.S. presidents have employed over the last 30 years. As mentioned earlier, the Michigan governor has one of the largest gubernatorial staffs in the country, giving the office the necessary resources to deploy in ways that can potentially help influence the Legislature, the media, and the public. More important, it provides the governor with the tools to exercise leadership and manage the executive branch in more direct ways. The governor's staff can help coordinate policies and functions across departments, along with providing logistical and operational support when needed.

Many claim that the next class of appointments key to a governor's success are the directors of the executive departments. These positions possess the authority and power over major public policy areas. Unlike the governor's staff, department director appointments are subject to the advice and consent of the state Senate. At the federal level, "advice and consent" has come to be defined as the U.S. Senate approving of the president's nomination by a majority vote. However, the 1963 Constitution defines "advice and consent" much differently for Michigan. Instead of forcing the Legislature to take positive action, the Michigan Constitution merely requires the state Senate to disapprove of an appointment within 60 session days after the governor's submission. If no action occurs, the Senate's "advice and consent" is considered to have been given and the appointment is made. Therefore no legislative action is needed to make an appointment, even to positions requiring the "advice and consent" of the Senate.

The governor has only a limited number of department positions to appoint, primarily because of state civil service laws that restrict the removal of state employees from office. Before the late 1930s, the Michigan governor or the heads of executive departments could remove individuals and make appointments to nearly every position within the executive branch.[40] After consecutive elections where the governorship changed from one political party to another and the subsequent turnover in state personnel through the selection of individuals based on party affiliation rather than merit, there arose strong public support for civil service reform.[41] In 1937, the Michigan Legislature finally passed legislation creating the state's first civil-service system that would manage the process for removing and appointing state employees. Three years later Michigan voters approved a constitutional amendment creating the Civil Service Commission, empowered to set appointment, removal, and salary standards for nearly all state employees.[42]

Despite the restrictions that the civil service system imposes, governors still have ample opportunity to make appointments outside the top-level political offices within the executive departments. For example, there are over 200 boards and commissions to which the governor makes appointments.[43] These boards and commissions have been created by legislation and executive reorganization orders and in some cases do not require the advice and consent of the Senate. For example, among those boards that do not require Senate approval are the Human Trafficking Health Advisory Board, the Middle Eastern Affairs Commission, and the 21st Century Education Commission.

There are, however, constitutional and statutory qualifications placed on some of these positions that can limit the individuals who can be considered for appointment. For example, Article V, Section 5 of the Michigan Constitution requires that a majority of the members appointed to the examining or licensing board of any profession "be members of that profession." In another case, the Board of Accountancy—through a statutory mandate—requires at least one of its members to be a full-time instructor of accounting above the elementary level at an accredited college or university.[44]

The final category of appointments that extends the governor's influence into government operations is the judiciary. Although Michigan has an election system for the selection of state judges, the governor has the authority to make appointments where there is a judicial vacancy under Article VI, Section 23 of the state Constitution. The person appointed then will stand for an election to fulfill the unexpired term of the vacated seat. One study of judicial selection found that 43.4 percent of all current Michigan judges were initially appointed to the bench.[45] The appointed "incumbent" rarely loses the election, which nearly ensures that the governor can reshape the state judiciary as vacancies arise. Governor Snyder appointed David Viviano (in 2013) and Joan Larsen (in 2015) to the Michigan Supreme Court, and both won their elections in the 2016 race. These appointments solidified the conservative majority on the court with five of the seven justices considered to be Republicans.[46]

Executive Orders and Privilege

There are two remaining gubernatorial powers that are often overlooked—executive orders and executive privilege. Executive orders provide the governor with the ability to unilaterally shape public policy by directing government officials to act or not act. All executive orders are based on either federal laws, the state Constitution, or state laws. Primarily governors will use one of the latter two sources as justifications for an order. The state Constitution provides Michigan governors with the ability to issue an order, with the approval of the House and Senate Appropriations Committees, to reduce state spending if there are insufficient funds. In 2015,

Governor Snyder issued an executive order reducing expenditures in 11 departments under that constitutional provision.[47]

Like many other state chief executives, Michigan governors possess the authority to withhold certain information from the press, public, and Legislature; this is the power of executive privilege. The rationale behind this ability is that governors and their advisors need the privacy to hold frank discussions about what are often important but highly sensitive public policy matters. In 2013, Governor Snyder claimed executive privilege in a court case that could have resulted in the disclosure of e-mails and other documents related to his administration's discussions of potential candidates for the Detroit emergency manager. Attorney General Bill Schuette explained that the "governor's verbal and written communications with those high level officials who advise him must be afforded protection and deference, to assure that such communications can be candid and confidential."[48]

Checks on the Governor's Power

Although the Michigan governor's powers are significant, there are checks on them that can be employed both inside and outside the executive branch. The state Constitution provides for a plural executive, with two independently elected department heads in the attorney general and secretary of state. Each position, therefore, has its own electoral power base and is not directly answerable to the governor. A third department head—the superintendent of public instruction—is also outside the control of the governor as that position is appointed by the State Board of Education, an entity whose members are elected at-large by state voters.

Another check is the state Legislature, which consists of full-time professional lawmakers and is one of the most well-resourced lawmaking bodies in the country (see chapter 7). Its members are well compensated and have sizable nonpartisan and partisan staffs, employing in total nearly 1,000 full-time staff members.[49] One account of the Michigan Legislature noted it is one of the "four or five most professional state legislatures in the country."[50]

In many states, professional legislatures are often the ones setting the state's agenda and providing executive branch oversight. However, that often has not been the case in Michigan where the governor typically provides direction on public policy matters while experiencing little, if any, oversight by the Legislature. Any number of reasons have been given for the lack of legislative leadership and success in the state of Michigan. Lawmakers tend to pursue their immediate need of reelection, which means they focus more on local interests and constituent concerns. They are also susceptible to gubernatorial favors, such as help with fundraising or listening to their advice on appointments. As one state political observer noted, "Any legislator who says he needs nothing from the Governor's office is either lying or stupid."[51]

However, there is a wide array of political science research that supports former Governor Engler's contention that term limits "killed the legislature in Michigan."[52] Passed in 1992, term limits in Michigan now restrict House members to six years of service while in the Senate it is eight years (see chapter 7). One study of term limits noted that "to know term limits is NOT to love them."[53] The general findings have concluded that term limits have shifted power to governors.[54] It is easy to see why. Term limits have created an environment where large-scale turnover of the legislative body is the norm. Within a 10-year period there are no senior legislators, which, in turn, greatly reduces the collective experience of the legislative body. The inexperienced lawmakers tend to not only defer to governors but to executive branch officials to a greater degree than their pre-term-limited predecessors. That dynamic has the potential to swing the imbalance of power even further in the direction of the governor.[55] Of course the weakening of the Legislature might not necessarily be bad if the institutional changes produce good policy outcomes. But, at least according to one study, the concentration of power in the executive tends to produce higher spending compared to when there is a governing structure where the governor and lawmakers share more balanced power.[56]

Gubernatorial Elections

Between the adoption of the 1835 Constitution and 2017, there have been 47 governors of the state of Michigan. From 1837 to 1966, Michigan governors were elected to two-year terms. In 1963, the state Constitution changed the terms to four years. In 1992, an amendment to the Constitution imposed a two-term limit. The only constitutional restrictions for gubernatorial candidates running for office are that they must be at least 30 years old and have been a registered voter in the state for four years before the election.

Between 1933 and 2014, Michigan has generally had a competitive two-party system for gubernatorial elections with the Republican Party winning eight elections and the Democratic Party seven. Recent elections have not been as competitive—at least when looking at the results. Governor Snyder won in 2010 with an 18 percent margin of victory. In 2014, however, he was reelected by only 4 percent. Democratic governor Jennifer Granholm had a 14 percent victory margin in her last election in 2006. Since the adoption of the two-term limit all incumbent governors have won their reelection campaigns, with John Engler, Jennifer Granholm, and Rick Snyder having left (or will leave) office without being defeated. During the 20th century three governors served more than 10 years in office: G. Mennen Williams (12 years); William Milliken (14 years); and John Engler (12 years). Table 6.2 illustrates the years in office, party affiliation, and partisan majorities in the Legislature for the most recent Michigan governors.

TABLE 6.2. Michigan Governors, Party Affiliation, Election Results and Legislative Context, 1969–2019

Governor	Party	Years in Office	Percent of Vote Earned[a]	Divided or Unified Government
William Milliken	Republican	1969–1971[b]		Republican Senate / Democratic House
		1971–1975	50.8	Republican Senate[c] / Democratic House
		1975–1979	52.2	Democratic Senate / Democratic House
		1979–1983	56.8	Democratic Senate / Democratic House
James Blanchard	Democrat	1983–1987	53.3	Republican Senate / Democratic House
		1987–1991	68.4	Republican Senate / Democratic House
John Engler	Republican	1991–1995	50.3	Republican Senate / Democratic House[d]
		1995–1999	61.5	Republican Senate / Republican House[e]
		1999–2003	62.2	Republican Senate / Republican House
Jennifer Granholm	Democrat	2003–2007	52.0	Republican Senate / Republican House
		2007–2011	57.1	Republican Senate / Democratic House
Rick Snyder	Republican	2011–2015	59.3	Republican Senate / Republican House
		2015–2019	52.1	Republican Senate / Republican House

[a]Percentages reported are percentage of the two-party vote. In each election various other candidates were on the ballot or received write-in votes, but the totals were insignificant. Data from 1970–2010 are taken from the *Michigan Manual 2013–2014* (http://www.legislature.mi.gov/%28S%28fs5zan2ps23dzs c1tzwykeda%29%29/mileg.aspx?page=MM2013-2014&chapter=9); data from 2014 are taken from the Michigan Secretary of State's office website (www.mich.gov/sos).

[b]William Milliken assumed office in 1969 when Governor George Romney resigned to take the position of secretary of the U.S. Department of Housing and Urban Development.

[c]The composition of the state Senate in this time period was evenly split between the parties, but Republicans organized the chamber because the Republican lieutenant governor cast the tie-breaking vote at the start of the legislative session.

[d]During 1993 and 1994, membership in the House was split evenly. The two parties came to a power-sharing agreement that let both control the chamber for a period of time including both parties' leaders alternating as Speaker of the House and equal membership on committees.

[e]Democrats controlled the House in 1997 and 1998.

Most modern Michigan governors have experienced divided government with the other political party controlling at least one chamber in the Legislature. Governor Williams served from the late 1940s to the early 1960s without the benefit of his Democratic Party controlling the House or Senate during that time. In 1968, Governor George Romney became the first chief executive since Governor Kim Sigler (who served from 1947 to 1948) to have the benefit of unified government. More recently, Governor Engler from 1995 to 1996 and 1999 to 2002 along with Governor Snyder from 2011 to 2019 (when he will leave office) have served alongside a Republican-controlled Legislature.

In terms of campaign finance restrictions (see chapter 10), Michigan has a long history of passing legislation to prevent corruption and bribery in elections dating back to the early 1800s, even before it became a state. As only a territory, Michigan passed laws in the 1820s dealing with legislative bribery.[57] In the late 1870s, Governor Charles Croswell helped pass reforms to the state election laws to more effectively deal with corruption and bribery along with closing saloons on Election Day.[58] In 1976, a comprehensive campaign finance law was passed, the Michigan Campaign Finance Act. In 1990, the U.S. Supreme Court upheld that law against a First Amendment challenge, noting that the prevention of political corruption in the electoral process is a compelling state interest.[59] More recent laws, such as Public Act 269 of 2015, have tended to relax some campaign finance regulations by raising contribution limits for political action committees, for example.

Gubernatorial Leadership in Troubled Times

As noted in chapter 1, Michigan has faced serious economic challenges during what has been called the "lost decade" beginning in the year 2000. Michigan governors faced these challenges in the years prior to the national economic recession. The rest of the United States entered the Great Recession at the end of 2007, which resulted from a housing market bubble along with the collapse of the financial sector. At the federal level, President George W. Bush secured from Congress the largest bailout of the financial sector in U.S. history. In Michigan, the effects of the Great Recession were immediately felt in the lagging sales of automobiles and in severe financial losses for the auto industry. Eventually President Bush approved a bailout of General Motors and Chrysler.

Even with the federal government's response to the Great Recession there were many lagging effects of the recession on state and local governments. The loss of jobs meant that government revenue through tax collection greatly declined, which took a toll on the state budget. In early 2009, before the unveiling of a new budget, Governor Granholm faced a $1.6 billion dollar shortfall in the upcoming fiscal year. General fund revenue had declined 7.9 percent from the previous year. Executive departments were asked to cut 8 percent from their budgets.[60] By the end of the year Granholm and the Legislature (including, at times, members of her own party) were at loggerheads. Although she signed the budget, Granholm declared "it is a budget I don't agree with and don't support." Continuing, she said, "It makes cuts that are too deep and are too painful for kids going to college, families keeping their families healthy and keeping their streets safe."[61]

In her last year as governor, Granholm pushed to restore many of the cuts made in the previous year. However, doing so proved impossible with the state facing a $1.58 billion budget deficit, Governor Granholm's own lame duck status, and with Republicans controlling the state Senate.[62] Working with Senate Majority Leader Michael Bishop, a Republican, and House Speaker Andy Dillon, a Democrat, Granholm closed the revenue shortfall and secured a new budget but without some of the previously cut programs she wanted to reinstate, even though some of the cuts to programs she wanted restored had not been included in the budget. The budget highlighted the fact that despite the significant powers governors can claim the Legislature is still an important and formidable player in state politics.

Under Governor Granholm, budget negotiations with the Legislature were generally contentious. In 2007 and 2009, the state government temporarily shut down after the governor and Legislature initially failed to agree on a budget. Senate Majority Leader Mike Bishop blamed Granholm: "She didn't understand the Legislature, and I don't think she particularly looked at the Legislature with the idea that they had an equal role in the process."[63] Former Republican governor William Milliken disagreed, however, noting that Michigan's problems "are not fixable alone by the chief executive. [Granholm] did not have full cooperation from the Legislature, which she should have. She had less than her share that she was entitled to of cooperation from Republicans."[64]

The relationship between the governor and Legislature greatly improved under Governor Snyder as Lansing experienced unified party control of state government for the first time since 2002. Despite working with a friendly legislature Governor Snyder still faced a reeling economy with a $1.8 billion deficit.[65] The first-year budget talks were also made more difficult because of Governor Snyder's pension tax proposal.[66] Despite significant opposition from Democrats, the American Association of Retired Persons, and other groups, Governor Snyder—and the Republican-dominated Legislature—secured approval of a budget within four months.[67] The same speedy budget process has occurred in each of Snyder's six years in office through 2016.[68]

During that time Snyder and the Legislature faced the ongoing fallout of the City of Detroit's bankruptcy, which began in July 2013 after the governor had appointed Kevyn Orr as emergency manager. Over the course of several months Orr failed to reach agreement with Detroit's creditors and unions in order to settle the city's debt. As a result, in July 2013 Detroit was forced to file for Chapter 9 bankruptcy in order to resolve its $18 billion in long-term debt. At the time, it was the largest municipal bankruptcy in U.S. history (see chapter 4).

By early 2014 Governor Snyder and other state leaders realized that without state help the outcome of the bankruptcy would have tremendous negative implications for not only Detroit but the entire state of Michigan. The governor worked with a variety of representatives from the city of Detroit, public employee unions, private foundations, and the state Legislature. To that end, by May 2014, Republican House Speaker Jase Bolger created the House Committee on Detroit's Recovery and Michigan's Future to craft legislation that would help mitigate the economic fallout from Detroit's bankruptcy. Speaker Pro Tem John Walsh, who chaired the committee, stated, "Detroit is still a driver of economic activity in the Great Lakes region and its failures and successes impact all of Michigan. We are taking action to ensure its bankruptcy is a new beginning rather than an end."[69] After a month of negotiations, a grand bargain was agreed to where the state provided $195 million to help settle the bankruptcy by minimizing the cuts in pensions. Included in the aid package was the creation of a commission that would oversee the review and approval of city budgets and contracts for at least 13 years.[70] In endorsing the bill, Democratic state Senator Tupac Hunter noted, "It makes pensioners as whole as possible."[71]

The only other contentious budgetary item between Snyder and the Republican Legislature was the 2014–15 road funding debate. Several months after a 2015 failed ballot proposal which was backed by Governor Snyder, he declared, "we're at an impasse," with the disagreement centering on how to pay for the bill.[72] Eventually the two sides came to an accommodation, with the governor signing the bill in November 2015. The episode, however, indicates that governors will face disagreement and conflict with the Legislature even with the presence of unified state government.

Another crisis Governor Snyder faced was the Flint water crisis, which came to light in late 2015 and early 2016. High levels of lead had been discovered in Flint's drinking water after the city decided to switch from using the Detroit water system and, in a separate decision, the Flint emergency manager decided to use the Flint River as a temporary water source in April 2014. More importantly, a series of early reports began to paint a picture of government failure and indifference—by federal, state, and local elected and appointed officials, including the Michigan Department of Environmental Quality (MDEQ), the regional office of the Environmental Protection Agency, and by the state-appointed emergency manager sent to Flint. The Flint water crisis captured national—and even international—media attention as more information was discovered and released to the public.

Regardless of how much culpability rested with his office specifically, Governor Snyder did respond to this major challenge by late 2015 and early 2016. In late September 2015, the governor publicly acknowledged that Flint's water was a problem, and pledged to take action in response to the high lead levels. Distribution of water filters and bottled water followed, and, in early October, Governor Snyder called for Flint to reconnect to the Detroit water system and also created a five-member Flint Water Advisory Task Force to investigate the crisis. In late December 2015, the Task Force's preliminary report placed most of the responsibility for the crisis on Snyder's administration, particularly the MDEQ, which did not treat water safety as a high priority and failed to properly follow federal Environmental Protection Agency rules. The findings resulted in the quick resignation of MDEQ director Dan Wyant and MDEQ communications director Brad Wurfel.

By early January 2016, more revelations about the crisis put greater pressure on the governor to respond with a quick and complete solution. On January 5, Synder declared a state of emergency in Flint, and about two weeks later he asked President Obama to declare Flint a major disaster area in order to trigger federal aid to the city. The governor activated the National Guard to help the state police and others distribute bottled water and water filters to Flint residents. Flint was the first substantive topic of his 2016 State of the State message, and in that speech he again apologized to the citizens of Flint and said that government had failed them. By the end of the month Snyder and the Legislature approved a $28 million aid package to Flint to purchase water filters, medical aid, and provide children health assessments.[73] A month later the state appropriated an additional $30 million to provide water bill credits of up to 65 percent for residents and 20 percent for business, and in June the state agreed to send $165 million to pay for lead pipe replacements and the ongoing costs of water.[74]

The Flint water crisis deals directly with state-local government relations in Michigan, this book's fourth theme. The governor's appointments of emergency managers in both Detroit and Flint provide a direct connection between local decision making and state government. State departments, especially the MDEQ, essentially downplayed or even ignored the early warnings regarding high lead levels in Flint's water. Snyder's own Flint Water Advisory Task Force's final report, issued in March 2016, highlighted the systematic failures at the state level that resulted in "the discounting of profound public health concerns and indifference to Flint's residents' plight." The report also highlighted some of the fundamental problems that result when emergency managers replace local elected officials in the decision-making process: "emergency managers made key decisions that contributed to the crisis, from the use of the Flint River to delays in reconnecting to [Detroit's water system] once water quality problems were encountered."[75]

More fundamentally, the Flint water crisis raises questions concerning executive leadership and accountability. How much Governor Snyder knew—and how early he knew it—became a much-discussed topic in the state. In an interview with the *National Journal* in January 2016, Governor Snyder acknowledged that the Flint water crisis could be regarded as his "Katrina," because it was also a disaster and would reflect negatively on his leadership and legacy as governor.[76] But another parallel might be made. This could also be considered Governor Snyder's Watergate—it was caused by the decisions and actions of people (not a natural disaster like Hurricane Katrina), and it left a number of people asking U.S. Senator Howard Baker's question about President Richard Nixon during the Watergate hearings, "What did he know and when did he know it?"[77]

Despite promising in his 2016 State of the State address to release all of the relevant e-mails from his office that involved the Flint crisis, critics have claimed that Snyder and his administration have not been fully transparent. For example, the day after his State of the State message, Snyder's office did release a batch of e-mails, but a number of them were heavily redacted (including one that was completely redacted). The governor's ability to pick and choose what to disclose results from a combination of executive privilege powers and the state's decision to exempt the Governor's Office from the Michigan Freedom of Information Act. However, despite the redactions, Snyder has not shown any Nixon-like stonewalling tactics and has said, "I want to cooperate with all the investigations."[78] By

June of 2016, Snyder had released 18 batches of e-mails consisting of over 180,000 pages of documents.[79]

Even if the Flint crisis is not Snyder's Watergate, it does raise questions about his leadership and the state's responses to local concerns. By the end of 2016, Republican attorney general Bill Schuette had charged nine people with crimes—eight state employees and one City of Flint worker.[80] Although the governor and his staff had not been subject to any criminal charges by that time, then House Democratic leader Tim Greimel called on Snyder to resign, noting that "Michigan residents need to have trust in the governor and we need to have a state government that is transparent and accountable." Greimel opined that the "only way to ensure those two things are to have the governor resign."[81] Regardless of the ultimate outcome of the criminal investigations, the Flint crisis has brought to the forefront the dark side of executive power along with the struggles Michigan faces in finding the right balance between state-local control over public policy issues.

Conclusion

The Michigan governor possesses significant formal powers. Combined with a politically gifted politician and a legislative branch weakened by term limits, a governor has the potential to dominate state government and public policy matters. That does not mean the governor will successfully lead on each issue. For example, Governor Snyder struggled as he attempted to assume a leadership role in fixing the state's roads system in 2014 and 2015. His plans for legislation to fund roads stalled in the Legislature. After that, Governor Snyder actively promoted Proposal 15-1 in 2015, the so-called roads and tax statewide ballot proposal. This was a compromise proposal that ended up with a complex plan that would eliminate the sales tax on fuel; increase statewide sales tax from 6 to 7 percent; and increase the state's Earned Income Tax Credit. The proposal also sought to provide additional funds to local governments and to the School Aid Fund (see chapter 11). The proposal failed miserably.

However, the overall structure, powers, and political dynamics in state government result in a system where the Legislature might win a tactical battle against the governor but more often loses when it comes to an overall policy outcome. As two gubernatorial scholars have noted, "The American system of checks and balances constrains but does not cripple its chief executives."[82]

The reason that the traditional rough-and-tumble political process between the governor and legislative branch favors the former has as much to do with the lack of political will to counter the executive branch on policy disputes as it does with the crippling effect of term limits restrictions on the Legislature (though the two factors are not mutually exclusive). The Legislature still has the means at its disposal to prevail in disputes with the governor. But lawmakers must have the will and persistence necessary to overcome what often can be long and aggravating battles against a determined executive. Until lawmakers commit to fulfilling their constitutional roles it is likely that the general trend of more political and policy authority being concentrated in governors will continue.

WEB RESOURCES

The *Michigan state government* webpage provides useful summaries and links to each executive branch department. From the home page (michigan.gov) click on "Government" and then "Executive Branch."

The *Council of State Governments* compiles and maintains data on state governments going back to 1935. From their home page (knowledgecenter.csg.org/kc/) click on "Policy & Research," then "Government," and then "Executive Branch."

The *Michigan Senate* maintains an alphabetic listing of all gubernatorial appointments, including the date(s) the Senate receives the appointment along with the date when the term expires. From the home page (www.senate.michigan.gov/default.html) click on "Rules & Appts," and then "Governor Appointments."

The *Michigan Legislature* maintains an archive of all executive orders of Michigan governors dating to 1993. From the home page (www.legislature.mi.gov/) click on "Executive Orders" to view gubernatorial executive orders organized by year.

The *National Governor's Association* (www.nga.org/cms/home.html) provides lots of information about state governors and gubernatorial elections, and a best practices section on various state public policies, such as health care, jobs, education, and ways to improve intergovernmental relations.

NOTES

1. Nathan Bomey and Matt Helms, "Detroit Bankruptcy Over; Emergency Manager Resigning," *USA Today*, December 10, 2014, http://www.usatoday.com/story/news/nation/2014/12/10/detroit-bankruptcy-exit/20192289/

2. 1963 Michigan Constitution, Article V, Section 30.

3. David G. Chardavoyne, "The Northwest Ordinance and Michigan's Territorial Heritage," in *The History of Michigan Law*, ed. Paul Finkelman and Martin J. Hershock (Athens: Ohio University Press, 2006), 17.

4. Jack Ericson Eblen, *The First and Second United States Empires, Governors and Territorial Government, 1784–1912* (Pittsburgh: University of Pittsburgh Press, 1968), 100–101, 203.

5. 3 Stat. 769 (1823).

6. Chardavoyne, "Northwest Ordinance and Michigan's Territorial Heritage," 23.

7. Susan P. Fino, *The Michigan State Constitution* (New York: Oxford University Press, 2011), 11.

8. Article 5, Section 3, Michigan Constitution of 1850.

9. Article 8, Section 1, Michigan Constitution of 1850.

10. John A. Fairlie, "The State Governor, II," *Michigan Law Review* 10 (April 1912): 461.

11. Article IV, Section 7, Michigan Constitution of 1908 and State of Michigan, *Papers in the Matter of the Removal of John W. Jochim, Secretary of State, Joseph F. Hambitzer, State Treasurer, and John G. Berry, Commissioner of the State Land office* (Lansing: Robert Smith, 1895), 109–10.

12. Bruce A. Rubenstein and Lawrence E. Ziewacz, *Michigan: A History of the Great Lakes States* (Wheeling, IL: Harlan Davidson, 2008), 222; and Richard Elling and Peter Kobrak, "The Bureaucracy: An Ambiguous Political Legacy," in *Michigan Politics and Government: Facing Change in a Complex State*, ed. William P. Browne and Kenneth Verburg (Lincoln: University of Nebraska Press, 1995), 145.

13. Article V, Section 37, Michigan Constitution of 1908.

14. Article III, Section 8, Michigan Constitution of 1908.

15. Fino, *Michigan State Constitution*, 18.

16. Article VI, Section 22, Michigan Constitution of 1908.

17. David Houghton, "Michigan: Four Constitutions, Four New Beginnings," in *The Constitutionism of American States*, ed. George E. Connor and Christopher W. Hammons (Columbia: University of Missouri Press, 2008), 438–39.

18. In 1958, the Legislature passed a law giving the governor the ability to submit executive branch reorganization plans to the Legislature, subject to the disapproval of either chamber. All but one of the reorganizations plans were rejected. See Legislative Service Bureau, *Michigan Manual, 2013–2014* (Lansing: Legislative Service Bureau, 2014), 271.

19. Fino, *Michigan State Constitution*, 112.

20. The 20-department restriction meant the consolidation of approximately 140 different commissions, boards, bureaus, and agencies into 19 departments through the approval of the Executive Organization Act of 1965, MCL 16.101. See Albert L. Sturm and Margaret Whitaker, *Implementing a New Constitution: The Michigan Experience* (Ann Arbor: Institute of Public Administration, 1968), 119.

21. Thad L. Beyle, "The Governor's Formal Powers: A View from the Governor's Chair," *Public Administration Review* 28 (November–December 1968): 540–45.

22. Joseph A. Schlesinger, "The Politics of the Executive," in *Politics in the American States*, ed. Herbert Jacob and Kenneth N. Vines (Boston: Little, Brown, 1965), 207–38.

23. For a detailed look at the increase in gubernatorial powers in the 1960s and 1970s, see Larry Sabato, *Goodbye to Good-Time Charlie: The American Governorship Transformed* (Lexington, MA: Lexington Books, 1978).

24. Most of that increase can be attributed to governors receiving the line-item veto power. Thad L. Beyle, "Governors: Elections, Campaign Costs and Powers," in *The Book of the States* (Lexington, KY: Council of State Governments, 2005), 201. For an up-to-date listing of gubernatorial powers, see "Table 4.4. The Governors: Powers," in *The Book of the States* (Lexington, KY: Council of State Governments, 2015), 171–72.

25. Formal powers include the presence of separately elected executive branch officials; tenure potential; appointment power; budget power; veto power; and the governor's political party control of the Legislature. Personal powers include electoral mandate; governor's position on the state's political ambition ladder; personal future of governors; and the governor's job performance rating in public opinion polls.

26. Margaret Ferguson, "Governors and the Executive Branch," in *Politics in the American States: A Comparative Analysis*, 10th ed., ed. Virginia Gray, Russell L. Hanson, and Thad Kousser (Washington, DC: CQ Press, 2013), 227.

27. See "Table 4.3. The Governors: Compensation, Staff, Travel, and Residence," in *The Book of the States* (Lexington, KY: Council of State Governments, 2015), 169.

28. Barry L. Van Lare, "The Governors' Office," in *The Book of the States* (Lexington, KY: Council of State Governments, 2009), 183.

29. Executive Reorganization Order No. 2015-1, Creation of Department of Health and Human Services.

30. Monica Davey, "Governor of Michigan Vetoes Bill on Guns," *New York Times*, January 15, 2015, A20.

31. Amy Bailey, "Granholm Vetoes Abortion Bill," *Grand Rapids Press*, October 11, 2003, A5.

32. "Overrides Are Rare," *Grand Rapids Press*, August 3, 2002, A6; Bernard Klein and Joseph Cepuran, "The Politics of Gubernatorial Leadership," in *Michigan Politics and Government: Facing Change in a Complex State*, ed. William P. Browne and Kenneth Verburg (Lincoln: University of Nebraska Press, 1995), 90–91.

33. Charlie Cain and Mark Hornbeck, "Engler's Image Takes Beating in Stunning Override," *Detroit News*, August 14, 2002, 8A.

34. Thad Kousser and Justin H. Phillips, *The Power of American Governors: Winning on Budgets and Losing on Policy* (New York: Cambridge University Press, 2012), 195.

35. Bernard Klein and Joseph Cepuran, "The Politics of Gubernatorial Leadership," in *Michigan Politics and Government: Facing Change in a Complex State*, ed. William P. Browne and Kenneth Verburg (Lincoln: University of Nebraska Press, 1995), 90.

36. Jon C. Teaford, *The Rise of the States: Evolution of American State Government* (Baltimore: Johns Hopkins University Press, 2002), 61.

37. Jonathan Oosting, "Michigan Gov. Rick Snyder Signs 'Solid' $49.5 Billion Budget Short on Money for Medicaid Expansion," *MLive.com*, June 13, 2013, http://www.mlive.com/politics/index.ssf/2013/06/michigan_gov_rick_snyder_signs_3.html

38. "Gov. Rick Snyder: Budget Reflects Focus on Making Michigan Bet-

ter, Safer, Stronger," press release, June 30, 2014, http://www.michigan.gov/snyder/0,4668,7-277----,00.html

39. *Michigan Manual, 2013–2014* (Lansing: Legislative Service Bureau, 2014), 274; and "Governor Appointments," Michigan Senate webpage, http://www.senate.michigan.gov/Appointments/governor_appointments.htm

40. Robert G. McCloskey, "The Case for 'Foot in the Door,'" *National Municipal Review* 34 (March): 128.

41. Gregory M. Saltzman and Shlomo Sperka, "Public Sector Collective Bargaining in Michigan: Law and Recent Developments," in *Collective Bargaining in the Public Sector*, ed. Joyce M. Najita and James L. Stern (New York: Routledge, 2015), 129.

42. Richard Elling and Peter Kobrak, "The Bureaucracy: An Ambiguous Political Legacy," in *Michigan Politics and Government: Facing Change in a Complex State*, ed. William P. Browne and Kenneth Verburg (Lincoln: University of Nebraska Press, 1995), 147.

43. "Alphabetical Listing of Michigan Boards and Commissions," Michigan.gov, http://www.michigan.gov/snyder/0,1607,7-277-57738_23228-249058--,00.html

44. MCL 339.721, Act 299 of 1980.

45. Charles R. Toy, "How Should We Select Our Judges?," *Michigan Bar Journal*, August 2010, 14.

46. Jonathan Oosting, "Gov. Rick Snyder Appoints Judge David Viviano to Michigan Supreme Court," *Mlive.com*, February 27, 2013, http://www.mlive.com/politics/index.ssf/2013/02/gov_rick_snyder_appoints_judge.html

47. Executive Order No. 2015-5, "Implementation of Expenditure Reductions under Section 20 of Article V of the Michigan Constitution of 1963."

48. Chad Livengood, "Snyder: Block Emails on EM," *Detroit News*, October 21, 2013, A9.

49. National Conference of State Legislatures, "Size of State Legislative Staff," http://www.ncsl.org/research/about-state-legislatures/staff-change-chart-1979-1988-1996-2003-2009.aspx

50. Thomas H. Little and David B. Ogle, *The Legislative Branch of State Government* (Santa Barbara, CA: ABC-CLIO, 2006), 321.

51. Thad Kousser and Justin H. Phillips, *The Power of American Governors: Winning on Budgets and Losing on Policy* (New York: Cambridge University Press, 2012), 38.

52. Alan Rosenthal, *The Best Job in Politics: Exploring How Governors Succeed as Policy Leaders* (Washington, DC: CQ Press, 2012), 32–33.

53. Carol S. Weissert and Karen Halperin, "The Paradox of Term Limit Support," *Political Research Quarterly* 60 (September 2007): 516.

54. John M. Carey, Richard G. Niemi, and Lynda W. Powell, "The Effects of Term Limits on State Legislatures," *Legislative Studies Quarterly* 23 (May 1998): 271.

55. Richard J. Powell, "Executive-Legislative Relations," in *Institutional Change in American Politics: The Case of Term Limits*, ed. Karl Kurtz, Bruce Cain, and Richard G. Niemi (Ann Arbor: University of Michigan Press, 2007), 138.

56. George A. Krause and Benjamin F. Melusky, "Concentrated Powers: Unilat-

eral Executive Authority and Fiscal Policymaking in the American States," *Journal of Politics* 74 (January 2012): 98–112.

57. Zephyr Teachout, *Corruption in America* (Cambridge: Harvard University Press, 2014), 114.

58. Don C. Henderson, *The Red Book for the Thirtieth Legislature of the State of Michigan* (Lansing: W. S. George & Co., 1879), 513.

59. *Austin v. Michigan Chamber of Commerce*, 494 U.S. 652.

60. Associated Press, "Michigan Budget Proposal to Address $1.6 Billion Shortfall," *MLive.com*, Feb. 11, 2009, http://www.mlive.com/politics/index.ssf/2009/02/michigan_budget_proposal_to_ad.html; Senate Fiscal Agency, "Michigan's Economic Outlook and Budget Review," December 21, 2010, http://www.senate.michigan.gov/sfa/Publications/BudUpdates/EconomicOutlookDec10.pdf, p. 1; Tim Martin, "More Michigan Budget Cuts Planned for 2009–2010," *Oakland Press*, May 15, 2015, http://www.theoaklandpress.com/general-news/20090515/more-michigan-budget-cuts-planned-for-2009-10

61. Peter Luke, "State Shutdown Averted," *Grand Rapids Press*, October 31, 2009, A1.

62. Mark Hornbeck and Karen Bouffard, "Granholm Pushes Plans to Build Jobs, Economy," *Detroit News*, February 4, 2010, 1A; Peter Luke, "Budget Forecast: Michigan Faces $1.58 Billion Deficit," *MLive.com*, Jan. 11, 2010, http://www.mlive.com/politics/index.ssf/2010/01/post_16.html

63. Karen Bouffard, "How Granholm Handled Economic Woes Clouds Legacy," *Detroit News*, December 15, 2010, A1.

64. Ibid.

65. Karen Bouffard, "Michigan Recovery Battles with $1.8B Deficit," *Detroit News*, January 15, 2011, A1.

66. Paul Egan, "Snyder's Budget Calls for 'Shared Sacrifice,'" *Detroit News*, February 18, 2011, A1.

67. Peter Luke, "Signature Makes It Official," *Grand Rapids Press*, June 22, 2011, A1.

68. Karen Bouffard, "Governor Signs $49B Budget," *Detroit News*, June 27, 2012, A3; "Gov. Snyder Signs 2014 State Budget," *Manistee News Advocate*, June 14, 2013, 1A; Paul Egan and Kathleen Gray, "Snyder Signs $54.5-Billion Budget That Lacks Road Fix," *Detroit Free Press*, June 17, 2015, http://www.freep.com/story/news/local/michigan/2015/06/17/governor-snyder-sign-state-budget/28855399/; Kathleen Gray and Paul Egan, "Michigan Lawmakers Finalize $55-Billion State Budget," *Detroit Free Press*, June 8, 2016, http://www.freep.com/story/news/politics/2016/06/08/lawmakers-set-wrap-up-54-billion-budget-week/85597092/

69. Jonathan Oosting, "State Money for Detroit? New Michigan Panel to Consider 'Grand Bargain' Legislation, Oversight," *MLive.com*, May 6, 2014, http://www.mlive.com/lansing-news/index.ssf/2014/05/state_money_for_detroit_new_mi.html

70. Jonathan Oosting, "Michigan Senate Approves 'Grand Bargain' in Detroit Bankruptcy Case, $195M for Pensions," *Mlive.com*, June 3, 2014, http://www.mlive.com/lansing-news/index.ssf/2014/06/michigan_senate_approves_histo.html

71. Kathleen Gray, "Michigan Senate OKs Historic $195M Detroit Aid Pack-

age," *Detroit Free Press*, June 4, 2014, http://archive.freep.com/article/20140603/NEWS06/306030043/Detroit-bankruptcy-pensions-artwork

72. Jonathan Oosting, "Snyder: Road Funding Negotiations Have Reached 'an Impasse' in Michigan Legislature," *MLive.com*, Oct. 13, 2015, http://www.mlive.com/lansing-news/index.ssf/2015/10/snyder_road_funding_talks_reac.html

73. Emily Lawler, "Michigan Gov. Rick Snyder Signs $28M Aid Bill for Flint Water Crisis," *MLive.com*, January 29, 2016, http://www.mlive.com/news/index.ssf/2016/01/michigan_gov_rick_snyder_signs.html

74. Damon Maloney, "Gov. Snyder Signs $30 Million Budget Bill," abc12.com, February 26, 2016, http://www.abc12.com/news/headlines/Gov-Snyder-signs-30-million-budget-bill-370275451.html; and David Eggert, "Snyder Signs Budget with $165M More for Flint," *Detroit News*, June 29, 2016, http://www.detroitnews.com/story/news/politics/2016/06/29/snyder-budget-flint/86521044/

75. Flint Water Advisory Task Force: Final Report, March 2016, 1 and 62, http://media.graytvinc.com/documents/FINAL+FWATF+REPORT+21March20161.pdf

76. Ron Fournier, "Snyder Concedes Flint Is His 'Katrina,' a Failure of Leadership," *National Journal*, January 18, 2016; accessed January 22, 2016, http://www.nationaljournal.com/s/352793/snyder-calls-flint-his-katrina-catastrophic-failure-leadership

77. This question was repeated many times, including in an article by David A. Graham, "What Did Governor Know about Flint's Water, and When Did He Know It?," *Atlantic*, January 9, 2016; accessed January 22, 2016, http://www.theatlantic.com/politics/archive/2016/01/what-did-the-governor-know-about-flints-water-and-when-did-he-know-it/423342/

78. Tim Skubick, "Attorney General's Flint Investigation: No One Can Get Away from a Crime," fox2detroit.com, February 9, 2016, http://www.fox2detroit.com/news/flint-water-crisis/87791628-story

79. Governor Snyder, press release, June 21, 2016, http://www.michigan.gov/snyder/0,4668,7-277-57577-387125-RSS,00.html

80. Robert Allen, "6 State Employees Criminally Charged in Flint Water Crisis," *Detroit Free Press*, July 30, 2016, http://www.freep.com/story/news/local/michigan/flint-water-crisis/2016/07/29/6-state-employees-criminally-charged-flint-water-crisis/87697834/

81. Brian McVicar, "Michigan Lawmaker Calls on Gov. Rick Snyder to Resign over 'Indifference' to Flint Water Crisis," *MLive.com*, March 2, 2016, http://www.mlive.com/news/index.ssf/2016/03/house_democratic_leader_calls.html

82. Kousser and Phillips, *Power of American Governors*, 260.

7 ✦ Michigan's Legislature

KEVIN G. LORENTZ II AND TIMOTHY BLEDSOE

The Michigan Legislature is the principal policy-making institution of state government, vested with the legislative power of government. Housed in the Michigan State Capitol in Lansing, the Legislature represents the "people's voice" in state government, composed of elected representatives tasked with mediating divergent interests and translating such needs and wants into laws.

A Brief History of the Michigan Legislature

Michigan's Legislature has undergone several iterations, although its basic structure and authority has remained relatively stable since Michigan became a state in 1837. Michigan's first Constitution (drafted in 1835) created a bicameral legislature, consisting of a House of Representatives and a Senate.[1] Representatives would serve a term of one year while senators would be elected biennially concurrent with the state governor. In addition to general lawmaking duties, the Legislature was also responsible for funding (and promoting) a system of improvements designed to encourage internal development and future immigration to Michigan.[2]

Successive legislatures, reorganized following adoption of a new state constitution, retained this basic structure although legislative powers, terms of office, and seat apportionment would undergo significant revisions. The Constitution of 1850, for example, increased the size of both the House and Senate, extended terms for state representatives to two years, and required biennial sessions.[3] While leaving intact most of the 1850 constitutional structure, the 1908 Constitution altered the scope of the Legislature's authority (see chapter 2). For instance, the governor was afforded a line-item veto for appropriations bills, allowing chief executives to veto specific line items without opposing a bill in its entirety (see chapter 6). In addition, local municipalities were extended the legislative power to adopt and amend their charters, called "home rule" (see chapters 4 and 5), freeing the state Legislature from considering local legislation, which had dominated earlier legislatures.[4]

Michigan's present Constitution, enacted in 1963 and since amended, was a significant rewrite in terms of modernizing and streamlining state government. Structurally, senators saw their numbers increased to 38, with their terms of office expanded to four years (along with the executive branch officers). The House was expanded to 110 members serving two-year terms. While the Constitution maintained some old practices, the Legislature saw its powers both expanded and constrained. For example, the Legislature was prohibited from enacting a graduated income tax or capital punishment. Alongside these prohibitions, though, the new Constitution expanded legislative powers through new grants of authority, incorporating phrases "as prescribed by law" or "as provided by law" throughout the document, authorizing new legislation in the areas of public health, environmental affairs, and energy, among others.

Today's Legislature continues to reflect the arrangement embodied in the 1963 Constitution, and works to address the challenges faced by Michigan's society. Through its historical evolution, the Legislature is empowered to combat the state's economic decline, although several constitutional amendments have affected the Legislature's lawmaking powers and general structure, most notably the implementation of term limits for state legislators and executive officers (see below). It is within these confines that Michigan citizens collectively engage in a forum tasked with addressing and ultimately solving the state's public policy issues.

General Structure of the Legislature

Like most state governments, the Michigan Legislature is bicameral, with a 38-member Senate (elected to four-year terms concurrent with the governor) and a 110-member House of Representatives (elected to two-year terms). While the number of legislators is constitutionally fixed, the size of individual districts changes every 10 years according to population, with each district containing as nearly an equal number of persons as possible. Following the 2010 census, state House districts contained approximately 90,000 residents and each Senate district had about 260,000 persons. For each district, constituents elect one representative or senator to represent them in Lansing, and therefore they are considered "single member districts."

Qualifications to become a senator or representative (usually preceded by "state" to indicate a state-level official) are the same for each chamber and are set by the Constitution. Accordingly, legislators must be a citizen of the United States, at least 21 years of age, an "elector" (i.e., resident) of the district he or she represents, and must not have been convicted of subversion or a felony involving a break of public trust within the past 20 years. Once elected, legislators are prohibited from holding another constitutional or civil office from the State of Michigan or a subordinate governmental entity. Legislators must also remain uninvolved in any contractual obligation with the State of Michigan or any political subdivision thereof, causing a conflict of interest that would hinder the objectivity of a legislator in performance of her or his duties (Article IV, Sections 7–10, and Article XI, Section 8). Finally, via a constitutional amendment in 1992, legislators are limited to serving six years (i.e., three terms) in the House and eight years (i.e., two terms) in the Senate (Article IV, Section 54).

While in office, legislators enjoy several privileges in conducting their duties. Senators and representatives are immune from civil arrest and court proceedings. For example, legislators cannot be sued for performing their duties, some of their records are protected from judicial subpoenas, and they cannot be questioned for their speech on the House or Senate floors. However, legislators are still subject to criminal proceedings and arrest, while each chamber maintains strict ethical standards in upholding legislator conduct. In extreme instances, each chamber may expel a member for breaching these provisions with the concurrence of two-thirds of its members.[5] In matters relating to the qualifications and elections of its members, each chamber is sole judge, meaning that the House or Senate resolves any challenges that may arise. Finally, legislators are compensated for their service, with such enumeration determined by the State Officers Compensation Commission every two years. For example, during the 2017–18 session, legislators were paid an annual salary of $71,685 and an expense allowance of $10,800, with supplemental salaries for House and Senate leadership.

Each legislature continues for two years, divided into annual sessions beginning at noon on the second Wednesday of January (e.g., the 98th Legislature lasted from January 7, 2015 to January 11, 2017). Each session continues until members agree to adjourn *sine die* (Latin for "without day"), with annual sessions normally ending in December of each year. Daily sessions normally occur on Tuesdays, Wednesdays, and Thursdays, although each chamber sets its own schedule and meeting times. Periodic recesses of both houses occur throughout the year. Special sessions of the Legislature may be called by the governor, but such sessions are limited to the subjects placed before it by the governor. Regardless of the type of sessions, each chamber records its proceedings in its journal, which is periodically published, representing a public record of the Legislature's work.

Institutional Powers, Responsibilities, and Processes

Like its predecessors and federal counterpart, the Michigan Constitution of 1963 invests the legislative power of the state government in the bicameral Michigan Legislature (Article IV, Section 1). Besides general lawmaking, the Legislature is empowered specifically to do the following:

- implement and promote the civil rights and liberties contained within the Michigan Constitution's Declaration of Rights (Article I);
- regulate elections within the state (Article II);
- regulate hours and conditions of employment (Article IV, Section 49);
- pass "suitable" laws for the protection and promotion of public health (Article IV, Section 51);
- provide for an annual, public audit of state finances and public spending, including the appointment of an auditor general to oversee said audit (Article IV, Section 53);
- create additional judicial courts and judgeships (Article VI, Section 1);
- support a system of free public education, including public institutions of higher education (Article VIII, Section 2);
- manage state-owned land and, by two-thirds vote, create additional state land reserves (Article X, Section 5); and
- levy taxes to cover the state's general expenses (Article IX).

While broad, the Legislature's plenary power is not absolute. The Legislature is constrained in its ability to limit the rights guaranteed under Article I's Declaration of Rights, including prohibitions on the abridgment of free speech, free press, equal protection, double jeopardy, and denial of habeas corpus, among others. The Constitution specifically forbids the Legislature from promulgating the death penalty as a suitable punishment for any crime (Article IV, Section 46). In terms of fiscal policy, the Legislature is forbidden from supporting nonpublic educational institutions with public funds (Article VIII, Section 2), enacting a graduated income tax, and cannot raise the sales and use tax beyond the constitutional limitation barring a constitutional amendment (6 percent as of 2017) (Article IX, Sections 7–8). The Legislature is also precluded in several circumstances from delegating its taxing and legislating powers to other bodies or institutions, or both.

Recent constitutions have constrained the Legislature's plenary authority by introducing elements of direct democracy. The 1908 Constitution, in particular, introduced limited versions of both the initiative and the referendum, while a 1913 amendment added the recall.[6] Voters now could initiate legislation themselves, reject laws passed by the Legislature, and recall elected officials, mechanisms that Michigan's citizens have used occasionally since. The 1963 Constitution has maintained all three direct democracy instruments while affording voters additional avenues with which to influence state policy making (Article II, Section 9). The Legislature is empowered to submit laws directly to voters for assent (generally a majority of votes cast), while any constitutional amendment proposed by the Legislature must be submitted to a general vote for approval (Article XII). Likewise, the current Constitution has maintained the practice begun in 1850 of submitting a ballot question to the electorate every 16 years regarding general constitutional revision. While there are limitations to voters' initiative, referendum, and recall powers (see chapter 11), Michigan remains among only 15 states that afford its citizens power to intervene directly in the lawmaking process and, in some instances, circumvent its popular representatives.

Besides its lawmaking duties, the Legislature also provides oversight of the various executive branch agencies, departments, and officials. Executive branch officials routinely testify before legislative committees regarding programs and budgetary matters, allowing legislators to ensure that the laws passed and appropriations made are being carried out appropriately and in accordance with the Legislature's intent. Legislators also investigate matters of public importance and disasters, examining the state government's response and recommending changes. A recent example concerns the lead contamination of Flint's water supply (see chapter 15). Following the public outcry and political fallout, the Legislature impaneled a special joint committee to explore the various state and local agencies' responses and how existing policies failed. Hearing over 18 hours of testimony from experts, bureaucrats, elected officials, and private citizens, the committee recommended several statutory and bureaucratic changes. In particular, the committee urged: adoption of stronger clean water standards; changes to existing agencies' operating procedures; reform of the state's emergency manager law; and a series of ameliorative programs for Flint's recovery.[7]

Besides hearings, the Legislature also provides oversight through its "advice and consent" and impeachment powers. Several executive branch department heads, board members, and commissioners must be confirmed by the Michigan Senate before assuming their duties, having been nominated by the governor (see chapter 6).[8] However, the Legislature, through statutory law, has limited the gubernatorial appointment power in a number of ways, including eligibility requirements for appointees, involving the Speaker of the House and the Senate majority leader in consultative roles, requiring selection from among a list of nominees, or mandating that appointments reflect certain territorial divisions of the state. Such oversight is an important check the Legislature uses to maintain the separation of powers among the three branches of state government. Finally, the Legislature holds sole power to declare and try impeachments of state officials. Under the Constitution, civil and political officers can be impeached for "corrupt conduct in office or for crimes or misdemeanors" committed while in office (Article XI, Section 7).

Legislative Elections, Redistricting, and Recalls

In Michigan, a total of 148 individuals are elected to the Legislature to represent the diverse (and oftentimes conflicting) interests and viewpoints of roughly 10 million people living in the state. Not surprisingly, legislative elections matter a great deal in policy making. Elections are partisan, meaning that candidates run as a member of a political party (although a person may run as an independent candidate). Assuming an individual meets the qualifications noted above—and is not subject to any of the stated proscriptions—interested persons run in their respective party primaries, held in August during even-numbered years, with winners advancing to the general election in November. In either case, a candidate needs only to achieve a plurality to secure election (also known as the "first-past-the-post" system). Successful candidates take their seats as members of the Legislature the following January.

Becoming a candidate is simply a matter of paying a fee of $100, forming a candidate committee, and notifying the Secretary of State.[9] Candidates who expect to raise less than $1,000 for their campaign can file a reporting waiver.[10] When filing the required paperwork to run for office (i.e., by May of election years), individuals identify whether they intend to run in the Democratic or the Republican primary. Candidates in contested primaries spend the spring and summer working to raise money among friends and relatives, and also among Lansing lobbyists who command well-funded political action committees (PACs). Lists of likely primary voters are used to do targeted mailings and prepare voter contact lists for door-to-door campaigning. Candidates seek to differentiate themselves by winning endorsements from key interest groups held in esteem by primary voters within the party. After the party primary in early August, winning candidates turn their attention to the November general election. With many districts gerrymandered to favor one party or the other, general election campaigns often produce little energy or excitement, especially in midterm elections (i.e., election years that fall in the middle of a president's term of office). On the other hand, in the few competitive districts that remain, vast outside resources can be poured into races to try and impact electoral outcomes.[11]

Every 10 years, after the census, the Legislature is tasked with redrawing district boundaries for the Michigan House, Michigan Senate, and U.S. House. This redistricting for U.S. House seats is made more complicated by the state's regular status as a net loser in reapportionment (see table 1.1), as congressional seats have shifted from states with little or no population growth to those growing at high rates. Michigan lost a congressional seat after the census in 1980, 2000, and 2010; after the 1990 census it lost two. Michigan's stagnant or declining population has important consequences for its political clout in Washington, and this is best seen in its shrinking congressional delegation. Consequentially, a declining federal stature means fewer federal dollars allocated to the state, limiting federal options that may assist the state in redressing its economic hardship.

The most recent redistricting following the 2010 census saw the Republican Party holding all the cards with majorities in the state House and Senate, the governorship, and the state Supreme Court (legal challenges often arise over redistricting; see chapter 8 for more on the "partisanship" of the state Supreme Court). The redistricting process begins when committees in the two chambers hold public hearings and hear testimony about the need for a transparent process that yields a fair and balanced map of legislative districts. Behind the scenes, though, skilled consultants hired by the two parties work quietly and out of sight to produce maps that maximize the number of safe seats for the party, with a "safe seat" defined as one that can be held even against a strong partisan tide for the other side. When the redistricting plan comes to the floor, the map proposed by the majority party always prevails, and may even garner a few votes from minority party members as a result of various side deals.

The impact of each decennial redistricting map will be felt for the following 10 years, most obviously as legislative majorities are cemented in place. Less obviously, the maps create so many safe districts that often the only election that matters is the party primary. This makes candidates, and incumbent office holders, exceptionally deferential to more ideologically extreme groups that swing primary contests and less attuned to more centrist voters who constitute most of the district but who may not participate in a primary election.[12] Given this highly partisan milieu, policy making often takes on an ideological slant, affecting the types of policies deemed acceptable for consideration while coloring the relationship between the Legislature and the other organs of government. State-local government relations, for example, can become localized partisan face-offs, while proposals that are designed to respond to challenges faced by the state are often screened for their partisan appeal rather than efficacy.

In the event that a legislator is unable to complete his or her term of office, a vacancy occurs. Normal procedures for filling vacancies include the governor calling a special election, although the governor has discretion to not call one if the vacancy occurs near a general election (and would be filled in a timely fashion anyway).[13] Michigan voters, however, also may recall, or prematurely remove, elected officials. The Constitution allows all elected officials, save judges, to be recalled upon a petition signed by 25 percent of the number of persons voting in the last election for governor within the respective electoral district. Specific mechanisms for recall, however, were left to the Legislature.

The use of recall against sitting state legislators has been limited since it was introduced. Between 2000 and 2011, for example, most recalls that made it to the ballot were directed against local, noncounty and school board officials, with less than 0.5 percent of all recall efforts targeting state legislators. Indeed, only two legislators faced recall elections during this period: Speaker of the House Andy Dillon, a Democrat, in 2008; and Representative Paul Scott, a Republican, in 2011. Speaker Dillon survived recall, but Representative Scott was successfully recalled from office. The rarity of sitting legislators being recalled in Michigan is reinforced in that Scott was only the third legislator to ever be recalled from office, as state Senators Phil Mastin and David Serotkin, both Democrats, were recalled in 1983.[14] While recall elections are possible, causal vacancies are considerably more common in the Michigan Legislature.

"Citizen Legislators": Michigan's Experiment with Term Limits

In Michigan, a particular electoral characteristic—term limits—has had a profound effect on the functioning of Michigan state government generally and on the Michigan Legislature in particular. Unlike the vast majority of American state legislators, Michigan legislators face mandatory retirement from office. Approved in 1992 via a citizen initiative (Proposal B in that year) and incorporated into the state Constitution (see Article IV, Section 54), legislative term limits restricted the lifetime tenure of legislators in both chambers, with state representatives able to serve up to three terms (six years) and state senators limited to two (eight years). The adoption of term limits occurred during a particular peak in the popularity of term limits across the country in the early 1990s, with a total of 21 states implementing some form of state-level legislative and executive term limits.[15] While the virtues of term limits were debatable, term limit movements tapped into public dissatisfaction with high reelection rates, unease with long-serving leaders in state legislatures, and a generic disenchantment with government at all levels.

Among the states with term limits, Michigan's ban is considered one of the most stringent due to its short terms and lifetime duration.[16] As a result, the post-1998 term limits environment has seen significant turnover in both chambers' memberships. Michigan's term limit policy affected legislators' terms beginning on January 1, 1993. Due to its four-year terms, the Michigan Senate did not feel the impact of term limits until 2002, when 27 senators (out of 38) were constitutionally barred from reelection. House members, due to their two-year terms, were subject to removal earlier, starting with the Legislature that began in January 1999. During the 1998 state House elections, as a result, 64 state representatives (out of 110) were barred from running for reelection, resulting in the largest turnover for the Michigan House since 1933 and the single largest among all states with term limits.[17] Not surprisingly, cycles of "legislative classes" have become routine, where large mandatory removals (or "graduations") occur every six years in the House and every eight years in the Senate.

The loss of veteran legislators has affected the functioning of the Michigan Legislature in several structural and institutional ways, hampering its ability to respond to the state's challenges. Beyond changes in membership—and the subsequent removal of long-serving legislators—term limits have affected the leadership characteristics in both chambers. Before the implementation of term limits in 1998, the average level of experience (or number of years served prior to becoming leader) for an incoming Speaker of the House was 11.4 years, while an incoming Senate majority leader was 7.7 years.[18] Since then, new speakers have assumed their role with well less than four years of legislative experience, while their Senate counterpart has also had less experience than his or her predecessors. For example, during the 98th Legislature (2015–16), Republican

Speaker of the House Kevin Cotter assumed the speakership after serving for four years (two terms), while Republican senator Arlan Meekhof became Senate majority leader after only one four-year term; during the 99th Legislature (2017–18), Representative Tom Leonard (R-DeWitt) became Speaker, again after only serving four years in the House, because Cotter had served his three two-year terms and therefore was term-limited out of office. Other leadership positions (including committee chairs and coveted positions on high-profile committees) have also seen an increase in the number of freshmen occupants, with new members having to be trained quickly given the time constraints and rapid turnover.[19]

Even more troubling, however, is the loss of "institutional memory," the collective knowledge shared by senior members imparted to junior members through the normal operating of the legislative process. Term limits have robbed the Michigan Legislature of the traditional "apprenticeship" period, where members would cultivate knowledge of not only the legislative process but also policy expertise, guided by experienced legislators. Term limits reduce the time to accumulate such reputations and knowledge, diminishing the significance of cooperation and policy expertise, while raising the incidence of short-term thinking and behavior. This has certainly influenced the Legislature's approach to the state's economic challenges, with emphasis on short-term "fixes" that ignore the long-term plights facing Michigan. "There seems to be no interest in long-range vision anymore," said Maxine Berman, who served in the state House for 14 years (1983–96).[20] Indeed, many other long-term legislators and political reporters have lamented the rise of new legislators who focus more on personal agenda items and securing future job prospects, including becoming lobbyists.[21]

As a result, the collegiality among members has undergone revision in the post-term-limits period. While friendships among legislators have continued, the frequency of such friendships across partisan lines has diminished, with most friendships and networks being based on shared partisan/ideological or regional ties.[22] The potential inability for legislators to bridge differences over policy alternatives through personal friendships, especially given the diverse economical and regional differences in Michigan, is troubling, as political conflict becomes more partisan and personalized rather than issue-based. Likewise, the number of colleagues who legislators find "influential," or sources of information for political and legislative activity, has declined, while increasingly the members who are deemed influential are party and chamber leaders. Scholars have suggested that influence in the post-term limits Michigan House, for example, has become centralized and colored in a partisan hue more than before.[23] Cooperation is often no longer guided through an issue-focused, nonpersonalized manner; rather, it has become couched in terms of partisanship.

Consequentially, the information sources (and, by extension, sources of control) have shifted from legislators themselves to other actors, both within and outside the Legislature proper. Once a bastion of information and leadership, committee chairs are now considered less informed, experienced, and capable by legislators, largely due to the centralization of power in the hands of chamber leadership.[24] Chairs have become extensions of the leadership, with instances of insubordination or inability to deliver on a bill resulting in leaders circumventing committees in the legislative process (e.g., removing a bill from a committee's purview). The inability of committee chairs to manage conflict (and now more likely to suppress it in favor of smooth operating) has caused legislators to often defer to other actors in acquiring information, including their fellow committee members, the governor, or outside groups, especially lobbyists and interest groups.

Term limits are thought to have increased the governor's power relative to the Legislature (see chapter 6), but a shift in influence has occurred elsewhere too. In particular, term limits appear to have benefited lobbyists and interest groups in Michigan in two ways. First, lobbyists and interest groups have become influential in terms of agenda control and in being top sources of political and policy information for legislators. They have actively filled the gap produced by the loss of long-serving members, providing their services in a mutual-fulfilling way. Second, lobbyists and interest groups seeking to change the status quo are emboldened by large and regular legislative turnover. As legislators opposed to a lobbyist's policy positions are replaced by new ones, lobbyists have an easier time in advocating and achieving their preferred policy changes, effectively meaning they can wait out the careers of unfriendly legislators.[25] This is not to say that lobbyists and interest groups have entirely benefited from term limits. The loss of institutional memory is detrimental not only to the Legislature itself but also to lobbyists who work hard to cultivate long-standing relationships with influential legislators. Having to reestablish such relationships (and many at that) every few years, while subsequently training political novices in basic legislating, requires a substantial investiture of time and resources by lobbying firms and interest groups.[26]

Term limits have had an additional, somewhat hidden, effect in terms of democratic accountability. Following a November general election, on average two-thirds of the chamber will be effective "lame ducks." That is, not only are members from the class of representatives departing that year lame ducks, but members of the class departing two years hence are effective lame ducks as well. This allows for the moving of highly controversial measures (like "right to work," which is discussed below) during the Legislature's lame duck session (i.e., the period between the election and when the new Legislature convenes in January), making it harder for citizens to hold their elected officials accountable for their legislative decisions. While evidence of this is only anecdotal, it appears that the volume of bills moving in lame duck sessions has increased in the era of term limits, thus harming a key attribute of representative democracy.

Relatedly, the governor (and by extension the bureaucracy) has seen an increase in relative power vis-à-vis the Legislature after term limits. Specifically, the ability of the governor to control the legislative agenda (i.e., which items the Legislature considers) has significantly increased after the imposition of term limits. Many Michigan legislators report that the governor's level of influence either increased or remained the same in terms of who made the important decisions concerning certain policy issues after term limits came into effect.[27] Additionally, legislative party leaders saw their influence increase as well, while committees and committee chairpersons saw their relative influence decline. Moreover, bureaucrats serve as information sources, albeit potentially biased ones, providing the Legislature with information aimed at achieving a particular policy objective of the gubernatorial administration. Finally, given any previous political or legislative experience (or both) he or she might have, the governor may have an experiential advantage compared to the less experienced legislature, especially in the Michigan House due to its shorter terms and overall six-year service limit.[28] The net effect of these changes is a governor with considerably more authority over the lawmaking process compared to before term limits were introduced, affording him or her an opportunity to exact a bill he or she deems acceptable, requiring less negotiation with legislators.

According to one comprehensive study, term limits in Michigan generally have not fulfilled the goals envisioned by its proponents in Michigan.[29] The Michigan Legislature, particularly the House of Representatives, has witnessed an erosion of its norms of cooperation, institutional memory, and institutional power versus the governor and bureaucracy. The rise of partisan acrimony is in line with the centralizing of influence in the hands of party and chamber leadership, while emphasis on fulfilling short-term, personal political goals has complicated the Legislature's efforts to adequately address Michigan's economic decline. Moreover, lobbyists and interest groups have seen their salience and influence rise considerably as nascent legislators turn to them for the policy expertise and institutional know-how today's "veteran" legislators are unable to provide. Collectively, these developments have caused a significant decline in the level of professionalism within the Michigan Legislature, which previously ranked among the most professionalized in the country.[30] While proponents have succeeded in limiting the tenure of long-serving legislators, the deleterious results mean that the cure may be worse than the disease.

Legislative Parties and Leaders

It is impossible to overstate the importance of political parties, and party leaders in particular, in the Michigan Legislature. Indeed it is the majority party leaders who control the office budgets for all members and both legislative party organizations, or caucuses. Names and jurisdictions of all committees are formally determined by the rules each chamber adopts at the beginning of a new legislature, but in practice the majority party's leadership determines these as well as the individual memberships of committees, including their minority party members. The majority leadership maintains an iron grip on bringing bills to the floor, bringing up favored bills and passing them quickly and preventing other bills from seeing the light of day. Motions and amendments from the minority are typically unceremoniously gaveled down. Even the ability to speak on the floor can fall victim to a loud gavel, which in turn signals a technician to turn off the microphone.

The Speaker of the House is both the presiding officer and leader of the majority party in the House of Representatives. Even though the lieutenant governor formally serves as presiding officer (but in practice is rarely in attendance), the majority leader exercises similar political clout in the Senate. Majority floor leaders serve as the second ranking officers in both chambers. Additional party leaders—speaker pro tempore, caucus chair, assistant floor leader, and so forth—are typically appointed by the party leader.

In the pre-term-limits era, party leaders were individuals who spent years mastering the legislative process and building relationships within their party caucus. They gained knowledge and expertise that won them the support of their colleagues as they proved themselves in their diligent committee work or as effective assistant leaders. Term limits short circuit this apprenticeship. It is rare for a freshman to be elected caucus leader, so as a practical matter House leaders serve either two or four years and Senate leaders typically serve one four-year term.[31] This means that maneuvering for leadership slots is almost continuous, especially in the House.

Becoming a caucus leader, and ideally a leader of the majority party caucus, involves careful planning and extensive effort. An early component involves outreach to major groups aligned with the party. On the Republican side, these would likely include the Michigan Chamber of Commerce, the Michigan Manufacturers Association, and Right to Life of Michigan. On the Democratic side, the United Auto Workers, the Michigan Education Association, and the AFL-CIO might be targeted. These outreach efforts seek the organization's aid and endorsement, as well as the organization's financial resources.

Today, all aspirants for caucus leadership form leadership PACs, which are fundraising devices distinct from their candidate campaign committees. Leadership PACs are legally permitted to raise and spend money in larger increments than candidate committees. Leadership aspirants seek financial support from the many groups that maintain active lobbying operations in Lansing. They then take this money and make contributions to candidates of their party who stand a good chance of winning election. While all incumbent candidates of the party are good bets to win reelection, the key to a successful leadership bid is often in identifying good prospects, or those candidates who stand a good shot of winning. This is the trickiest part of mounting a successful leadership bid, given the whopping turnover with each election cycle induced by term limits, but it is made easier if you have won the support of one or more of the major players mentioned above.

Thus, political parties dominate the modern Michigan Legislature, more than in the past and perhaps more than in most other states.[32] Legislative politics is a team sport, and the team with 56 or more seats in the House of Representatives and 20 or more seats in the Senate rules the day as the majority party. Minority party members are left to watch the action, draw their paychecks, and plot a strategy that will allow them to claim the majority at the next election. Love them or hate them, political parties are the engines that run the Michigan Legislature.

How a Bill Becomes a Law, Michigan Style

The legislative process in either chamber begins with a call from a legislator to the Legislative Service Bureau to request a bill draft. The Legal Division of the Legislative Service Bureau consists of a team of attorneys whose job it is to prepare drafts of bills, joint resolutions, and amendments to bills at the request of individual legislators. The first page of the draft bill provides spaces for signatures of the sponsor and any cosponsors he or she can find. Adding a large number of cosponsors shows broad support for the bill and enhances its prospects for moving through the legislative process.

After introduction, the leadership of each chamber then decides which committee should receive the bill. The bill's sponsor will likely informally approach the chairperson of the committee to secure a hearing for the bill. If a hearing is held on the bill (many bills receive no committee hearing, and thus die), the sponsor will usually be the first witness to testify. Other witnesses may or may not be called at the discretion of the committee chair. Once all witnesses are heard, amendments may be offered by any committee member, with the committee clerk calling the roll for a vote to decide whether to adopt each amendment. A similar process moves the bill out of committee and to the floor by a simple majority vote.

Bills are read three times in each chamber, typically by title only. First reading is done as bills are initially introduced, enrolled, and referred to committee. Second reading occurs when bills come out of committee and move to the floor. This is when amendments may be offered and possibly even voted on by all members of the chamber. However, the majority party leadership often uses the "power of the gavel" to reject, without votes, amendments from the minority and add, again without votes, amendments considered friendly.

Floor debate may take place after the third reading and before a recorded roll-call vote, but this, too, is at the discretion of the majority leadership. The presiding officer may decline to recognize members of the minority who wish to speak to the bill, and may stop their speech and have their microphone silenced at any point, again with a simple swing of the gavel. At this point the presiding officer in each chamber opens an electronic board for voting. In the Senate, votes are timed with members typically required to vote within 60 seconds. No time limits exist in the House and the vote will stay open as long as the presiding officer chooses to leave it open. If the majority leadership struggles to get to a majority of votes, the vote could stay open for hours.

Aside from constitutional amendments, votes to expel members, veto overrides, and several more specialized matters, a simple majority of 56 votes in the House or 20 votes in the Senate is sufficient for passage. However, because the Legislature and governor share the legislative power, bills must pass both chambers in exactly the same form before they are sent to the governor for signature. According to the Constitution (Article IV, Section 27), bills take effect 90 days after the end of the legislative session, or roughly April 1st of the following year. However, each chamber may grant "immediate effect" to a bill by a two-thirds vote. In the Senate, a roll call vote is held to seek two-thirds approval for immediate effect, but in the House, by tradition, immediate effect is granted by yet another swing of the gavel.

A Legislator's Work and Schedule

The daily and weekly lives of Michigan legislators follow a regular rhythm. The Legislature is normally in session Tuesdays through Thursdays, with the House holding committee meetings in the mornings and full session in the afternoons while the Senate reverses this pattern. Many (if not most) legislators commute to Lansing each day. Others make weekly trips arriving on Tuesdays and departing Thursday afternoons; those from the Upper Peninsula may go home only every two or three weeks. The "90-minute rule" is a rough guide to legislative behavior: if a legislator can travel one way in 90 minutes or less they do; otherwise they stay overnight.

If lobbyists and interest groups want to capture the attention of legislators, and they often do, food and drink are inevitably involved. Luncheons on the days when the Legislature is in session will produce a hungry and receptive crowd. Dinners are typically more intimate gatherings of lobbyists with a select group of legislators.

Likewise, legislators host fundraisers in Lansing, with a continental breakfast being the most affordable option. Fundraising luncheons and after-work receptions yield eager groups as well. Indeed, long-standing custom requires legislators to bring a special food from their districts to the chamber to commemorate the passage of their first bill. No alcohol is allowed, though, as a representative whose district included Detroit Metropolitan Airport learned once when he showed up with 110 minibottles courtesy of a major airline.

Mondays and Fridays are usually spent in the district attending public meetings and hosting "coffee hours." In contrast to members of the U.S. Congress, no monies are available for state legislators to rent office space in their districts, so most have no storefront where constituents can drop in. Meetings on Saturdays are not uncommon either, nor are visits to church on Sundays likely to go without one or two brief political conversations. The job of a legislator is not a nine-to-five, Monday-through-Friday occupation; rather, legislators are almost continuously "on call."

A Case Study in Response to Challenges: Right to Work

With the governor's signature affixed, Michigan became the nation's twenty-fourth "right to work" (RTW) state on December 11, 2012. The monthlong battle had concluded in victory for RTW advocates. "I think this is what's best for Michigan," remarked Republican governor Rick Snyder, arguing that the measure was about promoting job growth and making sure "workers have the right to choose who they associate with."[33] Opponents, meantime, posited that RTW represents a not-so-subtle attack on unions, while at its extreme is a harbinger of reduced wages and economic insecurity.[34] Indeed, Michigan's RTW controversy had as much to do about the state's economic decline as it did to do with partisan rancor: a fight between two diametrically opposed segments of the state's sociopolitical environment, while demonstrating one of the ways that the Legislature has addressed the state's economic hardship.

Right to work proponents believed that the law would free workers from financially supporting organizations (i.e., unions) which they do not support, while also benefiting Michigan's economy by making it more attractive to businesses. The Republican House Speaker at the time, Jase Bolger, described the measures as "pro-worker," not "anti-union"; he also commented that, "Today means new jobs and better careers for Michigan workers. Today means more freedom for those workers to determine which organizations they want to choose [to join]."[35] Critics, meantime, argued the converse: the law would not only hamper unions and their ability to negotiate but it would also mean a general wage reduction for all workers, hurting rather than helping the economy.[36] As Representative Jon Switalski, a Democrat, stated, "This is being forced down people's throats. We're left with a divided state. We're left with people angry."[37]

While perhaps a bit too forceful in its connotation, "angry" nonetheless was an apt description for the thousands of protesters who descended on Lansing in the weeks leading up to RTW's passage. Successive rallies were held throughout Lansing and in the State Capitol building itself, leading to sometimes-violent clashes with police. The protests hit their apogee on December 11, 2012, when upwards of 12,500 pro- and anti-RTW demonstrators descended upon the Michigan State Capitol.[38] Their goal was to send a clear message to the legislators besieged in the House and Senate chambers who were giving their final assents to the law. "As we can see from the spectacle outside, this is a very divisive issue for our state," said Representative Tim Greimel, the incoming House Democratic leader.[39] Speaker Bolger, however, described the day as "historic" and urged passage of the legislation.[40] While the protests were mostly peaceful, there were clashes between protesters and police involving pepper spray, although fighting also erupted between RTW supporters and opponents, including the tearing down of a tent set up by Americans for Prosperity, a group that backed the law.[41]

At the time the measure was being considered by the Legislature, Michiganders were divided over whether RTW would economically benefit or disadvantage the state, as 43 percent said the law would "help" the economy, while 41 percent believed it would "hurt."[42] Opponents of the law have been quick to seize on data that show a decline in union membership in Michigan—down from 16.3 percent of all employed workers to 14.4 percent in 2016—as proof that the law was meant to reduce union membership. The trend is also noteworthy given Michigan's drop from being the seventh most unionized state in 2013 to the eleventh in 2014.[43] In addition, union leaders have highlighted the economic effects nonunion workers face, including reduced salaries, benefits, and disposable income. However, proponents of the law counter with data that show an increase in union membership between 2014 and 2015—from 14.5 percent of all employed workers to 15.2 percent—as evidence that there is no link between RTW and union membership.[44] As of early 2017, experts cautioned that the full impact of RTW was yet to be fully understood. For instance, since contracts existing before RTW went into effect are immune to the law's provisions until the old contracts expire, there remains considerable potential that the rate of decline witnessed thus far will accelerate years to come. Whether or not this will be accompanied by a counterwave of job and wage growth, as proponents assert, remains an open question.

The Legislature's role in RTW, however, has demonstrated both its ability and inability to respond to Michigan's economic decline. While RTW was criticized by opponents for being a form of political revenge, observers can look toward the Legislature's role in crafting a law designed to bolster economic growth and development within the state. At the same time, however, critics have argued that RTW demonstrated that such lawmaking endeavors have been hyperpartisan in nature, ultimately dividing public and elite opinion at a time when broad cooperation is necessary for fundamental change. Indeed, following the passage of RTW, there was much distrust between important—and powerful—segments of the political establishment. Governor Snyder, for example, found his relationships with many labor officials and Democratic legislative leaders strained or nonexistent. The end result is that much political capital was spent on an issue that could have a fundamental effect on the Michigan economy. Similar challenges (e.g., the Flint water crisis) will require cooperation across and within the state's governing institutions, necessitating interparty and interbranch communication, which appears to have been damaged post-RTW. While partisan majorities can promulgate change, the challenges Michigan faces are better tackled with a broad, united sociopolitical front, rather than a hostile political environment that achieves not unity and success, but discord and potential failures.

Conclusion

The Michigan Legislature has both shaped and been shaped by the social and economic forces that have buffeted the state in the modern era. As Michigan has struggled to keep pace with the economic and population growth of states in the South and West, battle lines have sharpened within the state over stagnant and ever-declining resources. Pitched partisan and intraregional battles have become commonplace, despite the necessity of a united front to redress Michigan's decline. Ultimately, these are the battles fought out in the Legislature—and they affect all elements of state government, local government, and society more broadly.

Nonetheless, Michigan's socioeconomic environment requires increasingly greater cooperation and support between Lansing and the state's local authorities. While the state Legislature is concerned with the overall decline of the state, oftentimes how government responds to such challenges requires a coordinated local response. Thus, it is necessary that the state Legislature treats its preeminent role with great care, addressing and empowering the state's municipalities and agencies as the "vanguard" of Michigan's recovery, a task entrusted solely to the Legislature.

Yet plagued by term limits and districts gerrymandered to secure the safe election of candidates from one party or the other, our legislators today may be poorly prepared to meet these challenges. Political inexperience and an excessive deference to partisan extremists back home make for a debilitating blend in performing the tasks of lawmaking that are arguably tougher than in generations past. Michigan's recovery, nonetheless, requires an active legislature, one that can play its part effectively.

WEB RESOURCES

The *Michigan Secretary of State* provides current boundary maps for Michigan's legislative districts. From their home page (www.michigan.gov/sos) click on "Elections in Michigan," and then "Information for Voters." Under "Registering and Voting" you will see a link for "Legislative Districts."

The *Michigan Legislature* (www.legislature.mi.gov) offers one-stop shopping for almost everything you might want to know about the Legislature. The list of links on the left side of the page take you to current members of both the House and the Senate, committees, rules for each chamber, bills introduced and their current status, and much more.

The *Michigan Campaign Finance Searchable Database* contains all campaign statements filed with the Bureau of Elections. From the Secretary of State's website (www.michigan.gov/sos) click on "Elections in Michigan," then "Campaign Finance Disclosure," and finally "Searchable Database Downloads & Statistics." You can peruse the database based on numerous categories; simply click one to begin your search.

The *Michigan House of Representatives* (www.house.mi.gov) provides various information pertaining to the lower chamber, including representatives, House leadership, legislation, committees, and links to the Democratic and Republican caucuses.

The *Michigan Senate* (www.senate.mi.gov) provides information on senators, chamber leadership, legislation, and committees (click on the links running at the top of the page). Under "Related Sites," you can visit each party's respective caucus page for more specific news and legislative priorities for the Democrats and Republicans.

NOTES

1. The first Legislature was composed of 16 senators and 50 representatives.

2. Christopher J. Carl, "Michigan's Four Constitutions," Research Brief No. 13, Legislative Service Bureau, 1994, 1; Christopher J. Carl and Ted Rusesky, "The Michigan Legislature: A Look through History," Michigan Legislative Council, 2002, 5–7.

3. Carl, "Michigan's Four Constitutions," 2; see also Willis F. Dunbar and George S. May, *Michigan: A History of the Wolverine State*, 3rd rev. ed. (Grand Rapids, MI: William B. Eerdmans, 1995), 312–14.

4. Carl, "Michigan's Four Constitutions," 4; Carl and Rusesky, "Michigan Legislature," 23–24.

5. Only four individuals have ever been expelled from the Michigan Legislature: Representative Milo Dakin (1887), Representative Monte Geralds (1978), Senator David Jaye (2001), and Representative Cindy Gamrat (2015).

6. See Dunbar and May, *Michigan*, 445–54.

7. Joint Select Committee on the Flint Water Health Emergency, "Final Report of the Joint Select Committee," October 19, 2016, https://misenategopcdn.s3.amazonaws.com/99/publications/Final%20Report%20of%20the%20Joint%20Select%20Committee.pdf

8. See Michigan Constitution 1963, Article III, Sections 2–3 and 6–7. Note that the 1963 Constitution modified how the consent system proceeds compared to earlier renditions. Instead of formal assent being required per se, the Constitution requires that the Senate must *disavow* a nomination within 60 session days; otherwise, no action by the Senate constitutes a formal endorsement.

9. Candidates may also elect to secure ballot access through a petition drive.

State representative candidates must produce 200 valid signatures; state Senate candidates 500.

10. See Michigan Public Act 388 of 1976, Section 169.224.

11. See, for example, the Michigan Campaign Finance Network's reports on campaign fundraising and spending in Michigan. One report, "Michigan's 2014 Legislator Campaigns: $44.3M," details the spending in competitive and noncompetitive districts in 2014 (www.mcfn.org/press.php?prId=220). See also the State of Michigan's campaign finance disclosure database at the Secretary of State's website (www.mich.gov/sos).

12. For a discussion, see David W. Brady, Hahrie Han, and Jeremy C. Pope, "Primary Elections and Candidate Ideology: Out of Step with the Primary Electorate?," *Legislative Studies Quarterly* 32, no. 1 (2007): 79–105.

13. Michigan Constitution 1963, Article V, Section 13. The Legislature is empowered to prescribe the specific procedures for such special elections.

14. National Conference of State Legislatures, "Recall of State Officials," last modified September 11, 2013, http://www.ncsl.org/research/elections-and-campaigns/recall-of-state-officials.aspx

15. See Christopher Z. Mooney, "Term Limits as a Boon to Legislative Scholarship," *State Politics and Policy Quarterly* 9, no. 2 (2009): 205–6.

16. James M. Penning, "Michigan: The End Is Near," in *The Test of Time: Coping with Legislative Term Limits*, ed. Rick Farmer, John D. Rausch Jr., and John C. Green (Lanham, MD: Lexington Books, 2003), 33.

17. Carl and Rusesky, "Michigan Legislature," 39; Penning, "Michigan: The End Is Near," 34.

18. Penning, "Michigan: The End Is Near," 35.

19. Relatedly, the Michigan Legislature is the "youngest" in terms of members' average ages among the 50 states. The average age of a Michigan state representative is 48.5 years, while a Michigan state senator is 51.6 years old on average (for a legislature-wide average of 49.8 years). This parallels other term limit states, which have "younger" memberships. See National Conference of State Legislatures, "Who We Elect: The Demographics of State Legislatures," last modified December 1, 2015, http://www.ncsl.org/research/about-state-legislatures/who-we-elect.aspx

20. Quoted in Penning, "Michigan: The End Is Near," 37.

21. For discussion, see, generally, Penning, "Michigan: The End Is Near," and Marjorie Sarbaugh-Thompson, Lyke Thompson, Charles D. Elder, John Strate, and Richard C. Elling, *The Political and Institutional Effects of Term Limits* (New York: Palgrave Macmillan, 2004).

22. Sarbaugh-Thompson et al., *Political and Institutional Effects of Term Limits*, 122–26.

23. Ibid., 126–32.

24. Ibid., 138–41.

25. Ibid., 63–4.

26. Penning, "Michigan: The End Is Near," 39–40.

27. Sarbaugh-Thompson et al., *Political and Institutional Effects of Term Limits*, 180–83.

28. See ibid. for review.

29. For an elaboration, see the "scorecard" in Sarbaugh-Thompson et al., *Political and Institutional Effects of Term Limits*, 191.

30. See Peverill Squire, "Measuring State Legislative Professionalism: The Squire Index Revisited," *State Politics & Policy Quarterly* 7, no. 2 (2007): 211–27.

31. Penning, "Michigan: The End Is Near," 35–36.

32. See Boris Shor and Nolan McCarty, "The Ideological Mapping of American Legislatures," *American Political Science Review* 105, no. 3 (2011): 530–51.

33. Quoted in David Eggert, "Snyder, GOP Leaders Announce Plans to Pass Right-To-Work Law," *MLive.com*, December 6, 2012, http://www.mlive.com/politics/index.ssf/2012/12/snyder_gop_leaders_announce_pl.html

34. Richard Zullo, "What 'Right to Work' Would Mean for Michigan," Institute for Labor and Industrial Relations, University of Michigan, http://irlee.umich.edu/Publications/Docs/RightToWorkInMichigan.pdf#zoom=100

35. Quoted in Tim Martin, "Michigan Right-To-Work Foes Consider Legal Options, Gear Up for Elections after Bills Are Signed into Law," *MLive.com*, December 12, 2012, http://www.mlive.com/politics/index.ssf/2012/12/michigan_right_to_work_democra_2.html

36. Zullo, "What 'Right to Work' Would Mean for Michigan."

37. Quoted in Tim Martin, "Michigan on Verge of Becoming Right-to-Work State as Lawmakers Cast Historic Vote," *MLive.com*, December 11, 2012, http://www.mlive.com/politics/index.ssf/2012/12/michigan_right_to_work_approva.html

38. See British Broadcasting Company, "Michigan Passes 'Right-to-Work' Legislation," *BBC.com*, December 11, 2012, http://www.bbc.com/news/worl-us-canada-20682190

39. Quoted in Martin, "Michigan on Verge."

40. Quoted in Martin, "Michigan Right-to-Work Foes."

41. British Broadcasting Company, "Michigan Passes 'Right-to-Work' Legislation."

42. Associated Press, "Poll: Michigan Evenly Divided on Right-to-Work Law," *MLive.com*, March 31, 2013, http://www.mlive.com/politics/index.ssf/2013/03/poll_michigan_evenly_divided_o.html

43. Bureau of Labor Statistics, "Union Members: 2016," U.S. Department of Labor, February 9, 2017, http://www.bls.gov/news.release/pdf/union2.pdf; Bureau of Labor Statistics, "Union Members in Michigan—2015," U.S. Department of Labor, February 9, 2017, https://www.bls.gov/regions/midwest/news-release/UnionMembership_Michigan.htm

44. Bureau of Labor Statistics, "Union Members in Michigan—2015," U.S. Department of Labor, February 9, 2017, https://www.bls.gov/regions/midwest/news-release/UnionMembership_Michigan.htm

8 • Michigan's Court System

MARK R. BEOUGHER AND MARK S. HURWITZ

Michigan's court system comprises the third branch of the state's political institutions. To better understand this system, the structure of Michigan's courts, the methods used to select judges, the often-contradictory goals that the public sets for our judges, as well as the book's themes are considered. Each of these elements is critical to understanding Michigan's court system.

The structure, institutions, process, and people of the court environment make up the court system. Some of the institutions and processes can be thought of as "rules of the game," and refer to the set of formal and informal guidelines that attempt to control people and government actors within a particular area.[1] If we understand the rules of a particular institution or process, then we can hopefully better understand how and why particular decisions are made. Understanding institutions and processes, however, does not fully explain how and why the Michigan judicial system behaves the way it does. The people within those institutions—the judges—often claim that by putting on the black robe they put aside their personal preferences. Studies have repeatedly shown that they are just like the rest of us, however; they have perspectives that influence how they make decisions.[2] Judges may also be held to a difficult standard. On one hand we want judges to make decisions according to the law, rather than bow to the whim of the public or their own preferences. On the other hand, we sometimes want our judges to be aware of the concerns of society as a whole when making their decisions, the rationale being that since judges hand down decisions that affect our everyday lives, we should be able to hold them accountable when they make mistakes. It is difficult, if not impossible, to achieve both of these goals at the same time. Throughout its history Michigan has adopted rules that have shifted the balance between accountability and independence in its judicial system. Throughout this chapter the effects on how the judicial system has responded to problems facing the state are on full display.

General Structure of Michigan's Court System

The hierarchical court structure in Michigan is fairly typical across the United States. The Michigan Supreme Court—as the court of last resort—is at the top. Below it stands the Michigan Court of Appeals, which handles all appeals from lower courts. Those at the bottom, and from which the appeals come, are the circuit and district courts, which are primarily trial courts in the state (see fig. 8.1).[3] Another principle in the organization of courts is jurisdiction, which refers to the type of cases each has the legal authority to hear. Jurisdiction can apply to the specific geographic area that a court hears cases from, the subject matter of the cases that the court has the authority to rule on, or the stage of the judicial process of the cases presented in that court.[4] Courts with original jurisdiction—defined as the court that first conducts a trial—perform the function of determining guilt or innocence in criminal trials and liability in civil trials. Also at this level, the trial courts determine what evidence can be considered at trial, instruct juries as to their obligations, and hand out sentences. In contrast, courts can have appellate jurisdiction when tasked with determining whether prejudicial legal errors occurred during the original trial that could have influenced the outcome of the trial. When a court exercises appellate jurisdiction it does not consider new evidence or make determinations of fact. Although both district and circuit courts have appellate jurisdiction over certain types of cases, their primary role is as trial courts with original jurisdiction. Conversely, while the Michigan Supreme Court has original jurisdiction over a small number of types of cases, its primary function is to serve as an appellate court. The Michigan Court of Appeals acts only as an appellate court.[5]

Like other hierarchical court systems, Michigan's judges are required to follow the precedents created by higher courts.[6] This means district and circuit courts have less independence than the Michigan Court of Appeals, which in turn has less independence than the Michigan Supreme Court.[7] Precedents are legal decisions handed down by appellate courts that provide a basis for how a law or legal issue is to be followed. When appellate courts make a decision on a legal issue, that decision provides guidance to lower courts should that issue arise in a subsequent case. That is, decisions by the Michigan Supreme Court are supposed to control the actions of the

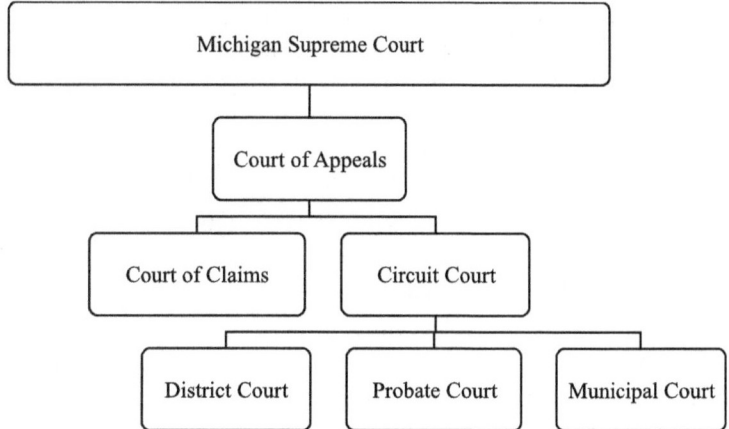

Fig. 8.1. Hierarchy of Michigan's Court System
Source: Adapted from the Court Statistics Project, http://www.courtstatistics.org/Other-Pages/State_Court_Structure_Charts/Michigan.aspx

Michigan Court of Appeals, which in turn should control the actions of trial courts. If a judge misapplies or ignores precedent from a higher court, his or her decisions can be overturned on appeal. Michigan's Supreme Court also has more independence than the Court of Appeals or any lower court because it can control which cases it hears. In Michigan, trial courts and the Court of Appeals have no control over which cases they must hear and, as such, are at the mercy of what comes before them. The Supreme Court, however, can pick and choose the cases it hears.

Trial Courts

Although district and circuit courts in Michigan do have appellate jurisdiction over some matters, the primary role of both is as trial courts. District courts occupy the lowest level of trial courts in the state of Michigan, and constitute a vast majority of Michigan citizens' interactions with the judicial system. Michigan has 105 district courts with 276 judges.[8] District courts have exclusive jurisdiction over all civil litigation up to $25,000, including landlord-tenant proceedings, land contract forfeitures, small claims, and summary matters that can be decided with minimum formality.[9] In the criminal field, district courts handle all misdemeanors where punishment does not exceed one year, including the arraignment, setting and acceptance of bail, trial, and sentencing. The district court also conducts preliminary examinations in felony cases. A small claims division for civil cases up to $3,000 is also provided in district court. In these cases, litigants agree to waive their right to a jury, rules of evidence, representation by a lawyer, and the right to appeal from the district judge's decision. If either party objects, the case is heard by the general civil division of the district court.

District judges may appoint magistrates, who are subordinate judges. Their job is essentially to reduce the burden placed upon district judges by handling lesser or preliminary issues in the court. Magistrates may set bail and accept bond in criminal matters; accept guilty pleas; and sentence for traffic, motor carrier, and snowmobile violations, as well as dog, game, and marine law violations. Magistrates may also issue search warrants and arrest warrants authorized by the prosecutor or municipal attorney.

The 57 circuit courts in the state of Michigan have supervisory control over the district courts. Decisions made at the district court level can be appealed to the circuit courts. Circuit courts also have appellate jurisdiction over appeals from probate court and state administrative agencies. In addition, circuit courts have original jurisdiction in all criminal cases where the offense involves a felony or certain serious misdemeanors; civil cases over $25,000; family division cases; and drain code condemnation cases (i.e., where eminent domain powers can be asserted if a property owner does not allow a right-of-way for a drain project).[10]

Michigan is divided into judicial circuits along county lines. Some circuit courts have jurisdiction over a single county, while others are composed of multiple counties. In multicounty circuits, judges travel from one county to another to hold court sessions.[11] The number of judges within a circuit is established by the state Legislature to accommodate required judicial activity.

The family division of the circuit court has exclusive jurisdiction over all family matters such as divorce, custody, parenting time, support, paternity, adoptions, name changes, juvenile delinquency and child protective proceedings, emancipation of minors, parental consent waivers, and personal protection proceedings. The family division also has ancillary jurisdiction over cases involving guardianships, conservatorships, and proceedings involving the mentally ill or developmentally disabled.[12]

Courts of Limited or Special Jurisdiction

Michigan has a number of trial courts with limited or specialized jurisdiction, which are courts with authority to hear only specific kinds of cases. For instance, the Court of Claims has jurisdiction limited to hearing claims against the State of Michigan. As a general rule, a state cannot be sued without its consent. Michigan granted that consent by establishing the Court of Claims, which has exclusive jurisdiction in all claims; however, the State Administrative Board is vested with discretionary authority in claims under $1,000. In a controversial move the Court of Claims was moved from the 30th Circuit Court, located in Ingham County, in 2013.[13] Now, Judges on the Court of Claims are nominated by the state Supreme Court from state Court of Appeals judges and sit in Lansing.

The probate court presides over cases pertaining to admission of wills, administration of estates and trusts, appoints guardians and conservators, and deals with the treatment of mentally ill and developmentally disabled persons. There is a probate court in each Michigan county, with the exception of 10 counties that have consolidated to form five probate court districts. Each district has one judge, and each of the remaining counties has one or more judges depending in large part on the population and caseload within the county.[14]

Appellate Courts

The Michigan Court of Appeals is an "intermediate" appellate court between the state Supreme Court and the district and circuit courts. The Court of Appeals must hear all appeals by right from lower courts. In certain circumstances, such as when a defendant in a criminal trial pleads guilty, parties do not have an absolute right to appeal. If such a defendant wishes to have his or her appeal heard, he or she must file for leave (i.e., permission) to appeal. Michigan Court of Appeals hearings are held before panels of three Appeals judges in Detroit, Grand Rapids, Lansing, or Marquette. The panels are frequently rotated so that the same three judges do not always make decisions together. The decision of the majority of the panel is final except for those cases reviewed by the Michigan Supreme Court.[15]

The Supreme Court is Michigan's court of last resort and is based in Lansing. Through the principle of "discretionary jurisdiction," the Court is not required to hear all of the appeals that are sent to it each year. Each year, the Supreme Court receives over 2,000 applications for leave to appeal from litigants primarily seeking review of decisions by the Michigan Court of Appeals. Every Supreme Court justice is responsible for reviewing each case to determine whether leave should be granted. The Court issues a decision in all cases filed with the Clerk's Office. Cases that are accepted for oral argument may be decided by an order, with or without an opinion. These orders may affirm or reverse the Michigan Court of Appeals, remand (i.e., send back) a case to the trial court, or accept as correct the Court of Appeals' opinion. The Supreme Court typically grants leave to those cases of greatest complexity and public import, where additional briefing and oral argument are essential to reaching a just outcome.[16] Cases come before the Court during a term that starts August 1 and runs through July 31 of the following year. The Court hears oral arguments beginning in October of each term, and decisions are released following the arguments throughout the term.

In addition to its judicial duties, the Michigan Supreme Court is responsible for the general administrative supervision of all courts in the state. This administration is accomplished through the State Court Administrative Office (SCAO), which is responsible for monitoring the performance of all lower courts. It is also tasked with implementing any changes to court structures or judicial positions. As part of efforts to reduce state expenditures under Governor Rick Snyder's administration, the SCAO has helped to orchestrate a "right-sizing" plan that has reduced the number of judges in Michigan by 40, saving an estimated $175 million since it was enacted in 2013.[17] The SCAO also establishes rules for practice and procedure in all courts in Michigan.

Overview of Judicial Selection and Retention Methods

As opposed to the federal judicial system in which nearly all judges are appointed by the president, states have adopted an array of judicial selection methods.[18] One can generally classify these methods into one of four general categories of selection: appointment, partisan election, nonpartisan election, and "merit systems."[19] In reality, however, judicial selection systems in many states, including Michigan, cannot be categorized as one particular type, as they often apply a hybrid of several selection methods.[20] In fact, few states use only one selection method for all levels of their court system.

Appointment

Some states follow the process of executive appointment and provide their governor with the ability to appoint judges to the bench, while a few states give the power of appointment to their legislatures.[21] Regardless of the judicial selection system in place within most states, a significant percentage of judges first come to the bench through appointment. This is due to the fact that in the majority of states governors are empowered to fill the seats of judges who leave the bench before their terms are completed. These are referred to as "interim appointments." Not surprisingly, those interim judges who are appointed to fill these terms are likely to win any subsequent election, since incumbents have many electoral advantages; however, studies show interim appointees are more vulnerable to lose their first election than other incumbent judges.[22]

Only six states continue to use appointment as the primary method of all judicial selection. Some argue that using appointment to select judges has an advantage because judges who are appointed do not have to fear reelection and thus arguably have greater independence. Critics point out that appointment systems generally have few mechanisms to remove "bad" judges or judges whose decisions deviate from those of the majority of the population.[23] But, since appointed judges in most states do not have lifetime tenure, as federal judges do, they are aware that their reappointment is not guaranteed, and thus there is more accountability for state-appointed judges than there would be for life-tenured federal judges.[24]

Partisan Elections

At one time, the majority of states used a form of partisan election in choosing their judiciary.[25] Partisan elections became in vogue during and after the populist era surrounding the presidency of Andrew Jackson.[26] Some scholars have argued that there are a number of benefits to partisan judicial elections.[27] First, judges should be more accountable to the citizens since they rely on their votes for reelection. Thus there should be fewer instances of "out of control" or "bad" judges in states with elections. Second, political parties are able to recruit and select candidates whose views are similar to theirs. Third, party identification allows voters to differentiate between candidates who they otherwise have very little information about.[28] Perhaps the greatest argument for partisan elections is that they appear to bring qualified judges to the bench. Recent studies have shown that appellate judges elected through partisan elections write longer and better opinions than judges selected through other methods.[29]

Despite these potential benefits, fewer states employ partisan elections today due to a number of deficiencies, both perceived and actual.[30] Electing judges through partisan elections makes it extremely difficult to maintain the image of judges as being neutral arbiters of the law. When a law passed by a Republican state legislature and signed into law by a Republican governor is overturned by a supreme court that has a majority of its members elected as Democrats, is the decision about the law or the politics? Would it be different if the legislature and governor were Democrats and the supreme court consisted of a majority of Republicans? Additionally, partisan judicial elections have become increasingly expensive over time.[31] Perhaps the most damning criticism involves the scant evidence showing that partisan elections make judges more accountable at the ballot box, as incumbent judges enjoy extremely high levels of re-election regardless of their judicial record.[32]

Nonpartisan Elections

The use of nonpartisan elections to choose and select judges came about in large part due to concerns over the influence of political party machines in the late 19th and early 20th centuries.[33] Nonpartisan elections were thought to be a solution to the negative aspects of merging political parties with judges while retaining the accountability benefits of direct elections. The belief was that by removing parties from judicial elections voters would make their decisions based more on the merits of the individual candidates rather than on party affiliation. It was also believed that nonpartisan elections would not be as costly as partisan elections have proven to be.[34] In reality, nonpartisan elections have proven to retain a number of the perceived problems of partisan elections while providing little to no additional benefits.[35] In fact, the cost of these elections is rising in proportion to the cost of partisan elections. Also, voter participation in nonpartisan elections is lower than in partisan elections. In addition, the removal of party identification has not resulted in voters making more informed decisions regarding candidates. Studies have shown that voters in states with nonpartisan elections are more likely to base their decisions on alternative factors such as name recognition or the position of the candidate on the ballot; or they figure out the partisanship of the candidate and then vote accordingly, if in fact they vote at all for a judicial candidate.[36]

Merit System or "Missouri Plan"

So-called merit systems, otherwise known as the Missouri Plan—as that was the first state to adopt this selection system—involve a combination of appointment and electoral systems.[37] Although there are several variations, the merit system generally involves a process whereby a commission of legal and lay experts nominates a small number of candidates for a judicial vacancy. The governor is then tasked with appointing one of these nominees to fill the position. Within a relatively short time period following the appointment, usually no more than 18 months, the judge is required to stand for a retention election in which voters decide whether she or he should remain on the bench. The essence of successful merit-based systems lies in the independence, impartiality, diversity, and expertise of the nominating commission.[38] Commissions also must have the resources and ability to vet the individual candidates.

To the extent that merit-based systems have failed to produce highly competent judges it has largely been the result of failures to achieve a combination of these aspects within the nomination commissions.[39] Also, the use of retention elections as a means of ensuring accountability retains many of the same problems associated with election systems. Like election selection systems, there is little real evidence that "merit" systems result in greater levels of accountability or diversity.[40] Additionally, since candidates stand in retention elections without opposition, many voters are confused as to what the purpose of the election is, which often results in low participation levels.[41] Yet another problem with the merit system is the increasing politicization of retention elections. Groups that are angered by decisions made by sitting judges have mounted aggressive campaigns against retention, often based upon single issues. The costs associated with defending against these campaigns have sometimes made retention elections as expensive as general elections.[42] In the end, merit-based judicial selection often does not live up to the benefits promised by its supporters.[43]

Michigan's Judicial Selection System

When Michigan became a state in 1837, its first Constitution placed the power to appoint Supreme Court justices in the hands of the governor. Lower court judges were selected by voters in direct elections. The process of gubernatorial appointment was ended with the adoption of the Michigan Constitution of 1850, which provided that all judicial officers would obtain their seats through partisan elections, with interim vacancies to be filled by the governor. The system of partisan election of all judicial officers in Michigan remained the norm for the next 89 years despite repeated and organized efforts at reform.

In the early part of the 20th century, spurred by the national movement away from partisan involvement in judicial selection, the American Bar Association and judicial reform groups supported a number of reforms that eventually became the merit system of judicial selection noted above. In Michigan, efforts to replace the partisan election of judicial officers with a commission-nominated appointment system reached its culmination in the 1930s. Several attempts to reform the Constitution to remove elections from the judicial selection process failed in the 1930s. Voters were not willing to support an amendment that removed their ability to directly elect judges. There was support, however, for the removal of political parties from judicial elections. The first step toward limiting the role of political parties in judicial elections was taken in 1938 when the Legislature passed a law removing party designations from judicial ballots. The following year, the citizens voted to approve a constitutional amendment that mandated the selection of all judges in the state be made through nonpartisan elections. The Michigan Supreme Court subsequently interpreted the language of the amendment to restrict partisan judicial elections for all judges but not the justices of the Supreme Court. The resulting hybrid arrangement is still present in Michigan today. All judicial officers in Michigan except Supreme Court judges obtain their positions in nonpartisan elections. Supreme Court justices are first nominated by party conventions but run on nonpartisan ballots in the general election.[44] As is the case in most states throughout the country, a large number of Michigan's judges first receive their positions through interim appointments.[45] This is due to the fact that Michigan governors have the power to fill any judicial seats that become vacant before the judge or justice's term is complete.[46] Judges who are interim appointees must stand for election during the next election cycle. Once a judge is appointed, he or she is allowed to be referred to as "Judge" or "Justice" on the ballot, thus acknowledging their status as an incumbent. Nationally, judicial incumbents are elected at a rate of over 90 percent.[47]

Controversies about Michigan's Judicial Selection System

A good example of the problems associated with how Michigan selects its Supreme Court justices can be seen in the end of the career of former chief justice of the Michigan Supreme Court Elizabeth Weaver. After twice being elected to the Michigan Supreme Court after being nominated by the Republican Party, Justice Weaver resigned amid growing anger with her Republican colleagues on the Court. In her resignation speech, Justice Weaver described what she saw as a broken system:

> The open discord on this court over the last 10 years is not really so much about clashes of strong personalities, but rather is the re-

sult of the formation of power blocks [sic] of justices usually joining together with a majority of four votes to promote agendas of political parties and special interests; personal interests, philosophies, and ideologies, and biases and prejudices.[48]

For a majority of her 10 years on the Michigan Supreme Court, Weaver predominately voted along with other Republican-nominated justices in favor of conservative causes. However, toward the end of her tenure, after she was removed from her position as chief justice, she began to have repeated conflicts with the other Republican nominees of the Supreme Court. On a Court with seven members in which a majority of four is needed, she often referred to the Republican majority as the "Gang of Four," bemoaning their lockstep allegiance to policies initiated by former Republican governor John Engler, who initially appointed most of them. During this time period she stopped voting along with the other justices who were nominated by the Republican Party on the Court and instead sided with the Democratic nominees. By choosing to resign while Democratic governor Jennifer Granholm was in office, Weaver ensured that a judge favorable to the Democratic Party would replace her, as Granholm would be responsible for appointing Weaver's interim replacement. In fact, in August 2010 Governor Granholm appointed Judge Alton Davis to serve out the remaining few months of Justice Weaver's term. This decision led to Democrats temporarily becoming the majority on the Michigan Supreme Court, and was met by shock and anger by Republican Party officials.[49] Saul Anuzis, a Michigan representative to the Republican National Committee at the time, described Weaver's resignation as "politics at its worst" and "borderline unethical."[50] In particular he believed that it was "a slap in the face" to all of the Republican supporters who had worked to get her elected to two terms. At the time, many Republicans believed that Justice Weaver's decision had more to do with her removal as chief justice than it had to do with any ideological concerns she might have had with the court.[51]

In his first election as the incumbent, Justice Davis was defeated at the polls by Republican nominee Judge Mary Beth Kelly in November 2010, an election in which Republicans across Michigan did quite well (including electing Rick Snyder as governor), and Democrats fared quite poorly. Thus, Justice Weaver's attempt to change the Supreme Court with her resignation was not successful. That said, whether Justice Weaver's decision to align with Democratic nominees on the Court was based upon genuine disagreements over the law or her anger at being driven out of her position as chief justice, the facts surrounding the situation do not paint Michigan's method of judicial selection in a good light. Although several studies have shown no difference in levels of judicial independence based on types of elections, and that the legitimacy of the judiciary is not affected by elections,[52] there is a potential of undermining the public's trust in the judiciary if judges are seen as making their decisions based upon political rather than legal grounds.

Money and Judicial Campaigns in Michigan

Former Supreme Court justice Marilyn Kelly noted in 2013, "The truth is that Michigan's nonpartisan Supreme Court elections have taken on a highly partisan cast and have become increasingly politicized over the past fifteen years. Moreover, money from undisclosed sources matters more and more."[53] The cost of judicial elections at all levels has been dramatically increasing in Michigan as well as the country as a whole. While this has been true for the nonpartisan election of lower level judicial officers, it is most striking in the case of the election of Supreme Court justices.[54] Overall campaign spending on Supreme Court elections in Michigan has been increasing since 2000, but saw a dramatic increase between 2008 and 2014. In particular, the amount spent by outside groups has skyrocketed.[55]

The amount spent on Michigan Supreme Court campaigns has steadily risen since 2000, but has been supercharged since the U.S. Supreme Court handed down its decision in *Citizens United v. Federal Election Commission* in 2010.[56] In *Citizens United*, the U.S. Supreme Court struck down the longstanding federal ban on corporate and union independent expenditures in elections. The two Michigan Supreme Court election cycles that followed *Citizens United* saw record spending from business and corporate sources. A great deal of this money comes from a new type of political action committee, which have come to be referred to as "Super PACs." Super PACs, born out of the U.S. Supreme Court case *SpeechNOW.org v. FEC*, are able to raise and spend unlimited amounts of money from any source during a campaign so long as they do not coordinate with an individual campaign. Even though Super PACs must disclose and report their donors, the contributors themselves may be organizations that are not required to disclose how they raised the funds they donated to the Super PAC. In recent years many who have given to Super PACs that spend funds trying to impact the outcome of an election in Michigan were not from the state of Michigan.[57] Thus, Michigan is facing a situation in which more money is being pumped into the election process while at the same time the people have less knowledge of who is giving it. Although it is legal for both corporate and nonprofit entities to spend unlimited amounts in campaigns, studies have shown that in large part it has been probusiness groups that have spent the most and gained the most influence.[58] This has been true for judicial candidates of both of the major parties.

Studies have also shown that how a state selects its judges plays an important role in how much influence corporate donations have over judicial behavior. In those states with partisan elections for the state supreme court, justices are significantly more likely to receive more campaign donations from business groups as well as being more likely to vote in favor of business litigants when their cases are in front of them.[59]

One of the biggest changes that has occurred in Michigan has been the prevalence of "dark money" in Supreme Court elections. So-called dark money refers to campaign spending that does not have to be reported to state election officials. In order to avoid having to report these expenditures the money must be spent on "issue" advertisements that do not support or attack a particular candidate. In Michigan during 2012, $13.8 million of the $18.9 million spent on television advertisements came from dark money. In 2014, nearly $4.7 million of the $7.2 million spent on television advertising was spent on issue advertisements.[60] The 2016 election cycle saw a dramatic reduction in the money spent on Supreme Court campaigns, but dark money still accounted for the vast majority of advertising.[61] Combined, the Michigan Chamber of Commerce and a Super PAC that represented Michigan realtors spent $1.4 million on issue ads in support of incumbent justices.[62] The total raised by all of the candidates in reported donations was just $1.5 million, with the challengers raising a total of less than $86,000.[63] One fact shows the true one-sided nature of the campaign and the spending advantage that side had: none of the challengers or their supporters aired a single television advertisement.[64] In each of these elections, the dark money that pays for issue ads was not reported to Michigan election officials, thus making it impossible to determine who the donors were.[65]

Michigan Courts in an Era of Economic Downturn

Michigan's judicial system has been center stage in the efforts to respond to the financial problems that have plagued the state in recent decades. As various legislatures and governors have proposed laws and initiatives designed to address the overall economic decline in the state, justices of the Michigan Court of Appeals and Supreme Court have been placed in the position of determining which actions are permissible under the Michigan Constitution. Time and again it has been Michigan appellate courts that have had the last say in whether these proposals are allowed to take effect. For example, beginning in 2011, efforts by Governor Snyder's administration to help alleviate shortfalls in pension obligations by forcing current teachers to pay more into retirement plans came to fruition only after the state Supreme Court found those actions to be constitutional.[66] In addition, when the Legislature passed and Governor Snyder signed into law "right to work" legislation that was designed to make Michigan a more attractive business environment, it was ultimately the decision of the Michigan Supreme Court that allowed it to remain the law of the state.[67]

State responses to the economic downturn have also placed Michigan courts in the role of adjudicating disputes between state and local governments. The Snyder administration's efforts to deal with economic problems in cities and school districts through the use of emergency managers and special school districts has been repeatedly challenged by local authorities as unconstitutional invasions upon their sovereignty (see chapters 3, 4, and 15).[68] Statewide ballot initiatives, such as one that legalized the use of medical marijuana, have been challenged in courts by local governments who want to limit their effects. Perhaps most damaging to local governments have been court decisions that limit the ability of local governments to raise revenue through taxes and fees.[69]

At the same time that Michigan courts have been enmeshed in efforts to solve some of the state's economic woes and resolve conflicts between the state and local governments, they have also been directly affected by the economic downturn in the state between 2000 and 2010. The judicial system has been forced to deal with smaller budgets, fewer judges, and the negative societal effects brought about by the economic downturn.[70] Day-to-day trials and assorted legal matters are handled by hundreds of district and circuit judges who are asked to do the same job with fewer resources. At a time when the state's tax revenue has faced serious challenges, the judicial system has been forced to deal with the costs of adjudicating the huge numbers of civil and criminal cases that flood the docket. And this took place during an era in which Michigan judges had not seen a pay increase between 2003 and 2016, the longest such period of salary stagnation in the country.[71] Reductions in state budgets affect such things as the indigent defense system where those accused of crimes but who cannot afford to pay an attorney receive legal representation. In fact, the state ranks 44th in the country in the amount of money spent on indigent defense.[72]

The Role of Courts in State-Local Government Relations

Michigan courts are routinely asked to resolve disputes between the state and local governments. As the Legislature and governor have sought solutions to Michigan's economic downturn, it has often come into conflict with local governments. Nowhere has this been more contentious and problematic than in Governor Snyder's use of emergency managers to take over the management of troubled cities and school districts. Michigan governors have had the power to appoint emergency managers to take over the management of financially troubled local governments since 1988 and school districts since 1990. Before 2011, emergency managers were given broad powers including the ability to sell off city assets, eliminate departments, and reduce or eliminate pay to the local mayor or city council. In 2011, the Legislature passed and Governor Snyder signed into law Public Act 4, which expanded the powers of the emergency manager to include the ability to cancel contracts as well as to make any nonfinancial moves he or she felt were necessary. Governor Snyder placed emergency managers in charge of several majority-minority cities including Benton Harbor, Pontiac, Flint, and Detroit.[73] Public anger over the use of emergency managers lead to a state referendum in which citizens voted to strike down Public Act 4 (see chapter 11). In response, the Michigan Legislature passed a revised version of the law, which removed some of the expanded powers given to emergency managers under Public Act 4.[74] Any further citizen challenge to the law was foreclosed by the Legislature's inclusion of an appropriation request in the legislation, which by Michigan state law precludes challenge by referendum. Michigan courts played a role throughout this process. It was the Court of Appeals that found that the new law was constitutional. It was also the Court of Appeals that determined the limits to the powers of an emergency manager.

In *Kincaid v. City of Flint*,[75] the Court of Appeals was asked to determine the extent of emergency manager powers. The Michigan Supreme Court determined that Flint's emergency manager could not approve unauthorized water and sewer rate increases that did not conform with existing city ordinances. By establishing limits to the power of emergency managers the Court of Appeals took a substantial step toward shifting power back to local governments.[76] Subsequent to this decision, Flint experienced a massive water contamination crisis that was in large part due to its emergency manager's decision to use the Flint River as a temporary water source (see chapter 15). By the end of 2016, a number of state and local government employees, including two former emergency managers, had been indicted for their alleged role in the contamination of Flint's water.[77] These proceedings again put the courts at the center of an important state issue, and it will be the courts that determine which level of government is ultimately responsible to pay for what could be formidable damages, as well as possible criminal violations.[78]

Michigan courts have also been forced to intervene when the provisions of state ballot proposals conflict with local ordinances. The passage of the Michigan Medical Marijuana Act created a number of problems for both state and local governments. In *Ter Beek v. City of Wyoming*, the Michigan Supreme Court was faced with determining whether a local zoning ordinance that prohibited uses of property contrary to federal law, state law, or local ordinance preempted the Michigan Medical Marijuana Act. Ter Beek wanted to set up a medical marijuana growing facility in compliance with the Act, but faced prosecution from the City of Wyoming for engaging in behavior that violated local zoning laws. The Supreme Court found that the Act preempted local zoning ordinances and that Wyoming could not ban the growing of medical marijuana through reliance on federal law.[79]

What Do We Want Out of Our Courts? Balancing Independence and Accountability

The often-conflicting goals of judicial independence and accountability underlie many of our nation's arguments about the proper role of judges in our political system. Hardly a controversial U.S. Supreme Court decision is announced without members of an aggrieved group claiming that it is illegitimate because it was made by unelected, out of touch elitists. At the same time, many people look at the millions of dollars being donated to the campaigns of candidates who are running for a judicial office at the state level and wonder how that money could not influence how judges make decisions.[80] Thus, on one hand the ideal judge is one who has the expertise and integrity to make tough legal decisions that are based upon the law rather than their own political or personal preferences. On the other hand, the public expects judges to make decisions that are consistent with the overall morals and concerns of society as a whole. Whether one thinks a judge is acting appropriately largely is determined by one's opinion of the result.

Judicial independence is often measured by the amount of discretion that a judge has over the kinds of cases he or she hears, as well as the ability to use his or her personal judgment in making decisions without the risk of consequences.[81] Allowing judges discretion is a double-edged sword. By giving judges discretion we allow them to apply their legal expertise and life experiences to their legal decisions.[82] This is often a good thing. One can imagine a judge who is tasked with sentencing two criminal defendants. One defendant shows genuine remorse and has owned up to his actions and seeks to remedy them. The other is unrepentant and seeks to shift the blame for his actions onto someone else. In such a case it arguably makes sense for a judge to have the discretion to sentence the second defendant more harshly than the first.

However, the danger in giving judges such discretion is that it might be misused. Judges might utilize their discretion to further their own agendas or express their own biases. In the above example, allowing judicial discretion in sentencing has led to situations where judges hand down tougher sentences to members of minority groups.[83] It is for this very reason that legislatures have attempted to limit judicial discretion in many states, including Michigan. The fear of the abuse of discretion is one of the primary reasons that states such as Michigan have established hierarchical court systems with rules and norms designed to constrain judicial behavior and thereby limit judicial independence.

Several methods to limit the abuse of discretion and bring about more accountability (and thus less independence) apply to all levels of courts in Michigan. One simple way to do this is through popular elections. All judges in Michigan eventually face election, and the hope is that regular and competitive elections will increase judicial accountability.[84]

The method of judicial selection adopted by a state has the potential to drastically influence judicial behavior. For example, studies have shown that in states where judges are elected they are more likely to hand down the death penalty in years when they are up for election than in nonelection years.[85] Methods of judicial selection mirror the themes of accountability and independence that underlie our discussion of institutional constraints upon judicial behavior. To the extent a state attempts to insulate judges from accountability from the populace or elected officials it has the potential to increase the ability of judges to act independently. Conversely, when states select judges through elections there is at least the potential for greater accountability.[86]

Beyond elections, when a Michigan judge's abuse of discretion rises to the level of misconduct he or she may be removed from the bench in one of three ways: judges may be impeached by a majority vote of the state House of Representatives and convicted by a two-thirds vote of the state Senate; the governor may remove a judge upon the concurrent resolution of two-thirds of the members of both houses of the Legislature; or on the recommendation of the Michigan Judicial Tenure Commission (MJTC), the Supreme Court may censure, suspend, retire, or remove a judge. The most common method of judicial removal or censure involves the MJTC.[87]

The MJTC was created after Michigan voters passed an amendment to Article 6, Section 30 of the Michigan Constitution in August 1968. The commission "strives to hold state judges, magistrates, and referees accountable without compromising the essential independence of the judiciary." The commission has nine members who each serve three-year terms. Judges from the Court of Appeals, circuit courts, probate courts, and courts of limited jurisdiction each elect a judge from their respective court. Three members are chosen by the Michigan Bar Association from its membership. The final two members of the MJTC are nonjudges who are appointed by the governor. Proceedings of the commission are not open to the public. The MJTC can recommend that the Supreme Court censure, suspend, retire, or remove a judge or justice. Grounds for such a recommendation include conviction of a felony, physical or mental disability, misconduct in office, persistent failure to perform his/her duties, or habitual intemperance or conduct that is clearly prejudicial to the administration of justice.[88]

The MJTC has power over the highest justices in Michigan's court system. On January 21, 2013, Supreme Court justice Diane Hathaway resigned after the MJTC filed a formal complaint alleging "blatant and brazen violations" of judicial conduct rules. Justice Hathaway was one of a record five Michigan judges who were removed from the bench or forced to retire in a four-year period in the early 21st century.[89]

Independence vs. Accountability: Guns in Michigan Schools

On March 4, 2015, Joshua Wade decided to attend his little sister's choir performance at Pioneer High School in Ann Arbor, Michigan.[90] While he claims that he did not intend to cause a stir, the fact that he was openly carrying a pistol on his belt created quite a commotion.[91] School officials quickly notified the police who, upon arrival, escorted Wade to the lobby of the auditorium. After a brief detention they allowed Wade to return to his seat with his firearm still openly presented on his belt. According to Michigan state law, since Wade had a permit to carry a concealed weapon, he was permitted to carry the weapon on school grounds so long as it was not concealed. Following the performance, an Ann Arbor Pioneer school official identified Wade to the audience and announced that he had been carrying a gun.

The events of that night quickly escalated into a series of policy changes and lawsuits. Ann Arbor's school board voted to ban the open carry of firearms on school property. In response to this ban, Ulysses Wong and the Michigan Gun Owners association filed suit to challenge Ann Arbor's policy. On September 22, 2015, Circuit Court judge Carol Kuhnke upheld Ann Arbor's ban on open carry on school grounds. Judge Kuhnke's decision was in apparent contradiction to a 2012 Michigan Court of Appeals decision that prevented a library from banning guns on its property.[92] Not surprisingly, the decision was met in some circles with joy, while in others it was met with outrage. In December 2016, the Michigan Court of Appeals upheld Ann Arbor Public Schools' ban on guns on campus.

This case presents an example of the often-contradictory demands placed upon our judicial system. On one hand, we look to our judges and justices to serve as protectors of the individual liberties of our citizens. According to this line of thought, judges should be able to act independently from public pressure in order to preserve the rights guaranteed by the Constitution. Wade and other open carry advocates argue that since both the Second Amendment to the U.S. Constitution and Michigan law allow the open carry of firearms in public schools, Judge Kuhnke may not have followed precedent when she upheld Ann Arbor's ban. As Wong's attorney summed up the opinion of the open carry advocates, "I think that the judge decided to ignore state law."[93]

To supporters of Ann Arbor Public Schools' decision to ban guns, Judge Kuhnke's decision was sound as it reflected the desires of the community she represents and what they would consider common sense. A vast majority of Washtenaw County residents were against allowing the open carry of guns on school property. As a judge who is elected by the citizens of Washtenaw County, Judge Kuhnke could not help but to have noticed that a majority of the people who put her in office were in favor of keeping the ban. To supporters, her actions represent how important it is to have a judicial system that is accountable to the citizens.

Ultimately, Wong's case against Ann Arbor Public Schools will continue to make its way through the judicial process and be appealed to a higher court. It will be the job of the Michigan Supreme Court to decide if Judge Kuhnke's and the Michigan Court of Appeals' decisions were in error. It is important to note, however, that the appellate judges who will likely review this case will face the same conflicting pressures that Judge Kuhnke faced. Like Judge Kuhnke they will be asked to independently review the issues and make a decision based upon the law, while at the same time being accountable to the people who elected them. What will be different is that the rules that govern behavior on the Michigan Supreme Court are different from those that governed Judge Kuhnke in the Circuit Court. By examining how these different rules influence the balance between independence and accountability we will be able to understand why Michigan's judicial system works the way that it does.

Conclusion

A 2008 study by the University of Chicago ranked Michigan last of all the states in the union in regards to judicial independence.[94] That study defined judicial independence as the likelihood that a judge would side with a judge from an opposing party on a particular issue.[95] If the current rules regarding how judges are elected in Michigan create a situation where business interests have more influence, is it surprising that the probusiness solutions of the Snyder administration have largely been supported by the courts? This is not intended to be a critique of Governor Snyder's policies or the specific policies adopted by the Legislature, but rather an explanation for the behavior of Michigan courts during this period of crisis. What is important to note is that the rules that govern the structure of Michigan's court system, as well as the selection of its judges, limit the ability of the judiciary to act as an independent force. The selection and retention rules as they exist in Michigan have dramatically tipped the scales toward accountability and away from independence. For the citizens of Michigan, judges appear to be more accountable to the political parties and special interests that fund their increasingly expensive campaigns than they are to the average voter. Is this a problem that needs to be solved?

What is clear is that the way judges and justices behave has more to do with the institutions in which they work. All judges work within the confines of the existing rules and will thus be incentivized and constrained in similar ways. If we want to change how the judicial system works we need to change the rules by which it is governed.

WEB RESOURCES

The *Michigan Courts* website (www.courts.mi.gov) offers a wealth of information on different aspects of the Michigan court system including links to cases decided by the courts (including briefs and opinions), details on the administration of the court system, as well as news, reference, and educational materials.

The *Michigan Supreme Court Historical Society* (www.micourthistory.org) is a nonprofit organization that serves the public by collecting, preserving, and displaying historical information related to the court system in Michigan. The website also includes a great deal of historical information on courts in Michigan.

The *Michigan Campaign Finance Network* (www.mcfn.org/) is a nonprofit organization that tracks money in Michigan politics. It includes over 25 years of information and data on Michigan Supreme Court elections.

The *National Center for State Courts* (www.ncsc.org/) focuses on judicial reforms. The organization's website includes information on state courts across the country in myriad areas including different types of courts, budget and finance information, sentencing, court-media relations, and many others.

The *Brennan Center for Justice* (www.brennancenter.org) is housed at the New York University School of Law and is a nonpartisan institute that focuses on improving democracy and justice. The Brennan Center's website contains information on different areas of possible reforms, proposals for reforms, and research conducted on topics such as judicial elections and court reforms.

NOTES

1. Douglas C. North, "Institutions," *Journal of Economic Perspectives* 5, no. 1 (1991): 97–112.
2. Laura Langer, *Judicial Review in State Supreme Courts: A Comparative Study* (New York: State University of New York Press, 2002).
3. Michigan Courts: One Court of Justice, "Courts," 2015, accessed November 1, 2015, http://courts.mi.gov/education/learning-center/curriculum-resources/pages/michigan-court-system.aspx
4. Ibid.
5. Ibid.
6. Ibid.
7. Jeffrey Allan Segal and Harold J. Spaeth, *The Supreme Court and the Attitudinal Model* (New York: Cambridge University Press, 1993).
8. State of Michigan, Michigan Courts, "Types of Courts," http://courts.mi.gov/self-help/center/general-information/pages/types-of-courts.aspx; accessed February 14, 2017.
9. Ibid.
10. Ibid.
11. Ibid.
12. Ibid.
13. Ibid.
14. Ibid.
15. Ibid.
16. Ibid.
17. State Court Administrative Office, "Home," accessed November 1, 2015, http://courts.mi.gov/administration/scao/Pages/default.aspx

18. Federal bankruptcy and magistrate judges are not Article III judges and are thus not appointed by the president.
19. Chris W. Bonneau and Melinda Gann Hall, *In Defense of Judicial Elections* (New York: Routledge, 2009).
20. Elizabeth Wheat and Mark S. Hurwitz, "The Politics of Judicial Selection: The Case of the Michigan Supreme Court," *Judicature* 96 (2013): 178–88.
21. Bonneau and Hall, *In Defense of Judicial Elections*.
22. Melinda Gann Hall and Chris W. Bonneau, "Does Quality Matter? Challengers in State Supreme Court Elections," *American Journal of Political Science* 50 (January 2006): 20–33.
23. Peter D. Webster, "Selection and Retention of Judges: Is There "One" Best Method?," *Florida St. University Law Review* 23 (1995): 1.
24. Langer, *Judicial Review in State Supreme Courts*.
25. Herbert M Kritzer, *Justices on the Ballot: Continuity and Change in State Supreme Court Elections* (New York: Cambridge University Press, 2015).
26. Jed Handelsman Shugerman, *The People's Courts: Pursuing Judicial Independence in America* (Cambridge: Harvard University Press, 2012).
27. James L. Gibson, *Electing Judges: The Surprising Effects of Campaigning on Judicial Legitimacy* (Chicago: University of Chicago Press, 2012).
28. Ibid.
29. Chris W. Bonneau and Damon M. Cann, *Voters' Verdicts* (Charlottesville: University of Virginia Press, 2015).
30. Mark S. Hurwitz and Drew Noble Lanier, "Diversity in the State and Federal Courts: Change and Continuity," *Justice System Journal* 29 (2008): 47–70.
31. Brennan Center for Justice, "Research," accessed December 14, 2015, https://www.brennancenter.org/research
32. Ibid.
33. Mark S. Hurwitz, "Judge Lopez Torrez and New York's Trial Judge Nominating Process," *Justice System Journal* 28 (2007): 243–46.
34. Shugerman, *People's Courts*.
35. Bonneau and Cann, *Voters' Verdicts*.
36. Melinda Gann Hall, *Attacking Judges: How Campaign Advertising Influences State Supreme Court Elections* (Stanford: Stanford University Press, 2015).
37. Wheat and Hurwitz, "Politics of Judicial Selection."
38. Webster, "Selection and Retention of Judges?"
39. Bonneau and Cann, *Voters' Verdicts*.
40. Hurwitz and Lanier, "Diversity in the State and Federal Courts."
41. Bonneau and Cann, *Voters' Verdicts*.
42. Ibid.
43. Todd A. Curry and Mark S. Hurwitz, "Strategic Retirements of Elected and Appointed Justices: A Hazard Model Approach," *Journal of Politics* 78, no. 4 (2016): 1061–75.
44. Wheat and Hurwitz, "Politics of Judicial Selection."
45. Charles R. Toy, "How Should We Select Our Judges?," *Michigan Bar Journal* (August 2010).
46. Michigan Constitution, Article VI, Section 1.

47. Brennan Center for Justice, "Research," accessed December 14, 2015, https://www.brennancenter.org/research
48. Electablog, "News and Commentary," accessed December 5, 2015, http://www.eclectablog.com/2010/08/mich-dems-get-gift-from-state-supreme.html
49. Ibid.
50. Ibid.
51. Ibid.
52. Gibson, *Electing Judges*.
53. Joanna Shephard, "Justice at Risk: An Empirical Analysis of Campaign Contributions and Judicial Decisions," American Constitution Society for Law and Politics, 2013; accessed November 18, 2016, http://www.acslaw.org/ACS%20Justice%20at%20Risk%20(FINAL)%206_10_13.pdf
54. Ibid.
55. John S. Klemanski, "Trends in Michigan Supreme Court Elections 2000–2012," *Michigan Academician* (2013): 289–309.
56. Michigan Campaign Finance Network, "MI Sup. Ct. 1984–2014," http://mcfn.org/uploads/documents/MISupCt84_14table.pdf, accessed December 12, 2015.
57. Ibid.
58. Ibid.
59. Ibid.
60. Ibid.
61. Michigan Campaign Finance Network, "Republican Michigan Supreme Court Nominees Have a $2.8-Million Money Advantage," http://www.mcfn.org/node/5964/republican-michigan-supreme-court-nominees-have-a-28-million-money-advantage, accessed November 15, 2016.
62. Ibid.
63. Ibid.
64. Ibid.
65. Michigan Campaign Finance Network, "MI Sup. Ct. 1984–2014."
66. Bonneau and Hall, *In Defense of Judicial Elections*.
67. Paul Egan, "Supreme Court Upholds Right-to-Work for State Workers," *Detroit Free Press*, July 29, 2015.
68. Chastiny P. Dawsey, "Emergency Manager Lawsuit Going to Michigan Supreme Court," *Detroit Free Press*, November 17, 2012.
69. *Bolt v. City of Lansing*, 587 N.W.2d 264 (Mich. 1998)
70. State Court Administrative Office, "Home," accessed November 1, 2015, http://courts.mi.gov/administration/scao/Pages/default.aspx
71. National Center for State Courts, "Survey of Judicial Salaries," 40, no. 2 (January 2016), https://www.ncsc.org/FlashMicrosites/JudicialSalaryReview/2015/resources/CurrentJudicialSalaries.pdf, accessed February 14, 2017.
72. National Legal Aid & Defender Association, "Defender Resources," accessed November 25, 2015, http://www.nlada.org/Defender/Defender_Evaluation/Michigan_Evaluation/
73. Minority-majority cities are those where minority ethnicities represent the majority of the population.

74. Jonathan Oosting, "Critics Expected to Test Michigan's New Emergency Manager Law at Ballot Box, in Court," *MLive.com*, January 2, 2013.
75. 821 N.W.2d 555 (Mich. 2012).
76. Ryan Felton, "Michigan Appeals Court Limits Authority of State-Appointed Emergency Managers," *Detroit Metro Times*, June 16, 2015.
77. Dominic Adams, "New Charges Announced in Flint Water Crisis," *MLive.com*, July 29, 2016.
78. Emily Lawler, "Involuntary Manslaughter among Crimes Considered in AG's Flint Water Crisis Probe," *MLive.com*, February 9, 2016.
79. *Ter Beek v. City of Wyoming*, 297 Mich App 446 (2015).
80. Michigan Campaign Finance Network, "MI Sup. Ct. 1984–2014," accessed December 12, 2015, http://www.mcfn.org/MSC1984_2014.php
81. Gerald R. Rosenberg, "Judicial Independence and the Reality of Political Power," *Review of Politics* 52, no. 3 (1992): 369–98.
82. Walter Evans and Frank Gilbert, "The Case for Judicial Discretion in Sentencing," *Judicature* 61 (1977): 66–72.
83. Shawn D. Bushway, "Judging Judicial Discretion: Legal Factors and Racial Discrimination in Sentencing," *Law & Society Review* 35:733–764.
84. Bonneau and Hall, *In Defense of Judicial Elections*.
85. Richard R. W. Brooks and Steven S. Raphael, "Life Terms or Death Sentences: The Uneasy Relationship between Judicial Elections and Capital Punishment," *Journal of Criminal Law and Criminology* 92, nos. 3–4 (2002).
86. Todd A. Curry and Mark S. Hurwitz, "Strategic Retirements of Elected and Appointed Justices: A Hazard Model Approach," *Journal of Politics* 78, no. 4 (2016): 1061–75; Todd A. Curry and Mark S. Hurwitz, "Institutional Effects on the Careers of State Supreme Court Justices," *American Review of Politics* 35, no. 1 (2016): 44–64.
87. Michigan Constitution, Article VI, Section 25.
88. Michigan Constitution, Article VI, Section 30.
89. L. L. Brasier, , "Troubling Trend: When Michigan Judges Need Disciplining," *Detroit Free Press*, December 7, 2014.
90. Lori Higgins, "Judge Rules Ann Arbor School District Can Ban Guns," *Detroit Free Press*, September 23, 2015.
91. Ibid.
92. Ibid.
93. Ibid.
94. Klemanski, "Trends in Michigan Supreme Court Elections 2000–2012."
95. Ibid.

- Political Actors and Processes

9 • Political Parties and Interest Groups in Michigan

JAMES M. STRICKLAND AND LOGAN T. WOODS

Michigan enjoys a diverse political environment, which includes a great diversity of opinions and ideas. With this, however, comes contentious politics: the expression of opposing policy preferences by organized groups within political or governmental settings.[1] This chapter examines how associations of individuals seek political influence in Michigan by attempting to affect state policy as well as how they might represent Michigan citizens' interests on a national level. Such associations consist of both state and substate party organizations that nominate candidates for office, and interest groups that lobby elected officials. Both political parties and interest groups play an important role in politics as linkage institutions; each, in their own way, provides a connection between citizens and their government. The chapter is centered on the history of these associations as well as the effects of these associations on Michigan's government today; parties are considered first with interest groups following. In each section, some key concepts are introduced before turning to a discussion of their relevance to Michigan's political system. This encompasses state government responses to challenges as well as state-local government relations—parties nominate candidates for office that eventually become state and local policymakers and interest groups lobby for their own ideas for policy solutions.

Historical Party Control in Michigan

The first major political party to form in Michigan was the Democratic Party. By 1832, five years before Michigan was granted statehood, the party had a presence. Early parties in Michigan were composed of many factions—for example, the Democratic Party consisted of the office-holding, the conservative, the radical, and the western factions. At the time, members of the Democratic Party were largely immigrants from western New York who were "poor and inclined to be radical."[2] What was referred to at the time as the radical faction of the Democratic Party consisted of farmers and laborers, who were characterized by their opposition to banks and slavery.[3] The Democratic Party platform included opposition to monopolies, equal rule of law for all, equal rights, and other positions that were steadfastly antiaristocratic in nature. For much of Michigan's history before 1854, the Democratic Party dominated statewide elections. These included elections for governor and state Legislature, although the party was sometimes split into conservative and radical factions, and by geographic loyalties.

The second major political party to form in Michigan was the Whig Party, organized in 1834.[4] While the constituents of the Democratic Party were largely poor, supporters of the Whig Party were mostly well-to-do. Despite success in the elections of the early 1840s, the Whigs were mostly a minority throughout Michigan's early history and were split between radical and conservative wings. The radical wing of the Whig Party consisted of Whigs opposed to slavery, and the radical Whig politicians tended to be younger than the conservative Whig politicians.[5] By the mid-1840s, as intraparty fractures became deeper, many Whigs began to support candidates nominated by third parties—particularly the Free Soil Party and the Know-Nothing Party, a nativist third party intended to limit the political influence of immigrants and Roman Catholics.[6] The fractures of the Whig Party were largely responsible for its failure to gain control of Michigan's government from Democrats after 1841.

The modern Republican Party formed in 1854, uniting several antislavery parties and the antislavery wings of other parties. The first meetings of the Republican Party took place in Jackson, Michigan, and in Ripon, Wisconsin. In Michigan, the Republican Party formed from remnants of the Free Democrat Party and more radical wings of the Democratic and Whig Parties.[7] While these prior partisan identities led to infighting within the new party, the preference for preventing additional slave states from being admitting into the Union was enough of a unifying factor to give the party strength. In 1854, the year of its founding, the Republican Party gained control of Michigan's state government. Subsequently, Democrats did not win an election for statewide office for another three decades.

Michigan has had several distinct periods of one-party control. With few exceptions, the Democratic Party controlled state government from

1837 to 1854.[8] For the next 80 years, however, Republicans consistently won statewide elections and presidential contests in Michigan. Since the 1932 elections, control of state government has vacillated between the two parties, but Republicans have reemerged at the state level since the mid-1990s. While the state's congressional delegation consisted mostly of Republicans until the late 1960s, Democrats had a stronger presence through the 1980s and 1990s, but after the 2002 elections, Republicans have had a majority of congressional seats. At the presidential level, a plurality of Michiganders voted for the Democratic candidate between 1992 and 2012. This, in turn, has awarded all of Michigan's electoral votes to those Democratic candidates. However, due in part to Republicans' successes in other statewide elections and sizable number of electors, Michigan has continued to attract considerable attention from candidates, parties, and outside groups during recent presidential elections.[9] In the 2016 elections, the Republican Party maintained control of the state government and the Republican nominee for President, Donald Trump, won a majority of the popular vote to gain the state's 16 Electoral College votes by a razor thin margin of less than 11,000 votes out of nearly five million cast.

Minor Political Parties in Michigan

Minor political parties (sometimes referred to as "third parties," although the two may not be equivalent under Michigan law) have a long history in Michigan and at times have had a prominent presence in municipalities across the state, despite being largely absent at the state level.[10] Early minor parties in Michigan included the Free Soil and Liberty Parties, of which the latter was the first antislavery party active in the state.[11] From 1900 to 1920, the Socialist and Prohibition Parties' top-of-the-ballot candidates consistently drew approximately 2 percent each of the total ballots cast. In 1912, Theodore Roosevelt's National Progressive Party received strong support in Michigan, winning more than 38 percent of the popular vote in the presidential election. Support for the party, however, was largely centered on Roosevelt's candidacy and it ceased to exist by 1916 when Roosevelt retired from national politics. In the 20th century, prominent minor parties in Michigan included the Human Rights, Libertarian, and Green Parties. While the Human Rights Party was active mostly in Washtenaw County in the 1970s and eventually merged with the Michigan Socialist Party, the Libertarian and Green Parties continue to regularly nominate candidates for statewide office. Candidates from these parties rarely receive more than 2 percent of the vote, although in

2016 the Libertarian Party candidate for president, Gary Johnson, received approximately 3.5 percent of the popular vote. The Tisch Independent Citizens Party, founded by antitax activist Robert Tisch in the 1970s, managed to gain some attention in statewide elections in the late 20th century but never gained more than 7 percent of the vote. In 1992, the party became affiliated with the U.S. Taxpayers Party, which later became the Constitution Party. The Tisch Independent Citizens Party is the most recent party (other than the Republican and Democratic Parties) to have qualified as a major party in Michigan, in 1992.[12]

Three Components of Political Parties

One way of examining political parties is through the lens of V. O. Key's "tripartite" model, which argues that parties consist of three elements: party in the electorate; party in government; and party as organization.[13] Party in the electorate focuses on individual members of the public and their attachment to a political party. Party in government refers to candidates running for office and elected officials who have a party affiliation. Finally, party as organization centers on the officials, staff, operatives and others who work to get the party's candidates elected to office. It is valuable to consider each of the three legs of Key's tripartite model in the context of Michigan politics. Doing so allows for a nuanced examination of the parties by giving proper attention to each of the different elements.

Party Identification in Michigan

A key component of party in the electorate is "party identification"; this is the level of attachment that an individual has toward a political party, or the level of importance the person attaches to being associated with that party.[14] While we cannot directly observe party identification because most parties do not require formal membership, the partisan leanings of individuals in the electorate are often used to measure the levels of party support. In some states, voters are required to declare a party affiliation when they register to vote, which makes it easier to measure or estimate party identification. Michigan, however, does not ask voters to declare their party loyalties when registering, and major parties do not maintain public records of how many residents identify as partisans.[15] Therefore, proxy measures are the only indicators of party identification and strength, with surveys asking respondents which party they identify with being the most common method of measuring party identification.

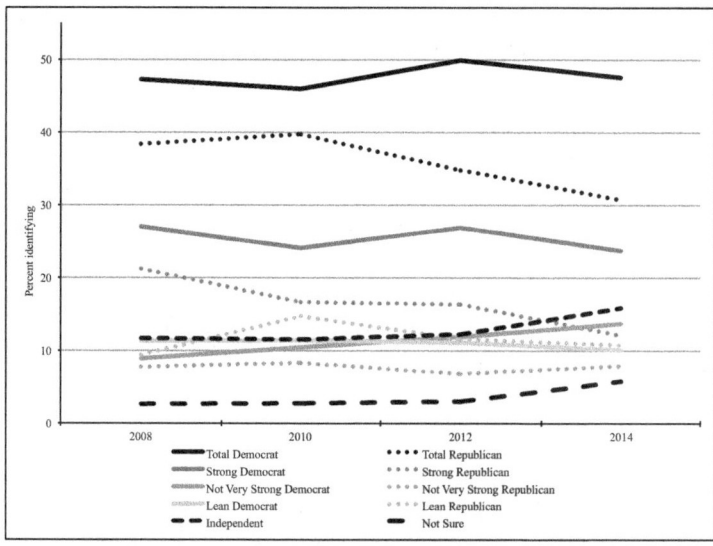

Fig. 9.1. Party Identification in Michigan, 2008–2014
Source: Cooperative Congressional Election Study.
Note: Data are from an online survey implemented by researchers who study various topics including ideology and party identification (Stephen Ansolabehere, "CCES, Common Content, 2008," Harvard Dataverse, 2010, accessed January 2016, http://hdl.handle.net/1902.1/14003; Stephen Ansolabehere, "CCES Common Content, 2010," Harvard Dataverse, 2012, accessed January 2016, http://hdl.handle.net/1902.1/17705; Stephen Ansolabehere and Brian Schaffner, "CCES Common Content, 2012" Harvard Dataverse, 2013, accessed January 2016, http://hdl.handle.net/1902.1/21447; Brian Schaffner and Stephen Ansolabehere, "CCES Common Content, 2014," Harvard Dataverse, 2015, accessed January 2016, http://dx.doi.org/10.7910/DVN/XFXJVY). Party identification is captured by a seven-point scale in which respondents may choose the strength of their partisan identities (from "strong Democrat" to "strong Republican," with independents being in the middle). "Total" Democrat and Republican are aggregations of the three gradients of the strength of party identification.

In recent years, Democrats have had a sizable advantage in party identification in Michigan. Between 2008 and 2014, Democrats have had a significant advantage over Republicans in terms of the percentage of people saying they identify with the party (see fig. 9.1). For instance, in 2008 nearly 48 percent of Michiganders said they were Democrats compared to only about 38 percent saying they were Republicans. Between 2010 and 2014 the gap between Democratic and Republican identification only grew, with Democrats more than doubling their lead in party identification over this time. Several other trends are apparent from the data. First, the percentage of weak party identifiers ("not very strong" and "lean" categories in fig. 9.1) in both parties and independents rose between 2008 and 2014. Second, the percentage of strong partisan identifiers of both parties declined in the same time period. In particular, this trend was most pronounced among self-identified "strong" Republicans. In most categories of party identification measured by these data—strong Democrat or Republican, not very strong Democrat or Republican, or lean Democrat or Republican—Democrats have held an advantage over Republicans with the exception of those who say they lean to one party or the other. Such trends may help to explain partly Michigan's increasing lean toward Democratic presidential candidates between 1992 and 2012. However, it runs counter to the successes that Republicans have had in other statewide elections (i.e., for governor, secretary of state, and attorney general) as well as the 2016 presidential race where, as noted above, Donald Trump won a slim majority of votes in the state (see chapter 10 for more on why this was the case).

Political Parties in Michigan Government

While party identification is focused on the electorate, party in government is often centered on elected officials. In recent years, much attention has been paid to how elected officials from the different parties have become polarized. Party polarization has been a popular topic of conversation among scholars and pundits alike as the Congress has become increasingly polarized over the last 40 years.[16] One way of capturing party polarization, or the ideological distance between the two major parties, in Michigan state government is to examine the ideological distance between the median Democratic and Republican members of the Michigan Senate and Michigan House of Representatives.

The Michigan Legislature has also seen its share of polarization, although polarization has typically been greater in the Michigan Senate than in the Michigan House, with the exception of a period between 2003 and 2008 when the polarization levels were roughly equal between the two chambers. The greater levels of polarization in the Senate were at a time when Michigan experienced extended periods of unified government; however, Republicans controlled the Senate with much larger majorities than they did in the House, and Democrats controlled the House for a brief period in this time frame. The period of relatively equal polarization within the two chambers coincided with a time of divided government; Michigan had a Democratic governor in Jennifer Granholm, the state Senate was controlled by Republicans and the state House was controlled by Republicans for two years and Democrats for two years. This split control of government may have led to the period of less partisanship and more pragmatism.

Another way to examine party in government is elected officials' ideo-

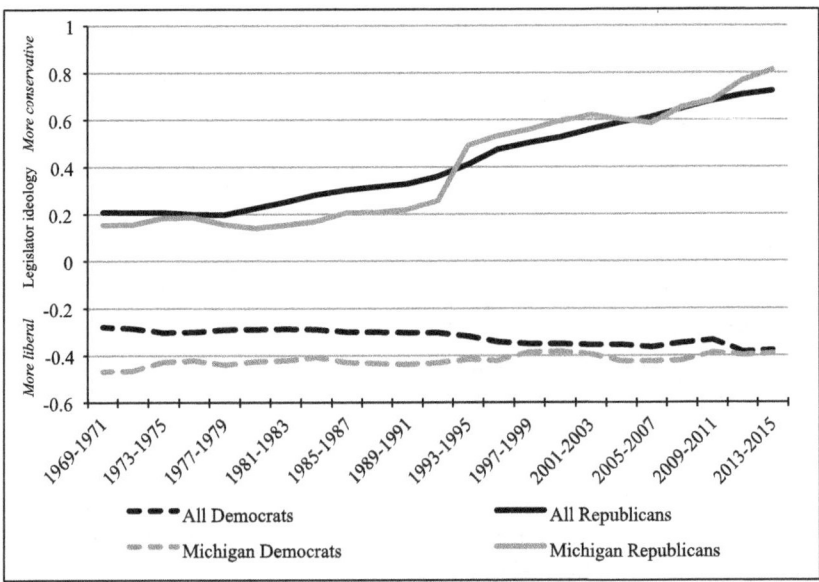

Fig. 9.2. Average Ideology of Members of Congress, by Party, 1969–2015
Source: DW-Nominate scores; see Royce Carroll, Jeff Lewis, James Lo, Nolan McCarty, Keith Poole, and Howard Rosenthal, "DW-Nominate Scores with Bootstrapped Standard Errors," VoteView.com, 2015, accessed January 2016, http://voteview.com/dwnomin.htm
Note: These scores are measurements of ideology frequently used by political scientists to predict voting patterns in legislative assemblies. Scores are based on the prior voting decisions of incumbent legislators. A low value indicates that a legislator has a more liberal voting history than those with high values, who voted more conservatively.

logical positions. Figure 9.2 illustrates the ideological scores of members of both parties in Congress, both as a whole and only those from Michigan from 1969 through 2015. The ideological position of all Democrats has been relatively unchanged during this time, with only a slight shift toward more liberal positions; Michigan Democrats also remained generally stable ideologically only showing a slightly more conservative trend over this time. Republicans, however, show a different pattern; after about 1994, Republican legislators—both as a whole and among the Michigan delegation—became much more conservative. Comparing Michigan representatives to all partisans nationwide, it is interesting to note that before the mid-1990s Republicans from Michigan were slightly less conservative than their fellow partisans while Democrats were slightly more liberal than their fellow partisans. Since this time, however, members of the Michigan congressional delegation from both parties have, on average, been very similar ideologically to other members of their party; in some years they have been slightly more ideologically extreme. It is noteworthy that the shift in ideology among Michigan Republicans came after the historic 1994 elections, which saw Republicans nationally win enough seats in the U.S. House to take control of the chamber for the first time in 40 years.

Party as Organization in Michigan

Central to all political parties is the goal of winning and then maintaining elective office so they can implement their preferred policies. To help in this effort, political parties form large organizational structures to help candidates get elected. Michigan election law mandates that "groups participating in elections form and register committees," the duties of which include fundraising and making expenditures. In practice, when a political party forms a state central committee, that committee governs the statewide party and sets bylaws by which all member party organizations abide.

Membership on the party committee includes both citizens and elected officials who are members of that party. An important distinction must be made here. Membership on the *party committee* is different than membership in the *state party* generally. As noted above, there is no consistent process for tracking membership in political parties. The United States does not have a party system that requires specific membership in a political party; hence the need to use survey data or party registration data for estimates of those in the electorate who identify with a particular party.

In Michigan, the Republican State Central Committee consists of regular members who are elected by the congressional district parties or nominated by the committee chairman; ex-officio members (i.e., statewide elected officials); nonvoting members (i.e., leaders of independent Republican organizations); and paid members (i.e., members who have made a contribution within the previous eight years). Similarly, the Democratic State Central Committee includes members elected by congressional district-level committees, members of the Democratic National Committee from Michigan, and congressional district and county chairpersons. State election law provides that committees be formed for county, congressional district, and state-level parties.[17] The state central committees are the decision-making authorities for the state parties when there is not a state party convention occurring.[18]

The Democratic and Republican Parties in Michigan have multiple levels of organization, and all levels play distinct roles in the efforts of the party across the state. According to its bylaws, the Michigan Republican Party consists of three party committees: the state party committee, the party committee for each congressional district, and the county executive committees.[19] Similarly, the bylaws for the Michigan Democratic Party describe the party as being composed of precinct, county, congressional district, and state-level organizations.[20] Michigan election law details the guidelines and procedures that state, congressional district, and county parties must follow, including rules for nominating processes and the scheduling of party conventions. There are also numerous party clubs and organizations that exist on local levels, at times supported by party committees and at times independent of them.

State Parties

State-level party organizations have several duties as prescribed by both their own bylaws and the laws that govern the state of Michigan. Similar to district and county parties, state parties are governed by committees and executive committees, each with discrete duties. State law mandates that state central party committees circulate notifications of the state convention to the county party chairs, declare all donations and expenditures to and by that committee, and name treasurers and other officers as the party deems appropriate.[21] Michigan state central committees are also tasked with crafting the bylaws that govern party organizations in Michigan when a state convention is not occurring, creating the procedure that sends party delegates to the national party convention, and coordinating with the relevant national party.

County and Congressional District Parties

State party organizations across the United States are notoriously uneven in their organizational resources and capacities. Some raise and spend more money than others, some have more professional staff than others, among numerous other differences. The unevenness of party organizations continues when considering lower-level party committees. Michigan is no different in this regard as county parties and congressional district parties are very different across the state. County parties in Michigan are in some cases constrained by the state party in their duties and governing rules and in other cases given a wide berth to determine their policies. Congressional district parties and party committees are also set forth in the bylaws of the Michigan Republican and Democratic state parties; there is one district committee in each congressional district in the state. In terms of how these two types of party organizations operate, county parties and congressional district parties differ across Michigan on a number of levels. For example, county parties differ in terms of whether or not membership requires a financial contribution (e.g., the Leelanau County Democratic Party requires annual dues while the Washtenaw County Democratic Party does not).

Differences also exist for the structures of these organizations including the duties of county party executive committees, which include allocation of precinct delegates and filling positions as necessary on the county party committees.[22] Duties of the county party committees include supporting local grassroots organizations and approving the bylaws set forth by the executive committee, among other duties that might be set forth by the executive committee or by state law. County parties are also obligated to hold a county party convention of precinct delegates at which delegates to the state party conventions are chosen and, frequently, county party bylaws are adopted.[23]

Much like county parties and their committees, there are differences in how congressional district parties and committees organize and operate. For example, there are no executive committees in the Republican district committee organizations, whereas the Democratic Party bylaws require the creation of both a district committee and an executive committee for that district. In terms of mission, the stated purpose of the Twelfth Congressional District Republican Committee, for instance, includes duties such as "promoting active citizenship through the Republican Party" and "supporting Republican Party candidates seeking elective office at the local, county, state, and federal levels as determined by the District Committee."[24] Other congressional district party committees are not as well organized and do not have as specific a purpose behind their existence.

Measuring Party Strength through Fundraising

All of the activities of a state party and many of the differences between county and congressional district party organizations across the state can be tied to fundraising. Indeed, party organizations need revenue to operate. State parties and their subsidiaries generate revenue through donations. Here again, however, there are great differences across the United States. For instance, during the 2016 election cycle, the Louisiana Democratic Party raised just $13,500 while the California Democratic Party raised over $24 million.[25] That same year the Florida Republican Party raised over $10 million while the Wyoming Republican Party raised only $78,000.

During the 2016 election cycle in Michigan, the two major state parties were relatively quiet. The Michigan Democratic Party raised roughly $3.2 million, while the Michigan Republican Party countered with slightly more than $1.75 million. There are, however, other party organizations in Michigan (and other states) that also raise money to further the cause of the party. For instance, both Republicans and Democrats have campaign committees devoted to helping candidates for the state House and state Senate get elected. In 2016, the House Republican Campaign Committee of Michigan raised over $2.5 million and the Michigan House Democratic Fund raised nearly $1.9 million. There was greater disparity in the state Senate committees with the Michigan Republican Senate Committee raising over $1 million and the Senate Democratic Fund of Michigan raising less than $400,000.

In 2014, however, both the Michigan Republican Party and Michigan Democratic Party reported raising about $5.5 million. In addition, the state House and state Senate committees were more active as the House Republican Campaign Committee raised over $2.4 million while its Democratic counterpart raised nearly $2 million. On the Senate side, the Michigan Senate Republican Campaign Committee raised $1.3 million while Senate Democratic Fund of Michigan raised only about $750,000.[26] These data reveal an important point about party activity in presidential years (e.g., 2016) and midterm years (e.g., 2014). In presidential election years, state parties are often quieter than in midterm years because of the presence of national party money flowing into the state.

These fundraising dollars help the parties with a core activity—helping candidates running for office in the state get elected. Obviously, different party organizations can do more or less to help candidates with these varying levels of funding during an election year. Funding of these party committees also ebbs and flows with the election calendar. Party organizations tend to raise much more during election years than they do in nonelection years.

Another Core Job of the Party: Candidate Nominations

In addition to helping candidates get elected to office and furthering the agenda of the party, party organizations have another important duty—helping select candidates for the general election through candidate nomination processes. Depending on the office, parties in Michigan nominate candidates through different processes. Most candidates are selected through primary elections, which are similar to other elections in that voters go to the polls and cast a ballot; the administration of this election is done by the state government. Because Michigan does not collect party affiliation data when a person registers to vote, party registration and membership are not required to vote in primary elections in Michigan. Michigan, therefore, has a system of "open" primaries where any individual who is registered to vote can vote in either the Democratic or Republican primary (but not both). Some candidates for office—the State Board of Education, university boards like the University of Michigan Board of Regents, and Michigan Supreme Court justices—are solely selected through party convention. In addition, in some instances, parties have chosen to have caucuses that are controlled by the party rather than the state, as in a primary. For example, in 2004 Democrats in Michigan elected to have a caucus at the presidential level; one notable feature of this particular caucus was that Democrats permitted participation through an online vote.

As of 2016, Michigan law stipulated that the presidential primaries for both parties be held on the second Tuesday in March.[27] However, the date of the Michigan presidential primary has changed many times. In general, the trend of presidential primary contests in Michigan (and to a certain extent the rest of the United States) has been to hold the primary elections earlier in the year, a phenomenon known as frontloading. Through the 2000s, many states moved their primary election dates earlier in the year to attempt to gain more influence in the election, as primary elections determine who runs in the general election. Michigan generally fits this trend as the 1980 presidential primaries were held on May 20 while the 2008 presidential primary elections were held on January 15. However, in the last two election cycles Michigan has moved its primary date a bit later in the calendar (as have some other states); the 2012 presidential primaries were held on February 28 and the 2016 presidential primaries were held on March 8. This was in response to new rules imposed by the national parties and Michigan's experience after the controversial decision in 2008 to move the presidential primary so early in the process.[28]

Interest Groups and Lobbying in Michigan

Americans have traditionally been suspicious of "lobbyists" and their "special interests."[29] They can hardly be blamed given the occasional scandals involving state officials and well-heeled powerbrokers. Despite such scandals and mistrust, however, most Americans have favorites among organized interest groups that advocate for causes they care about. Today, tens of thousands of interest groups are active at the federal and state levels trying to influence policy, and adult Americans have a higher probability of being associated with an interest group than of voting.[30] The policy positions that organized interests advocate for are incredibly diverse. Moreover, there are numerous kinds of interest groups, and their lobbyists fulfill multiple roles within policy-making processes. Even though the U.S. Constitution protects rights to assemble peaceably and petition government for policy change, not all interest groups take advantage of these rights to the same extent or in the same manner.

Lobbying in Michigan has changed a lot since the 1940s. In particular, more groups and individuals than ever before spend more money than ever before trying to influence policy made in Lansing. Importantly, numerous multiclient firms that consist of teams of lobbyists working in tandem have emerged in recent decades. Throughout the period studied in this chapter, lobbying in Lansing has become more crowded, competitive, and professional. The amount of information available about such influence is contingent on the types of disclosure laws enforced.

Tracing the Development of Michigan Interests

The 20th century saw the development of new ethics and disclosure laws within the American states. Such laws serve the purposes of regulating and making known the actions of hired lobbyists, interest groups, and other political entities.[31] In other words, they provide interesting glimpses into the world of lobbying that only insiders often get to see. Since the laws provide for regular registration and reporting by lobbyists, we can turn to lobbying disclosure records to see how lobbying has changed in Michigan over time. Fortunately, records of lobby disclosure in Michigan date to the late 1940s, thereby providing rich information on the development of organized interests. Lobby laws in Michigan are administered by the Bureau of Elections within the Department of State, and historical records are maintained by the Library of Michigan in Lansing.

The first law on lobbying transparency in Michigan was signed by Governor Kim Sigler on June 17, 1947. The law (Public Act 214 and also known as the "Legislative Agent Act") initially required paid lobbyists to register with the secretary of state's office. The law did not require any reporting of information beyond the names of those who chose to register.[32] Consequently, only the names and addresses of compliant lobbyists and interest groups from that period were publicly disclosed, leaving little information about their activities other than that reported by journalists. Despite these limitations, the records provide insight into how lobbying in Lansing has grown and diversified over time.

Lansing's community of lobbyists and interest groups began to expand rapidly in the early 1980s (see fig. 9.3). From the 1950s through the early

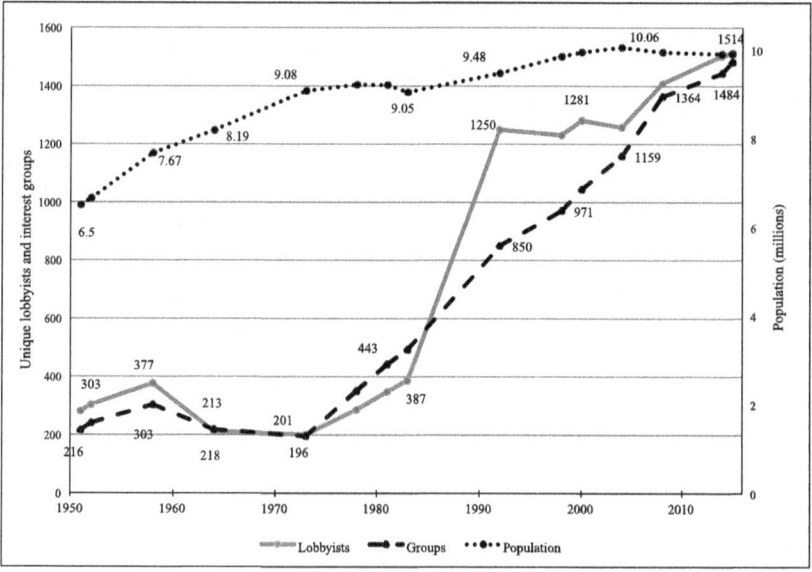

Fig. 9.3. Number of Interest Groups and Lobbyists in Michigan versus Population Growth, 1952–2015
Source: Figures compiled by authors from lists originally maintained by the Michigan Secretary of State.

1970s, the number of lobbyists and interest groups remained relatively stable, with even a small dip in numbers during the 1960s. In the 1980s, however, more and more interest groups began to appear, and many more individuals began to register as lobbyists in Lansing. In fact, totals of lobbyists and their clients have grown more than sevenfold between the 1970s and 2015. This growth contrasts with Michigan's population (also plotted in fig. 9.3, which did not increase at the same rate) but mirrors lobbying growth seen in some other states around this time.[33]

Existing accounts of lobbying activity may suggest a few potential causes of the rapid growth of lobbying in Lansing. Political scientists Virginia Gray and David Lowery proposed a theory of why some states have larger communities of interest groups than others.[34] To them, totals of registered interests reflected the size of a state (in terms of constituents) and its politics (which energizes interest groups to mobilize). Since Michigan's totals of registered interests are only moderately correlated with its population, political factors may help to explain the growth of lobbying. Gray and Lowery suggested that government growth and the potential for policy change may each contribute to increased lobbying.[35] Other political factors that may have contributed to increased lobbying in Michigan include the presence of ballot initiatives (see chapter 11), more instability of partisan control, the imposition of term limits (see chapter 7), or increased numbers of legislative staff.[36]

To help identify the causes of lobbying growth, one can also consider changes in the diversity of registered interests in Lansing. Examining the diversity of interests in the types of groups that are registered to lobby is a helpful starting point. Between 1951 and 2007, Lansing's community of interest groups changed in composition.[37] Despite little movement in the ratio of for-profit to nonprofit interests, some types of interest groups increased their lobbying efforts much more than others. In 2007, the most numerous types and totals of for-profit interest groups in Lansing were organizations related to healthcare (146), business services (143), manufacturing (126), and banks (84). The lobbying activities of each of these sectors were much smaller in 1951 when only 13 healthcare organizations, 25 service firms (e.g., the Michigan Chain Stores Association, or Michigan Movers Association), four manufacturers, and six banks registered to lobby, among other for-profits. Shifts of similar magnitude also occurred among nonprofit interest groups. In 2007, the most common types and totals of nonprofits were groups related to education (130), sports and hobby leagues (48), environmental causes (20), and groups related to police and firefighters (41). This is in contrast to 56 years earlier when only 10 educational organizations, 3 sports leagues, 3 environmental groups, and 3 police or firefighter groups were registered. In general, while all types of registered interest groups have increased dramatically in number over the past six decades, for-profit interests continue to dominate the lobbying community in Lansing. Groups related to health care, service firms, and manufacturing enjoy the greatest numerical advantages, but may not always advocate for the same policies.

Political Influence, Transparency, and Ethics

Laws that are intended to make lawmakers more accountable to their constituents may play some role in explaining the rapid increase in the totals of registered lobbyists and interest groups. Since such laws are intended to provide members of the public and media with information about the activities of lawmakers, lobbyists, and other political actors, the strength (or enforcement) of these laws may determine how much information they actually deliver. Tracing the ebb and flow of special-interest influence on Michigan politics is more challenging than determining how many individuals and groups were registered to lobby. There is some evidence, however, that lobbying in Michigan has become more professional (e.g., with more formal education and training, more full-time positions) between the 1950s and more recent years. This is due in part to improvements in transparency and ethics laws.

Michigan's first lobbying transparency law in 1947 contained few enforcement provisions.[38] In an opinion issued in 1949, Michigan's attorney general Stephen John Roth stated that the law "does not in fact undertake to regulate the activities of lobbyists. Licensing [i.e. registration] and regulation are not synonymous terms."[39] While the original act required that lobbyists register with the secretary of state, pay a filing fee, and maintain records of expenses for six years, the law did not require lobbyists to report their activities or even register on a regular basis. While the state's attorney general was responsible for enforcing the law, the office was given few resources for prosecuting violations of the law. Moreover, numerous attempts were made throughout the 1950s to repeal the act. It was not until the passage of House Bill 551 in 1958 that lobbyists were required to register on an annual basis. However, a study of Michigan lobbyists found that numerous interest groups still did not register and that no lobbyist had ever been prosecuted under the law.[40]

Following the failure of an income tax reform proposal in April 1962, Governor John Swainson requested that Attorney General Frank Kelley investigate whether any lobbyists had violated standards of ethical conduct while lobbying against the proposal. Kelley's investigation found that two particular lobbyists, both of whom represented large automotive companies, were likely effective in having persuaded several state senators to change their votes from "yea" to "nay." Other senators reported "vicious" and "unbearable" pressure from other lobbyists as well.[41] Apart from the pressure applied during the tax reform debate, Kelley's investigation recorded numerous informal tactics used by Lansing lobbyists in the early 1960s. Upon being questioned, numerous lobbyists reported regularly buying drinks and meals for lawmakers. They also stated that lawmakers had come to expect such perks continually. Some lobbyists reported maintaining hospitality suites in local hotels for lawmakers, and other lobbyists reported that lawmakers frequently turned to them to secure jobs for relatives from their employers. Lawmakers were reported to have asked for and received numerous gifts from lobbyists, including cruises, golf trips, cigars, and beverages. Upon concluding his investigation, Kelley recommended the enactment of a new lobbying law that included enforcement provisions.

It was not until 1978 that a stronger lobby transparency law was enacted in Michigan.[42] Act 472, known as the "Lobby Act," created more specific registration and reporting criteria for lobbyists and their employers, and included numerous bans on gifts to legislators. It also empowered the secretary of state's office to forward cases of suspected noncompliance to the attorney general for investigation. While the secretary of state's office had created rules for enforcing the law by November 1980, a coalition of more than 100 lobbyists, businesses, and professional associations filed a lawsuit that challenged the law's constitutionality. The law was deemed an infringement on free speech by an Ingham County circuit judge in October 1981. Within a year, however, the Michigan Court of Appeals had reversed this ruling (see *Pletz v. Secretary of State*), and in September 1983, the Michigan Supreme Court refused to hear the second appeal, effectively upholding the appeals court's ruling. While the reporting requirements of the lobby law had been weakened, most aspects of the law were deemed constitutional. The Michigan Legislature has since modified the law several times, including making changes to the reporting requirements and implementing prohibitions on legislators accepting honoraria for speeches or other public appearances.

Michigan's 1978 Lobby Act is likely a major cause of the rapid increase in lobby registrations in the 1980s. Throughout the litigation process and following the decision of the Supreme Court, the total of both registered lobbyists and interest groups increased by roughly 400 percent. The more specific registration criteria of the act encouraged interest groups to register *all* their lobbyists in hopes of avoiding violations. William Browne and others argue that the act's implementation involved an adjustment period in which interest groups cautiously registered more individuals as lobbyists than required.[43] Moreover, the law appeared by some accounts to have reduced the number of perks received by Lansing legislators.[44] As lobbyists and their clients became more familiar with the law's requirements, registration figures began to level off.

In addition to being more regulated, there is evidence that lobbying in Lansing was becoming much more sophisticated by the early 1990s. Throughout a series of interviews conducted with several influential contract lobbyists in the summer of 1994, political scientists Virginia Gray and David Lowery found that lobbying in Lansing was becoming more lucrative and competitive than ever before.[45] One lobbyist claimed that it was not unusual for lobbyists to arrange with legislators to get certain bills introduced to the Legislature only for those same lobbyists to be paid to lobby against those bills.[46] Similar to the actions of infamous lobbyist Jack Abramoff, this maneuver would involve lobbyists lobbying *against* the interests of their clients at least temporarily.[47] Other lobbyists alleged that competition was increasing because more people were entering the lobbying business. Indeed, since so many interest groups had come onto the policy-making scene in Lansing, legislative business was said to be more arduous than ever before.[48] When asked about the competitive advantages of hiring multiclient lobbying firms over using in-house lobbyists, some lobbyists emphasized that the political donations of their lobbying firms gave them greater access to and influence over lawmakers. It was claimed that such firms were becoming powerful players in Michigan politics. Indeed, "money and people, that's the name of the game," according to one lobbyist.[49]

Recent Developments in Michigan Lobbying

Today, hundreds of individual lobbyists, interest groups, and lobby firms consistently spend more than $35 million per year trying to influence policy in Lansing. While reported spending on lobbying has set new records in recent years, Lansing's lobbyists are not immune to fluctuations in the state's economic performance. Reported spending on lobbying varied greatly during the period of the Great Recession and back to the early 2000s.[50] While reported spending recovered to its prerecession levels by 2011, spending has leveled off after reaching a new record in 2012, but appeared to be heading for more records by the middle of the 2010s.

Since reporting standards remain lax compared to other states, however, total spending in Lansing may be greater than the data indicate. Little is known about the individual expenses of particular interest groups since lobbying firms that represent multiple clients are not required to report which expenses are made on behalf of each of their clients.[51] Lobbyists also are not required to report personal expenses for lawmakers that cost below particular thresholds. Michigan's current lobbyist reporting requirements place it in the bottom fourth of states in terms of how many requirements exist,[52] and in 2012 the state received an "F" grade for lobbying disclosure from the Center for Public Integrity.[53] Despite lax reporting standards, firm-level spending totals are available. Among the Lansing lobby firms that have consistently spent the most money on lobbying efforts in the mid-2010s were Governmental Consultant Services, Inc., James H. Karoub Associates, Kelley Cawthorne, RWC Advocacy, and the Michigan Health and Hospital Association. It remains to be seen how Michigan's newest campaign finance law (signed by Governor Rick Snyder in January 2016) may affect lobbying in Lansing, if at all.

One other development may have increased the influence of lobbyists in Michigan politics: the implementation of legislative term limits. In November 1992, as part of a larger national movement, Michigan's voters approved a constitutional amendment imposing term limits on numerous state officials (see chapter 7). Legislatures in which term limits are in effect tend to experience greater turnover among lawmakers, thereby lowering average policy knowledge among lawmakers.[54] These greater informational asymmetries between new lawmakers and lobbyists, agency officials, and others may have exacerbated the influence of professional lobbyists, many of whom market policy expertise and familiarity with legislative processes.[55] At the same time, however, term limits may have reduced the value of cultivating personal relationships with lawmakers by limiting the amount of time such individuals may serve in office. In addition, with term limits, more former lawmakers may market their personal connections to gain lobby contracts.[56] When interviewed in 2014, one lobbyist also attributed increased lobby expenditures to term limits, since lobbyists must spend more money to develop relationships with new legislators.[57]

Conclusion

Michigan political parties have experienced periods of influence, competition, and irrelevance. While the Republican Party has enjoyed more years of influence throughout Michigan's history, this has not always been the case. Both the Republican and Democratic Parties have multiple levels and have sometimes experienced more influence at different levels of government or in different geographic areas. The state, congressional district, and county-level branches of the parties have different responsibilities and interact differently with state officials. Importantly, despite a steady decline of strong partisan identifiers among Michigan's voters, legislators from Michigan (both in Lansing and Washington) continue to exhibit strong partisan trends in their roll-call voting records.[58] In fact, such polarization is becoming more pronounced over time as the median lawmakers of the two parties diverge. Such polarization may be a consequence of a lack of electoral competition. Michigan experienced several periods of domination by one party in its early history, followed by a period of electoral competitiveness. But that dynamic appears to be on the decline relative to its levels in much of the 20th century, as Republicans have swept the elections for state-level statewide office for much of the early 21st century.

With all the money that is spent on campaigns and lobbying in Michigan, it is easy to assume that interest groups and lobbyists successfully divert public policy away from the preferences of voters. It is important to remember, however, that not all the thousands of interest groups and lobbyists in Lansing lobby for the same opinions or ideas. In fact, as the political salience of different issues waxes and wanes, various interest groups may find themselves forming alliances with new partners or even former opponents.[59] Moreover, campaign donations or lobbying serve purposes other than influencing public officials and their decisions in office. Since interest groups have tended most often to make campaign contributions through their political action committees and lobby already-friendly lawmakers, such efforts may simply be attempts to keep friendly lawmakers in office, maintain access to them, or educate them on the merits of the group's position.[60] There are numerous interest groups in Michigan that each serve particular constituents, and their lobbyists fulfill a number of important roles in the policy-making process. Despite Americans' suspicion of special interests and their lobbyists, such associations fulfill important roles by representing diverse groups and articulating their preferences before lawmakers. Michigan politics can be characterized in part by the various associations that seek power in the state, whether those groups are political parties or organized interests. In addition, both are constantly seeking to advance policy agendas that can have an impact on countless issues in Michigan.

WEB RESOURCES

The *Michigan Democratic Party* (www.michigandems.org) and the *Michigan Republican Party* (www.migop.org) have websites that provide information about state and substate party organizations and their staffs, issue positions of the party, and information and support for candidates running on their party label.

The *Michigan Department of State's Bureau of Elections* provides a wide range of information about Michigan lobbyists, including a copy of Public Act 472 of 1978, the lobby registration act. From the Secretary of State's website (www.mich.gov/sos) select "Elections in Michigan" and then "Lobby Disclosure."

The *National Institute for Money in State Politics* provides campaign fundraising and spending data for a variety of organizations, including party organizations, political action committees, and nonprofit organizations. From the webpage (www.followthemoney.org), go to "Our Data" and select "State Overviews"; use the drop-down menu to select "Michigan" and select a year; scroll down to "Party Committees" for information about party fundraising and spending; and "Top Contributors" to see interest group/political action committee activity.

The *Michigan Campaign Finance Network* (www.mcfn.org) is a nonpartisan organization that tracks money in Michigan politics. They conduct research on campaign contributions and their relationship, if any, to election outcomes and public policy decisions.

NOTES

1. Charles Tilly and Sidney Tarrow, *Contentious Politics* (Oxford: Oxford University Press, 2006).
2. Floyd Benjamin Streeter, *Political Parties in Michigan 1837–1860: An Historical Study of Political Issues and Parties in Michigan from the Admission of the State to the Civil War* (Lansing: Michigan Historical Commission, 1918).
3. Ibid., 31.
4. Ibid.
5. Ibid., 38.
6. Ibid.
7. Ibid.
8. Ibid.
9. Daron R. Shaw, *The Race to 270: The Electoral College and the Campaign Strategies of 2000 and 2004* (Chicago: University of Chicago Press, 2006).
10. Major and minor parties differ in multiple ways under Michigan law. Major parties hold primary elections to nominate their candidates while minor parties must hold caucuses (Michigan Compiled Laws 168.532). The campaign finance laws that govern major and minor party candidates also differ, particularly with respect to the eligibility of candidates to receive money from the Michigan state campaign fund (Michigan Compiled Laws 169.265). County chairpersons of major political parties are also permitted to challenge the appointment of an election inspector based upon the inspector's party affiliation while Michigan law does not provide the same power to the county chairperson of a minor party (Michigan Compiled Laws 168.674).
11. Streeter, *Political Parties in Michigan*.
12. State governments are responsible for determining thresholds for parties to appear on official ballots. Such thresholds are frequently referred to as "ballot access laws" and are responsible for keeping election ballots within manageable lengths. In the state of Michigan, different rules apply to major political parties and to minor political parties. Major parties are defined legally as those whose principal candidates received more than 5 percent of the vote within the last general election for the office of secretary of state. Minor parties are defined as those that failed to reach this threshold. Since 1854, candidates from the Republican and Democratic Parties have consistently received enough votes for their parties to be classified as major parties in Michigan.
13. V. O. Key Jr., *Politics, Parties, and Pressure Groups*, 3rd ed. (New York: Thomas Y. Crowell, 1952). This concept of parties has been challenged by some, arguing that parties consist of even more elements and should be thought of as "networks" of actors. See, for example, Mildred A. Schwartz, *The Party Network: The Robust Organization of Illinois Republicans* (Madison: University of Wisconsin Press, 1990); J. P. Monroe, *The Political Party Matrix* (Albany: State University of New York Press, 2001); Jonathan Bernstein, "The Expanded Party in American Politics," PhD diss., University of California, Berkeley, 1999; Seth E. Masket, *No Middle Ground: How Informal Party Organizations Control Nominations and Polarize Legislatures* (Ann Arbor: University of Michigan Press, 2009); and Kathleen Bawn, Marty Cohen, David Karol, Seth Masket, Hans Noel, and John Zaller, "A Theory of Political Parties," *Perspectives on Politics* 10, no. 3 (2012): 571–97, for this perspective.

14. Ken Kollman, *Outside Lobbying: Public Opinion and Interest Group Strategies* (Princeton: Princeton University Press, 1998), 422.

15. Michigan Compiled Code § 168.615c.

16. Pew Research Center, "The Polarized Congress of Today Has Its Roots in the 1970s," 2014; accessed February 2016, http://www.pewresearch.org/fact-tank/2014/06/12/polarized-politics-in-congress-began-in-the-1970s-and-has-been-getting-worse-ever-since/

17. Michigan Campaign Finance Act of 1974.

18. Democratic State Central Committee of Michigan, *Rules*, last modified 2016, http://www.michigandems.com/sites/default/files/Rules%20of%20the%20MDP%20%28updated%20January%202016%29.pdf

19. Michigan State Republican Committee, *Bylaws*, last modified 2012, http://rightmi.com/wp-content/uploads/2013/01/MRSC-BYLAWS-2-4-12.pdf

20. Democratic State Central Committee of Michigan, *Rules*, last modified 2016.

21. Michigan Compiled Codes Chapter 169.

22. The bylaws for both the Michigan Democratic Party and the Michigan Republican Party include rules and provisions for county executive committees and county party committees. Members of the county executive committees are elected during the relevant county party convention, and typically hold terms of two years. Elected officials from that county who are party members are also frequently named to the executive committee of that county.

23. Michigan Compiled Code § 168.592.

24. Twelfth Congressional District Republican Committee Bylaws, last modified 2016, http://12cdrc.org/docs/12thDistrictCommitteeByLawsFinal

25. These data can be found at the National Institute on Money in State Politics (http://www.followthemoney.org).

26. National Institute on Money in State Politics, last modified 2016, http://www.followthemoney.org/election-overview?s=MI&y=2012

27. Michigan Compiled Code § 168.613a.

28. David A. Dulio, "Madness in Michigan: A Microcosm of Elections American Style," in *Campaigns and Elections American Style*, 3rd ed., ed. James A. Thurber and Candice J. Nelson (Boulder: Westview Press, 2009), 269–304.

29. Lester Milbrath, *The Washington Lobbyists* (Chicago: Rand McNally, 1963), 298.

30. Scott H. Ainsworth, *Analyzing Interest Groups: Group Influence on People and Politics* (New York: W. W. Norton, 2002), 3.

31. There is wide variation between U.S. states in the numbers and types of laws that affect the political activities of these actors. Other targets of ethics and disclosure laws often include elected and appointed state officials, political parties, and political action committees (PACs).

32. Frank J. Kelly, "Lobbying Investigation Report of Attorney General Frank J. Kelley to Governor John B. Swainson, August 16, 1962."

33. Virginia Gray and David Lowery, *The Population Ecology of Interest Representation: Lobbying Communities in the American States* (Ann Arbor: University of Michigan Press, 1996).

34. David Lowery and Virginia Gray, "The Population Ecology of Gucci Gulch, or the Natural Regulation of Interest Group Numbers in the American States," *American Political Science Review* 39 (1995): 1–29.

35. Gray and Lowery, *Population Ecology of Interest Representation*, 71.

36. Frederick J. Boehmke, "The Initiative Process and the Dynamics of State Interest Group Populations," *State Politics and Policy Quarterly* 8 (2008): 362–83; Christopher Z. Mooney, "Lobbyists and Interest Groups," in *Institutional Change in American Politics: The Case of Term Limits*, ed. Karl T. Kurtz, Bruce Cain, and Richard G. Niemi (Ann Arbor: University of Michigan Press, 2007); Marjorie Sarbaugh-Thompson, Lyke Thompson, Charles D. Elder, John Strate, and Richard C. Elling, *The Political and Institutional Effects of Term Limits* (New York: Palgrave Macmillan, 2004); Kyle T. Kattelman, "Legislative Professionalism and Interest Group Concentration: The ESA Model Revisited," *Interest Groups and Advocacy* 4 (2015): 165–84; Gray and Lowery, *Population Ecology of Interest Representation*; Virginia Gray and David Lowery, "State Lobbying Regulations and Their Enforcement: Implications for the Diversity of Interest Communities," *State and Local Government Review* 30 (1998): 78–91.

37. Virginia Gray and David Lowery, "The Institutionalization of State Communities of Organized Interests," *Political Research Quarterly* 54 (2001): 265–84.

38. Legislative Service Bureau, "Research Report: History of Lobbying Legislation" (Lansing, MI: Legislative Service Bureau, 1965).

39. Opinion no. 866.

40. Walter Dale De Vries. "The Michigan Lobbyist: A Study in the Bases and Perceptions of Effectiveness," PhD diss., Michigan State University, 1960.

41. Kelly, "Lobbying Investigation Report," 8.

42. Lobbyists were strictly regulated (at least temporarily) during Michigan's Constitutional Convention of 1962. "Convention agents" (i.e., lobbyists) were required to maintain more detailed records of their attempts to influence the convention proceedings. Similar regulations were enforced during Pennsylvania's convention five years later.

43. William P. Browne, Kenneth VerBurg, Delbert J. Ringquist, John S. Klemanski, and Charles Press, "Influencing Michigan Politics," in *Michigan Politics and Government: Facing Change in a Complex State*, ed. William P. Browne and Kenneth VerBurg (Lincoln: University of Nebraska Press, 1995).

44. Joanna Firestone, "State's Lobbyist Law Thins Out 'Gravy Train,'" *Detroit News*, March 16, 1984.

45. Virginia Gray and David Lowery, "The World of Contract Lobbying," *Comparative State Politics* 17 (1996): 31–40.

46. Ibid., 34.

47. David Lowery and Kathleen Marchetti, "You Don't Know Jack: Principals, Agents, and Lobbying," *Interest Groups and Advocacy* 1, no. 2 (2012): 139–70.

48. Gray and Lowery, "World of Contract Lobbying." 35.

49. Ibid., 37.

50. Rich Robinson, "State Lobbying Down $2.3M in 2009: Reporting Gaps Obscure Complete Spending Picture," *Michigan Campaign Finance Network*, February 22, 2010, accessed January 14, 2016, http://www.mcfn.org/press.php?prId=94

51. Jonathan Oosting, "Which Lawmakers Got the Most Free Lunch? Michigan Lobbying Topped $37M in 2014," *MLive.com*, February 18, 2015; accessed January 14, 2016, http://www.mlive.com/lansing-news/index.ssf/2015/02/which_lawmakers_got_free_lunch.html

52. James M. Strickland, "Disentangling the Effects of Lobbying Regulations on Interest Registrations in the American States, 1988–2013," paper presented at the Ninth Annual Conference on Empirical Legal Studies, November 2014, Berkeley, CA.

53. Chris Andrews, "Michigan Gets F Grade in 2012 State Integrity Investigation," Center for Public Integrity, March 19, 2012; accessed January 14, 2016, http://www.publicintegrity.org/2012/03/19/18188/michigan-gets-f-grade-2012-state-integrity-investigation

54. See Mooney, "Lobbyists and Interest Groups," for a concise review of research on term limits and lobbying.

55. It remains to be determined whether the many resources (such as staff assistants) available to Michigan lawmakers help to counter or condition the influence of lobbyists in the state's term-limited legislature. In the absence of such staffers, lobbyists might play a larger role in drafting laws and providing lawmakers with information about policy. See Michael B. Berkman, "Legislative Professionalism and the Demand for Groups: The Institutional Context of Interest Population Density," *Legislative Studies Quarterly* 26 (2001): 661–79.

56. As of January 2015, Michigan's "revolving door" law was among the weakest in the nation. Unlike in most other states, which prevent former lawmakers from registering to lobby for specified periods of time after leaving office, former legislators in Michigan are allowed to receive compensation for lobbying immediately upon leaving office, except in the case of resignations.

57. Justin A. Hinkley, "Which Lobbyists Interact with Your Lawmakers? Lansing Lobbyists and Lawmaker Term Limits Clash to Create 'the Potential for Sloppiness,'" *Lansing State Journal*, November 15, 2014, accessed January 23, 2016, http://www.lansingstatejournal.com/story/news/local/capitol/2014/11/15/michigan-lobbying-m-potential-sloppiness/19103893/

58. Royce Carroll, Jeff Lewis, James Lo, Nolan McCarty, Keith Poole, and Howard Rosenthal, "DW-Nominate Scores with Bootstrapped Standard Errors," *VoteView.com*, 2015, accessed January 2016, http://voteview.com/dwnomin.htm

59. Gray and Lowery 2004.

60. Frank R. Baumgartner, Jeffrey M. Berry, Marie Hojnacki, David C. Kimball, and Beth L. Leech, *Lobbying and Policy Change: Who Wins, Who Loses, and Why* (Chicago: University of Chicago Press, 2009); Richard L. Hall and Alan V. Deardorff, "Lobbying as Legislative Subsidy," *American Political Science Review* 1 (2006): 69–84.

10 ✦ Elections and Political Participation in Michigan

JOHN A. CLARK

Many citizens pay the greatest attention to their government during election campaigns. That attention presumably helps them make informed decisions about who should represent them in our democratic system; most democratic countries, including the United States, are actually indirect democracies (sometimes called "republics"), in which citizens elect representatives to make policy on their behalf.[1] Few Americans pay much attention to how elections are conducted, and some ignore policy making and the actions of government until the next round of elections appears on their radar screen. As a result, elections are at best a blunt—but critical—instrument for influencing policy.

Elections and political participation reflect the themes of this book in a broad sense. By choosing their representatives and leaders, voters determine who the elected officials will be in the state-local government relationship. In some cases, elections and their outcomes can be seen as a reaction to decline, as voters seek to identify candidates who they believe can best respond to the challenges of decline. Indeed, elections are the chief means by which citizens influence the direction of public policy in most democracies. When one candidate wins the governorship instead of another, for example, the policy agenda of the state can be altered dramatically. Moreover, election outcomes are sometimes the result of a citizenry that is unhappy with how government has performed since the previous election, and in this way can be seen as responses to challenges. State-local government relations are also an important dynamic in elections given that all elections are administered at the local level. And finally, elections have not always been conducted in the same way they are today; adaptation, political maneuvering, and changes in state laws are seen throughout the history of Michigan elections. These issues, and others, are explored in the pages that follow.

Types of Elections in Michigan

Elections are complex and multistep processes. Voters in Michigan, like citizens in other states, have the opportunity to participate in several types of elections. A state law passed in 2005 set four possible months for elections to be held: February, May, August, and November. In 2015, the February election was replaced with the date of the presidential primary in presidential election years (typically determined the year before). Not all jurisdictions will have elections at all of these times, but consolidating the dates can save money for the local jurisdictions that must pay for them.

When many Americans think of elections, they think only of the one-on-one matchups that occur during the fall general election campaign period. However, at the beginning of the process, there may be many more than two candidates. *Primary elections* are used by major political parties to select their nominees for most offices. In Michigan, the primary for offices other than president is held in August. Since the advent of term limits for the state Legislature (see chapter 7), some primaries have attracted large fields of candidates to battle for their party's nomination. Michigan's election law stipulates that only political parties that received 5 percent of the vote in the prior election for the office of secretary of state can use the primary for selecting nominees. Smaller parties must use a caucus or convention for their nominations. Nonpartisan primaries are used to select the general election candidates for judgeships other than the state Supreme Court; Supreme Court candidates are nominated at party conventions but appear on the general election ballot without party affiliations (see chapter 8).

General elections are the elections that are more familiar to most Americans as they are the head-to-head competitions that are used to select officeholders. General elections are held on the first Tuesday after the first Monday in November for federal and state offices. Some local jurisdictions (e.g., school boards) can set their own election timing. The timing of the primary leaves a relatively short window for candidates to contest the general election. Most state-level elections in Michigan are partisan, which means that candidates are nominated by political parties and their party affiliation appears on the ballot. Nonpartisan elections are used to select officeholders for positions including local school boards, community college boards, and judges and justices in the state court system. Many municipalities use nonpartisan elections in odd-numbered years to select their elected officials including some mayors (although townships continue to hold partisan elections in even-numbered years).

Recall elections allow voters to remove elected officials from office before their terms are complete. Michigan is one of 29 states (plus the District of Columbia) that allows recall elections. Under the state Constitution, the number of signatures required to place a recall question on the ballot is equal to 25 percent of the total vote cast for that office in the previous election. The threshold is so high that even getting a recall question on the ballot can be difficult. For example, more than 3 million voters participated in the 2014 gubernatorial election, meaning nearly 800,000 valid signatures would be necessary to place a recall on the ballot. Recalls are often threatened by political opponents but few ever make it all the way to the ballot and even fewer are successful in removing someone from office. Indeed, only three state legislators have been successfully recalled under this provision: Democratic senators Phil Mastin and David Serotkin in 1983 and Republican representative Paul Scott in 2011. Democratic Speaker of the House Andy Dillon survived a recall election in 2008.[2] In each instance, the recall effort centered on disagreements over public policy rather than criminal activity or personal scandal. On the other hand, recalls of local elected officials—such as school board members—are much more common in terms of both qualifying the question for the ballot and the success of the recall.

Michigan voters also have the opportunity to vote on matters of public policy through the use of *initiatives* and *referendums*. While there are differences in how ballot measures qualify for voter consideration (see chapter 11), they are similar in that they give citizens some control over the adoption of legislation or the approval of constitutional amendments. The façade of direct democracy at the ballot box often hides very expensive battles among organized interests seeking to affect public policy. For example, the Moroun family spent more than $31 million in 2012 on a ballot proposal to prevent construction of a new bridge that would compete with the family-owned Ambassador Bridge connecting Detroit with Windsor, Ontario.[3]

Michigan Elections and State-Local Government Relations

Federalism in the United States can create a complicated and uneasy relationship between the federal, state, and local governments. Election law and administration reveals some of that uncertain relationship. Most election law and administrative responsibility falls to U.S. state governments. However, there are notable examples of federal preemption in election matters. For example, the 15th and 19th Amendments to the U.S. Constitution expanded suffrage to African Americans and women, respectively, and the 26th Amendment lowered the voting age to 18. Similarly, the 17th Amendment mandated the direct election of U.S. senators and the 24th Amendment eliminated the poll tax. At the statutory level, the 1965 Voting Rights Act and the 1993 National Voter Registration Act (also known as the "Motor Voter" law) both sought to reduce barriers to voting, whether because of racial discrimination or overly strict registration laws. The Help America Vote Act (2002) mandated that states modernize their voting equipment and maintain statewide voter registration lists.

The responsibility for most election law and administration is left to the states, which may in turn delegate some responsibility for election administration to local governments. Local administration is most obvious on Election Day, as voters typically participate at a polling place located in their designated voting precinct. An average precinct tends to have up to a few thousand voters. Even though elections are administered locally, the state provides a number of standards for election administration. For example, state law (MCL168.31(k)) requires that all local election officials be trained and accredited, which is accomplished through a state-run accreditation course of instruction. Furthermore, local election officials must maintain accreditation through a continuing education program every two years (MCL 168.33(4)). There also are standards of operation required by the state, covering everything from technical standards of ballot production to the physical layout of a polling place (e.g., to ensure voter privacy), as well as steps required to confirm a voter's identity.

The strong state-local connection in Michigan has been noted in other chapters of this book. That connection also is true as it relates to elections. State election law regulates both state-level and local-level elections when it comes to voter qualifications, voter registration, and campaign finance reporting. In Michigan, state election law also provides that specific decisions about the qualifications and the nomination process of local candidates be determined by a city's charter (Michigan Election Law Act 116 of 1954, Chapter XV). For example, in 2012 Detroit voters approved a revision to the city's charter that changed city council elections from nine at-large seats to seven district seats and two at-large seats, effective for the 2013 elections. Other local election initiatives include local decisions to require term limits for local officials. Some local governments in Michigan have chosen to adopt term limits for their mayors, including Farmington

Hills, Cheboygan, Bay City, Livonia, Troy, Hillsdale, and Rochester Hills.[4] In a rare circumstance, the term-limited mayor of Rochester Hills ran as a write-in candidate in 2015 and won.[5] State election law regarding township elections (Act 116 of 1954, Chapter XVI) tends to impose more regulations for these offices than for municipal offices in the state.

Local elections comprise a large percentage of the overall number of offices sought and candidates filing to run. After all, these elections would include any county-level election, as well as municipal, township, and school district elections. County-level and township elections in Michigan are held in even-numbered years and are partisan, but as an outgrowth of the Progressive Era, most other local elections are held in odd-numbered years and are nonpartisan.

Statewide Rules Governing Elections in Michigan

The U.S. Constitution says very little about how elections are to be conducted. Instead, states largely set their own rules governing elections. Important rules in Michigan include how candidates qualify for the general election ballot, campaign finance regulations, the drawing of legislative districts, and term limits.

Nominations and Ballot Access

Candidates obtain ballot access in the general election through a variety of nomination mechanisms. Michigan has used an open primary system to nominate major party candidates for most offices for more than 100 years.[6] In an open primary, a voter does not have to register as a party member to participate in that party's nominating process. Voters select nominees for only one party, but the determination of which party's nominees to select is made in the privacy of the voting booth. In contrast, closed primaries occur in states that require a declaration of party affiliation when registering to vote and limit party primary participation to only those who are registered as affiliates of that party. The open primary in Michigan is used to select nominees for governor, U.S. Congress (both House and Senate), the state Legislature, and county offices.

Nominees for other statewide offices are selected at state party conventions, including candidates for lieutenant governor, attorney general, secretary of state, the trustees of three state universities (i.e., the University of Michigan, Michigan State University, and Wayne State University), and the State Board of Education. Ironically, candidates for state Supreme

Court justice are nominated by the parties at their conventions, but candidate party affiliations are not listed on the general election ballot (see chapter 8). Convention delegates are assumed to be party loyalists who have the best interests of their parties in mind. They frequently attempt to balance the ticket in terms of region, gender, race, and ideology. Nevertheless, factional divisions within the party can emerge, such as when a Tea Party–backed candidate unsuccessfully challenged the sitting lieutenant governor Brian Calley for renomination at the 2014 Republican convention.[7]

Signatures from registered voters are required for major party candidates to get on the primary ballot, and the number of signatures varies depending on the office. For example, major party candidates for the U.S. House of Representatives must gather 1,000 signatures to qualify for the primary ballot, with the primary winner getting automatic access to the general election ballot. Minor party candidates are nominated by their party conventions, but independent candidates (i.e., those not running on an established party's label) need 3,000 signatures to qualify for the general election. For some offices (although not the U.S. Congress), a filing fee can be paid in lieu of signatures. The number of signatures may seem trivial, but the stakes are high. U.S. Representative Thaddeus McCotter resigned his seat in 2012 after failing to submit the appropriate number of valid signatures on his nominating petitions to qualify for the 2012 primary.

Presidential nominations are a special case of the more general nomination process. Nominations are formally made by delegates at each party's national convention during the summer of a presidential election year. Between 1916 and 1928, Michigan's major parties used primary elections to select delegates to the national conventions, but the delegates were not required to support particular candidates. From 1932 to 1968, national convention delegates from Michigan were selected at the state party conventions.[8] Since the national parties made reforms that began following the 1968 election, the nomination contests (mainly primaries and caucuses) that occur in the states determine the allocation of delegates to specific candidates. The specific delegate allocation process in each state is determined by a combination of state law and state party rules in the context of the rules set by the national party organizations. In Michigan, the laws surrounding presidential nominations have sometimes conflicted with party rules. For example, national Democratic Party rules prohibited delegate allocation via an open primary in 1980, forcing Michigan Democrats to forego the state-run primary in favor of a party-run caucus. Four years later, a Democratic state Legislature temporarily abolished the state-run presidential primary altogether, forcing Republicans to create their own caucus system. When state Democrats opted for a caucus in 2000, the winner of the meaningless primary—and the only candidate on the Democratic ballot—was fringe candidate Lyndon LaRouche with fewer than 15,000 votes.[9]

In 2007, the Michigan Legislature enacted a new law that had the effect of making the state's presidential primary closed instead of open. Although prior party registration was not required, voters would have to request in writing the partisan ballot they wished to receive. The information identifying which voters selected which party's ballots was made available only to the state parties and was not otherwise disclosed to the public. The law also set the date for Michigan's presidential primary to be held on January 15, 2008, outside the time frame allowed by national Democratic and Republican Parties. The violation kept the Democratic candidates from campaigning in the state, and both national parties penalized the state by cutting the delegate allocation to the national convention by half.[10] The Legislature modified the law for the 2012 presidential nomination contest by removing the disclosure exemption for the ballot selection data. The same system was used in 2016, when both parties used the state-run primary for the first time since 1992.[11]

Campaign Finance

Campaigns for elective office are governed by a complex web of regulations when it comes to raising and spending money. Candidates for state and local offices must abide by state campaign finance laws, while candidates for president and the U.S. Congress (i.e., federal offices) follow a different set of national laws. At all levels, spending on campaigns occurs both inside and outside the regulatory framework.

As in federal elections, there are limits on how much an individual can contribute to a candidate's campaign in Michigan. Individual contributions to the campaigns of state representatives are capped at $1,000 and of state senators at $2,000. Individuals can contribute up to $6,800 in total to the campaigns of candidates for statewide offices. There are higher limits for contributions to candidates from political action committees (PACs) and party committees.[12]

In addition to direct contributions to candidates, individuals and groups can spend unlimited amounts of money to affect election outcomes so long as they do so independently of candidates' campaigns. These so-called independent expenditures have long been a part of the fabric of campaigns. Their use at the national level has exploded with the rise of "super PACs" and various tax-exempt organizations that spend exorbitant sums on television ads and targeted mailings. In Michigan, only campaign spending that explicitly asks citizens to vote for (or against) a candidate is considered campaign activity and thus subject to regulation; all other activity falls outside of the regulatory context. The amount of money that went toward candidate-focused television advertising that was done outside of the regulatory system nearly doubled between 2010 and 2014, from $22.9 million to $42.9 million. Combined with $11.4 million in independent expenditures that were regulated, roughly 40 percent of the spending on state elections in 2014 was not under the control of the candidates themselves. In the gubernatorial race, only a third of the spending was under the control of the candidates, while the rest was spent by outside groups.[13]

Michigan law allows for partial public funding for gubernatorial campaigns. To qualify, candidates for the major party nominations must be able to raise $75,000 in contributions of $100 or less during the primary phase of the campaign. Each $1 in qualifying contributions is matched by $2 in public funding up to a maximum of $990,000 in public funds for the primary. In 2014, Democratic gubernatorial candidate Mark Schauer received the maximum in public funds for the primary stage of the campaign even though he was running unopposed for his party's nomination.[14] In the general election, eligible candidates receive $1,125,000 in public funds. However, they must agree to limit contributions from their immediate families to $50,000 for the election cycle and limit expenditures to $2 million for each election (i.e., primary and general) for which they receive public funds. These limits can be waived if opposing candidates receive contributions of $340,000 or more from their immediate families.[15]

While the public funding of gubernatorial elections is part of state election law, participation is voluntary for the candidates. In recent years many candidates have eschewed the public funding system in favor of raising private funds far in excess of the limits of the public funding system. The 2006 gubernatorial race was the most expensive in Michigan history. Republican candidate Dick DeVos and his wife, Betsy (who became U.S. secretary of education in President Trump's administration), poured $35.5 million of their own money into his unsuccessful campaign to unseat incumbent Democratic governor Jennifer Granholm. The amount was reported to be the most ever spent by a Republican candidate self-funding their campaign for governor in any state. Because DeVos's contributions to his own campaign were so high, Granholm received the maximum allowable public funding without having to limit her campaign expenditures. In total, nearly $80 million was spent on this single election.[16]

Redistricting

The U.S. Constitution mandates a national census every 10 years so that the membership of the U.S. House of Representatives from each state can be reapportioned to take into account population shifts in the country. Once the number of representatives from each state has been determined, states draw the boundaries of their legislative districts. The process of redistricting has been called "the most political activity in America"[17] because the composition of each district affects who will be elected from it. As a result, control over the redistricting process can give one party a tremendous advantage in helping its candidates get elected.[18] Some critics argue that gerrymandered districts (i.e., districts drawn to benefit one party or group) allow elected officials to choose their voters rather than voters choosing their representatives.

Different states have different rules for the drawing of district lines. In Michigan, state legislative and congressional districts are drawn through the legislative process and signed into law by the governor. It was not always so. The 1963 Michigan Constitution (Article IV, Section 6) created a bipartisan apportionment commission to draw district lines. The state was divided into four geographic regions, and each political party earning 25 percent of the vote for governor in the preceding election appointed a commission member from each region. The commission proved to be unworkable. Because it was unable to reach a consensus, the responsibility for drawing state legislative districts ended up in the hands of the state Supreme Court three straight times (1968, 1972, and 1982). In 1982, the Court ruled that the composition of the apportionment commission violated the principle that population rather than geography should determine representation.[19] Since the 1990 census, the Legislature has drawn district lines.

Republicans controlled the House, Senate, and governorship in Michigan following the 2010 elections, which gave them unfettered control over the redistricting process. How successful were the redistricting efforts of Michigan Republicans? Their party controlled nine U.S. House seats prior to redistricting, and they maintained those seats after the new lines were drawn. The state lost one seat due to a decline in population since the previous census, and that loss was absorbed by the Democrats.[20] The true mark of Republican success in redistricting, however, is how they managed to hold the majority of the House delegation. In both the 2012 and 2014 elections, Democratic candidates for the U.S. House of Representatives together received a slight majority of the popular vote, but Republicans won nine of the fourteen seats. The average percentage of the vote for Democratic winners in the two elections was about 70 percent, while the average Republican victor received less than 60 percent of the vote. In 2016, Republican congressional candidates managed to win more votes than Democrats, but only by a very small margin (50.6 percent of all votes in these contests compared to 49.4 percent). The margins of victory in all districts were similar to those in 2012 and 2014 with GOP winners garnering roughly 60 percent of the vote with Democratic winners getting over 70 percent of the vote. These patterns demonstrate that GOP lawmakers in the state Legislature effectively packed Democratic voters into a relatively small number of districts while maximizing the number of seats likely to be won by Republicans.

Term Limits

Between 1990 and 2000, voters in 21 states enacted some form of term limits on state legislators.[21] In 1992, Michigan voters waded into the hotly debated topic of term limits with an amendment to the state Constitution that limited state representatives in Michigan to three two-year terms and state senators to two four-year terms. In addition, the governor, lieutenant governor, attorney general, and secretary of state were limited to two four-year terms. The amendment received support from 58.9 percent of voters that year.

The 1992 amendment adopted in Michigan also limited the number of terms that could be served by members of Congress. The terms of members of the U.S. House of Representatives were capped at three during any 12-year period, and U.S. Senators were limited to two six-year terms for any 24-year period. This section of the amendment was invalidated, however, when the U.S. Supreme Court overturned a similar law in Arkansas.[22] The Court's majority ruled that the U.S. Constitution set the qualifications for members of Congress and states did not have the authority to add to them. The Michigan constitutional amendment anticipated this outcome by asking members to voluntarily limit their terms of service to honor the wishes of voters. To date, only Republican congressman Dan Benishek voluntarily limited his terms in the U.S. House when he declined to run after serving a third term that ended in 2017. However, this decision came only after he seemingly reneged on his initial pledge to serve only three terms by announcing in March 2015 that he would seek reelection.[23] Later in 2015 he reversed course and decided not to run for a fourth term.[24]

The combination of term limits and heavily partisan (i.e., gerrymandered) districts creates an interesting dynamic in congressional and state legislative elections. First, it means that the most meaningful contest often is the party primary rather than the general election. Except under extraordinary circumstances, the general election becomes a foregone conclusion. Second, elections for the state House and state Senate frequently draw large fields of experienced candidates, especially when no incumbent is running, because state legislators are unable to retain their seats beyond the limits set in the state Constitution.

Voters in Michigan Elections

The state government sets the rules governing elections, but the aggregated decisions of Michigan voters determine who wins and who loses and, ultimately, who controls the direction of public policy. Voters in elections make two sets of decisions: first, whether to vote, and second, for which candidates they will vote.

Turnout in Michigan

In an electorally competitive state like Michigan, who votes—and who does not—goes a long way toward determining which candidates win and which lose. Political scientists have identified the types of people most likely to vote in a given election. Those with higher levels of education and income, with strong connections to their communities, and who feel a strong sense of duty or obligation to vote are more likely to cast a ballot. Older people are also more likely to vote than younger people. In addition, those who think of themselves as belonging to a political party or who may be mobilized by a labor union or a religious organization are more likely to vote. People also are more likely to vote when the election is close or when they become interested in a campaign.[25]

State laws can also influence the likelihood that individuals will vote by raising or lowering the barriers to participation. For example, there are differences in voter registration laws across states. In Michigan, citizens can register with the secretary of state's office when they obtain their driver's license or by sending a form to their city or county clerk. A person must be registered 30 days before an election in order to participate (a few states allow same-day registration). Those individuals serving sentences in prison cannot vote, but their voting rights are restored once their sentences are complete. A number of states, including Michigan, require voters to show some type of state-issued photo identification at the polls; voters in Michi-

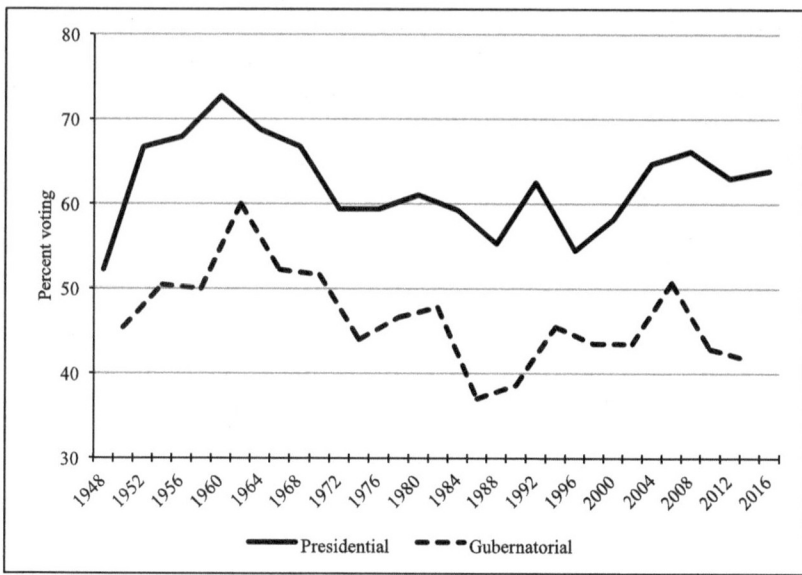

Fig. 10.1. Voter Turnout in Michigan, 1948–2016
Source: Years 1948–2014 are taken from the Michigan Secretary of State's Office, accessed November 18, 2016, http://www.michigan.gov/documents/sos/voter_stats_490816_7.pdf; 2016 data are from reports at the Secretary of State's Office, http://miboecfr.nictusa.com/election/results/2016GEN_CENR.html and http://www.michigan.gov/documents/sos/2016_RegVoterCount_511666_7.pdf

gan are able to vote if they are willing to sign an affidavit stating they do not have a state-issued identification. Some states have voting provisions that allow any voter to cast a ballot prior to Election Day, including early voting (which opens limited polling locations days or weeks ahead of Election Day) and so-called no-excuse absentee ballots (which allow anyone who wishes to vote absentee to do so).[26] Michigan, however, does not offer early voting or no-excuse absentee voting and voters must meet certain requirements or expect to be out of town in order to cast an absentee ballot prior to the election.[27]

Voter turnout varies across types of elections. Participation in general elections is typically higher than in primaries. Figure 10.1 displays the raw number of voters who participated in general elections during presidential and midterm election years (when gubernatorial elections take place in Michigan) from 1948 to 2016. Two trends are evident. First, turnout has been variable over time. After high points in the early 1960s, turnout declined in both presidential and gubernatorial years until 1986 at the gubernatorial level and 1996 at the presidential level (except 1992). Then, presidential turnout increased through 2008, dipped in 2012, and went up slightly in 2016. In governor's races, turnout went up after 1986 until 1994, when a small decline began (except 2006). Second, turnout in presidential election years is higher than in gubernatorial elections, and the difference seems to have grown larger over time.

Local Voter Turnout in Michigan

Academic research on voter turnout has tended to find fairly low turnout rates for local elections. Previous research on local turnout has found average local turnout rates of 34 percent[28] and 27 percent for mayoral elections.[29] Thomas Holbrook and Aaron Weinschenk estimated that typical mayoral election turnout was only 25.8 percent when over 300 mayoral elections across 144 cities were examined.[30] As Hajnal and Lewis have noted, "Nowhere is the turnout problem worse than at the local level."[31]

A similar result is found when examining local voter turnout in Michigan. For elections in which the mayor's office is on the ballot, the percentage of registered voters who cast a ballot in selected Michigan cities ranges from the teens to the mid-20s. In Warren (Michigan's third largest city, located in Macomb County north of Detroit), turnout was 15.1 percent in 2015. In August 2015, the winner of the mayoral primary in Grand Rapids received more than 50 percent of the vote (and thus avoided a runoff election in November), based on a turnout of 15.8 percent. In Detroit's 2013 mayoral election won by Mike Duggan, voter turnout was 25.4 percent of registered voters.

County clerks report turnout rates for all communities in their entire county, and some recent turnout results showed even lower rates. For example, Washtenaw County (which includes Ann Arbor) saw a 12.3 percent turnout rate in 2015, while Marquette County (Marquette) in the Upper Peninsula had only an 11.1 percent turnout rate in 2015.[32] In Oakland County, countywide voter turnout was 21.1 percent in 2015, with local-level turnout as high as 50.1 percent in Brandon Township, 49.6 percent in Huntington Woods, 27.4 percent in Farmington, and 27.3 percent in Clarkston, while the lowest turnout rates were found in Lyon Township (4.8 percent), Royal Oak Township (5.4 percent), and Hazel Park (9.9 percent).[33] Michigan's experience with voter turnout appears to be typical of that in other states, where turnout is highest in presidential elections, with drop-offs in midterm election years (i.e., the elections that take place halfway through a presidential term), and even lower turnout for local elections in odd years.

Michigan's Electoral History

Michigan lays claim to the founding of the Republican Party, which held its first convention in Jackson in 1854.[34] Republicans dominated the state's politics for almost 100 years starting in the 1850s. Democrats made some gains during the New Deal realignment of the 1930s,[35] but the two parties were not truly competitive on a statewide level until the 1950s.[36] Since the election of Democrat G. Mennen Williams in 1948, four Democrats and four Republicans have held the state's governorship with only one holding office for just a single term. Democratic presidential candidates carried the state in each election between 1992 and 2012, but Republicans won Michigan's electoral votes in eight of the prior 11 elections dating back to 1948. In 2016, Donald Trump returned Michigan to the Republican column by fewer than 11,000 votes (out of more than 4.7 million cast), one of the narrowest margins of any state that year and in Michigan's history.

This pattern of competitiveness suggests that candidates from both parties have the opportunity to win any given statewide election. A closer look at the returns suggests that some Michigan voters may be reacting negatively to the party controlling the White House. Under the current Michigan Constitution, governors are elected to four-year terms during presidential midterm elections. The gubernatorial candidate from the president's party has an uphill battle to win the governorship. Michigan's governor was of the same party as the president for just 24 of the 70 years between when Williams was elected governor in 1948 and the end of Rick Snyder's term in 2018. The pattern is even stronger in more recent years. The governor and president have shared a party label only eight of 30 years between Governor James Blanchard's first term and Governor Snyder's second term. Democratic governors Blanchard and Granholm were elected while a Republican was president, and Republican Rick Snyder was elected (and reelected) while Democrat Barack Obama was president. Only Republican John Engler in 1990 was first elected while a fellow Republican was in the White House during this time period.

Although the state as a whole has been competitive, individual elections may not be. Michigan often—but not always—supports the winning candidates in presidential elections. As noted, in elections for governor, voters are likely to vote for candidates who are not from the president's party. As a consequence, there can be a great deal of volatility over short time periods. Figure 10.2 shows the Republican percentage of the two-party vote (i.e., minor parties excluded) in presidential and gubernatorial elections between 1948 and 2016. The divergence between the lines demonstrates the volatility

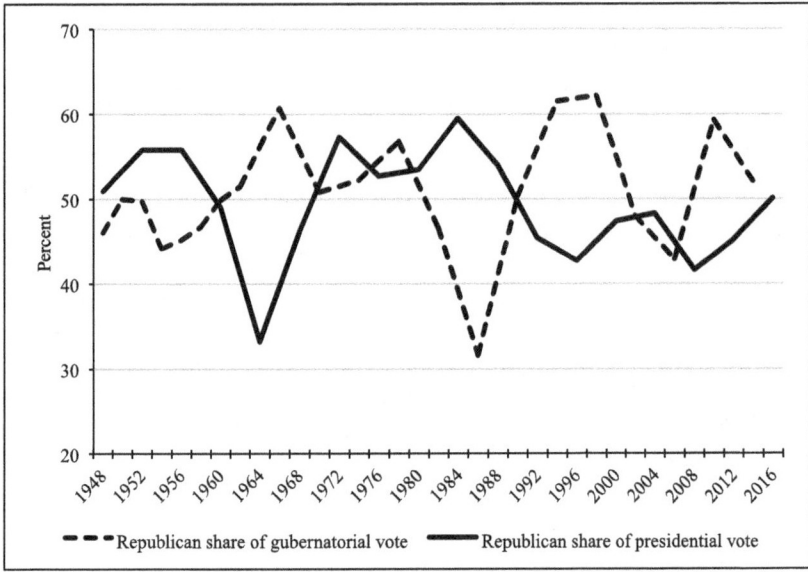

Fig. 10.2. Republican Share of the Two-Party Vote for President and Governor, 1948–2016
Source: Gubernatorial-year data are taken from the Michigan Legislature, "Michigan Manual 2015–2016," accessed November 19, 2016, http://www.legislature.mi.gov/(S(uz5rpp1s2pocpcqpdrxj3z34))/documents/2015-2016/michiganmanual/2015-MM-P0540-p0544.pdf; presidential-year data are taken from the "Atlas of U.S. Presidential Elections," Dave Leip, accessed November 19, 2016, http://uselectionatlas.org
Note: Percentages are of the two-party vote; minor party votes are excluded.

in election outcomes. The low point for Republicans was Democratic governor Blanchard's reelection landslide over William Lucas in 1986. Blanchard's victory came only two years after Republican president Ronald Reagan's large reelection victory over Walter Mondale (in Michigan and nationally) in 1984. Similarly, Democratic incumbent Lyndon Johnson's landside in the 1964 presidential election was followed two years later with a large reelection win for Republican governor George Romney.

These patterns suggest two possible conclusions. First, it appears that Michigan voters tend to support incumbents running for reelection. During this time period, only three governors lost reelection bids— Kim Sigler in 1948, John Swainson in 1962, and James Blanchard in 1990. Second, it appears that Michigan voters like to split their tickets in elections and across elections once presidential and gubernatorial elections were staggered.[37] As Peter Kobrak noted several decades ago, "Ticket-splitting is increasingly common, and when voters find appealing incumbents, they stick with them regardless of party affiliation."[38] A closer inspection of recent elections shows that the apparent volatility is largely limited to one important segment of the state's electorate, voters who do not identify with either the Republicans or the Democrats.

The 2012 Presidential Election in Michigan

Although Democratic presidential candidates had won Michigan's Electoral College votes in each election since 1992, Republicans sensed an opportunity for success in 2012. For one thing, Michigan had elected a Republican governor in 2010, and their party had secured large majorities in both chambers of the state Legislature. Their success stemmed in large measure from opposition to President Obama's policies, particularly his signature legislative achievement in health care reform, the Affordable Care Act (commonly known as Obamacare). Moreover, many GOP strategists doubted that Obama could replicate his success in turning out young and minority voters at the levels he did when he was first elected president in 2008.

The likelihood of a Republican win in Michigan was enhanced when the GOP selected former Massachusetts governor Mitt Romney as its presidential nominee. Romney was born in Michigan, where his father served as governor from 1963 to 1969. Members of his family had remained active in Michigan politics, although their electoral success was limited.[39] Romney's moderate, probusiness philosophy seemed to match well with that of fellow Republican governor Rick Snyder.

Unfortunately for Republicans, Romney never seemed to click with Michigan voters. For one thing, many voters had no recollection of his father's service as governor. Some of those Republicans who did remember had few fond memories of a moderate governor whose views no longer fit in a party that seemed to become more conservative over time. Moreover, Romney seemed out of touch with the state's voters. During the run-up to the 2012 presidential primary, his puzzling statement that Michigan's "trees are the right height" was followed with the proud admission that he and his wife owned a Ford Mustang, a Chevy truck, and two Cadillacs. Instead of demonstrating his support for American-made cars, the comment focused voters' attention on the enormity of his personal wealth.[40]

An opinion column Romney wrote for the *New York Times* in 2008 became an issue in both the primary and general election campaigns. Although it gave a fairly sophisticated argument about restructuring the auto industry, its headline—"Let Detroit Go Bankrupt"—made for an easy target in a state still heavily dependent on automobile manufacturing.[41] The bailout of the auto industry began in the waning days of the George W. Bush administration and continued under President Obama. The Obama campaign used the issue to contrast the Democratic Party's support for working people with Romney's seeming indifference to the plight of the manufacturing sector. Exit polls indicated that more than 60 percent of Michigan voters favored the federal government's bailout of the auto industry, and 76 percent of those voters chose Obama.[42]

The Romney campaign regularly listed Michigan as a state they were contesting, but relatively few resources were allocated to Michigan by either campaign.[43] Obama won the state with 54 percent of the vote, slightly down from the 57 percent he won in 2008.

The 2016 Presidential Election in Michigan

In many ways, the 2016 presidential election in Michigan paralleled the election of 2012. The state was again considered a battleground early on, but it was largely ignored for most of the campaign. In addition, the Democratic candidate seemed to be in control—until the very last days of the campaign, that is. When the votes were counted, Republican Donald Trump defeated Democrat Hillary Clinton by an incredibly slim margin. The Michigan result was repeated in several states that Obama carried in 2012, including Florida, Wisconsin, and Pennsylvania by narrow margins, and Ohio and Iowa more comfortably. Although Clinton won a victory in the national popular vote, Trump won the Electoral College vote and thus the presidency, with Michigan being a big boost to Trump's path to a large majority of electoral votes.

Trump's success and Clinton's struggles were foreshadowed in Michigan's presidential primaries eight months earlier. The large field of Republican candidates had essentially been winnowed down to four: Trump, Ohio governor John Kasich, and Senators Ted Cruz of Texas and Marco Rubio of Florida. A political novice, Trump had capitalized on his celebrity status to emerge as the frontrunner. He bucked Republican orthodoxy on free trade (he was against it) and abortion (he was not clearly against it, although his position fluctuated). His opponents, meanwhile, were battling to win the votes of more "establishment" Republicans. Trump won Michigan's primary with 36.6 percent of the vote, followed by Cruz and Kasich (24.7 and 24.3 percent, respectively). Cruz ran strongest in the Grand Rapids area, which is commonly thought of as a more conservative part of the state and includes large numbers of evangelical Christians. Kasich won Kalamazoo and Washtenaw Counties—both areas that have more moderate Republicans. Trump was successful almost everywhere else. Even so, more than six out of 10 Republican voters cast their ballots for someone other than Trump. Importantly, Trump showed strength in places like Macomb and Saginaw Counties, winning with some of his biggest margins in both areas. Voters in these counties, and others like them, responded to Trump's populist message on issues like trade, as Trump campaigned on issues including the North American Free Trade Agreement (NAFTA) that many in Michigan saw as the cause of the decline in the auto industry. This success would foreshadow similar success in the general election several months later.

While Trump was successful in his party's primary, Hillary Clinton's narrow loss to Vermont senator Bernie Sanders shocked most political observers. Clinton emerged as the Democratic frontrunner, while Sanders campaigned as the underdog. Like Trump, Sanders gained traction in Michigan with his opposition to free trade, in particular the Trans-Pacific Partnership (TPP) negotiated by the Obama Administration. Clinton won Wayne County (which includes Detroit) by a large margin, but it was not enough to carry the state; she lost by a margin of 49.7 percent to 48.3 percent. These results, again, foreshadowed results to come.

Publicly available opinion polls taken throughout the campaign showed Clinton with a small but consistent lead through much of the general election period. In 39 polls taken between June 2015 and November 2016, she led in all but three (two ties and one Trump lead).[44] The margins were mostly small, though, and they fluctuated with national trends. Clinton seemed to pull away following the first presidential debate, while Trump appeared to be closing the gap as the election neared.

The campaign dynamic changed in the final days before the election. After largely ignoring the state, both candidates sent surrogates to campaign in Michigan (including their children and vice-presidential running mates). Trump held rallies in Sterling Heights (which is in Macomb County) two days before the election and in Grand Rapids on the night before the polls opened. Meanwhile, Clinton held her own Grand Rapids rally a few hours before Trump's, and both her husband, former president Bill Clinton, and President Obama made appearances to energize her supporters. The sudden shift in attention to Michigan reflected a race that was closer than many observers realized. In the end, exit polls revealed that 13 percent of Michigan voters made their choice in the last week of the campaign. Trump won that group by a margin of 50 percent to 39 percent.

Comparing the 2012 and 2016 Elections and Party Coalitions

The election outcomes in 2012 and 2016—and in previous Michigan elections—seem to suggest that many Michigan voters must have voted for both Barack Obama and Donald Trump. Indeed, 12 counties where a majority of voters voted for Obama in 2012 saw majorities vote for Trump in 2016—Macomb, Saginaw, Bay, Eaton, Gogebic, Isabella, Lake, Manistee, Monroe, Shiawassee, and Van Buren. The vote totals, however, do not tell us which, nor do they give much indication of why, voters switched from a Democratic presidential candidate in 2012 to a Republican presidential candidate in 2016.

The exit polls from 2012 and 2016 can be used to compare voting patterns within the electorate, and provide some clues for Trump's victory.[45] For example, political scientists have long understood that one's connection to a political party (known as party identification) can be an important determinant of vote choice,[46] and it seems to be important in these elections. Overall, about 40 percent of Michigan voters identified as Democrats compared to 30 percent each for Republicans and independents. In both 2012 and 2016, party identifiers overwhelmingly voted for the candidate of their party. Nearly all voters in 2012 selected their party's nominee, with Obama receiving 95 percent of the votes of Democrats and Romney getting 96 percent of the votes of Republicans. The 2016 nominees did only slightly less well, with both Trump and Clinton receiving nine out of 10 votes cast by members of their parties. The stable choices of partisan voters stand in sharp contrast to independents. Obama and Romney split the votes of independents fairly evenly. In 2016, however, Trump won these voters by a 52 to 36 percent margin with an additional 10 percent of the vote going to minor party candidates. How significant was this difference? Had Clinton done as well as Obama in this group, she would have won the state and its Electoral College votes. In Michigan, a state with similarly sized blocs of Republicans and Democrats, the key for candidates is to hold their party's base and win independent voters.

Partisanship is not the only way to look at the differences across elections. Table 10.1 shows the percentage of the vote for Romney and Trump, the two Republican candidates, broken down by various categories of the electorate. Both candidates did better with male voters than with female voters. The gender gap was larger for Trump, however, as he ran better among men than Romney. Although it is interesting that Trump earned the same percentage of the vote among Michigan women as his fellow

Republican four years earlier, especially given some of the criticisms levied against Trump during (and after) the campaign. Both Republicans won a majority of the white vote, but neither found much support among African American voters. They tended to do better with higher income voters than with those making less. These patterns reflect consistent differences across parties in Michigan and across the United States.

In addition to a larger gender gap, there are some other differences worth noting across the two elections. Trump won the support of a higher percentage of voters from union households due to his rhetoric in support of protectionist trade policies and rebuilding the manufacturing sector. Similarly, Romney did better among those voters with college degrees compared to those who did not graduate from college, while the opposite was true for Trump. Trump's success in counties with lower proportions of college graduates has been noted in Michigan and nationally.[47] Moreover, Trump won twice as many voters who called themselves liberal in exit polls; these are likely voters who voted for Sanders in the Democratic primary but found themselves closer to Trump in the general election, again due to his criticism of free trade agreements like NAFTA and TPP.

Differences in turnout affected the 2016 vote outcome, too. The afore-

TABLE 10.1. Voter Characteristics and Support for Republican Presidential Candidates in Michigan, 2012 and 2016

Characteristic		Percent voting for Romney in 2012	Percent voting for Trump in 2016
Gender	Male	48	53
	Female	42	42
Race	White	55	57
	Black	5	6
Union household	Yes	33	40
	No	49	47
College Graduate	Yes	48	44
	No	43	49
Income	Less than $50k	36	42
	$50k or more	51	51
Size of Place	Urban	19	24
	Suburban	50	53
	Rural	53	56
Ideology	Liberal	7	14
	Moderate	39	42
	Conservative	83	79

Source: Exit polls reported by CNN in 2012 and 2016, http://www.cnn.com/election/2012/results/state/MI/president/, http://edition.cnn.com/election/results/exit-polls/michigan/president

mentioned change in partisan support among those who did not graduate from college was magnified by an increase in turnout among this demographic group. Voters without a college degree comprised 54 percent of the electorate in 2012 but increased to 58 percent in 2016. Turnout among rural voters increased from 19 percent to 27 percent, according to the exit polls. Romney defeated Obama by about 7 percentage points in this group, while Trump trounced Clinton by 20 points four years later.

Taken together, these differences demonstrate the point that Trump won votes from those who may have experienced a loss of economic opportunities in Michigan's changing economy. At an earlier time, plentiful manufacturing jobs created opportunities for upward mobility without having gone to college. Many of those jobs no longer exist, either due to outsourcing or to advances in technology and automation that made them obsolete. The newer jobs in the manufacturing sector are more likely to involve expertise in computer science, robotics, and engineering. Similarly, many rural areas have seen similar declines in jobs related to agriculture. Trump's pledge to "Make America Great Again" resonated with many voters who felt left behind by changes outside their control.

A high-profile target of Trump's message was Macomb County. Located on the northern edge of the Detroit metropolitan area, Macomb was home to the "Reagan Democrats" of the 1980s. These working-class whites defected from their party home to support the Republican presidential candidate. Candidates who could capture this demographic group in Michigan were likely to be successful on a national scale, making Macomb County something of a bellwether for national politics. Barack Obama won the county by almost 9 percent in 2008 and about 4 percent in 2012. In 2016, Donald Trump carried the county by more than 11 percent. In an election decided by less than 11,000 votes, Trump's 48,348-vote margin in Macomb County helped provide the cushion he needed to win the state.

Conclusion

Elections allow citizens to influence the direction of public policy; therefore, they help drive responses to challenges faced by the state. Michigan is a state with sharp divisions between the policy preferences of Democratic and Republican elected officials, so control of government matters for the kinds of policies that are enacted. In the general public, the size of the Democratic, Republican, and independent voting blocs are fairly similar. Because partisan voters usually support their party's candidates, control over election outcomes is determined by which candidates are best at turning out their fellow partisans and wooing voters who are not aligned with either party. These patterns result in a competitive and sometimes unpredictable state electorate.

In this context, aggregate voter preferences and election results in Michigan are almost always changing. Short-term stability can mask volatility over a longer time horizon. Elections are fundamental in a democratic system and their impact on Michigan's politics and government is difficult to overstate.

WEB RESOURCES

The *Michigan Secretary of State's* office (www.mich.gov/sos) offers a wealth of public information on voting and elections including data on voter turnout across the state, campaign finance, listings of candidates running for office, and others.

The *Michigan Campaign Finance Network* (www.mcfn.org) is a nonpartisan organization that tracks money in politics. It offers data, research, and reports on all types of money in Michigan politics.

Local county clerk's offices (a simple web search of a county name and "clerk" will produce specific offices) provide election administration information for local governments as well as voter turnout information for the county and its localities.

The *National Conference of State Legislatures* (www.ncsl.org) provides a great deal of information on election reforms in states across the United States.

NOTES

1. The United States and the states within it all are examples of indirect democracies. Some states, such as Michigan, also have provisions that allow something more akin to direct democracy where citizens vote directly on public policy issues (see chapter 11).

2. National Conference of State Legislatures, "Recall of State Officials," September 11, 2013; accessed February 2, 2016; http://www.ncsl.org/research/elections-and-campaigns/recall-of-state-officials.aspx

3. David Eggert, "Morouns Spend Record $31 Million Backing Anti-Detroit Bridge Proposal 6," October 26, 2012; accessed February 2, 2016; http://www.mlive.com/politics/index.ssf/2012/10/morouns_spend_31_million_alone.html

4. Michigan Municipal League, "Term Limits," accessed March 17, 2016; http://www.mml.org/resources/sample_docs/qa/faq_term_limits.htm

5. Bill Laitner, "Bryan Barnett Wins Third Term as Rochester Hills Mayor," *Detroit Free Press*, November 6, 2016; accessed November 25, 2016; http://www.freep.com/story/news/local/michigan/oakland/2015/11/06/bryan-barnett-elected-rochester-hills-mayor/75292266/

6. Arthur C. Millspaugh, "The Operation of the Direct Primary in Michigan," *American Political Science Review* 10, no. 4 (1916): 710–26.

7. Chad Livengood, "Lt. Gov. Brian Calley Gets Nomination over Nakagiri," *Detroit News*, August 23, 2014; accessed March 17, 2016, http://www.detroitnews.com/story/news/politics/michigan/2014/08/23/michigans-gop-state-convention-gets-underway/14489865/

8. Peter Kobrak, "Michigan," in *The Political Life of the American States*, ed. Alan Rosenthal and Maureen Moakley (New York: Praeger, 1984).

9. In contrast, more than one million voters participated in the Republican primary. Vice President Al Gore won the Democratic caucuses a few weeks later.

10. Barbara Norrander, *The Imperfect Primary: Oddities, Biases, and Strengths of U.S. Presidential Nomination Politics* (New York: Routledge, 2010), 77–78.

11. State of Michigan, Secretary of State, "Michigan Presidential Primary Facts and Statistics," November 2015; accessed February 2, 2016, http://www.michigan.gov/documents/MichPresPrimRefGuide_20863_7.pdf

12. State of Michigan, Secretary of State, "Contribution Limits for State Level Office," January 2016; accessed February 14, 2016, http://mertsplus.com/mertsuserguide/index.php?n=MANUALS.StateLevelOffices

13. Michigan Campaign Finance Network, "A Citizen's Guide to Michigan Campaign Finance 2014," October 2015; accessed February 14, 2016, http://www.mcfn.org/uploads/documents/MCFN_2014_Cit_Guide_Final.pdf

14. Michigan Campaign Finance Network, "A Citizen's Guide to Michigan Campaign Finance 2014."

15. State of Michigan, Secretary of State, "Quick Facts: Michigan's Public Funding Program—Gubernatorial Candidates Only," April 2009; accessed February 14, 2016, http://www.michigan.gov/documents/sos/Quick_Facts_Revised_04012009_with_MCL_references_274421_7.pdf

16. Michigan Campaign Finance Network, "2006 Citizen's Guide to Michigan Campaign Finance," June 2007; accessed February 14, 2016, http://www.mcfn.org/uploads/documents/MCFN_2014_Cit_Guide_Final.pdf. For one journalist's take on the race, see Tim Skubick, *See Dick and Jen Run* (Ann Arbor: University of Michigan Press, 2006).

17. Charles S. Bullock III, *Redistricting: The Most Political Activity in America* (Lanham, MD: Rowman and Littlefield, 2010).

18. Roger H. Davidson, Walter J. Oleszek, Frances E. Lee, and Eric Schickler, *Congress and Its Members, 15th Edition* (Los Angeles: CQ Press, 2016), 45–56.

19. The court relied on *Reynolds v Sims*, 377 US 533 (1964), in which the U.S. Supreme Court ruled that state legislative districts had to be drawn according to population. See William P. Browne and Kenneth Verburg, *Michigan Politics and Government: Facing Change in a Complex State* (Lincoln: University of Nebraska Press, 1995), 125–27, 177–78.

20. Michael K. Romano, Todd A. Curry, and John A. Clark, "Michigan: Republican Domination during a Population Exodus," in *The Political Battle over Congressional Redistricting*, ed. William J. Miller and Jeremy D. Walling (Lanham, MD: Lexington, 2013).

21. Term limit provisions have been revoked in six states, four via court decisions and two through legislative action. See National Council of State Legisla-

tures, "Term Limits," accessed March 1, 2016, http://www.ncsl.org/research/about-state-legislatures/term-limits.aspx

22. *U.S. Term Limits, Inc. v. Thornton*, 514 U.S. 779 (1995).

23. Todd Spangler, "Despite Term-Limit Pledge, Benishek to Seek Re-election," *Detroit Free Press*, March 24, 2015; accessed March 17, 2016, http://www.freep.com/story/news/local/michigan/2015/03/24/benishek-running/70389148/

24. Emily Lawler, "U.S. Rep. Dan Benishek Will Not Run Again, Leaving Competitive Congressional Seat Open in Northern Michigan," *MLive.com*, September 25, 2015; accessed March 17, 2016, http://www.mlive.com/lansing-news/index.ssf/2015/09/us_rep_dan_benishek_will_not_r.html

25. Jan E. Leighley and Jonathan Nagler, *Who Votes Now? Demographics, Issues, Inequality, and Turnout in the United States* (Princeton: Princeton University Press, 2013).

26. Roger Larocca and John S. Klemanski, "U.S. State Election Reform and Turnout in Presidential Elections," *State Politics and Policy Quarterly* 11, no. 1 (2011): 76–101

27. State of Michigan, Secretary of State, "Information for Voters," accessed February 28, 2016, http://www.michigan.gov/sos/0,4670,7-127-1633_8716---,00.html

28. Curtis Wood, "Voter Turnout in City Elections," *Urban Affairs Review* 38 (2002): 209–31.

29. Neal Caren, "Big City, Big Turnout? Electoral Participation in American Cities," *Journal of Urban Affairs* 1 (2007): 31–46.

30. Thomas M. Holbrook and Aaron C. Weinschenk, "Campaigns, Mobilization, and Turnout in Mayoral Elections," *Political Research Quarterly* 67, no. 1 (2013): 46.

31. Zoltan Hajnal and Paul Lewis, "Municipal Institutions and Voter Turnout in Local Elections," *Urban Affairs Review* 38 (2003): 645.

32. State of Michigan, Secretary of State, "Candidate Listings and Election Results–Local," accessed March 16, 2016, http://www.michigan.gov/sos/0,1607,7-127-1633_8722-103241---,00.html

33. Oakland County Clerk, "Oakland County, Michigan Official Results, Voter Turnout Report, November 3, 2015 General Election," accessed March 16, 2106, https://www.oakgov.com/clerkrod/elections/Documents/voter_turnout_11032015.pdf

34. William E. Gienapp, *The Origins of the Republican Party, 1852–1856* (New York: Oxford University Press, 1987), 104–6.

35. James K. Pollock and Samuel J. Eldersveld, *Michigan Politics in Transition: An Areal Study of Voting Trends in the Last Decade* (Ann Arbor: University of Michigan Press, 1942).

36. Browne and Verburg, *Michigan Politics and Government*.

37. Prior to 1966, governors were elected to two-year terms. Starting in 1966, the terms were extended to four years and elections held only in midterm years.

38. Kobrak, "Michigan," 105.

39. Mitt Romney's brother, G. Scott Romney, was a candidate for the Republican nomination for attorney general in 1998 and served on the Michigan State University Board of Trustees. Scott's first wife, Ronna, was a member of the Republican National Committee and twice ran for the U.S. Senate. Their daughter

Ronna Romney McDaniel was a member of the Republican National Committee and was elected chair of the Michigan Republican Party in 2015.

40. Charles M. Blow, "Mitt, Michigan and a Couple of Cadillacs," *New York Times*, February 24, 2012; accessed February 16, 2016, http://www.nytimes.com/2012/02/25/opinion/blow-mitt-romney-michigan-and-a-couple-of-cadillacs.html

41. Mitt Romney, "Let Detroit Go Bankrupt," *New York Times*, November 18, 2008; accessed February 16, 2016, http://www.nytimes.com/2008/11/19/opinion/19romney.html

42. CNN Election Center, "President: Michigan," accessed February 16, 2016, http://www.cnn.com/election/2012/results/state/MI/president/

43. David Eggert, "Election Results 2012: Obama Wins Michigan over Romney, Grabs 16 Electoral Votes," November 7, 2012; accessed February 16, 2016, http://www.mlive.com/politics/index.ssf/2012/11/election_results_2012_obama_wi.html

44. The polls are aggregated at http://elections.huffingtonpost.com/pollster/2016-michigan-president-trump-vs-clinton

45. Exit polls gather information from voters as they leave polling places or after they vote early or absentee. Though not perfect, they provide an important window into the minds of voters on Election Day. The exit polls used here were sponsored by a consortium of news organizations. They were reported by CNN at http://www.cnn.com/election/2012/results/state/MI/president/ for 2012 and http://edition.cnn.com/election/results/exit-polls/michigan/president for 2016.

46. Angus Campbell, Philip E. Converse, Warren E. Miller, and Donald E. Stokes, *The American Voter* (New York: John Wiley, 1960).

47. In Michigan, the pattern was identified by Michigan State political scientist Corwin Smidt two days after the election. For evidence at the national level, see Nate Silver, "Education, Not Income, Predicted Who Would Vote for Trump," *FiveThirtyEight*, November 22, 2016; accessed November 23, 2016, http://fivethirtyeight.com/features/education-not-income-predicted-who-would-vote-for-trump/

11 ✦ Ballot Proposals in Michigan

JOHN S. KLEMANSKI AND DAVID A. DULIO

Some argue that direct democracy—when citizens have an unfiltered say in making decisions that affect government policy—is the purest form of democracy. However, a state's direct democracy provisions often operate alongside the procedures and policy-making rules of representative democracy, combining to form what has been called a "hybrid" democracy.[1] In this chapter, we examine the major types of ballot proposals that comprise the direct democracy provisions possible in the state of Michigan. As part of that examination, we also note the way in which some Michigan ballot proposals require or can involve legislative action, which illustrates the hybrid nature of what is popularly considered direct democracy. Michigan is one of only 15 states that provides for all existing forms of direct democracy—initiatives, referendums, and recall elections.[2] The state of Michigan has some history of local and school board recall elections (where voters may remove a sitting elected official; see chapter 10), but the discussion here will focus on initiatives, referendums, and constitutional amendments.

Michigan is one of 24 states that allow state ballot proposals that are decided on by voters to help shape their policy making. How direct democracy works in Michigan is examined by outlining the different types of state ballot proposals that are used in Michigan. A brief history of the practice in Michigan is then offered, including how proposals qualify for the ballot. A discussion of how proposals have been used in recent years follows, especially with respect to important—and sometimes controversial—measures. The role of campaign spending in selected ballot proposal elections is also examined. Finally, selected ballot proposals that have had implications for state-local government relations are explored.

For purposes of this discussion, the various ballot proposals are divided into three categories—statutory initiatives, referendums, and constitutional amendments. Each has a somewhat different path to reach the ballot. First, there are *statutory initiatives*—these include any citizen-initiated proposals seeking to place a question on the ballot for the purposes of enacting a new state statute or amending a current statute.[3] Between 1963 and 2016, there were 13 statutory initiatives that qualified for the ballot, with seven approved by voters and six rejected (see table 11.1).

Second, *referendums* in Michigan can take two different forms, but both give voters input into the public-policy-making process—in keeping with the principles of direct democracy. The Michigan Constitution (Article IV, Section 34) provides for legislative referendums, which are laws passed by the Legislature but allow voters to make the final decision on whether or not a bill becomes a law. Between 1963 and 2016, 14 legislative referendums were sent by the Legislature for voter approval, with voters approving 10 proposals and rejecting four.

Michigan's Constitution also provides for the option of a voter referendum (called a "veto referendum" in some states), which grants powers to Michigan voters to "approve and reject laws enacted by the legislature" and placed on the ballot through a petition process (Article II, Section 9). With this type of referendum, citizens must collect enough petition signatures for a referendum question to be placed on the ballot. The threshold for petition signatures for a voter referendum is 5 percent of the total votes cast in the last governor's race. Between 1963 and 2016, 10 voter referendums were placed on the ballot through petition, with voters approving one referendum and rejecting nine.

TABLE 11.1. Michigan Initiatives, Referendums, and Constitutional Amendments, 1963–2015

Proposal Type (% of all proposals)	Total Number on Ballot	Number Approved	Percent Approved
Statutory Initiatives (11.6%)	13	7	54%
Referendums (21.4%)			
Legislative	14	10	71%
Voter (via petition)	10	1	10%
Constitutional Amendments (67%)			
Legislative	44	22	50%
Citizen-initiated (via petition)	31	10	32%
Total (100%)	112	50	45%

Source: "Initiatives and Referendums under the Constitution of the State of Michigan of 1963," March 2015, accessed May 15, 2015, https://www.michigan.gov/documents/sos/Initia_Ref_Under_ Consti_12-08_339399_7.pdf; proposal 15-1 was not included in this report, it was added by the authors to the total calculations.

Third, a proposal for a *constitutional amendment* may be placed on the ballot. Proposed amendments can reach the ballot in two different ways. One, the state Legislature may place a proposed amendment on the ballot (as occurred in May 2015, with the "roads and sales tax" proposal). Two, a proposed amendment may be placed on the ballot if supporters obtain enough valid petition signatures. The Michigan Constitution (Article XII, Section 2) requires that the number of petition signatures needed for a constitutional amendment proposal to qualify for the ballot be at least equal to 10 percent of the vote total in the previous governor's election. Constitutional amendments have been, by far, the most-used type of ballot proposition in Michigan. Between 1963 and 2016, 44 amendments have been placed in the ballot by the Legislature, with half being approved by the voters. In addition, 31 proposed amendments reached the ballot in this timeframe via voter petition, with 10 being adopted (see table 11.1).

Aside from those three major types of ballot proposals, there is one more kind of proposal that appears on the Michigan ballot. This type of proposal calls for a constitutional convention, or "ConCon," to revise the Constitution, and is automatically placed on the ballot every 16 years without requiring petition signatures. Such proposals have appeared on the ballot in 1978, 1994, and 2010—all were defeated, with 67 percent of voters rejecting the 2010 proposal. The next proposal for a constitutional convention will therefore appear on the November 2026 ballot.

Historical Use of Ballot Proposals in Michigan

The early history of ballot proposals in Michigan illustrates the kinds of issues brought to the ballot and which proposals voters have tended to support. With adoption of the 1908 Michigan Constitution, provisions for initiatives and referendums were approved, but strict requirements for ballot access at that time made it difficult for proposals to qualify for the ballot. Only eight proposals were placed on the Michigan ballot between 1914 and 1930, and voters rejected every one of them. In the early 1930s, the first two proposals that Michigan voters approved included a proposal to create a state liquor control commission (which still operates today) and an amendment to limit property taxes. In 1939, voters approved nonpartisan elections for state judges, which is how judges are selected currently (see chapter 8). The period between the 1940s and the adoption of the 1963 Constitution saw several proposals regarding the administration of state or local government. For example, voters approved a proposal to establish a civil service system in state employment in 1940, but proposals in 1942 and

1946 that would have allowed Wayne County to become a charter county both failed. Other issues during the 1940s that reached the ballot included establishment of a state revenue-sharing arrangement between state and municipal governments through the state's sales tax and a modification of the 15 mil property tax limit assessed by local governments (both were approved).[4] These two early proposals illustrate the long-standing interplay between state and local governments that is a major theme of this book.

The period after adoption of Michigan's Constitution of 1963 witnessed increased ballot proposal activity. In addition, the overall approval rate for these proposals has hovered around just under half (45 percent). As part of the sometimes-complex interplay between direct and representative democracy, the state Legislature has enacted six statutory initiatives within the allotted 40-day period after the proposed initiatives qualified for the ballot.[5] If the Legislature takes action, the new law is not subject to voter approval. Table 11.1 illustrates the types of proposals that reached the Michigan statewide ballot between 1963 and 2016.

As table 11.1 indicates, a large majority of all ballot proposals since 1963 have been proposed constitutional amendments—75 out of 112, or two-thirds of all proposals. This is interesting because, of the three major types of proposals, the qualifying signature threshold is highest for constitutional amendments. While it is more time-consuming and expensive to achieve this higher requirement, constitutional amendments, if approved by voters, are not subject to modification by the state Legislature or governor. Of course, the courts may ultimately determine that a voter-approved ballot proposal is unconstitutional, as the U.S. Supreme Court did in 2015 in the *Obergefell v. Hodges* case involving Proposal 2 in 2004—the constitutional amendment that banned same-sex marriage and had been approved by Michigan voters.

Some ballot proposals in Michigan have greatly influenced state policy. For example, in 1976, after 10 years of legislative inaction on the issue, Michigan voters overwhelmingly approved a "Bottle Bill" initiative, which put a 10-cent deposit on bottles and cans, and mandated that bottles and cans be returned for deposit or recycled. The Michigan Container Act initiative, known that year as Proposal A,[6] was extremely popular with voters. The proposal's supporters collected a record (at the time) of 400,000 petition signatures to put the measure on the ballot, with Governor William Milliken signing the first petition. Sixty-four percent of voters approved the proposal out of almost 3.4 million votes cast.[7] With a 95 percent average return rate on deposits, Michigan has the highest bottle return rate of all states (and is also the only state with a 10-cent deposit), including those with their own bottle deposit laws.[8]

One ballot proposal that perhaps has had the most significant impact on the way politics and government have operated in Michigan was the term limits constitutional amendment proposal approved in 1992. In the early 1990s, a group of term-limits supporters, concerned with many "career politicians" who seemingly held the same office for decades, started to pursue term limits for legislators around the country. This term limits movement gained momentum during this time after California, Colorado, and Oklahoma adopted them in 1990, and ultimately about 20 states adopted term limits for their state offices. In Michigan, a limit of two terms was placed on offices for governor, lieutenant governor, secretary of state, attorney general, and all state senators (who serve four-year terms). State representatives were limited to three two-year terms. Approved in 1992 (by a 59 percent to 41 percent margin), term limits first made an impact on Michigan state House of Representatives elections in 1998 and the state Senate in 2002.

In states such as California where citizen initiatives are frequently on the ballot, in one two-year election cycle voters may see as many as 10 or more ballot proposals. Other states, including Michigan, typically do not see that many proposals each election. The 2012 general election in Michigan was somewhat unusual as far as ballot proposals were concerned. There were six proposals on the ballot that year, with several quite controversial; all were rejected.

In Michigan and in other states, a wide range of proposals and issues have been brought to voters through the ballot proposal process. Over the years, tax policies have often reached the ballot in many states, as have legislative term limits and issues concerning the death penalty. In the early 21st century, several issues emerged and appeared on the ballot in a number of states, including both defense of traditional marriage and support of same-sex marriage; bans on hunting certain animals or animal welfare protections; increases in the minimum wage; and legalization of medical or recreational marijuana.[9]

Ballot Access for Statewide Proposals in Michigan

For proposals taking any of the citizen-initiated paths, the Michigan Constitution mandates that statewide ballot proposals garner a minimum number of valid petition signatures for the proposal to qualify for the ballot. The minimum number of signatures can vary, and different procedural rules apply depending on the type of initiative being proposed. For initiatives seeking to create new or to change existing statutes, the minimum

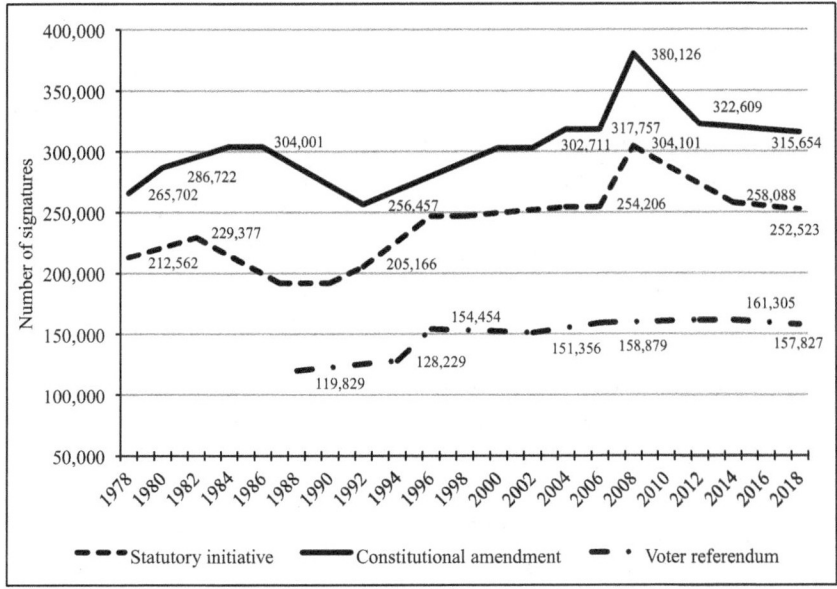

Fig. 11.1. Signature Requirements for Different Types of Ballot Proposals in Michigan, 1978–2018
Source: "Initiative and Referendum Petitions," State of Michigan, Secretary of State, March 2015, accessed April 6, 2015, https://www.michigan.gov/documents/sos/Ini_Ref_Pet_Website_339487_7.pdf

number of signatures to gain ballot access must be equal to at least 8 percent of the total votes cast in the last governor's election, and a minimum of 5 percent for referendum ballot proposals (Article II, Section 9). For initiatives seeking to propose constitutional amendments, a minimum of 10 percent of votes cast is required (Article XII, Section 2). According to the Michigan Secretary of State, the 2016 and 2018 election requirement for statutory initiatives was 252,523 signatures; for constitutional amendment proposals, 315,654 signatures; and for voter referendums on legislation, 157,827 signatures (see fig. 11.1 for petition signature requirements through to 2018).

While states differ on exactly how citizen-initiated proposals of all types qualify for the ballot, most states generally require a similar process: sponsors create the draft language for a ballot proposal (subject to the state's limits on number of words and whether the proposal must be limited to a single topic); a state office reviews the proposal based on any rules for clarity and word length; an official title and summary of the proposal are created; and petitions are circulated and signatures are collected. The state office in Michigan that reviews proposals is the Board of State Canvassers, a four-member bipartisan group appointed to four-year terms by the governor, with advice and consent from the Michigan Senate.

Once the petitions are circulated and the minimum number of signatures has been gathered, supporters file the petitions with the secretary of state's office. The Board of State Canvassers checks the validity of signatures and determines whether or not the minimum number of valid signatures has been gathered. Timing can be important here, and the state recommends that petitions be filed at least 160 days prior to the next general election to help ensure that the proposal will be placed on the ballot. If all conditions are met, the proposal qualifies for the ballot. If there is a general election that will be held in the current calendar year, the proposal, by law, must be placed on the November ballot. A large percentage of all ballot proposals in Michigan find themselves on the November general election ballot in Michigan rather than, say, an August primary election ballot. Some, however, employ tactics so that their ballot question is placed on the ballot in May or August, possibly for strategic reasons related to voter turnout differences in the different types of elections.

The minimum number of petition signatures required can be a major factor in how easy or difficult it is for a proposal to qualify for the ballot in a given state. Some states have much higher minimum requirements for proposals to be placed on the ballot. Moreover, while some states in the past banned the use of paid signature gathering for ballot proposals (in other words, volunteers must be used), in 1988 the U.S. Supreme Court overturned a Colorado ban on paid signature gatherers.[10] Over the past 30 years, the frequency of wealthy financial backers and professional petition management firms has been common in most states (including Michigan) and made it easier for proposals to reach the ballot.[11] This has been especially an issue in ballot proposal-heavy states such as California,[12] where obtaining enough signatures for ballot access can cost millions of dollars.[13] To put this in real numbers for the state of Michigan, figure 11.1 illustrates the minimum number of petition signatures required in selected years for constitutional amendments, statutory initiatives, and for voter referendums.

In the sections below, the recent experiences for the most commonly used types of ballot proposals in Michigan are examined. As noted in table 11.1, the overall approval rate between 1963 and 2016 has been less than half (45 percent), but there have been significant differences in approval between types of proposals. For example, citizen-initiated statutory initiatives have a 54 percent approval rate (out of a total of 13 proposals), while legislative referendums have had a 71 percent approval rate (10 out of 14 proposals).

Statutory Initiatives

A statutory initiative is an attempt to put a proposal on the ballot that will enact a new law or amend an existing law. The Legislature is required to enact, without modification, or reject any proposed statutory initiative within 40 session days once the proposal is approved for the ballot. If enacted by the Legislature, the original initiative would not be placed on the ballot. If the Legislature rejects the proposal, the original initiative goes on the ballot. Table 11.2 below offers a few selected state statutory initiatives that have been proposed over the years in Michigan. Because Michigan law allows this kind of initiative to first go to the Legislature for its action, it is considered to be an *indirect* statutory initiative. In the table's first example, the "Bottle Bill" initiative in the 1970s first went to the state Legislature after the proposal qualified for the ballot, but that body rejected the proposal. Therefore, it was placed on the ballot, where it was approved by a substantial margin.

There also are examples of the Legislature taking action prior to an initiative reaching the ballot. In 2013 and 2014, two statutory initiatives qualified for the ballot, but in both cases the Michigan Legislature took action that preempted these proposals from reaching the ballot. The two proposals were (1) a measure to ban public and private health insurance companies from covering abortions, unless individuals purchase a supplemental health

TABLE 11.2. Selected Michigan Statutory Initiatives Approved by Voters

Year	Proposal	Percent Voter Approval
1976	**Proposal A** The "Bottle Bill"—to prohibit use of nonreturnable containers and to require refundable cash deposits	63.7%
1982	**Proposal E** Enacting new legislation calling for a verifiable freeze on nuclear weapons between the United States and the Soviet Union, with transmission of this act to both U.S. and Soviet officials	56.6%
1996	**Proposal E** Enacting new legislation that allows up to three gambling casinos in the city of Detroit	51.5%
2008	**Proposal 08-1** Allow the use and cultivation of marijuana for specified medical conditions	62.7%

Source: "Initiative and Referendums under the Constitution of the State of Michigan of 1963," State of Michigan, Bureau of Elections, March 2015, accessed May 15, 2015, https://www.michigan.gov/documents/sos/Initia_Ref_Under_Consti_12-08_339399_7.pdf

insurance policy (which became Public Act 182 of 2013); and (2) a measure to require that decisions affecting hunting and fishing use scientific wildlife management principles (which became Public Act 281 of 2014).

Over the history of statutory initiatives in Michigan, there have been relatively few proposed, and subsequently approved by voters, compared to those that seek to amend the state's Constitution. In part, this has been due to legislative action within the 40-day time period. But it also is possible because supporters of a particular proposal know they can avoid legislative interference more easily when proposing a constitutional amendment rather than a state statute.

Another example of a statutory initiative by citizens was a 2008 medical marijuana proposal, which was approved by over 60 percent of Michigan voters that year. Legalized medical marijuana—and in some states, recreational marijuana—became hotly debated issues in the early 21st century. Changing values among voters had begun to emerge during this time, but most state legislatures were unwilling to act on these matters. As a result, several states have seen ballot proposals supporting recreational marijuana use and some states have approved these measures (e.g., California, Colorado, and Washington).

Citizen-Initiated Constitutional Amendments

Not all states that allow ballot proposals on constitutional amendments allow citizens alone to initiate the proposed changes to their state's constitution. For example, in Minnesota, Iowa, Indiana, and Wisconsin, state legislative approval of a voter-approved amendment is required. In Michigan, citizens may initiate a constitutional amendment without legislative approval. If approved, these ballot proposals generally represent a substantial change in how the politics of a state operates or in what ways the state's constitution provides for governmental structure and responsibilities, how it allocates power, or to what degree it protects the rights of citizens.

Earlier, we compared how easy or difficult it is for a proposal to be placed on the ballot. Gaining the required petition signatures is an important step in this process, but there are other factors in play as well. The resources needed to support the signature gathering effort, and even the petition distribution requirements, also can play a role. For example, some states (e.g., Nebraska and Wyoming) require that a certain percentage of petition signatures come from a minimum number of counties in the state.[14] Recent trends in Michigan suggest that supporters of a proposal prefer constitutional amendment proposal route rather than sponsoring state statute proposals. While it is more difficult to secure the higher threshold for petition signatures, a constitutional amendment is much more difficult for future voters to change, and especially for future legislators to make their own changes. Table 11.3 summarizes selected citizen-initiated constitutional amendment proposals in Michigan that voters have approved.

As table 11.3 illustrates, several important political and legal issues have been brought to voters through the constitutional amendment ballot proposal process. Michigan does not apply a state sales tax to food and prescription drug purchases, and has not done so since voters approved an amendment in the 1970s that removed these from the list of items to which the tax applies. As noted above, in the early 1990s, Michigan was one of about 20 states that supported term limits for its elected officials. Term limits for the state Legislature have certainly affected the way the state's politics and government have operated since the 1990s. While a complete consensus does not exist on the effects of term limits, several studies have noted the relative decline in power of term-limited state legislatures compared to governors, executive branch bureaucrats, and legislative staffers (see chapter 6).[15] In a study specific to Michigan, researchers found that one effect of term limits was to shift power away from legislators and toward lobbyists.[16]

TABLE 11.3. Selected Constitutional Amendment Proposals

Year	Proposal	Percent Voter Approval
	Citizen Initiated Constitutional Amendments	
1974	**Proposal C** to eliminate the sales tax and use tax on food and prescription drugs	55.5%
1978	**Proposal E** to establish limits on taxes that can be imposed (Headlee Amendment)	52.5%
1992	**Proposal B** to restrict the number of times a person can be elected to state office (term limits)	58.7%
2004	**Proposal 04-2** allows the marriage between a man and a woman as the only acceptable union	58.6%
2006	**Proposal 06-2** prohibits certain types of government affirmative action programs	57.9%
	Legislative Referral Constitutional Amendments	
1972	**Proposal A** to allow the state legislature to authorize a state lottery and the sale of lottery tickets	72.7%
1994	**Proposal A** to increase the state sales and use tax from 4% to 6% and to limit increases in property tax	69.1%

Source: "Initiative and Referendums under the Constitution of the State of Michigan of 1963."

In the decade of the 2000s, several ballot proposals centering on social issues appeared on many state ballots, including in Michigan. In 2004, about 60 percent of voters approved a constitutional amendment to define marriage as between a man and a woman only, but this was ultimately overturned by the U.S. Supreme Court in 2015. In 2006, voters in Michigan supported Proposal 2, a constitutional amendment to ban affirmative action programs in government or public schools and institutions of higher learning (unlike the amendment centered on marriage, this one was later upheld by the courts).

Of course, voters have not approved all citizen-initiated constitutional amendments over the years. Antitax proposals in 1980 (Proposal D) and 1981 (Proposal A) were both rejected by voters, as was a proposal limiting property taxes in 1992 (Proposal C). Proposal 02–3 in 2002, which would have given state classified employees the constitutional right to collective bargaining and arbitration, was rejected, as was a similar proposal in 2012 that covered both public and private employees (Proposal 12–2).

Amending the Constitution through Legislative Referral

Occasionally, the state Legislature will vote to put a constitutional amendment proposal before the state's voters. Since the proposal originates in the Legislature and not by citizens, it does not precisely fit the definition of direct democracy in the same way that a citizen-initiated amendment proposal does. Often, the Legislature decides that an issue is too controversial to enact on its own, and wishes to seek input from voters. For example, in 1972, the Legislature had taken up the matter of whether members of the Legislature would be allowed to resign during their term of office in order to accept another elected or appointed office. Since this dealt directly with their own offices, the state Legislature referred this proposal to the voters—who rejected it with 51.4 percent of the vote. Another proposal that year dealt with whether the state should authorize a state lottery. More and more states were considering ways to bolster their revenues, and a number of them placed such proposals on their ballots. In some states, in an effort to gain support for these measures, the states mandated that lottery revenues be earmarked for public education. In 1972, Michigan voters overwhelming supported creation of a state lottery, which promised, but did not mandate, that proceeds would go to the state's education system.

In 1994, the Legislature was reluctant to decide to increase the state sales tax on its own. The ballot proposal response to this was Proposal A, which was part of a restructuring of local property taxes to fund public school districts. Because this represented a tax increase, the Legislature sent this proposal to the state's voters. Despite the somewhat complicated nature of the proposal's intent and shift in taxes, voters approved the measure by a large margin (see table 11.3). Also in 1994, the Legislature sent a proposal to voters that would increase funds for a natural resources trust fund and establish a state parks endowment fund. Voters also approved this proposal by a large margin.

In May 2015, another controversial measure came to voters by legislative referral. In the years prior to 2015, the Michigan Legislature had failed to adequately fund the state's roads. Although everyone agreed the state's roads were in horrible shape, the state's leaders had reached an impasse on how to fund and fix Michigan's infrastructure. Therefore, a ballot measure was created and sent to voters (Proposal 15-1) that would have repealed the sales tax on gasoline, but would increase the fuel tax and add new fees for trucks. Most important, the state's sales tax would be increased from 6 percent to 7 percent. As part of an earlier bargain among state legislators, some of the funds raised through this ballot measure would go to public schools and local governments. Proposal 15-1 was crushed on Election Day. Four out of every five voters rejected the proposal, prompting longtime Michigan politics observer Bill Ballenger to call the proposal "one of the greatest ballot turkeys of all time."[17]

Ballot proposals through legislative referral highlight the sometimes uneasy and complex policy-making relationship between direct democracy and representative democracy in this hybrid system. Michigan's elected leaders were forced to deal with the state's crumbling roads after Proposal 15-1's defeat. Interpreting the May 2015 vote was a little complicated, because there likely were several different reasons why voters rejected the proposal. Antitax sentiment existed certainly, but some voters also did not like how complicated the proposal was, and some did not like the fact that funds from the "roads proposal" would be going for purposes other than fixing roads.

Referendums

The power of voters to approve or reject laws enacted by the state legislature is called the voter referendum power. This type of ballot proposal has the lowest petition signature qualifying threshold, at 5 percent of the vote totals from the previous governor's election (Michigan Constitution, Article II, Section 9). With a referendum petition, the filing deadline is 90 days following the final adjournment of the legislative session when the law was enacted. In addition, if voters pass a referendum measure, a future legislature may amend that measure (Article II, Section 9). Occasionally, a bill may be passed by the state Legislature and signed by the governor, but the legislation includes a provision that stipulates that the bill will not become law unless voters approve it in a referendum election. This includes any legislation that has preempted a statutory initiative proposal that had qualified for the ballot but did not reach the ballot due to legislative action. Therefore, similar to constitutional amendments, referendums can reach the ballot via petition or be referred by the Legislature.

Compared to other proposals, referendums are not used very much in Michigan. According to the Bureau of Elections, 24 referendums were placed on the statewide ballot between 1963 and 2016 (see table 11.1). Of those, 14 were placed on the ballot by the Legislature (10 were approved), while 10 were placed by citizen petition (1 approved). Among those legislative referendums approved by voters include a 1974 proposal to uphold Public Act 106, which authorized issuing bonds to help fund bonus payments to Vietnam veterans; a 1998 authorization of bonds for environmental protection programs; and a 2002 authorization of bonds for sewage and storm water projects. The lone citizens' referendum proposal approved by voters was a 1988 proposal to prohibit the use of state funds to pay for abortions for those receiving welfare.[18]

From the discussion above, it is apparent that a number of ballot proposals have been very controversial and have generated considerable interest. The section below traces the level of campaign spending activities for selected ballot proposal questions.

Financing Ballot Proposal Campaigns

Overall funding of political campaigns in the late 20th and early 21st centuries in the United States has become a huge enterprise. Campaigns for ballot proposals have tended to follow the recent trend toward greatly increased political campaign spending. In a number of states, supporters of a possible ballot proposal often seek out a wealthy individual who can underwrite a high-spending campaign. In Michigan, some of the wealthy families and individuals contributing to ballot proposal committees have included Jon Stryker (an architect and heir to Stryker Corporation, a medical supply company), Richard DeVos (the cofounder of Amway, now called Alticor, and whose son Dick was the Republican gubernatorial candidate in 2006) and the DeVos family, Al Taubman (a real estate developer), and Manuel Moroun (known for trucking companies and as owner of the

Ambassador Bridge, the border crossing between Detroit and Windsor, Canada). For example, in 2012, the Moroun-funded (through his holding company, DIBC Holdings Inc.) ballot question committee "The People Should Decide" spent over $31 million on Proposal 6. This proposal would have required voters to approve construction of any new bridge between Detroit and Windsor (at the time, the Ambassador Bridge was the only bridge between the two cities and was owned by Moroun's Detroit International Bridge Company, or DIBC). As reported by the *Detroit Free Press*, their $31 million estimate was low because Mr. Moroun spent millions of dollars on TV ads about the bridge issue prior to creation of the ballot question committee.[19] Other ballot proposals in 2012 had generated considerable controversy and campaign spending as well. Some of the six proposals, however, were typical of issues where there is little funding to either support or oppose, or issues where one side raises considerably more than the other. In 2012, regardless of spending patterns, all six proposals were rejected by voters in 2012. For example, on Proposal 12–1, the Emergency Manager Law, those on the winning side who rejected Public Act 4 spent about $2.25 million, while those supporting retention of the law spent about $125,000. Similarly, uneven spending occurred with Proposal 12–4 (the Home Healthcare Amendment proposal, which among others, would have given home health care workers collective bargaining rights), with about $28,000 spent in favor, but $8.65 million spent in opposition (which was the winning side).

Another proposal in 2012 with substantial spending differences was Proposal 12–5, which sought to limit the enactment of taxes. No money was spent by the winning opposition committees while almost $4 million was spent in a losing cause in favor of the proposal. The biggest spending difference occurred with Proposal 12–6, the bridge proposal. Committees in favor of the proposal spent over $31 million in a losing cause, while those in opposition spent about $1.6 million.

Occasionally, a proposal will see more balanced spending between those in favor and those opposed. Proposal 12–2, regarding public and private sector collective bargaining, featured almost identical spending by the two sides. Committees in favor of Proposal 2 spent $23.05 million, while those opposed spent $23.27 million. As seen with Proposal 6, spending lots of money does not mean that side will always win when it comes to ballot proposals. Given the controversy over some of the issues and the number of TV ads aired during the 2012 campaign,[20] the amounts officially reported are probably smaller than was actually spent.

Analyzing the amount of campaign spending on ballot proposals is useful because it illustrates the wide range of spending that can occur across different ballot questions and different elections. Despite the lack of evidence showing that campaign spending influences ballot question election outcomes, the overall amount of money spent on ballot proposals has grown tremendously in recent years. Two of the 2012 ballot proposals totaled at least $45 million each, with a third proposal that saw almost $32 million spent. According to one report, Michigan ballot committees in 2012 alone raised $141.4 million, which far outpaced the $107.6 million that was spent for *all Michigan state-level candidate campaigns* in 2010.[21]

In addition to the importance of campaign spending in many of these ballot question campaigns, another enduring ballot proposal dynamic has been the frequency with which ballot questions regarding local governments have appeared. State-local government relations can be complex and generate passions on both sides of an issue. In the notable cases examined below, the use of ballot proposals in establishing or restricting local government power, financing, and operations is clear.

Ballot Proposals and State-Local Government Relations

A number of ballot proposals have had a direct effect on local governments or state and local relations. This should not be too surprising, since state-level policy making often deals with local governments and the fiscal, political, legal, and administrative interactions between the state and its local governments. State financial assistance to general purpose local governments (e.g., revenue sharing) and to public school districts (through the School Aid Fund) receives a fair share of attention from state elected officials. As noted in a previous discussion, voters in Michigan also have directly weighed in on changes to state laws regarding local governments or amended the state's constitution in a way that has affected the operations and finances of local governments.

The Headlee Amendment, approved by voters in 1978, was part of an emerging nationwide taxpayers' revolt that included similar ballot proposals in California (Proposition 13) and Massachusetts (Proposition 2½) that appeared between 1978 and 1980. The Headlee Amendment limited certain state and local taxes, but the limits on local property tax revenues imposed by Headlee greatly restricted the ability of Michigan local governments and school districts to raise local operating funds. Local voters may pass waivers that can raise the limits imposed by Headlee, and this has happened in many Michigan cities over the years. At the same time, the

Headlee Amendment also required that state government fund any new state-required program or program expansion for local governments (so that there are no unfunded state mandates imposed on local governments).

Proposal A in 1994—a legislatively referred constitutional amendment proposal—also impacted local government finances in a direct way. Proposal A shifted government revenues away from property taxes but raised the state's sales tax from 4 percent to 6 percent. This proposal came for two reasons. First, many local governments and school districts had been severely constrained in their ability to raise revenues and provide services since enactment of the Headlee Amendment. Second, growing public debate had been occurring around the disparities between rich and poor school districts in Michigan. In short, wealthier communities could raise more money per pupil through their local property taxes than poorer communities could. Despite minimum per pupil allotments across all districts, the gap between spending by wealthy districts and poor districts was quite large by the early 1990s.

A major state-local government relations proposal in 2012 centered on emergency managers (EMs). Proposal 12–1 was a voter referendum issue that asked voters if Public Act 4 of 2011 should be approved or rejected. Sponsors of this proposal were unhappy with Public Act 4 and wanted voters to reject the proposal, which would result in the law being repealed. This Act had greatly expanded the powers of EMs compared to powers granted through previous legislation. Public Act 4 gave EMs some of the broadest powers in the nation. Emergency managers were individuals appointed to run the finances of cities that were experiencing severe financial problems and were near bankruptcy. That a number of Michigan cities were in financial distress is another example of the decline that Michigan has faced over the past 30 years. The state's appointment of EMs—who had power over all of a local government's financial decisions—was controversial, especially in those cities where managers already had been placed (e.g., Flint, Benton Harbor, Pontiac, and Ecorse). Voters narrowly rejected the proposal, with 52.7 percent of the voters casting a "no" vote, which repealed Public Act 4. However, after this vote, the Michigan Legislature enacted Public Act 436 of 2012, the Local Financial Stability and Choice Act, which provided for emergency managers again, but with more restricted powers, keeping in part with voter sentiment on Proposal 12–1. Voter rejection of Proposals 1 and 2 in 2012 illustrates a common interplay that exists between direct democracy and representative government. In both cases where the proposals were rejected, the Legislature acted (fairly quickly) in response to the vote. Legislative reaction to Proposal 2's vote was to enact legislation that codified voter sentiment, but also struck back at the state's labor unions by passing a new right-to-work law. In the case of Proposal 1, the Legislature was forced to write language into a new law that tempered the powers of emergency managers, per voter rejection of the expanded powers EMs had been granted by Public Act 4 of 2011.

Conclusion

The use of state ballot proposals as policy-making tools in Michigan can be a complex and sometimes highly technical issue. However, the topic deserves attention by students of state politics in part because of its increasing use by many states over the past 20 years. Moreover, the fact that direct democracy provisions are allowed in Michigan requires that students of politics and policy making examine how these provisions fit—sometimes uncomfortably—in the larger system of representative government that is the basis of U.S. politics. Some scholars have called this a hybrid democracy, as both representative and direct democracy principles operate at the same time. When reviewing the range of state initiatives that have been approved by voters over the past 40 years, it is clear that a number of very significant policies have been enacted directly by Michigan voters. For example, voters eliminated the sales tax on food and prescription drugs, as well as authorizing a system for reducing beverage can and bottle litter in the 1970s. In the 1980s, voters authorized establishment of a natural resources trust fund and a board to administer the fund, along with two bond proposals to fund environmental protection programs and state and local recreation projects.

In the 1990s, Michigan voters mandated term limits for state offices through a constitutional amendment, which changed how the state's politics and government operated in a fundamental way. In the 2000s, social conservatives became active in addressing several policy issues, and voters approved both a defense of marriage constitutional amendment (that was later overturned by the courts) and a ban on affirmative action programs in government (which was upheld). In the decade beginning in 2010, voters eliminated the personal property tax on businesses and allocated a portion of state use taxes to Michigan municipalities in the form of a local "community stabilization" share.

In reviewing the state ballot proposals since the 1970s, several trends emerge. First, Michigan voters so far have not been interested in convening a constitutional convention for the purpose of rewriting the 1963 Constitution. Second, there has been relatively little use (and therefore approval) of statutory initiatives. The few that exist have first been submitted to the Legislature for their action prior to being placed on the ballot. The petition signature requirement for constitutional amendments is only slightly higher (10 percent compared to 8 percent of the previous governor's election vote total), so supporters of an initiative often prefer the constitutional amendment route to avoid any potential legislative tinkering.

It should not be a surprise that there are many more attempts to put a proposal on the ballot than actually achieve ballot status. This is for a number of reasons, including legislative action on a piece of legislation that preempts a ballot question. But, just as likely, a proposal simply does not receive enough valid petition signatures to qualify (so petitions are not even submitted) or the petitions that were submitted were not certified as meeting the required minimum threshold. Often, time and money run out on supporters of a proposal. In addition, there are cases in which the courts rule that the proposal language does not meet the legal standards (often because it is overly broad).

Michigan's experience with ballot proposals reveals a strong connection with each of this book's themes. There is an important historical component to ballot proposals in Michigan as the process has been in place since just after the turn of the 20th century. After a slow start, Michigan has actively produced public policies through a wide variety of ballot measures. A number of funding-related proposals have specifically touched local general purpose or school district governments in Michigan. For example, the 2012 ballot proposals on the emergency manager law and collective bargaining for public and private sector workers would have affected how local governments operate, how they spend money, and how they are staffed. Ballot proposals can also be linked to decline in Michigan. As noted above, the proposal that brought term limits to the state has been linked to a decline in the power of the state Legislature relative to the governor and to lobbyists. As such, another lesson of ballot proposals in Michigan is that policies made in response to the state's challenges may themselves create problems. In addition, many ballot proposals since the 1970s have been attempts to respond to the challenges of the state's economic decline.

The role of ballot proposals in state policy making can be an intriguing one, especially when considering Michigan's experience compared to those states that have no direct democracy provisions. The relationship between the actions of our elected representatives and the policies decided by voters as part of Michigan's hybrid direct democracy process will remain a complex and an interesting lesson for students of state politics.

WEB RESOURCES

The *Citizens Research Council of Michigan* (www.crcmich.org) offers a number of resources on ballot proposals including "Reform of Michigan's Ballot Question Process," Report 386, January 2014.

The *Initiative and Referendum Institute* at the University of Southern California (www.iandrinstitute.org) is a nonpartisan educational organization that collects and distributes information on the initiative and referendum process across the United States.

The *National Conference of State Legislatures* (www.ncsl.org) maintains a comprehensive database for all states on ballot proposals by state, year, and topic.

The *Michigan Secretary of State's Office* (www.mich.gov/sos) provides information on the ballot proposal process in Michigan and campaign finance disclosure by ballot question committees. Of particular interest is the March 2015 document, "Initiatives and Referendums under the Constitution of the State of Michigan of 1963."

NOTES

1. Elizabeth Garrett, "The Promise and Perils of Hybrid Democracy," Fifth Annual Henry Lecture, *Oklahoma Law Review* 59, no. 2 (Summer 2006).

2. Michigan Manual, 2009–10, Chapter IX, Elections, "How an Issue Becomes a Ballot Proposal," accessed November 5, 2016, http://www.legislature.mi.gov/(S(50nxmumhzghotrw24boul4rx))/documents/2009-2010/michiganmanual/2009-MM-p0569-p0571.pdf

3. Ibid.

4. See Initiative and Referendum Institute for a history of initiative usage in Michigan, "Michigan: Statewide Initiative Usage 1914–2000," accessed November 5, 2016, http://www.iandrinstitute.org/docs/Michigan.pdf

5. See summary of rules at State of Michigan, Bureau of Elections, "Initiatives and Referendums under the Constitution of the State of Michigan of 1963," March 2015; accessed November 7, 2016, https://www.michigan.gov/documents/sos/Initia_Ref_Under_Consti_12-08_339399_7.pdf

6. Michigan law regarding the ballot proposal numbering system was changed in 1999 effective for the year 2000. Chapter XXII, Section 168.474a provides for a numbering system in which the "first 2 digits shall be the last 2 digits of the year of the election. The next digit or, if necessary, 2 digits shall indicate the chronological order in which the question was filed to appear on the ballot." Therefore, a 2018 ballot proposal would be designated 18–1, 18–2, and so forth, depending on when the proposal was filed. In the period between the 1970s through the 1990s, letter designations were typically given to proposals (Proposal A, Proposal B, and so forth). See "Michigan Legislature: Michigan Election Law (Excerpt), Act 116 of 1954, 168.474a Assignment of Number Designation to Appear on Ballot for Question Submitted on Statewide Basis," accessed November 5, 2016, http://www.legislature.mi.gov/%28S%28inamlgvvyoskgk55a5jp4t55%29%29/documents/mcl/pdf/mcl-168-474a.pdf

7. See Heritage Academies for a summary of the Bottle Bill, "About the Michigan Container Act," ftp://ftp.heritageacademies.com/ET/CurriculumCenter/NHAHistoryInteractive/Themes/BottleBill/BottleBill_popup.html; accessed November 5, 2016.

8. Container Recycling Institute, 2005, "Bottle Bills Promote Recycling and Reduce Waste," accessed November 5, 2016, http://www.bottlebill.org/about/benefits/waste.htm

9. See the National Conference of State Legislatures, "Ballot Measures Database," accessed November 6, 2016, http://www.ncsl.org/research/elections-and-campaigns/ballot-measures-database.aspx. The National Conference of State Legislatures maintains a comprehensive database on state ballot initiatives by topic, year, and state.

10. *Meyer v. Grant*, 486 US 414 (1988).

11. David S. Broder, *Democracy Derailed: Initiative Campaigns and the Power of Money* (New York: Harcourt, 2000).

12. David McCuan, Shaun Bowler, Todd Donovan, and Ken Fernandez, "California's Political Warriors: Campaign Professionals and the Initiative Process," in *Citizens as Legislators: Direct Democracy in the United States*, ed. Shaun Bowler, Todd Donovan, and Caroline Tolbert (Columbus: Ohio State University Press, 1998); and Peter Schrag, *Paradise Lost: California's Experience, America's Future* (Berkeley: University of California Press, 2004).

13. Norimitsu Onishi, "California Ballot Initiatives, Born in Populism, Now Come from Billionaires," *New York Times*, October 16, 2012; accessed November 5, 2016, http://www.nytimes.com/2012/10/17/us/politics/california-ballot-initiatives-dominated-by-the-very-rich.html?_r=0

14. Shaun Bowler and Todd Donovan, "The Initiative Process," in *Politics in the American States: A Comparative Analysis*, 10th ed., ed. Virginia Gray, Russell L. Hanson, and Thad Kousser (Thousand Oaks, CA: Sage/CQ Press, 2013).

15. John M. Carey, Richard G. Niemi, and Lynda W. Powell, "The Effects of Term Limits on State Legislatures," *Legislative Studies Quarterly* 23, no. 2 (1998): 271–300; John M. Carey, Richard G. Niemi, Lynda W. Powell, and Gary F. Moncrief, "The Effects of Term Limits on State Legislatures: A New Survey of the 50 States," *Legislative Studies Quarterly* 31, no. 1 (2006): 105–34; Jennifer Drage Bowser, Council of State Governments, "The Effects of Legislative Term Limits," *The Book of the States 2005*; accessed November 5, 2016, http://www.csg.org/knowledgecenter/docs/BOS2005LegislativeTermLimits.pdf

16. Marjorie Sarbaugh-Thompson, Lyke Thompson, Charles D. Elder, John Strate, and Richard C. Elling, *The Political and Institutional Effects of Term Limits* (Houndmills, England: Palgrave Macmillan, 2004).

17. Leonard N. Fleming and Gary Heinlein, "Michigan Voters Reject Proposal 1 Tax Hike," *Detroit News*, May 6, 2015; accessed November 8, 2016, http://www.detroitnews.com/story/news/politics/2015/05/05/proposalone/26952783/

18. Michigan Bureau of Elections, "Initiatives and Referendums under the Constitution of the State of Michigan of 1963," March 2015; accessed October 24, 2016, https://www.michigan.gov/documents/sos/Initia_Ref_Under_Consti_12-08_339399_7.pdf

19. Paul Egan, "With $31 Million, Manuel (Matty) Moroun Spends More

Than Anyone Ever on a State Ballot Proposal," *Detroit Free Press*, October 27, 2012; accessed April 11, 2015, http://archive.freep.com/article/20121027/NEWS15/310270139/With-31-million-Manuel-Matty-Moroun-spends-more-than-anyone-ever-on-a-state-ballot-proposal

20. Paul Egan and John Gallagher, "Michigan Voters Reject All Proposals; Emergency Manager Law Repealed," *Detroit Free Press*, November 7, 2012; accessed April 12, 2015, http://archive.freep.com/article/20121107/NEWS15/311070105/Michigan-proposals-emergency-manager-law

21. Michigan Campaign Finance Network, "Ballot Committees Have Raised $141 M," October 28, 2012; accessed November 5, 2016, http://www.mcfn.org/press.php?prId=167

◆ Public Policy Case Studies

12 ✦ Education Policy in Michigan

DOUGLAS CARR

National policy issues and politics often come to mind when discussing education policies in the United States. The role of the Department of Education, laws such as No Child Left Behind and the Every Student Succeeds Act, and even comparisons of how students in the U.S. stack up against students from other nations are common talking points. However, education policy is primarily controlled by state governments, which assign much of this responsibility to local school districts. In Michigan, higher education policies are likewise decentralized, with most decision-making responsibility resting with each university.

Michigan's Constitution (Article VIII, Section 2) states that "[t]he legislature shall maintain and support a system of free public elementary and secondary schools as defined by law." As a result, this responsibility has made education a major spending category in the state. A quick review of the Governor's Executive Budget for Fiscal Year 2016 shows that public education is one of the most important issues in the state in terms of spending. In fiscal year 2015, education was the second largest spending category, comprising about 31 percent of all expenditures. Education trailed only Health and Human Services (46 percent) that year, and greatly exceeded the next highest spending category—Jobs (10 percent).

As you read this chapter, consider the following questions about education in Michigan:

- Who is responsible for making and implementing education policy in Michigan?
- How are state governance and local economies shaping education funding? How does education funding shape education policy?
- What factors are driving the urgency in education debates?

- How has Michigan responded to poor academic performance?
- What is the role of the state government in local education and higher education?

Structure of K-12 Education Governance in Michigan

State Government

As noted above, education policy is primarily the responsibility of the states. National trends in education policy will play out uniquely in each state, and policies in Michigan also address challenges unique to the state. In Michigan, K-12 education policies are established by the state Legislature and implemented by the Michigan Department of Education. However, political accountability for state educational policies extends beyond these two bodies. The State Board of Education, which consists of eight board members elected to eight-year terms in statewide elections, oversees the Department of Education and advises the Legislature on education policy. These elected board members also select the state superintendent, who is the administrative head of the Department of Education and serves in the governor's cabinet.

The state government can create, dissolve, and exercise authority over local school districts. The state sets requirements such as curricular standards, the minimum number of days in an academic year, and standards for teacher certification. These centralized policies at the state level produce a common policy environment in public education throughout the state of Michigan.

Standardized testing is one example of where the state can have a dramatic impact on education policy. States each develop their own standardized tests, and in 2014 the Legislature required the Michigan Department of Education to develop a new test to replace the Michigan Educational Assessment Program (MEAP). This legislative action followed initial steps by the Michigan Department of Education to replace the MEAP with the Smarter Balanced exam, which was developed by a consortium of states.[1] Some legislators were concerned that the Smarter Balanced exam would erode local control over education because of its association with the national Common Core standards.[2] After using the MEAP for 44 years, a new test aligned with current state standards was clearly needed. However, when the Legislature disagreed with the Michigan Department of Education on what replacement exam should be used, the Legislature had the authority to require the Michigan Department of Education to instead develop what became the Michigan Student Test of Educational Progress (M-STEP).

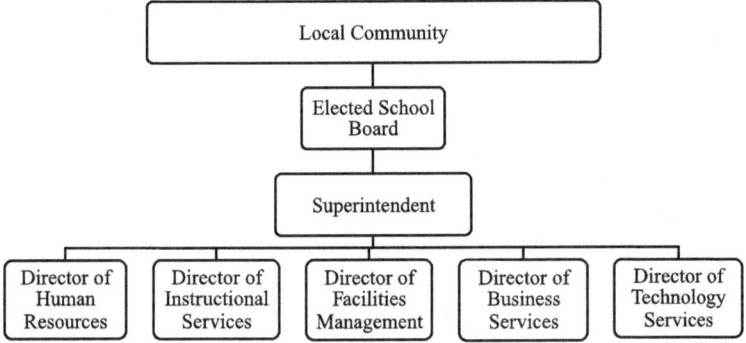

Fig. 12.1. Typical Local School District Organization
Note: The departments overseen by the superintendent in this chart illustrate an example of school district organization. The exact departmental structure will vary across school districts.

Local Governments

Traditionally, public education in Michigan has been provided by local school districts. School districts, a type of local government, are separate from counties, cities, and townships. School districts have elected boards of education in the same way that cities have elected city council members. It is important to note that a city and school district with the same name are separate governments and may have different geographic boundaries. Moreover, cities and counties do not have authority over school districts.

The political structure of local school districts is similar in many ways to state educational governance in Michigan. School board members for local school districts are elected by local voters. The school board develops policy for the school district and hires and oversees a superintendent who serves as the administrative head of the school district. Figure 12.1 illustrates the organization of a typical school district.

Local school districts also have responsibility over staffing and curriculum decisions. Public education in the United States has traditionally been responsive to and designed by individual communities that are served; residents who are not satisfied with the public education provided locally can hold the local elected school board accountable through regular school board elections and even through recall elections of elected board members.

Michigan also has intermediate school districts that encompass multiple school districts, usually organized by county. These intermediate school districts facilitate local district compliance with state requirements and provide educational resources to local school districts contained within their borders. For example, an intermediate school district may provide local school districts with training and educational resources for: instruction using Braille; conducting program evaluations; and instruction of bilingual students learning English.

While most intermediate school district boundaries in Michigan coincide with county borders, intermediate school districts and counties are separate governments. Also, similar to local school districts, intermediate school districts have a board of education that hires a superintendent. However, in many of the intermediate school districts, these board members are chosen by the local school board members of school districts that are served by the intermediate school district. Therefore, many intermediate school district boards are accountable to the elected local school district boards responsible for their appointment rather than directly accountable to voters.

City and county general purpose governments have little to do with education. Local school districts, intermediate school districts, and the Michigan Department of Education are responsible for the delivery of traditional public education in Michigan. As of the 2015–16 academic year, there were 56 intermediate school districts and 540 local school districts.[3]

Federal Government

While state and local governments are responsible for most educational policies, the federal government does influence local education. The federal government's role in elementary and secondary education has been defined by the Elementary and Secondary Education Act (ESEA) of 1965 and its reauthorizations. These include the No Child Left Behind (NCLB) Act of 2001 and the Every Student Succeeds Act (ESSA) of 2015. President Lyndon Johnson signed the ESEA into law in 1965, establishing a framework for providing federal funding for schools serving low-income families.[4] Reauthorizations of the ESEA have modified the federal role in education while still maintaining federal funding for schools serving students from low-income households. For example, the NCLB Act of 2001 defined a framework for student testing and holding schools accountable for student progress. The ESSA of 2015 shifts responsibility from the federal government to state governments for setting student performance targets, identification of academically struggling schools, and intervention in such schools. It also introduces academic standards measuring readiness for college and careers and adds pre-K education into the Act.[5]

While the ESEA and its reauthorizations are often the focus of discussion on the federal role in education, other federal laws also have had a significant impact on education. For example, the federal Family Educational Rights and Privacy Act (FERPA) establishes education records as private and gives parents of minors access to their children's educational records. Restrictions on the release of a student's educational records under the Act apply to primary, secondary, and higher education institutions.

Federal legislative influence in education is often realized through the promise of federal funding. For example, the ESEA and its reauthorizations offer federal Title I funding for schools serving low-income populations; however, compliance with the Act is required in order to qualify for these funds. By creating requirements for receiving federal funding, Congress is able to directly influence local education throughout the nation.

Court cases also determine the federal role in education. The 1954 U.S. Supreme Court decision in *Brown v. Board of Education* declared segregated schools unconstitutional, in violation of the equal protection clause of the 14th Amendment to the Constitution. The following year, the Supreme Court instructed that schools be desegregated with "all deliberate speed."[6] While well known, this is not the only federal court decision to have shaped U.S. education. For example, the Supreme Court ruled in 1988 that a school can censor a student newspaper without violating the First Amendment free speech and free press rights of student journalists.[7] Also, in 2002 it ruled that drug testing of students participating in extracurricular activities does not violate students' Fourth Amendment rights against unreasonable search and seizure.[8]

The decentralized nature of education policy is even seen in many federal education policies. Control over implementation of federal policy typically resides with the states. For example, this is seen in the NCLB, which left room for state policy, and in the ESSA, which expands the role of state policy in setting student performance targets. States are responsible for determining the standards that define educational performance targets for schools.

Structure of Higher Education Governance in Michigan

Higher education policies in Michigan are more decentralized than are K-12 policies. The 15 Michigan public universities offering bachelor's, master's, and doctoral degrees are each governed independently by a board of regents or a board of trustees that, depending on the university, is either elected or appointed by the governor. Community colleges in the state are organized around geographic areas, and residents living in a community college district elect the college's governing board. Each governing board makes independent decisions regarding policies for that university or college. Michigan's decentralized structure for higher education is unique among the states. Other states have some type of coordinating body for higher education, such as Massachusetts' Board of Higher Education or Missouri's Department of Higher Education.[9] The lack of such a coordinating body in Michigan means there is not a single board that manages and coordinates higher education budget and policy requests to the state Legislature. Instead, each university has more direct interaction with state legislators. Also, the Legislature is fully responsible for how state funding is allocated across the universities; in particular, the Legislature determines the formulas used to allocate state appropriations across universities.

The role of public community colleges and universities is also determined by the Legislature. While community colleges in Michigan have traditionally offered associate's degrees, authority to award some baccalaureate degrees was granted by the Legislature beginning in 2013 through Public Act 495.

Education Funding

Education funding provides a valuable lens through which education policy can be understood. The budget process forces policymakers to choose policy directions and prioritize policy goals. Not every idea can be funded, and the allocation of resources reflects the legislative body's policy preferences. This is true whether the legislative body is a local school board or the state Legislature.

The structure of education funding can also force difficult decisions. When insufficient funds are available to maintain the current budget of a school, additional funding must be secured (e.g., from tuition increases at universities) or cuts must be made to balance the budget. When a school district is unsuccessful at balancing its budget, state policymakers may step in to either enforce deeper budget cuts or provide additional revenue. The state Legislature holds an important role in educational policy, and education funding is a significant avenue through which the Legislature shapes education in the state.

K-12 Funding

When federalism exists in a policy arena, it is important to understand the fiscal federalism context of that policy. Fiscal federalism describes how different levels of government are involved in the funding and expenditures of a particular policy area (see chapter 3). Intergovernmental transfers, such as

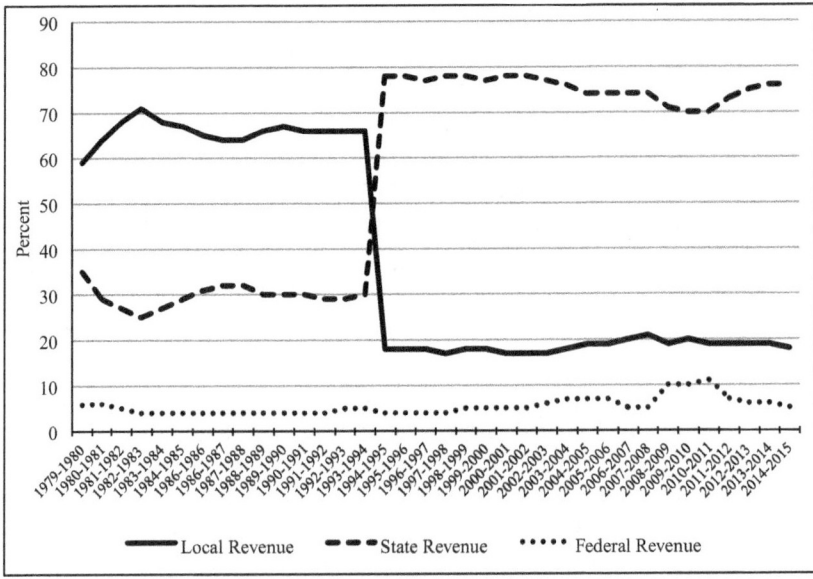

Fig. 12.2. Percent of K-12 Education Funding in Michigan by Source, 1979–2015
Source: Kathryn Summers, Senate Fiscal Agency, *Overview of K/12 School Aid*, Lansing, 2014; 2013-14 Bulletin 1011, Analysis of Michigan Public School Districts Revenues and Expenditures, Michigan Department of Education, February 2015; 2014-15 Bulletin 1011, Analysis of Michigan Public School Districts Revenues and Expenditures, Michigan Department of Education, February 2016.
Note: Excludes intermediate school districts.

state or federal funding for local school districts, often comes with strings attached (i.e., school districts must comply with certain requirements to qualify to receive the funding). For example, school lunches must meet certain federal nutrition guidelines in order to qualify for federal school lunch subsidies. A local school district can receive funding from the state, the federal government, and local taxes. Figure 12.2 details the percent of funding for public education in Michigan from each source.

Historically, local education in the United States was supported by a property tax, and Michigan is no exception. Funding education through local taxes aligns the benefits of local education to the local community with the costs of that education; residents pay for the education provided for their own community through a portion of their property taxes. Prior to property tax reform in Michigan, roughly two-thirds of education funding came from taxes levied by local school districts.

Proposal A, approved by voters in 1994, brought sweeping changes to property taxes in Michigan as part of a plan to reform the funding mechanism for schools. This significantly affected school districts because of their traditional reliance on funding from property taxes. School districts lost much of their ability to generate revenues through property taxes. Lost local revenues were replaced with funding from the state government, which was made possible by increasing the sales tax from 4 to 6 percent.[10] Since 1995, the vast majority of education funding has come from the state government, making local school districts more reliant on the state Legislature. Because of this, education funding is a significant issue for the Legislature, and changes in the state budget can have large effects on school finances.

A majority of state funding for local education comes from the School Aid Fund (SAF). This fund in the state budget is earmarked for education, and while a small portion of the fund is used for higher education (3.6 percent of the 2015–16 SAF budget), almost the entire SAF is used to support local early childhood, elementary, and secondary education (totaling just over $12 billion in the 2015–16 budget). A majority of this fund provides per-student funding to local schools, but state school aid also helps local school districts pay for special education, programs benefiting at-risk students, and early childhood programs. It also helps cover a portion of retirement benefits for teachers, operating costs for intermediate school districts, career and technical education, and early literacy programs.[11]

Higher Education Funding

Unlike public K-12 education, public higher education institutions charge tuition. Historically, tuition covered only a small portion of higher education costs, with the state subsidizing most of the costs at public higher education institutions. However, state funding per student has significantly declined over the past several decades. Figure 12.3 details state funding for public universities in Michigan and shows a drop in funding from almost $8,000 per student in 1997 to about $4,000 per student in 2013.

Funding to community colleges in the state saw decreases as well, although not as much as with university funding. In part, community college districts are taxing authorities, so they have a stream of revenue not available to Michigan's public universities. Funding from the state per community college student dropped from a little less than $2,500 per student in 1997 to about $1,500 per student in 2013, as illustrated by Figure 12.4.

Between 1997 and 2014, state funding per student in Michigan declined 51 percent for public universities and 30 percent for community colleges.

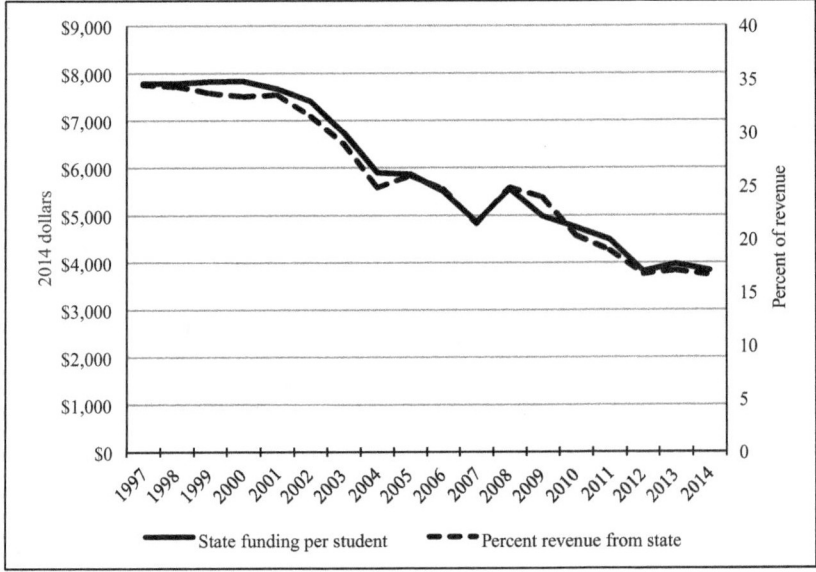

Fig. 12.3. State Funding of Public Universities, 1997–2014
Source: Integrated Postsecondary Education Data System, National Center for Education Statistics.
Note: Figures 12.3 and 12.4 detail funding for Michigan community colleges reporting data to the Integrated Postsecondary Education Data System at the National Center for Education Statistics. Data in these graphs has been adjusted for inflation using the Higher Education Price Index, which measures inflation in items purchased by higher education instructions; adjusting this data for inflation is necessary to provide meaningful comparison across time.

The percentage of community college and university funding coming from the state has experienced a similar decline. During the same period, state appropriations have gone from comprising 35 percent of total university revenues to 17 percent of total revenues, and community colleges have seen state appropriations decrease from accounting for 30 percent of total revenues to 17 percent of total revenues.

These decreases in state subsidies for higher education have forced public institutions to make up the difference from other funding sources. Since community colleges can levy property taxes, voters living in a community college district have the option of voting for property tax increases. However, with the dramatic decline in the housing market during Michigan's "lost decade," property tax revenues generally experienced significant declines. Public universities have largely turned to tuition increases to make up for these reductions in state funding. Michigan is not

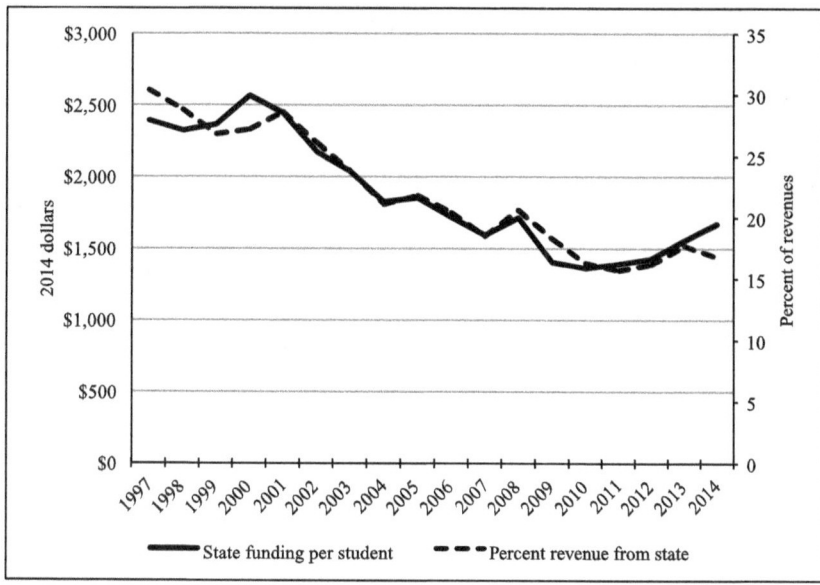

Fig. 12.4. State Funding of Community Colleges, 1997–2014
Source: Integrated Postsecondary Education Data System, National Center for Education Statistics.

alone in experiencing this trend of reduced state funding and increasing tuition;[12] one study linked 78 percent of tuition increases nationwide to reduced state funding.[13]

Policy Responses to Recent Crises: Modeling Policy Intervention

When studying policy responses to problems facing society, it is informative to consider the catalysts leading to the policies in question. As described by public policy scholar John Kingdon, policy intervention occurs when a problem exists, potential policy actions are being discussed, and the political environment supports a given policy intervention. This framework can be instructive when studying Michigan education policies.[14]

Policies are often created in response to a crisis. Before analyzing policy solutions and the political environment, consider the problems policymakers face when considering Michigan education policy. Financial crisis and academic achievement are problems driving education policy in Michigan.

Local school districts running out of money can force state intervention. Also, in Michigan and throughout the nation, poor academic performance in some school districts has attracted attention from policymakers. While low achievement can be relatively easy to identify, its causes are not. It is important to note how a problem is defined, because the way a problem is defined will direct the types of solutions that are implemented.

There are a number of different ways the problem of poor academic achievement can be described. Some view poor academic performance as the result of poor school leadership, arguing that school officials are not doing everything in their power to improve student achievement. The effectiveness of teachers whose students are not demonstrating adequate academic achievement is often questioned. A lack of educational support in the home is frequently identified as a significant academic barrier to students. And the challenges associated with poverty that families face are also blamed for hindering student achievement. The policy solutions considered depend greatly on which problem definition prevails in policy discussions.

The political environment will guide the selection of predominant problem definitions. While many stakeholders are present and significant debate exists as to the causes of poor educational achievement, the state Legislature is often seen playing a central role in developing policy responses. The state government has broad authority to respond to education crises, and a majority of education funding comes from the state.

With a conservative majority in both chambers of Michigan's state Legislature beginning in 2011, the Legislature during the 2010s predominately defined the academic achievement problem as resulting from a lack of accountability and adequate incentives for teachers and school administrators. This focus is not unique to public education; in recent years there has been significant emphasis on the need for accountability in the public sector, including in education.[15]

Discussion of potential solutions designed to increase accountability only have traction in the state Legislature in light of the above problem definition for low academic achievement. Without problems, solutions, and politics coming together to create windows of opportunity for policy change, discussions of increasing accountability would not result in new education policies. However, because of how educational problems, policy discussions, and the political environment have come together, state policies have focused on increasing accountability for both teachers and schools.

Policy Responses to Academic Performance in Michigan

Accountability of Educators

Teachers are now being held accountable for student achievement through annual performance evaluations. In 2015, the state Legislature required that a portion of each teacher's evaluation be based on student growth and assessment data.[16] Legislators believe this will provide the necessary incentive for teachers to focus on student outcomes. This focus on establishing appropriate incentives recognizes that people are motivated by incentive structures, and argues that incentives are necessary to ensure that teachers are looking beyond routine instruction and focusing on student achievement.

Opponents of linking teacher evaluations to student assessment data argue that factors beyond the control of a teacher significantly affect student achievement. Teachers of students facing educational barriers outside the classroom will be punished for factors beyond their control, and teachers in schools serving at risk populations will have difficulty achieving satisfactory performance as a result of the population they are serving. Opponents to this type of teacher evaluation also argue that this creates an incentive for teachers to avoid teaching in classrooms with at risk students.

Accountability through School Choice

In addition to creating new incentives for teachers, the state Legislature has pursued accountability for school districts through incentives creating competition for student enrollment. One motivation for creating this competition is to allow families to hold schools accountable through the mechanism of school choice. If families that choose to send their children to public school only have one schooling option, public schools are guaranteed enrollment numbers. However, if families have the option to send their children to a number of different publicly funded schools, then supporters of school choice argue that schools have an incentive to provide the best possible education in order to attract and retain students. Schools are very attentive to enrollment numbers because school funding is so closely tied to student enrollment.

This also provides families living in an area with poorly performing schools an alternative schooling option. Many poorly performing schools are located in lower-income areas where many families would struggle to afford a private school; the introduction of school choice provides these families with other public schooling options that do not require the family to pay tuition. In addition to the traditional options of private schooling and homeschooling, Michigan has pursued school choice through the schools of choice option and through charter schools.

The schools of choice option allows each school district the option to accept students who live outside the school district's borders. This option can be attractive to school districts because the increased student enrollment will bring increased state funding. Local school districts making this choice have a degree of control over the extent to which they will accept additional students. The local school board determines the total number of students who will be accepted from outside the district boundary along with which grades and school buildings are available for outside enrollment. Also the district decides whether they will accept students only from the same intermediate school district or also from surrounding intermediate school districts. School boards also have the option to enable intradistrict choice, allowing students living in the district to attend a school other than their normally assigned school.[17]

Charter schools are operated by private organizations that receive a charter to operate a public school. There is no tuition charge, so families are able to choose between a traditional public school and charter schools without concern over cost. Supporters point out that allowing school choice among public schools enables every family the opportunity to choose the best school for their children.

In Michigan, charter schools receive their funding from the state. State funding is calculated on a per student basis, creating an incentive for charter schools to attract and retain students. This funding mechanism is designed to give families a way to hold charter schools accountable. Schools that perform well will attract students and be rewarded with additional funding, while charter schools that fail to retain students will receive reduced funding.

In addition to enrollment-based funding, charter schools are held accountable by the entity granting the charter. The school charter, which is the legal framework authorizing a particular charter school, is designed to focus accountability on student performance rather than only focusing on compliance with state regulations. A school charter will stipulate student performance goals that must be met, and at the same time the charter school has greater operational flexibility in meeting the goals than would a traditional public school. This arrangement is intended to promote innovation while only rewarding successful charter schools.

In Michigan, school charters can be granted by the school board of a traditional public school district or intermediate school district, or by the governing board of a community college or public university. Each charter sets requirements for the school, including goals that must be met in order to maintain the charter. Performance of the charter school is monitored by the governing board that granted the charter; a poorly performing charter school may not receive a renewal of its charter, and a charter may also be revoked for poor performance.[18]

The state Legislature passed into law the legal framework for establishing charter schools in 1993. Since then, the number of charter schools and student enrollment in charter schools has grown significantly. By the 2014–15 academic year, there were 375 charter schools enrolling a total of 142,752 students; attendance in these charter schools accounted for 10.7 percent of total public school enrollment as of 2015.[19] This relative prevalence of charter school education brings additional attention to the debate regarding this new type of school.

Charter schools have a mixed record when it comes to improving educational attainment of students. Numerous studies have evaluated the effectiveness of charter schools, and the results have varied.[20] Charter school quality is uneven, and there is evidence of charter schools both outperforming and underperforming traditional public schools. While some charter schools are highly successful at improving student outcomes, it is also not uncommon for charter schools to close after a charter has been lost because the school has failed to meet the educational goals set forth in the charter. Opponents of charter schools point to the large number of charter schools that are unsuccessful at improving student outcomes. Supporters instead point to successful charter schools. By design, failing charter schools are not permitted to continue operating, and students are benefiting from innovative approaches at charter schools that are deemed successful.

Unintended Policy Consequences

Opponents of charter schools argue that school choice is bad for local communities because of the unintended consequences it can create. Without school choice, families using public schooling can only use their local public school. When school choice among public schooling options is introduced, the distribution of students in a school is no longer tied to geographic location. Instead, students may travel greater distances to enroll in a preferred school of choice district or attend a charter school.

The new patterns of school enrollment under charter schools have the potential to produce some unexpected results. If families are drawn to schools that reflect the family's own socioeconomic status, then school choice could actually increase school segregation. This would occur because socioeconomic status is related to race.[21]

Not all families find charter schools equally attractive. Families choosing charter schools tend to have more in common with families that choose private schools than they do with families that choose traditional public schools. Charter schools may be viewed as a no-cost alternative to private schooling, attracting families who would choose a private school if cost were not a barrier. In general, charter schools attract students from higher socioeconomic households than do traditional public schools.[22] This leaves traditional public schools with less diversity and a lower socioeconomic student body.

Those opposing charter schools also argue that charter schools divert necessary resources away from traditional public schools. Because school funding in Michigan is so closely tied to school enrollment, traditional public schools lose funding when students leave for a charter school. This diversion of education funding is difficult for traditional school districts because of fixed costs the districts face. While some costs, such as the number of teachers, are variable and can be adjusted according to year-to-year enrollment changes, costs including school building maintenance or pensions for retired teachers cannot be as easily adjusted.

State Takeovers

States are becoming directly involved in local education in schools that are failing academically or financially (both situations are sometimes called "academic bankruptcy"). Nationally, states are stepping in where local schools have consistently poor performance and removing local control by taking authority away from the elected school board. These actions are designed to "turn around" academically failing schools when the local school district has been unable to do so. By removing local control, a state is altering the traditionally accepted value of locally managed education in the United States. Unsurprisingly, these actions are quite controversial as local residents lose their ability to influence educational decisions.[23]

Consistent with this national trend, Michigan has begun removing local control over poorly performing schools. In 2012, the state transferred control of 15 of the lowest performing public schools in Detroit to a newly formed charter school district named the Education Achievement Authority. These new schools were charged with making the changes necessary to improve low test scores, with the intention that this new district would expand to include other low performing schools in the state. As has been the case with state takeovers elsewhere in the nation, significant controversy accompanied this action.[24] This controversy, along with continued poor academic performance at these schools, led to these schools being transferred to the newly created Detroit Public Schools Community District in 2017.[25]

Policy Responses to Financial Crisis

Understanding the Crisis: Student Enrollment Trends

Recent financial crises in some public school districts have been another clear problem for public education. Understanding these financial problems will provide insight into some recent policy decisions designed to respond to them. Many school districts have been experiencing declining enrollment. Historically this would not have caused serious problems for most school districts in Michigan because public education was primarily funded through the local property tax. Local property tax revenues are determined by property assessments and the tax rate, and they do not fluctuate with school enrollment. However, state funding for local education is calculated on a per-pupil basis, resulting in funding levels tied to school enrollment when state funding comprises a significant portion of local revenues. Prior to Proposal A, Michigan guaranteed school districts a minimum per pupil payment; school districts in communities with low property values would receive state funding to make up for the inability of those districts to raise higher levels of property tax revenue.[26] Only school districts in communities with significantly low property values would face revenues significantly influenced by student enrollment. However, since the passage of Proposal A, all school districts now see revenues significantly impacted by enrollment numbers. With roughly three-quarters of school funding now coming from the state and primarily based on per-pupil formulas, local education budgets are sensitive to enrollment trends.

This sensitivity to enrollment trends benefits education budgets when enrollment is increasing but hurts funding when enrollment is declining. Unfortunately for local school districts, declining enrollment has become the norm. According to official state data reported by the Center for Educational Performance and Information, statewide K-12 enrollment declined just over 11 percent from 2003 to 2015.[27] In short, Michigan is seeing fewer school-age children in the state. Furthermore, this decrease in enrollment is not uniform across the state; some districts have experienced very significant enrollment declines, while other schools have seen large enrollment increases, with such increases often resulting from school choice.

Comparing enrollment data from the Center for Educational Performance and Information over time identifies some noteworthy trends. Some schools have experienced significant enrollment growth. Between 2005 and 2015, 25 school systems experienced greater than 100 percent growth; all but two of those were charter schools, and the two traditional school districts in this list are small districts serving rural communities that increased enrollment by less than two dozen students. Crescent Academy in the City of Southfield was the fastest growing school system during this period, growing from 195 to 1,068 students. This charter school primarily enrolls students living in the Detroit school district and is an example of the relationship between charter schools and traditional public schools struggling with low student performance.

Michigan law permits traditional public schools to engage in competition for students along with charter schools. As noted above, public school districts have the option to become a school of choice, setting aside a set number of student seats for children living outside the school district. Some school districts have become schools of choice in an effort to maintain enrollment numbers; by enrolling students who live outside of the district, the school district is able to mitigate the financial effects of declining enrollment of students living in the district. This type of school choice is consistent with the goals of charter schools; accountability is introduced through competition for enrollment, and families have more schooling options for their children.

Declining enrollment has affected school districts in both large and small communities. For example, consider Albion Public Schools, which served a total of 547 students in 2015, and Detroit Public Schools, which served 47,959 students in the same year. Between 2005 and 2015, both of these public school districts experienced a 66 percent decline in enrollment.[28] Any district that loses almost two-thirds of its enrollment will face considerable financial strain simply because school funding is so dependent on enrollment. Significant enrollment declines in these and other school districts across the state stem from demographic shifts, resulting in fewer children living in a given school district, and school choice, as families choose to send their children to alternative schools such as charter schools.

Districts experiencing significant declines in enrollment and the associated decreases in funding will be faced with a difficult financial situation. Many school districts in this situation face significant "legacy costs," which are current costs resulting from past activities. For example, if a school district has not already set aside sufficient funds to pay for pensions or health insurance that was promised to retirees, current funds must be used for those legacy costs. These payments do not provide for current educational services, but instead pay for education provided in the past. If sufficient funds are not set aside for future benefits promised to current employees, the true cost of today's employees must be partially paid for in the future.

The use of current funds to cover legacy costs becomes especially problematic when a school district's budget shrinks. If legacy costs comprise a small portion of the overall budget, a school district can likely continue affording those payments. However, as a budget shrinks with reduced enrollment, legacy costs account for a larger portion of the overall budget. This makes it more difficult for the district to afford current educational costs.

Responding to Financial Crisis

State government intervention in the governance of local school districts in recent years frequently has been driven by financial crisis. Under Public Act 436 of 2012 (the Local Financial Stability and Choice Act), the state may impose constraints on local governments determined to be in financial emergency. This law applies to public school districts, since they are local governments. If a financial emergency is determined to exist, then a school district can choose between a consent agreement, under which the district agrees to specific actions in order to remedy the financial emergency, and a neutral evaluation, in which the school district will attempt to arrive at a settlement with those to whom the district owes money. An emergency manager, who will act in place of the school board and superintendent, is usually appointed only after a district unsuccessfully attempts to resolve the financial crisis through a consent agreement. As of the 2015–16 academic year, Benton Harbor Area Schools and Pontiac Public Schools were under a consent agreement, and Detroit Public Schools (which was later reorganized as the Detroit Public Schools Community District in 2017), Highland Park School District, and Muskegon Heights School District all had an emergency manager.

Local governments usually try to avoid bankruptcy because of the difficult sacrifices that emerge from bankruptcy proceedings. For example, as a result of the City of Detroit's bankruptcy, pensions for non-public-safety retirees were cut 4.5 percent.[29] When emergency managers are appointed, they take over the functions of the superintendent and elected school board; this limits local control over local education policies and decisions. An emergency manager is also given more authority than the school board, including the ability to alter negotiated union contracts. Broad authority is granted to the emergency manager for the purpose of doing whatever is necessary to avoid bankruptcy; however, the granting of this broad authority is unsurprisingly controversial. As with state takeovers addressing academic performance, a state takeover for financial reasons fundamentally alters the relationship between state and local education decisions.

In extreme cases, a school district may be dissolved by the intermediate school district containing it or by the state. Two school districts facing declining enrollments and financial crisis were dissolved in 2013: Inkster Public Schools in Wayne County and Buena Vista School District in Saginaw County. In these cases, the boundaries of the surrounding school districts were expanded to absorb the areas comprising the former school districts.

Higher Education Policy

The focus on accountability and incentive structures has not been unique to K-12 education. Recent state policies have also taken this approach in higher education. These policies have resulted when attention on accountability and incentive structures in the context of rising tuition and a desire for more college graduates in the state has combined with political pressure to contain tuition and encourage graduation.

Nationwide, there has been a push for performance funding in higher education. States with higher education performance funding formulas use university performance to determine a portion of the state's funding for each university. For example, in order to encourage greater graduation and retention of students, some states tie a portion of state funding to a university's graduation rates. There is significant variation in the performance metrics applied by the more than 20 states that have employed higher education performance funding, with some states having used more than a dozen different performance metrics.[30] Michigan incorporates performance funding into the state higher education budget, defining targets each year that universities must reach in order to qualify for the additional performance funding. This funding mechanism is designed to hold universities accountable for student outcomes and incentivize universities to increase performance in response to the performance funding.[31]

As noted above, higher education institutions have largely turned to tuition increases to compensate for decreased state funding. Higher education costs gain public attention, and the state Legislature has attempted to limit these tuition increases through incentive funding to universities. As is the case with state K-12 policy, we see accountability and incentive oriented policies enacted in response to challenges in higher education and in the context of political values held by lawmakers in Lansing. The Legislature typically sets a cap on tuition increases at public universities each year; universities that exceed this cap lose eligibility for the additional funding that is awarded based on university performance.

While there has been significant movement throughout the nation to use performance funding in higher education budgets, there is little evidence that these policies are responsible for improved outcomes. Periodically, Michigan universities will ignore the tuition cap and forego the additional state funding in order to have a larger tuition increase that generates (sometimes much more) additional revenue for the university. National studies have also failed to find a relationship between performance funding and student outcomes such as graduation rates.[32] This may be due to programs that are focused on assisting students at risk of not completing a degree, which the universities have been developing independent of any performance funding. Also, many of the factors leading to student success, such as student preparation during high school, are beyond the control of universities.[33]

Conclusion

Education policy is primarily the responsibility of state and local governments. The state exercises authority over local school districts, and most K-12 education funding in Michigan comes from the state. Higher education policies are largely overseen by the governing board at each college or university, and the state Legislature determines state funding for public colleges and universities.

Education funding decisions reveal legislative priorities and often receive significant public attention. Because most K-12 funding is provided by the state, public education funding is closely tied to student enrollment. This has resulted in declining revenues for many school districts because many districts have been experiencing declining enrollment. Higher education institutions have experienced significantly declining state subsidies per student, resulting in colleges and universities looking to tuition increases to make up for these reductions in funding.

Recent education policies have emphasized accountability and incentives. Policies have centered on key problems facing education in the state. Poor academic performance has been addressed by incorporating student achievement into teacher evaluations. School choice, including charter schools, has been used to promote accountability and provide incentives for schools. The focus on accountability and incentives is also evident through responses to financial crises. Public schools in Detroit have undergone several reorganizations, including creation of a separate district called the Education Achievement Authority, but which was then dissolved in 2017. Also, Detroit Public Schools was replaced by the Detroit Public Schools Community District. There has been significant state intervention to prevent bankruptcy, including appointing emergency managers and even calling for the dissolving of school districts facing financial emergencies. Performance funding incentives have been incorporated into higher education funding as well.

WEB RESOURCES

The *State of Michigan* (www.michigan.gov/education) as well as the *Michigan Department of Education* (www.michigan.gov/mde) provide a great deal of information on educational issues in Michigan.

The *National Center for Education Statistics* at the U.S. Department of Education (nces.ed.gov/ipeds) maintains the Integrated Postsecondary Education Data System. This database contains current and historical data on colleges and universities throughout the nation, and covers topics including enrollment, graduation rates, employees, revenues, and financial aid. Following the "Use the Data" link will provide a variety of statistical tools for accessing and analyzing the data.

The *Michigan School Data* website (www.mischooldata.org) provides a variety of data relating to accountability of individual school districts. A variety of statistics on student achievement and student enrollment can be downloaded for specific school districts using the links under "Kindergarten–12th Grade." Also, the "Dashboard & Accountability Scorecard" provides a summary of statewide education metrics.

The *Michigan Association of School Boards* (www.masb.org) is a good resource for policy issues facing local schools. Links to policy papers on current issues can be found by following the "Advocacy & Legislation" link and then clicking on "Legislative Priorities."

The *Michigan Senate Fiscal Agency* (www.senate.michigan.gov/sfa) provides current data on state appropriations for education. Data for K-12 funding is available by following the "Education Department" link. Data on higher education funding is available by following the "Higher Education" link.

NOTES

1. Lori Higgins, "New State Exam Requires Deeper Skills," *Detroit Free Press*, December 2, 2014.

2. "Michigan Unveils New Standardized Test to Replace MEAP," *Detroit News*, November 14, 2014.

3. "Number of Public School Districts in Michigan," accessed January 21, 2016, http://www.michigan.gov/documents/numbsch_26940_7.pdf

4. Janet Y. Thomas and Kevin P. Brady, "Chapter 3: The Elementary and Secondary Education Act at 40: Equity, Accountability, and the Evolving Federal Role in Public Education," *Review of Research in Education* 29 (2005): 29–50.

5. "Every Student Succeeds Act (ESSA)," accessed January 21, 2016, http://www.ed.gov/essa

6. For additional information on *Brown v. Board of Education* and the history of court decisions leading to this case, see the website for the Federal Judiciary: http://www.uscourts.gov/educational-resources/educational-activities/history-brown-v-board-education-re-enactment

7. *Hazelwood Sch. Dist. v. Kuhlmeier*, 484 U.S. 260 (1988).

8. *Board of Ed. of Independent School Dist. No. 92 of Pottawatomie Cty. v. Earls* (01-332) 536 U.S. 822 (2002). For a summary of additional U.S. Supreme Court decisions pertaining to education, see http://www.uscourts.gov/about-federal-courts/educational-resources/supreme-court-landmarks

9. For more information, see the State Higher Education Executive Officers Association: http://www.sheeo.org/

10. Susanna Loeb and Julie Berry Cullen, "School Finance Reform in Michigan: Evaluating Proposal A," in *Helping Children Left Behind: State Aid and the Pursuit of Educational Equity*, ed. John Yinger, 215–50 (Cambridge, MA: MIT Press, 2004).

11. Bethany Wicksall and Samuel Christensen, House Fiscal Agency, *School Aid*, November 2015.

12. United States Government Accountability Office, *Higher Education: State Funding Trends and Policies on Affordability* (GAO-15-151) (Washington, DC: U.S. Government Printing Office, 2014).

13. Robert Hiltonsmith, *Pulling Up the Higher-Ed Ladder: Myth and Reality in the Crisis of College Affordability* (New York: Demos, 2015).

14. John W. Kingdon, *Agendas, Alternatives and Public Policies*, 2nd ed. (New York: Harper Collins, 1995).

15. Brian M. Stecher and Sheila Nataraj Kirby, *Organizational Improvement and Accountability: Lessons for Education from Other Sectors* (Santa Monica, CA: RAND Corporation, 2004). eBook Collection (EBSCOhost). Accessed November 4, 2015.

16. The Revised School Code, MCL 380.1249.

17. Michigan Department of Education, *Schools of Choice*, 2013; accessed January 28, 2016, http://www.michigan.gov/documents/mde/choice1_279579_7.pdf?20160128141640

18. Gary Miron and Christopher Nelson, *What's Public about Charter Schools? Lessons Learned about Choice and Accountability* (Thousand Oaks, CA: Corwin Press, 2002).

19. National Center for Education Statistics, "Digest of Education Statistics: 2016," table 216.90, in *Public Elementary and Secondary Charter Schools and Enrollment, by State: Selected Years 1999–2000 through 2014–15* (Washington, DC: GPO, 2016).

20. Ron Zimmer, Brian Gill, Kevin Booker, Stéphane Lavertu, and John Witte,

"Examining Charter Student Achievement Effects across Seven States," *Economics of Education Review* 31 (2012): 213–24; Devora H. Davis and Margaret E. Raymond, "Choices for Studying Choice: Assessing Charter School Effectiveness Using Two Quasi-Experimental Methods," *Economics of Education Review* 31 (2012): 225–36; Ron Zimmer and Richard Buddin, "Charter School Performance in Two Large Urban Districts," *Journal of Urban Economics* 60 (2006): 307–26.

21. N. Lacireno-Paquet, T. T. Holyoke, M. Moser, and J. R. Henig, "Creaming versus Cropping: Charter School Enrollment Practices in Response to Market Incentives," *Educational Evaluation and Policy Analysis* 24 (2002): 145–58; M. Schneider, P. Teske, M. Marshall, and C. Roch, "Shopping for Schools: In the Land of the Blind, the One-Eyed Parent May Be Enough," *American Journal of Political Science* 42 (1998): 769–93.

22. J. S. Butler, Douglas A. Carr, Eugenia F. Toma, and Ron Zimmer, "Choice in a World of New School Types," *Journal of Policy Analysis and Management* 32 (2013): 785–806.

23. For example, the Arkansas State Board of Education dissolved the elected school board for the Little Rock School District, causing significant controversy. Greg Toppo, "More State Takeovers of Public Schools Possible," *USAToday*, February 9, 2015.

24. Mary L. Mason and David Arsen, "Michigan's Education Achievement Authority and the Future of Public Education in Detroit: The Challenge of Aligning Policy Design and Policy Goals," Working Paper No. 43, Education Policy Center at Michigan State University, 2014.

25. Shawn D. Lewis, "EAA at Beginning of End with New School Year," *Detroit News*, September 4, 2016; Nora Colomer, "Detroit School District to Take Over State-Run EAA Schools," *Bond Buyer*, November 9, 2016.

26. Susanna Loeb and Julie Berry Cullen, "School Finance Reform in Michigan: Evaluating Proposal A," in *Helping Children Left Behind: State Aid and the Pursuit of Educational Equity*, ed. John Yinger, 215–50 (Cambridge, MA: MIT Press, 2004).

27. Center for Education Performance and Information, 2015, [data file], retrieved from http://michigan.gov/cepi

28. Center for Education Performance and Information, 2015, [data file], retrieved from http://michigan.gov/cepi

29. In re City of Detroit, 14-cv-14872, Bankr. No. 13–53846 Chapter 9 (E.D. Mich. Southern Division 2015), LexisNexis Lexis 131174.

30. "The Effects of Performance Funding on Higher Education Outcomes: Testimony before the Michigan House Appropriations Subcommittee on Higher Education, March 21, 2012 (Testimony of Roger Larocca and Douglas Carr)."

31. Frank Schmidtlein, "Assumptions Underlying Performance-Based Budgeting," *Tertiary Education and Management* 5 (1999): 159–74.

32. Jung-Cheol Shin and Sande Milton, "The Effects of Performance Budgeting and Funding Programs on Graduation Rate in Public Four-Year Colleges and Universities," *Education Policy Analysis Archives* 12 (2004): 1–26; S. K. Woodley, "A Critical Analysis of the Effect of Performance Funding and Budgeting Systems on University Performance," DBA diss., Nova Southeastern University, 2005; J. Volkein and David Tandberg, "Measuring Up: Examining the Connections among State Structural Characteristics, Regulatory Practices, and Performance," *Research*

in Higher Education 51 (2008): 40–64; Jung Cheol Shin, "Impacts of Performance-Based Accountability on Institutional Performance in the U.S.," *Higher Education* 60 (2009): 47–68; N. W. Hillman, D.A. Tandberg, and J. P. K. Gross. "Performance Funding in Higher Education: Do Financial Incentives Impact College Completions?," *Journal of Higher Education* 85 (2014): 826–57; D. A. Tandberg and N. W. Hillman, "State Higher Education Performance Funding: Data, Outcomes, and Policy Implications," *Journal of Education Finance* 39 (2014): 222–42; D. A. Tandberg, N. W. Hillman, and M. Barakat, "State Higher Education Performance Funding for Community Colleges: Diverse Effects and Policy Implications," *Teachers College Record* 116 (2014): 1–31.

33. Roger Larocca and Douglas A. Carr, "The Effect of Higher Education Performance Funding on Graduation and Retention Rates," working paper, Oakland University, 2015.

13 ✦ Budget and Fiscal Policy in Michigan

MITCH BEAN

A state's fiscal policy and the decisions it makes about its own budget can have a major impact on a state's economy and the government's ability to respond to challenges. Among most other state policies, fiscal policies (i.e., taxation and spending) directly affect a state's economic health, through corporate tax rates and incentives to invest, as well as spending on infrastructure projects (e.g., roads) that support modern economic activity. These policies have the potential to reverse economic decline effectively enough to promote recovery, but policies also can fail to help—as well as create their own new set of new challenges. In the recent past, Michigan has suffered from serious economic decline, population loss, and, at times, new challenges created in part by policies intended to fix problems it faced. On matters such as state revenue sharing, shifts in taxes such as through Proposal A in the 1990s, and state tax limitation policies (e.g., the Headlee Amendment), the state also directly affects the budgets of its various local governments.

In this chapter, the economic challenges Michigan has faced during the last 20 years, the policy responses to those challenges, and the impact of those policy responses on resources available to state and local governments and state and local budgets are considered. The chapter begins with an overview of the boom, bust, and recovery cycle that has been present in Michigan's economy from the mid-1990s through the mid-2010s. While there are many factors that contributed to the decline of the state's economy over this period of time, one key dynamic that received special attention has been the dramatic structural changes in the Big Three automakers (Ford, Chrysler and General Motors) and the domestic auto industry generally.

In addition, an important part of understanding the story includes understanding certain statutory and constitutional requirements and how they affected responses and outcomes of state tax and spending decisions.

In Michigan, local units of governments—counties, cities, villages, and townships—deliver many of the services citizens rely upon. Local governments face a number of constraints on raising revenues and are dependent on the state for a major portion of their revenues. Many state tax and fiscal policy decisions impact local units of government as well as state government. The impact of the constraints local governments face, and the impact of state policymaker's decisions on local units, are also considered.

Michigan's Economy: Highs and Lows of the Last 20 Years

The Michigan economy has experienced stunning highs and lows during the last two decades. In the mid- to late 1990s, the state's signature industry, automobile manufacturing, captured over 70 percent of the U.S. market share of light vehicles (i.e., cars and light trucks) annually (see fig. 13.1). In addition, the overall automobile market was expanding, as total U.S. sales hit all-time highs and Michigan vehicle employment expanded and exceeded 346,000 workers. Through about 2007, overall light vehicle sales were fairly steady, but the Big Three's share of those sales dropped steadily to less than 45 percent of all sales by 2010. After the Great Recession, U.S. vehicle sales improved to nearly match their prerecession totals. However, the Big Three's share of the market was about 40 percent lower than what it was at its height. In addition, Michigan's employment in the light vehicle sector was about 50 percent lower than it was in 2000.

Beginning in 2001, the Big Three were facing a declining share of a smaller market and a drastic need to downsize and restructure. Later, after two of the Big Three (GM and Chrysler) emerged from separate structured bankruptcies, their market share stabilized. The light vehicle market came back strong as well and by May 2015 U.S. light vehicle annualized sales rate was 16.3 million units. Hence, the state's automobile sector had a stable share of a larger market and Michigan vehicle employment stabilized as well.

Michigan's job market was extremely strong in the mid- to late 1990s and the unemployment rate hit a record low of 3.2 percent in the spring of 2000. But beginning in 2001, state employment began to decline precipitously, and the state unemployment rate was the highest in the nation, exceeding 15 percent for several months in the fall of 2009.

The high point of Michigan's employment boom occurred in 2000, but over the next 10 years Michigan lost about 813,000 jobs—over 17 percent of the jobs below its high point in employment (see fig. 13.2). Employment increased in 2010 after the economy bottomed out in the wake of the Great

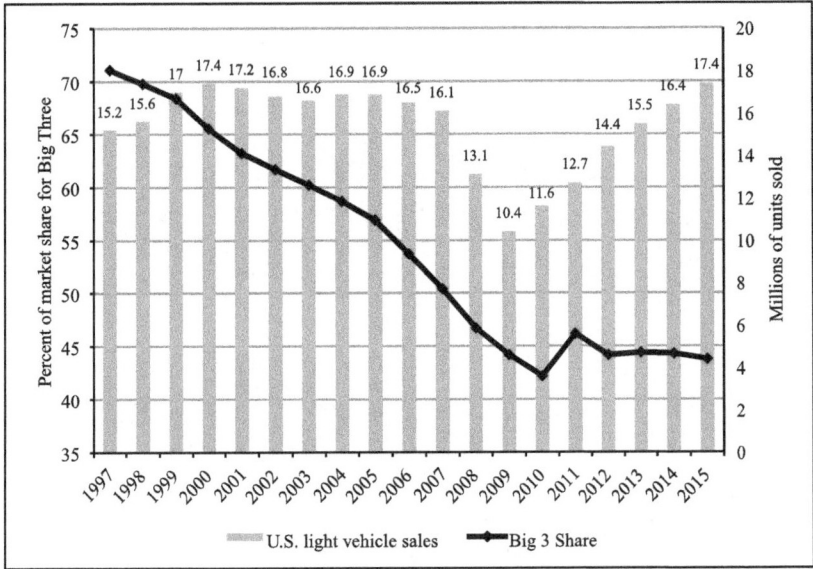

Fig. 13.1. U.S. Light Vehicle Sales and Big Three Market Share, 1997–2015
Source: Author's calculation based on data from the *Automotive News*, various issues.

Recession—but Michigan still had nearly 500,000 fewer jobs in 2014 than it did in 2000, even though the state saw some job growth after 2011. Job losses from 2000 to 2010 are almost entirely explained by losses in the automobile production sector and related jobs in the state economy affected by the losses in the vehicle sector. The state unemployment rate declined as the economy began to recover in 2010 and was close to the national average in the several years after that (see chapter 1). Some of the decline in the state unemployment rate was due to job creation, but some was also due to declines in the state labor force.

This necessitates a point of clarification about unemployment rates. The basic concepts involved in identifying the employed and unemployed are quite simple: people with jobs are *employed*; people who are jobless, looking for a job, and available for work are *unemployed*; the *labor force* is made up of the employed and the unemployed; people who are neither employed nor unemployed are *not in the labor force*.

The unemployment rate is the ratio of people who are unemployed to the total labor force. Two things affect this calculation: the number of jobs that are filled and the size of the labor force. If the numbers of jobs that are filled increases while the size of the labor force remains constant, the unemployment goes down. However, because it is a ratio, the unem-

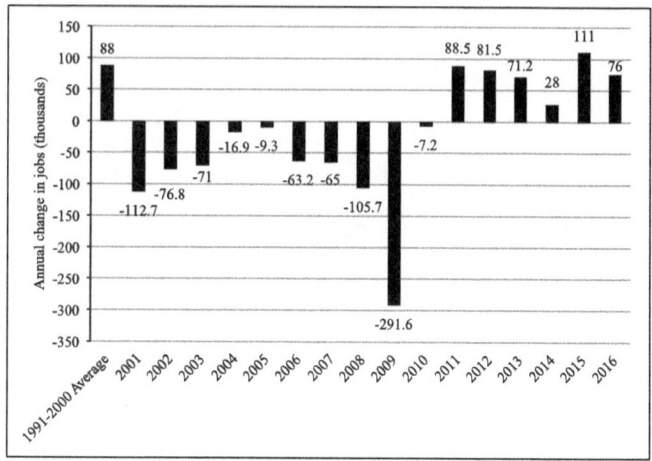

Fig. 13.2. Michigan Job Growth, 1991–2016
Source: Author's calculations based on figures from Michigan Department of Treasury, Office of Revenue and Tax Analysis (ORTA), as of 2016 Consensus Estimate.

ployment rate also declines if no jobs are created but the total labor force gets smaller. This is an important distinction because Michigan's *labor force* declined by over 400,000 persons from 2000 to 2014. Hence, lower unemployment rates were due in part to a smaller labor force and due in part to job creation. Some of the decline in the state labor force is due to demographics as older workers exited the labor force and some of the decline is due to discouraged workers who either dropped out of the labor force or moved out of state to find a job.

The good economic times the state experienced in the 1990s came to an abrupt halt beginning with the national recession in 2001. The contraction in the national economy was relatively mild and only lasted about six months, but economic growth in Michigan lagged behind the nation until after the Great Recession. As noted in chapter 1, Michigan saw deeper declines and more anemic recoveries in key areas like unemployment and economic growth during the first part of the 21st century. There is no wonder, then, why this period of time is known as Michigan's "single-state recession" and "lost decade."[1]

The State Budget and the Budget Process

The roles of the executive and legislative branches in producing the annual state budget are defined by the Michigan Constitution and a slew of enacted statutes. The process officially begins with the Consensus Revenue

Estimating Conference (CREC) every January, per the statutory requirements of the state's Management and Budget Act.[2] The Act requires that a revenue estimating conference shall be held in the second week of January and in the third week in May of each year. In addition, the Management and Budget Act mandates that the principals (i.e., voting members) of the conference shall be the state budget director or the state treasurer, the director of the Senate Fiscal Agency, and the director of the House Fiscal Agency, or their respective designees; that the conference shall establish an official economic forecast of major variables of the national and state economies; and that the conference shall also establish a forecast of anticipated state revenues. Forecasted revenues include the major revenue sources for General Fund/General Purpose (GF/GP) and the School Aid Fund (SAF). These include: state income tax collections; state sales tax collections; corporate income tax collections; Michigan business tax collections; other GF/GP revenues; lottery transfers to the SAF; and other SAF revenues.

The SAF and GF/GP are the state's two largest operating funds. The School Aid Fund is the largest and is constitutionally dedicated to K-12 schools and higher education (see chapter 12). In general, GF/GP is considered the state's discretionary source of funding and funds state departments such as the Department of Natural Resources or the Department of Military and Veterans Affairs. Some GF/GP funds go toward education and higher education as well. The third largest state fund is the Michigan Transportation Fund (MTF). The MTF receives the constitutionally dedicated transportation resources (which include federal funds, grants, fees, and so forth, while revenues refer to state and local taxes) that must be used for transportation related spending. The SAF and MTF also receive federal funds dedicated to education and transportation. There are other smaller state restricted funds but those are beyond the scope of this chapter.

The CREC's official forecast of economic and revenue variables must be determined by unanimous consensus among the principals, and are for the fiscal year in which the conference is being held and the next two fiscal years. In addition to economic and revenue forecasts, the May revenue estimating conference establishes expenditure forecasts for Medicaid expenditures and for human services caseloads and expenditures for the fiscal year in which the conference is being held, and for the following two fiscal years.[3] The January CREC is the official state economic and revenue forecast used by the executive branch to construct the budget that must be presented to the Legislature within 30 days after the Legislature comes into session each January for a seated governor, or within 60 days for a newly elected governor.[4]

The budget that the governor submits to the Legislature is based on the

January CREC revenue forecast, but may also include the use of beginning fund balances or recommended fund transfers and any recommended revenue enhancements such as new or increased fees or revenue from recommended tax changes. An important distinction between Michigan's budget (and most other state budgets) compared to the federal budget is that the Michigan Constitution requires the state to maintain a balanced budget. After the governor submits a budget to the Legislature, the Legislature can change it in any way it chooses. A shorthand description of the process that is often heard around the Capitol is "the governor proposes, and the Legislature disposes." The Legislature is responsible for passing a balanced budget each year based on the May CREC revenue estimate and any policy changes it has made affecting available resources. After a budget is approved by the Legislature it is sent to the governor for signature or veto. The CREC updates forecasts at least two more times after the budget is enacted, which allows the governor and Legislature to make any changes necessary to maintain a balanced budget.

After an appropriations bill is passed by the Legislature and signed into law by the governor, it permits the state to spend funds on a government program, but it is only in force during the fiscal year to which it applies. Unlike standing statutes, when the fiscal year ends the appropriation is no longer effective. It is important to note that an appropriation is not a mandate to spend; rather, the governor, with approval from the Legislature, may make adjustments to the spending plan should the revenue required not be available.[5] It is also important to note that the state Constitution specifies that "[n]o money shall be paid out of the state treasury except in pursuance of appropriations made by law."[6] The interaction of these two provisions has led to some interesting results for funding levels of statutory revenue sharing that are discussed below.

In Michigan, the governor has line-item veto authority (see chapter 6), but cannot unilaterally change the budget the Legislature sends to him or her. That does not mean that the state budget is a static document, however. As noted above, adjustments to the budget occur throughout the year as circumstances change. Adjustments to the budget can be made by transfer (administrative or legislative); through a supplemental appropriations bill; and by executive order budget reductions. A transfer shifts money between specific line items within a budget, but does not shift money between departmental budgets or change the amount of total appropriations. In most cases transfers require the approval of the Appropriations Committee in each chamber of the Legislature but do not require the vote of the full House or Senate.[7] A supplemental appropriation can add, reduce, or shift money between departmental budgets and change the amount of total appropriations. A supplemental appropriation is treated like any appropriations bill; it must be approved by majority votes of each chamber of the Legislature and be signed by the governor.

The authority for executive order budget reductions says in part, "The governor, with the approval of the appropriating committees of the house and senate, shall reduce expenditures authorized by appropriations whenever it appears that actual revenues for a fiscal period will fall below the revenue estimates on which appropriations for that period were based."[8] In practice, when changes to consensus revenue estimates indicate that a revenue shortfall to fund the current state budget will occur, the state treasurer and the state budget director officially inform the governor of the estimated revenue shortfall. The governor then informs the Legislature to expect to receive executive order budget reductions. Because Michigan has a strict separation of powers system, executive orders only apply to executive departments. Spending reductions to the judicial or legislative branches must be made through a negative supplemental appropriations bill.

Major State Revenue Sources

Revenues collected from state and federal sources determine resources available for expenditures on all state departments and state government services including education; these funds are also a major portion of local government resources. The revenues collected from state taxpayers are generally referred to as state-source revenue. Total resources include both state-source revenue and federal funding sources.

As of 2015, Michigan state and local governments levied a total of 60 different taxes (38 state taxes and 22 local taxes).[9] In addition to taxes levied by state and local governments, there are numerous fees that the various levels of government collect. Taxes at all levels of government are subject to important constitutional limitations that do not apply to fees, so the difference between taxes and user fees turns out to be more important than it might seem. The state Constitution and enacted statutes place limits on various state and local tax rates and the amount of total revenue that may be collected each year, whereas user fees are not subject to the same restrictions, with one exception. At the state level there is a restriction on the total amount of resources—including both taxes and fees—the state collects each year based upon a percentage of state personal income. A disagreement over what constituted a tax, and is therefore subject to these restrictions, and what constituted a fee came under some scrutiny in a 1998 state Supreme Court decision, *Bolt v. City of Lansing*. The Court laid out three criteria to distinguish a fee from a tax. User fees must serve a regulatory purpose rather than a revenue-raising purpose; be proportionate to the necessary costs of the service or commodity and imposed on those benefiting from the right/service/improvement supported by the fee; and are voluntary in nature. A tax, however, is levied to raise revenue for the general operation of government; levied to benefit the general public; and compulsory in nature.

In short, a fee may be thought of as a charge that permits an individual or other entity access to a government service or to a privilege granted by government, while a tax underwrites the provision of governmental services available to anyone, regardless of whether the tax has been paid by the individual benefiting from the service or not. For example, a toll on a bridge or highway permits a specific individual access to the bridge or highway. Therefore it is a fee. On the other hand, a gasoline tax, which also pays for bridges and highways, but confers no special access or privilege, is therefore a tax.

In most fiscal years, by far the largest single source of state revenue is federal resources. Federal resources have increased gradually over time. However, there were two significant infusions of federal funds into the state budget between fiscal year 2000 (FY00) and FY15 (see fig. 13.3). The first came during FYs 2009, 2010, and 2011 and were linked to the American Recovery and Reinvestment Act of 2009, one of the first major actions taken by President Obama after he was sworn in as president. The Act was an attempt to stimulate the national economy during the Great Recession and included billions of dollars for construction projects and other programs that injected funds into the economy. The second surge of federal dollars occurred in FY15 and came from roughly $2 billion for an expansion of the Medicaid program in Michigan as part of the Affordable Care Act (ACA; also known as Obamacare). After the ACA became law, Governor Rick Snyder and the Michigan Legislature decided Michigan would participate in the Medicaid expansion portion of the law (this was a step not all Republican governors and legislatures took). While, in this example of one year, the state saw Medicaid dollars increase, Medicaid caseload changes moving forward and changes in federal regulations will be the major determining factors of any future growth.

State-source resources are nonfederal resources collected from citizens and businesses by the state and consist primarily of state tax and fee revenue. As noted above, there are many taxes levied on the residents of

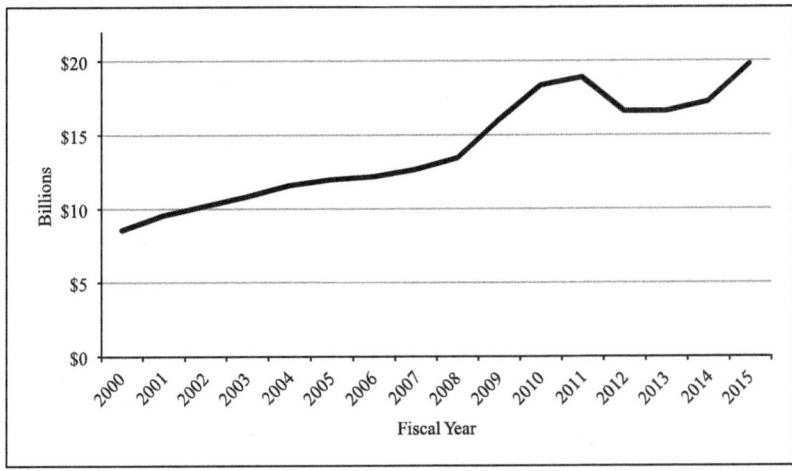

Fig. 13.3. Revenue from Federal Agencies in Michigan, Fiscal Years 2000–2015
Source: State of Michigan Comprehensive Annual Financial Report, various years.

Michigan. The state sales tax, for example, is a 6 percent tax collected when a consumer purchases an item to which the tax applies. The use tax is a specific excise tax levied at 6 percent on the use, storage, or consumption of some personal property not subject to the sales tax. Since 2011, the individual income tax has been levied at a rate of 4.25 percent of taxable income.

Sales and other usage taxes, like the gasoline tax, as well as net income taxes, tend to grow or decline with state personal income. Therefore, in an economic boom, revenue growth tends to accelerate as personal income accelerates, and in a recession, growth tends to slow as personal income growth slows. Transportation-related taxes from motor fuels and registration fees are constitutionally dedicated to transportation. Transportation related revenue peaked in 2004 and then began to decline into the mid-2010s. The amount of taxes the state collects from gasoline is complicated by the fact that as new vehicles have become more fuel efficient, due in part to higher federal standards, consumption has gone down. This also lowers the amount of tax collected. Flat or slower growth in registration fees reflected lower sales of vehicles, as they tended to last longer. The gas tax and vehicle registration fees were significantly increased in the legislation that the Legislature passed and Governor Snyder signed as part of the final plan to "fix the roads" in Michigan. In particular, the controversial plan increased the state's 19 cents-per-gallon gas tax by 7.3 cents; beginning in January 2017, drivers paid a total of over 26 cents per gallon of fuel purchased. In addition, the cost of vehicle registration was increased

20 percent. The entire package of changes generated $600 million of new revenue per year for transportation projects.

The State Education Tax, created as part of Proposal A in 1994, is levied on all property except industrial personal property; 100 percent of these funds are dedicated to the SAF. The State Education Tax and all property-related taxes are based upon the taxable value of the property as defined by law. Constitutional restrictions limit the yearly growth of taxable value to the rate of inflation or 5 percent, whichever is less. The amount the state collects from the State Education Tax is variable depending on market conditions. Factors such as inflation and changes in the housing market can cause the revenue to fluctuate from year to year. For instance, as property values plunged during the Great Recession, taxable values of property also decreased, which significantly restricted the growth of all property-related taxes collected. As home values (and therefore taxable values) rose after that, so did revenue from property taxes. However, restrictions stemming from Proposal A and the Headlee Amendment on revenue growth mean much of that growth is not realized in tax revenue.

Tobacco taxes include a tax on cigarettes and a separate tax on other tobacco products, such as cigars and smokeless tobacco. In terms of the total revenue for the state, tobacco taxes have declined beginning in the mid-1990s and are expected to continue that trend. Revenue from the state lottery is approximately 32 percent of all lottery sales and goes to the School Aid Fund. The remainder goes to prize payouts and to the retailers who sell the tickets. State revenue from the lottery tends to vary with total state personal income as well as other gaming alternatives that are available (e.g., Detroit's casinos), but growth has tended to be fairly slow since 2000.

Net business taxes include the impact of Michigan's Single Business Tax (SBT) refunds; refundable credits associated with the Michigan Business Tax (MBT); and Corporate Income Tax (CIT) collections. While the political maneuvering and debates underpinning them are beyond the scope of this chapter, it is important to know that the Single Business Tax was eliminated and replaced with the Michigan Business Tax in 2007, and the Michigan Business Tax was in turn replaced by the Corporate Income Tax in 2012. However, each of them still affects state revenues.

Business taxes that have been eliminated continue to affect state revenues because large multistate and multinational firms are often involved in lawsuits or negotiations with the Internal Revenue Service, or with other nations that last for several years and that lead to revised state and federal tax returns. Even though it was eliminated nearly a decade prior, during FY15, Single Business Tax refunds totaled about $20 million because of agreements (e.g., Michigan Economic Growth Authority tax credits) made while it was in effect. In the case of the MBT, firms who have outstanding claims for refundable credits, primarily associated with economic development programs are allowed to continue to claim the credits through the MBT. In fiscal year 2016, the value of MBT credits was roughly about $1.05 billion.

Tax expenditures are an important tax and budget policy issue, and are subsidies delivered through the tax code as deductions, exclusions, and other tax preferences. In other words, a tax expenditure is potential revenue that the state has chosen to forgo by reducing the amount of tax that households or corporations owe. Total tax expenditures exceed the amount of total revenue collected by the state from all taxes and fees that it levies each year. As an example of the importance of this state policy, consider that the Michigan Department of Treasury estimated that total tax expenditures totaled about $34.98 billion in FY16.[10] In other words, the state has relinquished nearly $35 billion in tax revenue during one year through incentives and other programs that benefit business and individuals. One of these tax expenditures that received a lot of attention in Michigan was the program that provided tax credits to film companies that made movies in the state.

Michigan has three major funds that draw on the total pool of resources: General Fund/General Purpose (GF/GP), the School Aid Fund (SAF), and the Michigan Transportation Fund (MTF). Each of these funds also receives federal resources. In any particular fiscal year, expenditures may be higher or lower than revenues credited to that year due to beginning fund balances, transfers to or from the "rainy day fund," and year-end balances.

Long-Term State Revenue Growth Trends

Total state tax revenues increased at an average yearly rate of 6.1 percent between FY95 and FY00, resulting in a total of a 31 percent increase over that five-year period. However, over the next 15 years, from FY00 to FY14, total state tax revenues grew at an average annual rate of only 0.7 percent; by contrast, average yearly growth of the Detroit Consumer Price Index over the same period was 2.2 percent. Therefore, during this time, inflation grew more than three times faster than state tax revenues. More important, in nominal (i.e., actual) dollars, while GF/GP revenue grew a total of 18.4 percent between FY94 and FY00, it decreased 15.6 percent from FY00 to FY14. In real (i.e., inflation-adjusted) terms, the GF/GP revenue picture actually gets much worse. In inflation-adjusted terms GF/GP revenue collections declined a total of 0.5 percent from FY94 to FY00, and declined over 46 percent from FY00 to FY14. Some of the dramatic decline in GF/GP resources was due to a slowing economy, but tax cuts were the major cause of the decline in total resources from taxes.

The SAF fared better at the start of the 21st century. Nominal SAF growth from FY95 to FY00 was about 42 percent. Like GF/GP, SAF growth slowed after FY00, but unlike GF/GP nominal SAF revenue growth remained positive. From FY00 to FY14 SAF revenue grew 16.5 percent. In real (i.e., inflation-adjusted) terms SAF revenue grew 22.2 percent from FY95 to FY00, but from FY00 to FY14, real SAF revenue declined by 25.8 percent. The primary reason SAF revenue growth was stronger than GF/GP is that most tax changes were designed in such a way that the School Aid Fund was "held harmless" to the changes.

Fuel taxes and registration fees are deposited into the Michigan Transportation Fund. The Michigan Constitution dedicates all taxes levied on motor fuels and vehicle registration fees for transportation purposes.[11] Gasoline tax revenues grew an average of 1.6 percent per year from FY85 to FY96, when the tax rate was held constant at 15 cents per gallon. On August 1, 1997, the gasoline tax was raised to 19 cents per gallon, after which gasoline tax revenue increased only 3.2 percent between FY98 and FY04. Gasoline tax collections peaked in FY02, remained fairly stable until FY04, and declined about 12.5 percent by FY14. The decline is due in part to technological advances that made motor vehicles more fuel efficient. Beginning in January 2017, Michigan phased in a change to the gasoline tax. The tax increased to 26.3 cents per gallon as part of the agreement reached by the Legislature and Governor Snyder as a way to fix the roads in Michigan and add a projected total of $1.2 billion to the funds used for road construction, including $600 million from the state's general fund.

Registration fees increased 82 percent from FY94 to FY04 when they peaked. From FY04 to FY14 revenue from registration fees were slightly lower or flat. The combination of flat to declining registration fees and declining fuel tax collections led to state-source MTF revenues peaking in FY04, but they declined roughly 5.5 percent by FY14. Also in January 2017, and as part of the aforementioned agreement to fix the roads, vehicle registration fees increased 20 percent (e.g., someone who paid $100 to register their vehicle would pay $120). Whether the increases in the gasoline tax or vehicle registration fees have a discernible impact on transportation-related revenue in Michigan is, again, beyond the scope of this volume.

A related impact of flat or declining MTF revenue is that the state has been in danger of losing part of the approximately $1.2 billion per year (as of FY14) of federal road funding that comes to Michigan. For the state to be eligible for the total possible allotment of federal highway funds, the federal government requires that states spend a certain amount of state resources on transportation purposes (e.g., a state "match"). In the four fiscal years starting in FY13 and running through FY16 the Legislature appropriated a total of $1.27 billion from the GF/GP budget for transportation purposes in part because MTF revenue was insufficient to meet the requirements for federal matching funds.

Long-Term Spending Trends

State spending changes each year, and often changes during the year when adjustments are made through supplemental appropriations, transfers, or executive order reductions. Available revenues determine how much the state can spend on state and local services such as infrastructure, education, and public safety. As one would expect, the impact of dramatic reductions in state resources led to dramatic budget reductions over the first part of the 21st century. The average yearly nominal growth rate of the combined School Aid Fund and General Fund/General Purpose was over 6.5 percent per year from FY93 to FY00. However, total nominal GF/GP and SAF revenues declined about $30 million during the period of FY01 to FY10. During this time, the yearly growth rate of total revenues was negative four times, and less than 1 percent three times.

One example of a particularly hard hit area of the state budget has been higher education (see chapter 12). Total appropriations for state university operations fell 25.2 percent between FY00 and FY12. Adjusted for inflation, university funding fell about 37 percent. In FY16 state university operations were funded at about 17 percent below FY00 funding levels when not adjusting for inflation. Part of the decline in higher education funding can be traced back to a 15 percent across-the-board cut for FY12 to all state universities in Governor Snyder's budget agreement with the Legislature. Snyder made the determination that these cuts would help stabilize the state's budget picture. Since that cut in FY12, the state has started to restore funding to state universities, but as of FY16 the funding was still not back to where it was pre-FY12.

While costs related to student instruction at public universities are funded by both state appropriations and the tuition and fees paid by students, the dramatic decline of state support for Michigan's 15 public universities has shifted their revenue reliance from state support to student tuition and fees. State appropriations provided about 45 percent of operating revenues for all 15 public universities in FY01 and tuition and fees provided 44.6 percent of funding for operations. By FY14, state funding fell to about 21.5 percent of funding for university operations while tuition and fees increased to about 71.3 percent of the total. Between FY01 and FY14, average tuition and fees charged to full-time in-state undergraduate increased 150.6 percent.[12] Many universities have large endowments from private donations and attract research grants from federal sources like the National Science Foundation and the National Institutes of Health as well as private companies and philanthropic organizations. However, these funds are generally restricted to specific purposes and unavailable to support general operating costs.

An area where funds have not shrunk is in the amount of federal dollars coming to Michigan from Washington, DC. Federal funds flowing into Michigan increased from about 27.3 percent of total appropriations in FY00 to about 43.1 percent in the FY16 budget. Federal funds are used primarily for human services and transportation. The large increase during the first part of the 21st century was primarily due to enhanced Medicaid payments that were part of the Affordable Care Act. This saw Medicaid rolls expand in Michigan, and as a result had more federal dollars flowing to the state. Federal funds come with numerous restrictions in terms of what they may be used for, and usually have some sort of matching requirement (e.g., the transportation funds noted above), which means a certain amount of state-source revenue must be spent in a particular way in order for the state to receive federal funds. For instance, in order for the state to receive all federal money allocated to the state for Medicaid (which provides health insurance for the poor) and Temporary Assistance for Needy Families (a welfare program that primarily delivers food stamps), the state must spend about $3.1 billion of state-source dollars in qualifying matching funds.

Short-Term and Long-Term State Debt

Another potential source of revenue for the state is borrowing. Generally speaking, the state government is forbidden from running a deficit (i.e., when expenditures are more than revenues; this is also different than the federal government, which incurred a deficit in each fiscal year between FY01 and FY17). However, in some special circumstances, the state government may take on debt. The state Constitution grants the state government authority to issue short-term debt to manage cash flow and long-term debt for other purposes. Long-term debt can be general obligation debt backed by the full faith and credit of the state, or it can be backed by a stream of tax revenue and is called a revenue bond.

Short-term debt to manage cash flow is authorized by Article IX, Section 14 of the state Constitution, which allows the Legislature to authorize the state to issue its full faith and credit notes backed by GF/GP revenue. Notes for short-term cash flow cannot exceed 15 percent of GF/GP revenues received by the state during the preceding fiscal year, and must be repaid no later than the end of the same fiscal year. Over the last 15 years, the state has borrowed between $1 billion and $1.3 billion per year to manage cash flow. The need to take on short-term debt can occur when disbursements (i.e., payments from the state treasury) are scheduled to be made before all the revenue to support them is received. In these instances the state has a cash-flow problem. For example, annual collections for the state income tax and the state's business tax are not due until mid-to-late April, or seven months after the fiscal year begins. However, many required disbursements that are supported by tax revenue go out monthly, which means the state needs short-term financing to manage cash flow.

Long-term general obligation debt is authorized by Article IX, Section 15 of the state Constitution. Long-term general obligation debt must be for a specific purpose. The process for taking on this kind of debt is also different from short-term debt. To take on general obligation debt requires a vote of two-thirds of the members elected to and serving in each legislative chamber to put the question on a statewide ballot; taking on this debt must be approved by a majority of voters in any general election.

A third option for taking on debt is a revenue bond. These are bonds issued by the state and backed by a specific stream of revenue; revenue bonds do not require a vote of the people. An example of a revenue bond that has constitutional and statutory authorization and limits is transportation bonding. Article IX, Section 9 of Michigan's Constitution states that "[t]he legislature may authorize the incurrence of indebtedness and the issuance of obligations pledging the taxes allocated or authorized to be allocated under this section, which obligations shall not be construed to be evidence of state indebtedness under this constitution." This language gives constitutional authorization for debt secured by constitutionally restricted transportation revenue, and indicates that transportation notes and bonds are not considered general obligation debt of the state.

This constitutional authority was put into effect by a 1951 statute, which authorizes the State Transportation Commission to issue notes or bonds by pledging as payment constitutionally restricted transportation revenue and anticipated federal revenue. State law limits transportation-related debt service to 50 percent of the previous year's constitutionally restricted transportation revenue. Another example is the School Bond Qualification and Loan program, which was established by the 1963 Michigan Constitution and amended by a 2005 law to provide a state credit enhancement and loan mechanism for school district bond issues. To meet the legal requirements in this instance, the bonds must be qualified by the state treasurer and the bond proceeds must be used for capital expenditure purposes.

Local Government Resources and Revenue Sharing

As of 2010, the state of Michigan had over 2,800 separate local governments; this total ranked 13th in the United States in terms of the raw number of local governments. Included in the state's system of local governments are 83 counties, 1,240 townships, 275 cities, and 258 villages. In addition, Michigan has 552 school districts, 57 intermediate school districts, 14 planning and development regions, and over 300 special districts and authorities. The number of school districts continues to change as charter schools across the state come and go, and as school district consolidations occur (see chapter 12).

Virtually all of the various local governing bodies receive resources from property taxes, 21 cities levy a city income tax, and most local units collect various fees. A large portion of the revenue these local governments have at their disposal, however, comes in the form of revenue sharing from the state. Revenue sharing payments (discussed below) go to cities, villages, and townships. School districts, which include public school academies (i.e., charter schools), and intermediate school districts, while they are their own local government entities, are treated differently and receive state funding through the School Aid Fund.

State revenue sharing consists of two parts: constitutional payments and what is commonly referred to as statutory revenue sharing payments. Both are based on sales tax collections. The formula for revenue sharing is defined in the state Constitution (Article IX, Section 10), which states that "[f]ifteen percent of all taxes imposed on retailers on taxable sales at retail of tangible personal property at a rate of not more than four percent shall be used exclusively for assistance to townships, cities and villages, on a population basis as provided by law." These constitutional revenue-sharing payments are guaranteed and made every two months based on actual sales tax collections.

The other component of revenue sharing is usually called statutory revenue-sharing payments. Even though the statute still dedicates 21.3 percent of sales tax collections levied at a 4 percent rate to statutory revenue-sharing payments, the state Constitution specifies that "[n]o money shall be paid out of the state treasury except in pursuance of appropriations made by law."[13]

The Constitution takes precedence over statute, and actual appropriations have fallen far below the statutory earmark. Cumulative cuts to local revenue sharing between FY01 and FY15 exceeded $5.5 billion. In FY15 alone the statutory revenue sharing for municipalities was about $550 million less than full funding. One of the effects of cuts to local units has been a reduction in public safety personnel. The Michigan Municipal League reported that budget constraints led to the loss of 2,315 police officers and more than 1,800 firefighters from FY01 to FY10.[14]

Restrictions on Local Government Revenue Raising Ability

A major factor adding to the financial problems of many cities is the set of constraints and limited revenue flexibility caused by constitutional and statutory limitations. Municipalities rely primarily on property taxes and intergovernmental revenue sharing to finance essential public services. In recent years, these sources have failed to keep up with the current level of services, much less rising costs. Structural constraints, such as the interaction of the Headlee Amendment and Proposal A (see chapter 3), have limited the collection of taxes on existing properties. Statutory revenue-sharing payments, as well as other state grants to local governments, have also been cut due to tighter state budgets. A combination of legislative term limits (i.e., inexperience) and more conservative (and anti-local government) majorities in the Legislature helped make revenue sharing to cities an easier target for state budget cuts.

Historically, Michigan's different constitutions have provided voters with strong local control over the level and purposes of taxation. However, the reaction of the Legislature has been to limit that power each time it is granted. For example, Article 7, Section 21 of the 1963 Constitution grants cities and villages the authority to levy a wide array of taxes in addition to property taxes "subject to limitations and prohibitions provided by this constitution or by law." Within one year of ratification of the 1963 Constitution, the Legislature reversed this broad local control by providing that no city may levy a tax except as expressly permitted by law: "except as otherwise provided by law and notwithstanding any provision in this charter, a city or village shall not impose, levy or collect a tax, other than an ad valorem property tax, on any subject of taxation, unless the tax was being imposed by the city or village on January 1, 1964" (1964, Act 243).

In 1978, Michigan voters approved a constitutional amendment commonly referred to as the Headlee Amendment that gave voters more power over the decision to incur additional taxes for debt and reduced their power more by imposing a recalculation of voter-approved millage to account for inflation. This amendment as well as later legislation took authority away from local officials and provided no way to make up for the lost revenue. The Headlee Amendment addressed local government finance in three ways:

- it limits the growth of local government property tax revenues by providing millage rollbacks whenever revenue from existing property grows by more than the rate of inflation, unless voters override the rollback;
- it requires voter approval for any new local taxes or increase in a tax rate not authorized at the time the amendment was adopted; and
- it requires that the state provide reimbursement for any additional costs resulting from new requirements mandated by state law.

In addition to the constraints that were already in effect, in 1994 the voters approved Proposal A, which included a limitation on assessment increases for individual parcels of property, excluding new construction, to 5 percent or the rate of inflation, whichever is less. This provision cost cities an estimated $300 million in 2014. In addition to the constitutional restrictions, there are statutory restrictions that are less favorable to local governments that the state Constitution requires or permits.

State Tax Policy Response after Proposal A

Proposal A was such a dramatic change in state tax policy that to get a clear picture of what it meant for Michigan, one must look at state tax policy before and after Proposal A. The change began in August 1993 when the Michigan Legislature passed, and Governor John Engler signed into law, Public Act 145 of 1993. This Act eliminated approximately $7 billion of property taxes, which had been the primary funding source for K-12 education, but it did not provide for any replacement revenues for schools at the time. The sources of revenue and the formula for funding public schools were dramatically changed once Proposal A was enacted the following year.

On March 15, 1994, Michigan voters approved Proposal A, which asked voters to increase the sales tax rate and dedicate the additional revenue to K-12 education. Proposal A also capped the rate of increase for property taxes, and reduced the state income tax rate. The Michigan Department of Treasury reported that Proposal A reduced taxes $674 million in FY94, and the cumulative cuts for the 10-year period from FY94 to FY03 associated with Proposal A would total over $17 billion. Beginning in earnest with Proposal A, some state policymakers have been looking to implement tax cuts whenever possible and restricting the rate of growth of taxes so that they grow less than the rate of inflation. As a result, it is estimated that Michigan reduced state and local tax revenues a cumulative 19-year impact of $51.1 billion from FY94 to FY13.[15]

Most of the impact was due to changes in the tax base, the tax rate, or credits associated with the individual income tax, the state sales and use taxes, state and local property taxes, and the state's primary business tax, which was the Single Business Tax until 2007, the Michigan Business Tax from 2007 until 2012, and which later became the Corporate Income Tax.[16] The base, rate, and credits were changed 119 times between 1993 and 2014. The cumulative impact of changes from FY95 to FY12 is estimated to be a reduction in revenue of about $25 billion. The sales tax rate was set at 6 percent in Article IX of the state Constitution when Proposal A was enacted. After Proposal A, the base was changed 57 times from 1995 to 2012. The cumulative effect of those changes was estimated to be a reduction in revenue of $2.8 billion from FY95 to FY12. Between 1994 and 2010, the use tax base was changed 46 times. The cumulative post–Proposal A revenue impact of these changes from FY95 to FY12 is estimated to be $2.75 billion. State and local property tax base, credits, and exemptions were changed 47 times from 1995 to 2012, and the cumulative effect of those changes reduced state and local revenues by an estimated $2 billion from FY95 to FY12. From 1994 until 2007, the SBT was the state's primary business tax. From 2007, when it replaced the SBT, to 2012, the MBT was the state's primary business tax. From 1994 to 2012 business tax rates, credits, and the base were changed 193 times. The cumulative revenue impact of these changes from FY94 to FY12 was a revenue reduction of nearly $26 billion.[17]

It is important to note that a tax change enacted in one year may not take effect until subsequent years. It is also important to note that changes may have a positive effect on revenue, a negative effect, or may be technical in nature and have little or no effect on revenue collections. Reductions mentioned above are net changes that include positive and negative impacts of base and rate changes.

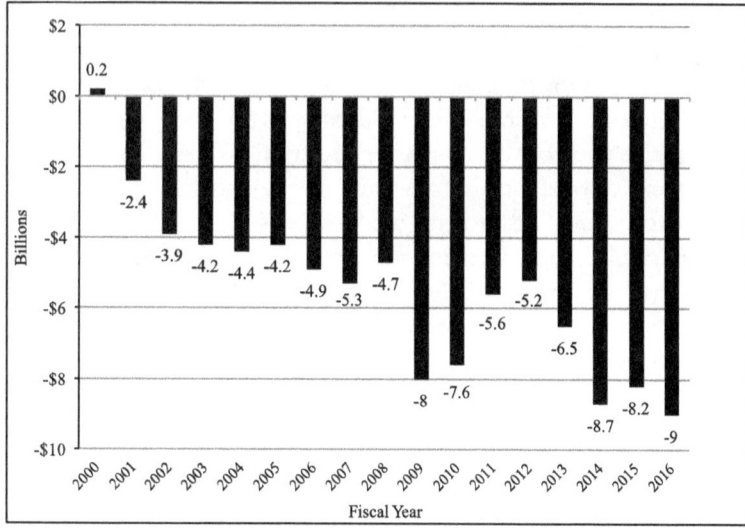

Fig. 13.4. State Revenue Collection Relative to the Constitutional Revenue Limit, Fiscal Year 2000–2016
Source: State of Michigan Comprehensive Annual Financial Report, various years, and May 2016 Consensus Estimate.

State Revenue Limit

Changes in tax policy over the years have affected the resources the state government has available to provide services such as infrastructure, education, and public safety. However, there is another factor that affects the resources Michigan has at its disposal; Michigan has a revenue limit that it may not exceed. Section 26 of Article IX in the Michigan Constitution provides a specific calculation for the limit on state-source revenues that may be collected and spent each year. The limit works out to be 9.49 percent of state personal income. Personal income is a good measure of economic activity. As economic growth expands or declines, personal income growth will increase or decline as well. The CREC provides estimates of the state's compliance with the limit for current and future fiscal years. After each fiscal year the official audited financial statements of the State of Michigan Comprehensive Annual Financial Report provide evidence of compliance with the limit. In FY00 state revenue collections exceeded the limit by about $160 million. But by FY01 they were over $2.4 billion below the limit and by 2014 they were about $8 billion below and have been about $8 billion to $9 billion below the limit each year thereafter (see fig. 13.4).

Personal income is a good measure of the state economic "pie," and the measure of where state government revenue collections stand in relation to the revenue limit is a good measure of the slice of the economic pie that funds state government each year. It also measures the size of state government and whether state government relative to the state economy is expanding or contracting.

Over the period of time reflected in figure 13.4, only a small portion of the growing gap between the revenue limit and revenue collections was due to the economy. Most of the difference was due to the tax cuts previously identified. It also indicates that the state tax base does not grow with the real state economy. For example, in addition to flat-to-declining revenue from fuel taxes and registration fees noted above, Michigan has relied on tobacco taxes to generate approximately $1 billion of revenue since the tax on cigarettes was increased to $2.00 per pack in 2005. Tobacco taxes generated about $1.18 billion in FY05, but collections declined to $957.5 million or by about 18.8 percent by 2013. So, on average, revenues declined about 2.3 percent per year. In inflation-adjusted dollars, the decline from 2005 to 2013 was about 30 percent or about 3.7 percent per year.[18]

Conclusion

The Michigan economy has experienced stunning changes in the last 20 years as the domestic auto industry soared to great heights in the 1990s but later suffered dramatic declines to a low point in 2009–10. Michigan went into deep recession and suffered because one of the state's primary industries, automobile production, suffered a dramatic loss of market share and job loss. As the auto industry has recovered market share and the market has grown the state economy started recovering as well.

Both during times of economic growth and times of significant economic decline, policymakers have relied on a supply-side approach that emphasizes tax cuts and incentives to stimulate economic growth. The state revenue limit demonstrates that due to tax cuts, incentives, and a tax structure that does not grow with the economy, the portion of the state economy that finances state government was about $9 billion lower in FY16 than it was in FY00.

The results of this approach have included a decrease in revenues for local governments and higher education in particular, which do not have the resources to invest in infrastructure and education. In addition, as the state cut funding and further restricted the ability of local governments to raise revenue, local governments were forced to reduce public safety personnel and cuts to higher education led to significant increases in tuition.

States and their cities need to successfully compete in the global economy in the 21st century. As such, Michigan's budget and fiscal policies play a large role in enhancing the state's importance in that economy, which includes making decisions that can attract business investment and jobs. At the same time, these policies can help provide its citizens opportunities for education and training, recreational opportunities, and cultural amenities. A state's fiscal and budgetary decisions help retain those already living in the state as well as attract new residents.

In order for a modern economy to prosper it must have access to an educated workforce, adequate infrastructure, public safety, and a system of courts, appropriate regulation, and a public safety net. In our society government either provides these public goods directly or contracts with the private sector to provide them. Whoever provides these public goods, taxes are required in order to pay the cost. A couple of questions worth pondering: Is the state investing enough in the public goods that an advanced capitalist economy relies upon? Is state tax policy as effective in stimulating the state economy as some believe?

WEB RESOURCES

The *Michigan House Fiscal Agency* (www.house.mi.gov/hfa) maintains hundreds of reports on the budget, revenue forecasts, and various fiscal issues going back as far as 1996 in the archives on its website.

The *Michigan Department of Treasury* (www.michigan.gov/treasury/; select Revenue, Economic, and Budget Data) maintains a reference library that contains the Annual Report of the State Treasurer, various tax reports, revenue reports, economic reports, and budget reports.

The *Michigan Senate Fiscal Agency* (www.senate.michigan.gov/sfa/) maintains historical and current data bases.

The *Citizens Research Council of Michigan* (www.crcmich.org) maintains an updated Outline of the Michigan Tax System and publishes numerous reports and studies.

NOTES

1. See, for example, Rick Haglund, "Analysis Shows 1980s Downturn Worse for Michigan than 'The Great Recession'," *Kalamazoo Gazette*, June 5, 2011, http://www.mlive.com/business/index.ssf/2011/06/analysis_shows_1980s_downturn.html, accessed November 23, 2015; Edward Hoogterp, "Great Recession Leaves Michigan Poorer, Census Numbers Show," *Michigan Business Review*, October 23, 2011, http://www.mlive.com/news/index.ssf/2011/10/great_recession_leaves_

michiga.html, accessed November 23, 2015; Monica Davey, "Michigan's Decade of Tarnish Seen in Census Report," *New York Times*, December 22, 2010, http://www.nytimes.com/2010/12/23/us/23michigan.html, accessed November 23, 2015; Melissa Anders, "Michigan's 'Well-Being' Dropped over Decade While Other States Improved," *Grand Rapids Press*, June 25, 2013, http://www.mlive.com/business/index.ssf/2013/06/report_michigans_well-being_dr.html, accessed November 23, 2015.

2. Act 431 of 1984; M.C.L. 18.1367; in addition to forecasting revenues, the CREC calculates the annual percentage growth in the basic foundation allowance provided for in the state school aid act of 1979, 1979 PA 94, M.C.L. (Michigan Compiled Law) 388.1601 to 388.1772; and estimates compliance with the state revenue limit established by section 26 of Article IX of the state Constitution of 1963; and pay-ins or payouts required under the countercyclical budget and economic stabilization fund.

3. Act 431 of 1984: M.C.L. 18.1367b.

4. Act 431 of 1984: M.C.L. 18.1363.

5. Section 20, Article V, Constitution of the State of Michigan.

6. Section 17, Article IX, Constitution of the State of Michigan.

7. Rules for Transfers are governed by the Management and Budget Act. M.C.L. 18.1393.

8. Section 20, Article V, Constitution of the State of Michigan.

9. *Outline of the Michigan Tax System*, Citizens Research Council of Michigan, May 2015.

10. *Executive Budget Appendix on Tax Credits, Deductions, and Exemptions, Fiscal Years 2015 and 2016*, Office of Revenue and Tax Analysis, Michigan Department of Treasury.

11. M.C.L. 257.801–257.810; Section 9, Article IX, State Constitution.

12. *Fiscal Focus: State Appropriations, Tuition, and Public University Operation Costs*, House Fiscal Agency, December 2013.

13. Section 17, Article IX, Constitution of the State of Michigan.

14. *The State of Our Communities*, Michigan Municipal League, 2015.

15. Douglas Drake, *Michigan's Tax Policies: Wrong Turns on the Path to Prosperity*, 2014, http://www.masb.org/drake-report.aspx (accessed November 23, 2015).

16. Tax revenue = tax rate × tax base – tax credits.

17. Details on each change are available in Drake, *Michigan's Tax Policies*, appendix tables 1-A, 2-A, 3-A, 4-A.

18. *Michigan's Cigarette and Tobacco Taxes 2013 Statistical Update*, Office of Revenue and Tax Analysis, Michigan Department of Treasury, November 2014.

14 ✦ Economic Development Policy in Michigan

RICHARD JELIER

Michigan is considered to be a dynamic model of early success rooted in agriculture, lumber, mining, and the economic miracle of the automobile age. The decline of Michigan's core industries in the latter half of the 20th century is deeply connected to the lack of economic diversity and overspecialization that has led to a rapid decline of once thriving cities. Some of the policy response to recent economic challenges and attempts at economic diversification are recounted through the lens of Michigan's last four governors—James Blanchard, John Engler, Jennifer Granholm and Rick Snyder—all of whom were elected to multiple terms. Finally, the key state-local government relationships summarized below emphasize the state's declining financial commitments to local government and the increasing use of state oversight. The use of the controversial emergency manager laws to exert state control over financially distressed local governments threatens a long-standing tradition of local autonomy and home rule in Michigan. In particular, the Flint water crisis has raised serious concerns about the efficacy and ethical appropriateness of the state role in usurping local control (see chapter 15).

From its early origins, economic development policy in the United States has been characterized by the importance of subnational policy developments and is shaped by both a federalist and capitalist matrix. State and local economic development is not a new governmental function in the United States and can be traced back to at least the New Jersey Legislature's decision in 1791 to incorporate Alexander Hamilton's private company, the Society for Useful Manufactures, as a vehicle for industrial development. More recent roles emerged after the Great Depression when southern states sought to lure industry with offers of tax relief, business subsidies, and cheap capital. Economic development planning soon became a function of every state, except Delaware, as a condition for receiving public works funds and eventually became universal elements of state government machinery.[1]

For state and local governments, the primary goals of promoting economic development seek to enhance the tax base and increase employment. At times, these objectives can conflict. For instance, a city can increase the tax base by attracting industries that are highly automated, which could also result in reduced job creation. In addition, supply-side tax abatement policies and programs often diminish tax revenues in hopes of increasing local employment.

Beginning in the period after World War II, three trends emerged that transformed state and local governments into becoming more proactive and entrepreneurial in their economic development responses: the redistribution of people and industry from the Rustbelt to the Sunbelt; the increasing internationalization of capital; and the reduction of heavy manufacturing employment. The scope and the scale of these regional shifts are remarkable. According to census figures, between 1950 and 1984, Western states grew by nearly 27 million people, while the South skyrocketed to an additional 43 million; Northeast and Midwestern states only grew by 25 million combined. In that 34-year period, California alone gained 15 million people, Texas more than doubled its 1950 population of 7.7 million to 16 million. Florida surged from 2.8 million to almost 11 million.[2] By the 1970s, serious economic deterioration in northern states elicited an aggressive policy response and intensified competition between states and localities. Industrial states such as Michigan embraced economic development incentives as a defensive response to perceived Sunbelt success with bidding competition for private industry.

For a while, expanded financial assistance from Washington, DC, also helped to lessen the decline of the Rustbelt. From 1955 to 1978 federal grants-in-aid to states and localities soared from $5.6 billion to $49.4 billion in constant (1972) dollars. Separate categorical programs climbed from 132 to 492 by 1978.[3] Since that time, national debt and deficits led to severe contraction of the federal system, forcing localities to build partnerships with the private sector to mitigate against the loss of funds left by the dismantling of many federal programs. In fact, since the 1970s, the incentives employed to nurture indigenous local tax bases have accompanied an overall decline in federal aid to states and localities. After the 1970s, the character of the economic development policy domain became qualitatively different from efforts in earlier years. A shift occurred from exclusive reliance on supply-side location incentives to more sensitive entrepreneurial and demand-side economic development policies. Demand-side policies such as business incubators, research and development investments, venture capital financing, small business support, and the development of export markets focused more on retention and expansion of existing business rather than capital attraction policies.

Economic development rose from a relatively marginal item on the political agenda of states to a central, perhaps even pivotal, issue. Indeed, after the 1970s, economic development became a universal public function of state government. By the mid-1980s, some estimated that more than 15,000 state and local officials nationwide were engaged in economic development as a primary activity.[4] As a result, gubernatorial State of the State addresses and speeches began to be studded with references to economic development strategies. As Peter Eisinger states, this devolutionary tendency in economic development policy is a core feature of our intergovernmental system:

> The invention and implementation of economic development policies are the responsibilities chiefly of numerous state and local governments. The task is shared by countless private organizations, such as chambers of commerce, and quasi-public bodies such as industrial development corporations. Most of these actors operate independently of one another. There is no federal department of economic development to offer guidance, nor is there a national development plan or coordinating body. Federal programs do exist, but their exploitation and implementation are left mainly to state and local officials and citizens' groups.[5]

Befitting our free enterprise system, the central structural feature of economic development policy in Michigan is that goals are best achieved through private sector activity supported by government. Public-private partnerships reflect that private businesses possess a crucial type of vision, expertise, management skill, and risk bearing. The state and local role hinges on the belief that while private investment is essential to the economic health of a community it will not take place in sufficient quantity or produce collective economic benefits without necessary public inducements. Federal initiatives have been essential at various times, but the overall U.S. role has been dwarfed by the energy, intensity, and ingenuity of state and local efforts. Yet, there is still a shared responsibility. The federal government sets the parameters through fiscal, monetary, and trade policies and its regulatory apparatus. Partially, as a result of this decentralization, striking regional inequalities exist across states and cities. Fierce interjurisdictional competition drives economic development policy. States "learn" what their neighbors and major competitors are doing and prudently seek to match or exceed those efforts or emulate other approaches.

Traditional approaches focus on capital attraction as key to stimulating economic growth. Rather than competing for a shrinking number of footloose firms, recent, more entrepreneurial economic development approaches emphasize homegrown firms. These retention and expansion efforts, sometimes referred to as economic gardening, may help to dampen some of the interjurisdictional and interstate competition that led to mayors, governors, and business leaders forming "raiding parties" that traveled to nearby states to prospect for businesses.

Historical Context in Michigan

Michigan's early history following statehood in 1837 was accompanied by rapid economic growth rooted primarily in agriculture, lumber, and mining industries. A decade earlier in 1825, the opening of the Erie Canal connected the Great Lakes with the Hudson River, New York City, and the Atlantic Ocean, precipitating Michigan's rapid development. The canal brought large numbers of people to Michigan while providing an inexpensive way to ship goods to market. Michigan's climate and fertile soil led to success in agriculture, especially wheat and fruit production along the coast of the Lake Michigan shoreline from Benton Harbor to Traverse City and extending up to the Grand Traverse Bay, which has come to be known known as the "fruit belt." Leading cash crops included corn, soybeans, sugar beets, as well as dairy and general livestock. By the 1850s, a rapid increase in cultivation occurred and the number of acres in Michigan under the plow more than tripled.[6] The making of cereal foods in Battle Creek, launched by W. K. Kellogg and C. W. Post, contributed greatly to the early Michigan economy. The importance of agricultural dominance and crop variety continues into the 21st century with more than a $50 billion impact on the state economy by 2016.

By 1844, iron and copper were discovered in the Upper Peninsula, creating the impetus for the construction of the Soo Locks, completed in 1855, allowing ships to travel between Lake Superior and the lower Great Lakes. By the end of the century, Michigan became the leading U.S. source for these ores. An astronomical amount of copper was mined. In fact, by the early 1870s, Michigan's ore production passed the 1 million ton mark, with production peaking in 1920. At one point, Michigan produced 90 percent of the nation's copper. Today, just two iron mines remain active.[7] After the Civil War, lumbering emerged as a seminal industry in Michigan, harvesting about a quarter of the nation's total lumber supply and sparking the furniture and papermaking industries in the state. In the latter half of the 19th century, over 33,000 acres per year of white pine were indiscriminately cut without reforestation.[8] Eventually, overlogging destroyed the lumber industry and widespread deforestation lead to rapid erosion of the topsoil. The ores would eventually be mostly extracted, too.

Michigan's modern story has been told around the world, with Henry Ford, R. E. Olds, the Dodge Brothers, William Durant, and Walter Chrysler sparking the 20th century's greatest wealth creation—the automobile industry. In 1910, Ford opened his first automobile factory in Highland Park, introducing humankind to the assembly line. Between 1900 and 1930 only Los Angeles grew faster than Detroit, and the Detroit population soared from 286,000 to nearly 1.6 million. Flint's population exploded from 13,000 to more than 156,000.[9] The growth of the auto industry foreshadowed the unity and activism of the labor movement, with Michigan home to the United Auto Workers (UAW), as well as a strong presence of the American Federation of Labor and Congress of Industrial Organizations. While the Great Depression hit Michigan hard, World War II's need for arms greatly boosted the industrial capacity of the state.

It is worth remembering that in the three decades from 1940 to 1970, Michigan's success in durable manufacturing resulted in a flood of workers migrating from other states and countries. During that period, Michigan's population climbed from 5.26 million to 8.88 million. If that same rate of growth from that era had continued, Michigan would have had more than 17 million people by the early 2000s.[10] Median household income in Michigan hovered consistently above the national average until 2001, but fell significantly below in the next 10 years (see fig. 1.4).

The trickle of imported foreign cars beginning in the 1960s soon became a flood; Michigan's overreliance on one economic sector—the auto industry—became readily apparent. This was heightened by the 1973 oil crisis, which negatively affected the Michigan economy, bringing both high unemployment and high inflation rates. Racial and urban unrest, combined with a reduction in the demand for unskilled labor, emptied out Michigan's cities and left a trail of economic devastation in its wake.

Decline in Michigan

Manufacturing's share of the U.S. gross domestic product shrank from about 27.2 percent in 1963 to about 12 percent in 2014. There was even more dramatic manufacturing decline in Michigan, falling from 48.2 percent in 1963 to historic lows of 17.9 percent in 2006.[11] By 2013, the auto industry recovery allowed manufacturing to rebound back to 19 percent of gross product share.[12] Michigan's relative downturn in manufacturing adversely affected every aspect of the state, but proved catastrophic for cities such as Flint, Pontiac, and Detroit (see chapter 4).

The economic collapse in Michigan and its cities is typical of the Rustbelt. It led to a new policy domain marked by extremely broad agreement on the desirability of substantial government involvement in search of economic diversification and the creation of private-sector employment. By the 1970s, this consensus for a vigorous state and local role in the economic development processes began to intensify, even crossing partisan lines, urban-rural divisions, racial cleavages, and regional boundaries.[13] Interestingly, when this expansion of the state and local role in the economic development process took shape, it was in stark contradiction to the national politics of the time where privatization, deregulation, laissez-faire approaches, and supply-side macroeconomic doctrines had taken root. In fact, as the national government grew more ideologically inclined, states and localities embraced economic and political pragmatism. In short, economic development policy in states and localities was driven less by ideology and more by trying anything and everything that might work to rejuvenate the tax base and create jobs. Some have described this approach as "shoot anything that flies, claim anything that falls." The old adage that there is no Republican or Democratic way to pick up the trash also held true for economic development policy in the 1970s and 1980s. Intervention by subnational government was justified on the grounds that it would stimulate private investment and was practiced by all municipalities regardless of political affiliation.

Barry Bluestone and Bennett Harrison's seminal work, *The Deindustrialization of America*, describes the kinds of economic devastation that afflicted older industrial economies such as Michigan's.[14] Unfortunately, relatively slow growth in service employment did not offset the loss of manufacturing jobs. The highly bifurcated occupational structure of the service economy also increased wage inequality in Michigan. Despite a call in the late 1980s by Peter Eisinger[15] and others to shift toward demand-side entrepreneurial economic development policies, research over the 1990s and 2000s clearly shows cities continuing, and even increasing, their focus on traditional industrial attraction incentives. Michigan in particular, consistently relies on these supply-side policies. Michigan cities are among the most active in use of industrial tax abatements in the nation.[16] Charles Mahtesian refers to these policies as "Romancing the Smokestack" or "Smokestack Chasing."[17] About one-third of local governments in Michigan granted property tax relief to manufacturing firms through industrial tax abatements in Public Act (PA) 198 of 1974. The evidence suggests that the use of tens of thousands of PA 198 abatements has not been successful in expanding Michigan's manufacturing sector, targeting declining segments of the economy rather than those with great growth potential.[18] Further, since the 1980s and 1990s, the subsidies cost municipalities more than $2 billion annually in forgone tax revenues, resulting in missed chances for local governments to use other types of development strategies and policies that might have better achieved a sustainable economic base that promotes diversification and new investments and jobs.[19]

In 2004, Michigan was 19th in a prosperity index, but slipped to 27th by 2007 and 33rd by 2011.[20] Noted economist Charles Ballard warned that if Michigan continues the poor rate of growth that began about 1999, in terms of per capita income decline relative to the national average, by 2035 Michigan would become the poorest state in the nation. He does not predict this will happen, but the trend illustrates the need to reverse the downward spiral with new economic development approaches in Michigan. Not only is Michigan becoming a poorer state but income inequality also has widened. In 1970 the top 5 percent held 15 percent of the state income; by 2009, the top 5 percent held more than 23 percent of total income.[21] A 2012 report from the Economic Policy Institute concludes that the top 1 percent in Michigan earns 25 times the state's average income compared to the bottom 99 percent, ranking Michigan as the 35th most unequal state in the country in terms of wage distribution. From 1979 to 2012, the top 1 percent in Michigan had a 115 percent jump in income while the 99 percent realized a 17 percent decline.[22]

In December 2015, the Census Bureau released its American Community Survey data, which highlighted key economic trends from 2010 to 2014. Median income declined during that period for three out of every four Michigan cities and villages. Adjusted for inflation, median income was down 8.7 percent while those living in poverty in Michigan rose 17 percent. More than one in six people in Michigan were living in poverty in 2015. In 2016, however, Michigan trended in a more positive direction. Median household incomes in the state rose 2.4 percent, the largest annual gain since the Great Recession. Despite the gains, median household income remained below prerecessionary levels.[23] Moreover, the state's unemployment rate has dropped steadily. In the mid-2000s it was worst in the nation but later improved to equal the nation's average, and some experts expected it to keep falling.[24] In August 2016 the rate fell to 4.5 percent, far from Michigan's peak unemployment rate of 14.9 percent in June 2009.[25]

Responses to Challenges

By the 1980s, the belief that successful state economies would depend heavily on the support and nurturance of the small business sector with high growth potential rather than continued overreliance on capital attraction strategies was becoming firmly entrenched in state economic development strategies. The stimulation of demand-side approaches to retain and expand existing businesses began to slowly change state economic development policies and priorities. Perhaps the economic development response to emergent challenges can best be told through the administrations of Governors Blanchard, Engler, Granholm, and Snyder. Each of these multiterm governors served after the beginning of the economic distress experienced by Michigan in the 1970s, and they all also emphasized economic development as a key strategic policy priority for the state.

Democratic governor James Blanchard (1983–91) campaigned and won on a simple slogan of "jobs, jobs, jobs." He inherited a $1.7 billion deficit, which was closed by cutting spending and raising the state's personal income tax. This was also aided by a temporary rebound from the automobile industry in 1985.[26] Blanchard launched the Governor's Commission on Jobs and Economic Development, a coalition of business, labor, education, and government leaders. He released Michigan's first economic development strategic plan, *Paths to Prosperity*, a strategy that concentrated Michigan's public policy on manufacturing-related businesses while also creating an environment that would stimulate innovation and new industry. The state also began to support venture capitalism. For instance, the Michigan Strategic Fund was created in 1984 to support small, innovative businesses that might not qualify for conventional financing, assisting companies at each stage of the business cycle, which continued through the Snyder administration.

Republican governor John Engler (1991–2003) used an executive order to reorganize the Michigan Jobs Commission into the Michigan Department of Career Development and the Michigan Economic Development Corporation. The Michigan Department of Career Development brought in career-related education (including adult, career and technology education, and postsecondary services), job training, and workforce development functions while separating out the economic development functions into the more specialized, quasi-public/private agency, the Michigan Economic Development Corporation. It adopted a corporate structure, more responsive to market conditions and business needs. Overall, the new organizations reflected the state consensus regarding the interdependence of education, workforce development, and economic development.

Governor Engler supported the supply-side concept of enterprise zones that was popular with many states at that time. In 1997, the Michigan Renaissance Zone Act established 11 enterprise zones across the state. The goal of the legislation was to serve as a catalyst for the economic revival of depressed urban and rural areas. By locating within a zone's boundaries, a business would be exempt from the Michigan Single Business Tax, Michigan personal income tax, operating property tax levies, and city income tax. By the end of the program in 2011, 41 Renaissance Zones had been established in the state. The Grand Rapids Renaissance Zone was considered to be the most successful in Michigan, generating hundreds of new investments and thousands of new jobs. Since January 1997, when the program started in Grand Rapids, the total private investment within the 10 designated zones in the city exceeded $251 million.[27]

In 1996, during John Engler's administration, new brownfield enabling legislation (Brownfield Redevelopment Financing Act, PA 381) restructured the process for determining liability for cleanup, created more flexible administration of brownfield sites, and established a brownfield redevelopment authority. According to the EPA, a brownfield is a property whose expansion, redevelopment, or reuse may be complicated by the presence or potential presence of a hazardous substance, pollutant, or contaminant. The act also established an incentive-based tax credit program to foster redevelopment of contaminated (actual or presumed) industrial and commercial sites. This sparked a tremendous amount of brownfield redevelopment in the estimated 10,000 brownfield sites in Michigan.

Engler's successor, Democratic governor Jennifer Granholm (2003–11) faced large structural deficits, limiting her ability to pursue her administration's economic development goals. However, Governor Granholm launched the Cool Cities Initiative in 2003 to attract and retain the "Creative Class" in Michigan (see chapter 5). Cool Cities rolled out a set of programs designed to support nominated redevelopment projects in large and small Michigan cities with a strong focus on promoting Talent, Innovation, Diversity and Environment (TIDE) that closely echoed Richard Florida's widely publicized recommended strategies for metropolitan economic development.[28] On one hand, modest funds were made available to localities to support specific TIDE projects, yet severe cutbacks in general revenue sharing in Michigan costs local governments millions in intergovernmental aid. This meant that cities were forced to make draconian cuts in programs that positively affected place-making investments (e.g., parks, infrastructure, and cultural amenities), which had been identified as key for attracting the creative class.[29] The Cool Cities program, the Main Street program, and the Blueprints for Michigan's Downtowns program all actually date from Governor Engler's administration.[30]

A popular perception exists that Michigan has been losing the "brain drain wars." The reality is more nuanced, however. Michigan is relatively successful in keeping its highly skilled graduates, but it has tended to be an unpopular destination for out-of-state graduates. Michigan, however, is not suffering from an unprecedented mass creative class exodus.[31]

In the last few decades, Michigan's disinvestment in higher education (see chapter 12) presents severe challenges in the state's attempt to reorient towards a creative class economy where TIDE factors are key building blocks for that transition. From 2001 to 2006, per capita spending on higher education was cut 30 percent; critics have argued that this was an unwise move in a state where the proportion of the population with a bachelor's degree already lagged behind the nation.

In efforts to promote further diversification of the state's economy, Governor Granholm promoted the SmartZones program across the state that promoted the creation of public-private partnerships and business incubators that would support select high-growth industries. Started in the early 2000s, SmartZones in Michigan foster collaborations among universities, industry, research organizations, government, and other community institutions in an effort to attract high-technology investments in the state. The program intended to stimulate the growth of technology-based businesses and jobs by aiding in the creation of recognized clusters of new and emerging businesses. The special focus here emphasized commercializing ideas, patents, and other opportunities surrounding corporate, university, or private research institute research and development efforts. The state's SmartZones provide distinct geographical locations where technology-based firms, entrepreneurs, and researchers can locate in close proximity to each other. The 11 original SmartZones locations comprised a critical mass of technology development assets. Statewide, the number of Zones increased from the original 11 to 15 (see table 14.1).

States such as Michigan pay an inordinate amount of attention to assessment and rankings of comparative business climates. State officials worry excessively about poor rankings and expend a lot of energy working to advertise favorable ones. Positive rankings carry substantial political weight. Tax policy plays an important symbolic role in the competition for investment. Republican governor Rick Snyder's (2011–19) first priority upon taking office was to reform what he considered a highly uncompetitive tax code. Under the governor's plan, the Michigan Business Tax was replaced by a 6 percent Corporate Income Tax on C corporations and a 4.25 percent

TABLE 14.1. Smartzone Service Areas in Michigan

SmartZone	Web Link and Description
MTEC SmartZone	http://www.mtecsz.com/
	Guides entrepreneurs and helps create high-tech jobs in Michigan's Keweenaw Peninsula through partnerships with the cities of Houghton and Hancock, Michigan Technological University, Keweenaw Economic Development Alliance, and Keweenaw Peninsula Chamber of Commerce.
Sault Sainte Marie Advanced Resources and Technology, Inc.	http://www.ssmartzone.com/
	Provides high-quality and economical new product development services for entrepreneurs and businesses by providing access to current manufacturing facilities; skilled engineering, business, and science personnel; and business training programs through a collaborative partnership between the City of Sault Ste. Marie, Lake Superior State University, the Michigan Economic Development Corporation, and the Michigan Small Business and Technology Development Centers.
GR Current	http://www.grcurrent.com/home
	Supports the creation of real solutions for high-growth industries such as health and life science, alternative energy, advanced manufacturing, agricultural processing, and defense to assist their clients in the commercialization of their innovative products.
Muskegon Innovation Hub	http://www.gvsu.edu/mihub/
	Creates a partnership with Grand Valley State University, the City of Muskegon, and the Michigan Economic Development Corporation, to be a key partner in the region's economic development ecosystem, supporting start-up businesses, entrepreneurs, and corporate innovation teams.
CMU Research Corporation	http://www.cmurc.com/
	CMURC is a nonprofit business accelerator focused on advancing economic development in the community by leveraging the resources of Central Michigan University, the Mt. Pleasant SmartZone, and its local, regional and statewide partners.
Mount Pleasant SmartZone Satellite Mid Michigan Innovation Center	http://cmurc.com/smartzone/Tech%20Park
	Mt. Pleasant SmartZone provides a home to incubation facilities and a launching space for companies to grow into their own development in the technology park, which is on university land.
Lansing Regional SmartZone	http://www.purelansing.com/LDFA
	Supports a cooperative effort with the Michigan Economic Development Corporation to stimulate the growth of technology-based businesses in the Lansing region. This is a partnership between the City of East Lansing, City of Lansing, Ingham County, and Michigan State University.
Southwest Michigan Innovation Center	http://kazoosmic.com/
	SMIC is an incubator/accelerator created to support life science ventures of all kinds, from the earliest startups to maturing companies. SMIC residents benefit from subsidized, low-cost laboratory, office, and conference space; high-quality scientific equipment and expertise; and a range of support services crucial to every life science business located in the Business Technology & Research Park at Western Michigan University.
Battle Creek Unlimited	http://www.bcunlimited.org/battle-creek-michigan-economic-development-site
	Battle Creek Unlimited (BCU), a private, nonprofit corporation, has received international acclaim serving as the business development arm for the city of Battle Creek, guiding the nation's first and most successful base conversion into Michigan's largest modern industrial park—the 3,000-acre Fort Custer Industrial Park.

TABLE 14.1.—*Continued*

SmartZone	Web Link and Description
Jackson Technology Park	http://enterprisegroup.org/ Supports the attraction, retention and expansion of new and emerging businesses focused on life sciences, advanced manufacturing, and alternative energy.
Ann Arbor SPARK	http://www.annarborusa.org/ Uses skills and knowledge to attract, develop, strengthen, and invest in innovative industries to help the Ann Arbor region thrive.
TechTown Detroit	http://techtowndetroit.org/ Detroit's business innovation hub. As the city's most established business accelerator and incubator, provides a powerful connection to a broad network of resources, catalyzing entire communities of entrepreneurs best poised to energize the local economy located within the Woodward Technology Corridor SmartZone.
OU INC	http://wwwp.oakland.edu/ouinc/ OU INC's focus is in the energy, medical device, and information technology sectors.
Macomb-OU INCubator	http://wwwp.oakland.edu/macombouinc/ Provide comprehensive development and support services to startup and emerging businesses, create and support an entrepreneurial climate, commercialize new technologies, expand and cultivate a defense corridor, attract investment and create new jobs in Southeastern Michigan in the targeted industries: defense, homeland security, advanced manufacturing, and technology.
Automation Alley	https://www.automationalley.com/Home.aspx Automation Alley is Michigan's leading technology business association, connecting companies and organizations with talent, resources, and funding to accelerate innovation and fuel Southeast Michigan's economy. Since its founding in 1999, the nonprofit has grown to include nearly 1,000 tech-focused members in business, education, and government, focused in five areas: advanced manufacturing, defense, entrepreneurship, international business, and talent development.

fixed individual income tax rate (see chapter 13). A C corporation under the United States federal income tax law refers to any corporation that is taxed separately from its owners. Also, several business tax exemptions and credits were eliminated altogether. Snyder's plan also included a tax on pensions to offset some costs of the tax cuts. In December 2012, Snyder signed right-to-work legislation (see chapter 7). Michigan, one of the states with the most labor union members and the birthplace of the UAW, became the 24th state to prohibit requiring workers to pay union dues or fees as a condition of employment.

By 2015, Michigan's overall business tax climate ranking had improved to 13th in the United States, according to the Tax Foundation. Yet many of Michigan's structural tax problems persisted. The state sales tax is applied to an ever-shrinking part of the state's economy. Efforts to implement a legislative tax on services in 2007 in a midnight legislative session in an attempt to avert a government shutdown over a $1.9 billion dollar deficit was handled so poorly that a tax on services will now likely remain off the table for a long time. Still, the economic argument in favor of taxing services in Michigan continues to be strong and advocated by many notable economists such as Charles Ballard. Michigan's regressive tax code and lack of revenues makes it difficult for the state to respond to challenges like infrastructure needs. In addition, if the percentage of income devoted to state and local taxes was the same as it was in the 1970s, then state and local governments would have about $7 billion per year more than they have now.[32]

Lack of state revenue diminishes the ability to adequately fund basic infrastructure like Michigan's roads, which have been deemed the worst in the nation. In 2014, only 17 percent of the state's roads were considered to be in good shape, 45 percent in fair condition, and 38 percent poor, according to the Michigan Department of Transportation Asset Management Council's dashboard.[33] Michigan has spent less per capita on its roads than any other state; in 2012, just $126 was spent per person on highways.[34] In 2015, after the state Legislature was unable to come up with a bipartisan plan for fixing the roads and bridges, voters handily rejected Proposal 1 (see chapter 11). This proposal was supported by Governor Snyder, and would have generated another $1.2 billion more per year for roads. In November 2015, the state Legislature returned their focus to the condition of Michigan's roads and revisited essentially the same legislation they rejected a year earlier. The revisited plan included a proposal for the first gas tax increase since 1997 (a 7.3 cents per gallon increase, and 11.3 cents per gallon for diesel beginning in 2017). Future gas tax rates will be indexed to inflation. Registration fees were also increased 20 percent. Governor Snyder signed the bill on November 10, 2015, calling it the largest investment of its kind in 50 years in Michigan. The tax increases were projected to generate about $600 million a year; the rest will be a general fund shift toward roads. Michigan Chamber of Commerce president Rich Studley stated, "All three of Michigan's leading industries—agribusiness, travel and tourism, and manufacturing—are heavily dependent on our roads and bridges and transportation system. This package will help us create and maintain jobs."[35]

Governor Snyder's big push for a second Detroit bridge crossing to Canada as an alternative to the Ambassador Bridge was another infrastructure issue of high impact on economic development in Michigan. The Ambassador Bridge, North America's number-one international border crossing, spans the Detroit River, connecting Detroit with Windsor, Canada. In 2013, Snyder and Canadian officials announced a U.S. presidential permit for the $2.1 billion New International Trade Crossing Bridge between Detroit and Windsor. Snyder indicated the bridge would bring jobs and improve the state's future. Despite the go-ahead, Manuel Moroun, who owns the 84-year-old Ambassador Bridge, continued his fight to block any rival bridge proposal. The Moroun family spent over $31 million of their own money to fund Proposal 6 in November 2012 (see chapter 11). The proposal would have amended the Michigan Constitution to require a public vote on all new construction of international bridge crossings if voters had approved it. With only 31 percent in favor, the ballot proposal failed.

The New International Trade Crossing project is now officially called the Gordie Howe International Bridge and could generate up to 10,000 temporary construction jobs and 25,000 indirect jobs during the four- to five-year building period. In the long term, the bridge is expected to employ 750 full-time employees in Michigan by 2035. Additionally, the construction of this new border crossing system is expected to generate or preserve, or both, as many as 25,000 jobs within Michigan and 70,000 jobs nationally.[36]

In a manufacturing state like Michigan, economic development strategies that aggressively support export activity are critical. The overall value of Michigan's exports had been steadily increasing, but in the past few years they have lost some ground to other states. No sector has a greater multiplier effect than manufacturing. Approximately 19,000 jobs are created for every $1 billion in export trade, according to the U.S. Department of Commerce estimates. In 1998, goods and service exports of $39.3 billion ranked Michigan fourth among the 50 states in export activity, up from $13.1 billion in 1987.[37] By 2014, Michigan companies exported $55.8 billion of trade goods, but fell to sixth in the country for jobs supported by exports and dropped four spots to eighth among states for total value of goods exported. In addition, 71 percent of that export trade was destined for just 11 countries. Transportation equipment accounted for about $25.9 billion, followed by $4.7 billion apiece in machinery and chemicals, and $3.1 billion in computer and electronic components. Agricultural exports have grown to $3.2 billion in recent years.[38] This helps explain why Governor Snyder conducted several trade trips to China. During Snyder's eight-day August 2015 mission, he made the case for Chinese companies to expand in Michigan and Chinese tourists to visit the state.

Opportunities for Michigan to expand into emerging markets especially for small and mid-size businesses exist but need nurturing by the public and nonprofit sectors. Eisinger describes the basic complexities of the export process and basic inertia as a foremost obstacle. Even if a firm can obtain the necessary financing to underwrite exporting, at a minimum a business must still: (1) identify and analyze appropriate markets; (2) adjust products for foreign specifications; (3) set prices; (4) conduct a marketing plan; (5) find a network of distributors; (6) overcome transportation problems, customs, foreign regulations, licensing, and tariffs; and (7) possibly arrange servicing of products. All of this transpires in the context of diverse languages and cultures.[39] Thomas Maguire, formerly of the U.S. Commercial Service, indicated that Michigan lacks adequate export assistance, focusing 90 percent of its energies on reverse investment and only 10 percent on promotion of export activity.[40] For the Michigan economy, export trade promises the greater stability that diverse foreign markets can provide over the business cycles of the traditional domestic market with its substantial uncertainty and turbulence.

Targeting select industries is a central element in state economic development strategic planning in determining which key industries deserve the most attention. From 1966 to 1979, spending by the private sector on research and development as a percentage of the gross national product hovered around 1.4 percent, which was not nearly as high as Germany and Japan.[41] The emerging entrepreneurial economy calls for a more vigorous role for state and local government in supporting research and development. Michigan has struggled to find its economic niche in its diversification from manufacturing—variously focusing on tourism, life sciences, alternative energy, and film industries.

The three-year experiment with film tax credits failed to produce the jobs and economic development expected. In 2011, Governor Snyder signed Public Act 291, replacing refundable film tax credits that were established in 2008 with a $25 million budget appropriation for the new Film and Digital Media Production Assistance Program run by the Michigan Film Office. To qualify for funding, an eligible production company must have had direct production expenditures or Michigan personnel expenditures of at least $100,000, or both. Yet, in 2015 Governor Snyder signed a law to end all film incentives. Critics contend few full-time industry jobs were created while the state paid out more than $250 million in incentives. In 2011, Snyder also signed into law Public Act 292, authorizing the Michigan Economic Growth Authority to enter into agreements to provide incentives for the construction of advanced battery manufacturing facilities, but later scaled back the offering, which required job creation in order for companies to receive the incentives.

Tourism in Michigan has not always been regarded as a key economic development tool, but the state has increasingly recognized the value of strategic investments in tourism as a key industry of the future. Around 2000, the state's commitment to tourism was less than a $5 million outlay. Under the Granholm administration, that commitment doubled to more than $10 million. Political support for tourism investment waned toward the end of Granholm's second term, but picked up again with Governor Snyder's strong support. In 2014, a record-breaking year for Michigan tourism, the state spent $12.4 million in out-of-state advertising. The industry captured in excess of $19.5 billion in domestic visitor spending and employed 214,000 workers. The "Pure Michigan" tourism campaign helped motivate more than 2.2 million visitors to the Great Lakes region and 1.9 million out-of-state visitors from across the nation traveled to Michigan. The Pure Michigan campaign generated $6.87 for each dollar spent on Pure Michigan advertising.[42]

In fact, the state even legislated a late school start to maximize Michigan's tourist season. In 2006, the Michigan State Board of Education mandated that all public schools in the state hold their first day of school after the Labor Day holiday, in accordance with the new post Labor Day school law. A survey found that 70 percent of all tourism business comes directly from Michigan residents and the shorter summer in between school years cut into the annual tourism season in the state.[43] However, a number of school districts have sought and received waivers from the Michigan Department of Education so they could begin their school year prior to Labor Day.

While the decline of Michigan's manufacturing sector is well documented, the rise of the land-based economy in Michigan (i.e., agriculture, tourism, forestry, and mining) is not yet fully recognized. Michigan's unique landscape produces more than 200 commodities, making the state second only to California in terms of crop diversity. The sector now accounts for over $101.2 billion of the state's economy annually, replacing manufacturing as the number-one industry. Michigan's food and agriculture system, with more than 10 million acres of farmland and 52,194 farms, accounts for 22 percent of the state's employment.[44] Yet, the three departments most connected to those industries, the Department of Agriculture, the Department of Natural Resources, and the Department of Environmental Quality, saw per capita spending cuts to their budgets of 60 percent, 64 percent, and 73 percent, respectively, during the five-year period after 2001.[45]

Michigan's emergent local economy, especially in the food and beverage industry is well documented, especially in Jaye Beeler's recent book, *Tasting and Touring Michigan's Homegrown Food: A Culinary Roadtrip*.[46] Perhaps this is best illustrated in the mitten state's 159 craft breweries, microbreweries, and brewpubs that are becoming a mighty economic engine for the state. As proudly proclaimed in the "Pure Michigan" statewide advertising campaign, "The Great Beer State" ranks fifth nationally in breweries. In 2014, the National Beer Wholesalers Association and the Beer Institute, Washington, DC-based lobbying groups, pegged Michigan's beer craze as a $2.664 billion annual contribution to the state's economy with 141 distributors and 16,744 retail establishments selling Michigan-made beer. All of that is estimated to have delivered $836 million in federal, state, and local taxes, and paid more than $320 million in federal and state excise taxes in Michigan. The local beer industry created 35,551 jobs with $1.04 billion in wages in Michigan.[47]

In March 2014, a group of bills were signed into law that included important changes to the laws regulating the brewing industry in Michigan. These positive changes to support the microbrewery industry include changing the definition of microbrewer by doubling the amount of beer that can be produced under that license, increasing the number of locations where a licensed brewer can produce, and allowing for self-distribution, among many other changes. Perhaps the boom can be further enhanced if both chambers of Legislature could further get behind Michigan's craft-brewing industry by addressing the state's high licensing laws, high excise taxes, and beer/wine wholesale monopoly. Michigan's small-batch distillers and spirit distributors are also getting on board by using only high-quality and pure Michigan ingredients—a new spirit venture capitalizing on Michigan's great agricultural heritage.

In Kent County alone, beer tourism accounts for more than $12.23 million a year, according to a recent study by Grand Valley State University professors Dan Giedeman, Paul Isely, and Gerry Simons. The beer industry, in addition to contributing to the growing perception of Grand Rapids as a thriving community, has contributed to an additional 14,000 hotel nights and an additional 42,246 visitors each year.[48] Grand Rapids was crowned Beer City USA, with Founders Brewing Co. there and Bell's Brewery in Kalamazoo ranked 17th and seventh, respectively, in the Top 50 largest U.S. craft breweries by sales volume.[49]

Finally, sustainability has become a critical economic development concept in recent years that Michigan can further capitalize upon. The primary focus of sustainability is on the "triple bottom line" of environmental stewardship, economic prosperity, and social responsibility. Some refer to it as the "Three E's" (economy, environment, equity), while others call it the "Three P's" (profits, planet, people). Michigan has been lagging behind the nation in advancing sustainable development strategies, yet that movement is growing. Michigan is not among the top 10 states in promoting sustainability, which has been led by California, Oregon, Washington, and New York, but has climbed to 19th place in recent sustainability rankings. The position is based on a number of factors including green industry projects per capita (e.g., renewable energy facilities, biofuels and biomass, recycling plants), LEED Certified Projects per capita, brownfield redevelopment funding, alternative fuel vehicles in use, and other factors.[50] West Michigan has been leading the way with an area-wide focus on LEED construction in both new buildings and renovation projects. A few years ago, the city of Grand Rapids had 58 percent of the LEED registered buildings in the state; West Michigan as a whole had 69 percent of LEED-certified buildings. Grand Rapids is recognized by Rick Fedrizzi, president of the United States Green Building Council, as having the most LEED-certified structures and square footage per capita of all the cities in the nation.[51]

State-Local Government Relations in Economic Development

The state's emergency manager laws, especially in the context of the Flint water crisis and the Detroit municipal bankruptcy, have understandably been the focus of a great deal of attention in state-local government relations in Michigan. However, the state, as described earlier in the chapter, has established the framework for many local government development efforts since the early 1970s. In particular, since PA 198 (1974), hundreds of local governments in Michigan have utilized industrial tax abatements in efforts to stem the loss of manufacturing jobs. The result has been tens of billions of dollars forgone in local tax revenues with limited effect on stemming the losses in the manufacturing sector.

Public Act 197 (1975) established downtown development authorities. Shortly thereafter, PA 450 (1980) created tax increment financing authorities. A community can capture property taxes that would have otherwise been paid to entities such as the library, community college, county, or transit system and instead use them for public improvements in specifically designated geographic zones. These authorities have been extensively used at the local government level to fund large-scale downtown development projects and day-to-day operations. In places like Grand Rapids, these tools have generated significant growth and billions of dollars of new private investment. They have been a reliable source of public sector funding even when municipal general fund budgets have experienced declining revenues and increasing financial hardship.

During the last two decades, the flagging economy, tax revenue shortfalls, and declining intergovernmental aid, juxtaposed with increased municipal employee health care and retirement costs, created extreme fiscal stress in localities throughout Michigan. One of the most controversial aspects of state-local relations continues to be the Michigan emergency manager law to deal with cities in financial collapse. The paternalistic relationship is long-standing. An early statute enacted was Public Act 72 (1990). The City of Flint's first emergency takeover ended in 2004, only for the state to take over Flint's finances again in 2011 (see chapter 15).

Michigan's aggressive emergency manager law has been mired in litigation and acrimony (see chapters 3, 4, 11, and 15). The law, which some view as a "takeover model," has survived a number of legal challenges. In 2012, Michigan voters rejected, by ballot referendum, the emergency manager law, PA 4 of 2011, by 52.66 percent only to see the Legislature pass and the governor sign another emergency manager bill into law (PA 436) less than two weeks later. That law, too, has survived legal challenges and persistent criticism. In 2016, an appeals court upheld PA 436 as not violating the constitutional rights of residents.

In 2012, responding to criticisms that the state should have acted more proactively to prevent emergencies, Governor Snyder created the Office of Fiscal Responsibility within the Treasury Department to assist local units of government. The state has also committed more than $234 million in aid for Flint, including $27 million to replace lead pipes.[52] The federal government has also authorized up to $170 million in infrastructure funds for communities such as Flint in a spending bill that passed in November 2016, averting a government shutdown after a lengthy battle over whether the federal government should help Flint. In October 2016, a joint select committee of the Michigan Legislature proposed sweeping changes in state government in response to the Flint water crisis (see chapter 15). The committee has proposed replacing the one-person emergency manager the state sends to financially distressed communities with a financial management team composed of a financial expert, a local government operations expert, and a local ombudsman.[53]

Part of the reason that localities are struggling financially is that Michigan reduced statutory revenue sharing, pushing problems down to vulnerable local governments (see chapters 4, 5, and 13). According to the nonpartisan Citizen's Research Council, more than $5 billion was diverted from the statutory revenue-sharing program between fiscal years 2001 and 2012. Detroit missed out on $732 million during that period and Grand

Rapids on $73 million.[54] The Michigan Municipal League contends that Michigan broke a social contract with its cities, and the result has been catastrophic for the state economy:

> Michigan cities and villages are the centers of our economy. They maintain the infrastructure and services that support the vast majority of our state's jobs. A recent study found that Michigan's metropolitan areas account for 89 percent of the state's jobs and 88 percent of its gross domestic product. The revenue sharing distribution formula was designed to appropriately compensate the communities that support us all and the higher costs they bear. Therefore, when that formula is underfunded, Michigan's entire economy suffers. Revenue sharing keeps our engines running.[55]

The statutory portion of revenue sharing has traditionally been distributed through a formula, not a per capita basis, which accounts for the significant variation in local governments' service and delivery needs, infrastructure maintenance, and fiscal capacity. Under Governor Snyder the statutory revenue sharing program was replaced with the Economic Vitality Incentive Program in 2011. But this did not restore state funding to localities to prerecession levels. Increased volatility and uncertainty in the revenue relationships between state and local governments has made the intergovernmental partnership difficult, and undoubtedly added to the severe fiscal stress or crisis experienced by many cities in Michigan (see chapter 3). Critics view it as a strong contributing factor to Detroit's eventual bankruptcy proceedings.

Clearly, Michigan's economic collapse was closely intertwined with the nation's lagging economic performance and eventually the global financial crisis in 2009. The U.S. government automotive industry rescue program eventually approved a financial bailout of General Motors and Chrysler. The federal government took over GM and Chrysler in March 2009. It fired GM chief executive officer Rick Wagoner, and required that Chrysler merge with Italy's Fiat. Between January 2009 and December 2013, the U.S. Department of Treasury invested a total of $80 billion, mostly in GM, through stock purchases. The bailout ended up costing taxpayers $9.2 billion. The bailout of the U.S. automobile industry ended on December 18, 2014, when the federal government completed a final sale of GM stock it held.[56]

No such bailout occurred for Detroit, which fell into state receivership and eventually filed for Chapter 9 bankruptcy on July 18, 2013. By doing so, it became the nation's largest municipal bankruptcy, with at least $18 billion in debt. Detroit was also the largest city by population to ever enter into Chapter 9 bankruptcy protections.[57] Since 1937, more than 600 Chapter 9 bankruptcies have occurred of cities, towns, villages, counties, and special-purpose districts in the United States.[58]

In December 2014, Detroit emerged from bankruptcy. Emergency Manager Kevyn Orr stepped down and Mayor Mike Duggan and the Detroit City Council regained control but continue to report to the Financial Review Commission, a state oversight board with broad powers to reject spending, borrowing, contracts, and labor agreements. After three years of managing the budget successfully, Detroit may come out of strict state oversight. In Detroit, long-term institutional corruption, out-of-control borrowing, and mismanagement are part of the legacy. Despite these steps, Detroit's future remains unclear. While the bankruptcy epitomized the worst-case scenario of failed municipal management and state neglect of its largest city, a productive relationship appears to have been built between Snyder and Duggan. Despite the emerging strength of the West Michigan economy, Michigan recognizes that the future health of the state economy is inexorably linked to a strong, revitalized Detroit. One year after exiting Chapter 9 municipal bankruptcy, Detroit was beginning to make some financial progress with a budget surplus for the first time in years. New investments in light rail (i.e., the QLine on Woodward Avenue) and the construction of a new stadium that is the home to Detroit Red Wings as well as the Detroit Pistons, and a venue for other events have renewed hopes for continued renewal, especially in the Woodward Corridor.

While the Detroit case provided fodder for larger concerns about local democracy, autonomy, state receivership, and economic development, it was the Flint water crisis that galvanized critics of the recent state role in local affairs. The crisis exemplified critics' worst fears about the potential negative consequences of the emergency manager law. The crisis grabbed national and even international attention, tarnishing Snyder's legacy. For weeks, negative news stories of failed government leadership permeated the airwaves.

At his 2016 State of the State address, Snyder accepted responsibility for the Flint water crises, blaming the bureaucracy, saying "what is so frustrating and makes you so angry about this situation is you have a handful of quote-unquote experts that were career civil service people that made terrible decisions."[59] Many Flint residents and a number of state and federal legislators placed the blame squarely on Governor Snyder. There were several calls for his resignation based on the belief that the administration knew about the toxins months before taking action and withheld critical information from the public. The business climate of Flint was already suffering from negative perceptions. The water crisis makes economic turnaround even more problematic for the city, and the negative publicity for Michigan makes it harder for the state to successfully turn around its economy as well.

Conclusion

In Governor Snyder's 2017 State of the State speech, he focused on the progress Michigan has made during his administration and outlined an accountability model for continuing strong economic growth and attracting new talent to Michigan. Snyder said, "Our proven track record shows how far we have come. But our vision, our persistence, and our commitment to our people is what proves just how far we have yet to go. Michigan has come back and now we're on a clear path toward our future."[60] He claimed the six years of his administration resulted in an economy that has been much more attractive to new businesses than it has been in decades. "In fact, since 2010 almost half a million jobs have been created in Michigan, which translates to roughly 200 news jobs a day for six years. This increase in jobs led to Michigan seeing its lowest unemployment rate in 15 years and 10 points lower than it was in June 2009."[61] While that rate slightly increased in early 2017, some view it as positive, as it means that more Michiganders had entered the workforce.

Balancing Michigan's assets in advanced manufacturing, food and agricultural industries, the Great Lakes, tourism, and the emerging health care sector against its liabilities—which include an aging infrastructure, racial and social polarization, and crucial skills deficits—will be a serious challenge. In addition, the economic turnaround for Michigan's key cities particularly on the east side of the state—Detroit, Flint, Pontiac and Saginaw—is far from realized. Moreover, the fact that Michigan is surrounded by the Great Lakes suggests more potential that is not fully realized. The importance of freshwater—to agriculture and tourism, to the emerging craft brewing industry, and in comparison to states with major drought challenges—places Michigan at the forefront of an emerging "blue economy."

As we look into the future, the efforts at economic diversification highlighted throughout this chapter will continue. For the immediate future, the governor has made talent attraction and reversing the decline in the state's population a high priority. While the 21st Century Infrastructure Commission was established in 2016, it is not clear where the necessary funds for critical improvements in infrastructure will come. The state is also prioritizing investing in its human infrastructure through the Skilled Trades Training Fund, targeting community colleges and skilled trade apprenticeship programs to develop the skills that will be needed to advance Michigan's economy.

The challenge for Michigan's government is to provide the right kind of state leadership to assist municipalities in economic turnaround and revitalization and avoid pressure-cooker policies for dealing with financially troubled municipalities. Unfortunately, while progress has been achieved in key strategic areas identified in this chapter (e.g., successful efforts to spur growth in cities such as Grand Rapids), the state is still searching for the right set of policies and interventions to reverse decline, avoid catastrophic events, and promote economic prosperity. Economic development policy will undoubtedly continue to be an area where Michigan leaders look to build on the successes that have been realized early in the 21st century and expand that growth and economic vibrancy to other areas of the state that are looking for the same kind of successes.

WEB RESOURCES

The *Michigan Economic Development Corporation* (www.michiganbusiness.org/about-medc/mission/) markets Michigan and provides the tools and environment to drive job creation and investment in the state. The site consists of press releases, events, news, and articles related to business in Michigan.

The *Michigan Department of Talent and Economic Development* (www.michigan.gov/ted/) allows the state to leverage its ability to build talent with in-demand skills while helping state businesses grow and thrive. Joining job creation and economic development efforts under one umbrella, the department consists of the Michigan Economic Development Corporation, the Michigan State Housing Development Authority, the Michigan Strategic Fund, and the newly created Talent Investment Agency.

The *Michigan Small Business Development Center* (www.sbdcmichigan.org/) enhances Michigan's economic well-being by providing counseling, training, research, and advocacy for new ventures, existing small businesses, and innovative technology companies.

The *Right Place* (www.rightplace.org/About-Us/Services-Support.aspx) through this website assists West Michigan entrepreneurs with a variety of programs.

NOTES

1. Peter Eisinger, *The Rise of the Entrepreneurial State: State and Local Economic Development Policy in the United States* (Madison: University of Wisconsin Press, 1988), 16.
2. Ibid., 56.
3. Advisory Commission on Intergovernmental Relations, *Significant Features of Fiscal Federalism* (Washington, DC: GPO, 1985).
4. Enid F. Beaumont and Harold A. Hovey, "State, Local, and Federal Economic Development Policies: New Federal Patterns, Chaos, or What?," *Public Administration Review* 45, no. 2 (Mar.–Apr. 1985): 327–32.
5. Eisinger, *Rise of the Entrepreneurial State*, 23.
6. Bruce Rubenstein and Lawrence Ziewacz, *Michigan: A History of the Great Lakes State* (Somerset, NJ: John Wiley and Sons, 2014), 144.
7. "Mining in Michigan: A Focus on Nonferrous Mineral Extraction Resource Guide," accessed November 15, 2016, https://www.michigan.gov/documents/deq/ICC_Mining_Guidebook_final_6-17-13_429204_7.pdf
8. Rubenstein and Ziewacz, *Michigan*, 177.
9. Public Sector Consultants, "Economic, Cultural and Political History in Michigan," chapter 1, in *Michigan in Brief, 2002–3* (Lansing, MI: Public Sector Consultants, 2002), 4.
10. Charles Ballard, "The Economic and Fiscal Background of Metropolitan Policies in Michigan," in *Sustaining Michigan: Metropolitan Policies and Strategies*, ed. Richard Jelier and Gary Sands (East Lansing: Michigan State University Press, 2009), 17.
11. Ballard, "Economic and Fiscal Background," 26.
12. Economic Policy Institute, *The Manufacturing Footprint and the Importance of U.S. Manufacturing Jobs*.
13. Eisinger, *Rise of the Entrepreneurial State*, 3.
14. Barry Bluestone and Bennett Harrison, *The Deindustrialization of America* (New York: Basic Books, 1982).
15. Eisinger, *Rise of the Entrepreneurial State*.
16. Laura Reese and Raymond Rosenfeld, "Local Economic Development in the U.S. and Canada: Institutionalizing Policy Approaches," *American Review of Public Administration* 34 (2004): 277–92.
17. Charles Mahtesian, "Romancing the Smokestack" *Governing* 8 (1994).
18. Gary Sands and Laura Reese, "Michigan's Industrial Tax Abatements," in *Sustaining Michigan: Metropolitan Policies and Strategies*, ed. Richard Jelier and Gary Sands (East Lansing: Michigan State University Press, 2009).
19. Gary Sands and Laura Reese, "Michigan's Industrial Tax Abatements," in *Sustaining Michigan: Metropolitan Policies and Strategies*, ed. Richard Jelier and Gary Sands (East Lansing: Michigan State University Press, 2009), 57.

20. "The Economic and Fiscal Background of Metropolitan Policies in Michigan," in *Sustaining Michigan: Metropolitan Policies and Strategies*, ed. Richard W. Jelier and Gary Sands (East Lansing: Michigan State University Press, 2009), 17–44.

21. Ballard, "Economic and Fiscal Background," 25.

22. Judy Putnam, "Lopsided Income Growth Hurts Michigan Economy," *Michigan League for Public Policy*, January 26, 2015, accessed November 15, 2016, http://www.mlpp.org/lopsided-income-growth-hurts-michigan

23. Kristi Tanner, "Michigan Posts Its Largest Income Gain since the Recession," *Detroit Free Press*, September 15, 2016.

24. Mathew Dolan, "5 Trends to Watch in Michigan's Economy," *Detroit Free Press*, January 2, 2016.

25. Martin Lavelle, "How Tight Is Michigan's Labor Market?," Federal Reserve Bank of Chicago, Detroit Branch, October 11, 2016, http://michiganeconomy.chicagofedblogs.org/?p=939

26. Paul Brace, *State Government and Economic Performance* (Baltimore: John Hopkins University Press, 1993).

27. "City of Grand Rapids," accessed November 15, 2016, http://grcity.us/design-and-development-services/Economic-Development/Pages/Renaissance-Zones.aspx

28. Richard Florida, *The Rise of the Creative Class and How It's Transforming Work, Leisure, Community and Everyday Life* (New York: Basic Books, 2002).

29. After serving on the Cool Cities Evaluation Taskforce, this chapter's author realized the limitation of the Cool Cities Initiative.

30. June Manning Thomas, "Michigan's Urban Policies in an Era of Land Use Reform and Creative-Class Cities," in *Sustaining Michigan: Metropolitan Policies and Strategies*, ed. Richard Jelier and Gary Sands (East Lansing: Michigan State University Press. 2009).

31. M. Curtis Hoffman and Jeremy Pyne, "The Brain Drain Wars: Characteristics of Recent Movers into and out of Michigan," in *Sustaining Michigan: Metropolitan Policies and Strategies*, ed. Richard Jelier and Gary Sands (East Lansing: Michigan State University Press, 2009), 292.

32. Ballard, "Economic and Fiscal Background," 27.

33. "Transportation Asset Management Council," accessed November 15, 2016, http://www.mcgi.state.mi.us/MITRP/Data/PaserDashboard.aspx

34. Eric D. Lawrence, "State of Michigan's Roads Go from Poor to Terrible," *Detroit Free Press*, March 29, 2015.

35. Jonathan Oosting, "Snyder Signs Long-Term Road Funding Plan: It's about Investing in Michigan's Future," *MLive Media Group*, November 10, 2015.

36. "New International Trade Crossing Proposal," September 2011, accessed November 1, 2016, http://www.michigan.gov/documents/snyder/NITC_Overview_362601_7.pdf?20141027054942

37. "A Profile of U.S. Exporting Companies, 1997-1998," U.S. Department of Commerce, United States Census Bureau, Foreign Trade Division, accessed February 11, 2017, https://www.census.gov/foreign-trade/aip/edbrel-9798.pdf

38. Chad Halcom, "Trade Report: Michigan Exports $55.98 B in Goods," *Crain's Detroit Business*, April 9, 2015.

39. Eisinger, *Rise of the Entrepreneurial State*.

40. Richard Jelier, "The Significance of Nonprofit and Public Sector Collaboration in Facilitating International Trade in West Michigan," *International Journal of Economic Development* 2, no. 4 (2000): 477.

41. Eisinger, *Rise of the Entrepreneurial State*, 81.

42. *The Economic Impact of Travel in Michigan: Tourism Satellite Account Calendar Year 2014* Tourism Economics: An Oxford Economics Company, 2014, accessed February 11, 2017, http://www.michiganbusiness.org/cm/Files/Reports/Michigan-2014-Tourism-Economic-Impact.pdf

43. "Michigan Tourism Business," accessed July 25, 2010, http://www.imakenews.com/tourism/index000142517.cfm

44. "Department of Agriculture and Rural Development," accessed November 1, 2016, http://www.michigan.gov.mdard

45. Ballard, "Economic and Fiscal Background," 32.

46. Jaye Beeler, *Tasting and Touring Michigan Homegrown Food: A Culinary Roadtrip* (Traverse City, MI: Arbutus Press, 2012).

47. "Beer Serves America: Economic Impact of the Beer Industry, 2014 Data, Michigan," accessed November 1, 2016, www.beerservesamerica.org/state-and-congressional-district-data

48. "Beer Tourism Draws Visitors to Kent County," *Forum: A Newsletter for the Grand Valley University Community*, October 26, 2015, https://www.gvsu.edu/cms4/asset/22C74362-091D-313E-BB6F7FC60974CE65/forum_ind_10.26(3).pdf

49. "Brewers Association, A Passionate Voice for Craft Brewers," accessed November 15, 2016, https://www.brewersassociation.org

50. Adam Burns, "Green Guide–Sustainability Rankings," *Site Selection Magazine*, 2013, accessed February 11, 2017, http://siteselection.com/issues/2013/jul/sustainability.cfm

51. Richard W. Jelier and Norman Christopher, "Building a Triple Bottom Line Sustainability Model in Michigan," in *Sustaining Michigan: Metropolitan Policies and Strategies*, ed. Richard Jelier and Gary Sands (East Lansing: Michigan State University Press, 2009).

52. Jonathan Oosting and Michael Gerstein, "Expert: Without Filter, No Water Safe from Lead Pipes," *Detroit News*, September 28, 2016, accessed February 11, 2017, http://www.detroitnews.com/story/news/michigan/flint-water-crisis/2016/09/28/snyder-flint-water-crisis/91213822/

53. Paul Egan, "Flint Report: Fix Law on Emergency Managers," *Detroit Free Press*, October 19, 2016.

54. Jonathan Oosting, "How Michigan's Revenue Sharing 'Raid' Cost Communities Billions for Local Services," *MLive Media Group*, April 13, 2103.

55. Diane Bukowski, "The Great $6.2 B Revenue Sharing Heist—Michigan Municipal League Report," *Voice of Detroit*, March 3, 2014.

56. The stock purchases by the federal government also included holdings of Ally, GM's finance arm. It was the sale of this stock that was the final move in the bankruptcy.

57. Monica Davey and Mary Williams Walsh, "Billions in Debt, Detroit Tumbles into Insolvency," *New York Times*, July 19, 2013.

58. Gosia Wozniacka, "Stockton Bankruptcy Is Hard Hit for City Retirees," *Boston Globe*, June 27, 2012.

59. Jason Sickles, "Michigan Governor Snyder on Flint: Terrible Decisions Were Made," Yahoo News, January 22, 2016.

60. Rick Snyder, *2017 State of the State*, accessed January 31, 2017, at http://www.michigan.gov/snyder/0,4668,7-277-74857_78766---,00.html

61. Snyder, *2017 State of the State*.

15 ✦ Flint's Water Crisis

A Case Study in Historical Context, Decline, Responses to Challenges, and State-Local Government Relations

PAUL ROZYCKI

The events surrounding what came to be known as the "Flint water crisis" became an international media sensation by 2016. But as the full story of the city's contaminated water began to unfold, it became clear that this volume's themes were a helpful framework for understanding the events that occurred. Examining the *historical context* of Flint helps provide a background to the events and decisions leading up to and surrounding the water crisis. Like many industrialized urban centers in the United States, and Michigan in particular, Flint saw a remarkable economic and population growth in the first half of the 20th century, but experienced an equally remarkable *decline* during the latter half of the century. Such decline led to a number of attempts to lead the city back to economic recovery. However, as several other chapters in this book have demonstrated, public policy *responses to challenges* are not always successful—and in some cases, have had unintended consequences that created their own set of problems on top of those the policy was supposed to address.

The water crisis in Flint also speaks directly to the book's fourth theme—*state-local government relations*. The appointments by Michigan governors of emergency managers to the city of Flint, in addition to being a particular response to a challenge, increased tensions between state and local officials over the years. Moreover, some of the decisions leading to the crisis included competing attempts by emergency managers in both Detroit and Flint to save money for their cities. As water problems became more serious in Flint, a breakdown in state-local relations unfortunately led to a situation where state government officials ignored or downplayed the increasing complaints made by local officials and Flint residents about water quality in the city.

Flint's Historical Context

The early history of Flint is a story of a community that rose and fell with changing technology and changing opportunities. Each change brought with it a new crisis and a new response, often based on the remnants of Flint's previous economic base. In 1819, Jacob Smith, considered Flint's first settler, established a trading post with the Ojibway Indians along what is now the Flint River. That trading post proved to be a useful connection between the Michigan lumber industry in the Saginaw and Detroit areas. By 1855 the settlement became a city and, for much of the second half of the 19th century, built its success on Michigan's lumber and timber industries. These industries and the profits gained from them laid the groundwork in Flint for the city's next dominant industry—the carriage manufacturing business. The availability of both lumber and skilled workers made Flint a major manufacturing hub for the horse-drawn-carriage industry.[1]

The next evolution in Flint, however, would begin to shape the city into what it became best known for—the automobile industry. As the "horseless carriage" began to take over the nation's roads in the early 20th century, those who made horse-drawn vehicles were in an ideal position to make the transition from a fading carriage business to the newly emerging automotive industry. After a brief beginning in Detroit, the Buick Motor Company moved to Flint in the early 20th century and brought with it a range of auto suppliers. Along with Buick, the city became home to a host of now forgotten automobile companies, such as Dort, Little, Flint, and Mason. By 1908, Buick was the largest manufacturer of automobiles in the nation, and, under the leadership of William C. Durant, it became the centerpiece for a new consolidated auto company, General Motors. Though Durant would have a checkered career with GM, the company he founded would emerge as a giant in the auto industry for much of the 20th century. Also, GM became the engine that drove both the explosive growth of Flint when the company opened plants, and later to the city's dramatic decline when it closed some of these same plants.

Flint was also central to the establishment of the United Automobile Workers, a major force in the labor movement of that era. In late 1936 and early 1937, the UAW's "sit-down strikes" at several GM facilities in

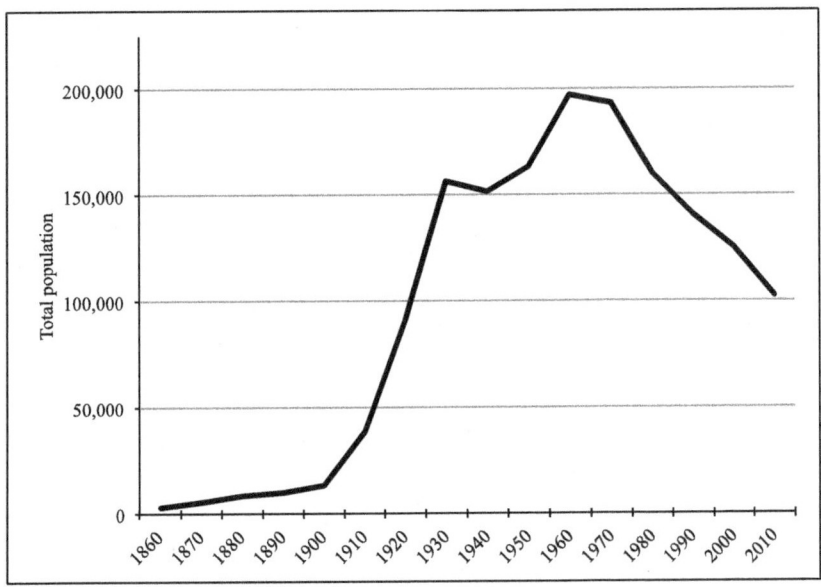

Fig. 15.1. Population of Flint, Michigan, 1860–2010
Source: U.S. Census Bureau, "Census of Population and Housing," reports for Michigan, various years, accessed November 21, 2016, http://www.census.gov/prod/www/decennial.html

the United States built on similar actions in Europe. The largest of these strikes came in Flint, and included a 44-day strike at the Chevrolet No. 4 plant that centered on a bitter dispute with General Motors. The impasse was finally settled when GM recognized the union as the sole bargaining agent for its autoworkers. The strike, and the recognition of the UAW, is considered one of the key events in the formation and success of the labor union movement in the United States.[2]

The growth of GM and the creation of a working relationship with the UAW led to a dramatic growth in both Flint's population and economic prosperity for the city's population. Long before GM, Flint was a small town. Through the end of 1800s there were fewer than 10,000 people living in the city (see fig. 15.1). As the 20th century began, however, there was tremendous growth; Flint started to boom and saw a tenfold population increase between 1900 and 1930. While population dipped between 1930 and 1940, the growth continued until the city's population peaked in 1960 at roughly 196,000 residents (this made Flint the second largest city in Michigan at the time). Much of this growth was due to the fact that more than 80,000 workers were employed by GM in Flint and in surrounding Genesee County at the time. Since that peak, however, population has steadily declined; by 1990, population was down to a level last seen in 1940. In 2010, population hovered around 100,000, only to drop below that mark by 2014.[3]

The prosperity of that era was led by a triad of major forces that led Flint to its best years. The combination of GM, the UAW, and the Charles Stewart (C. S.) Mott Foundation provided the funds and the leadership for many of Flint's proudest accomplishments. These included a nationally regarded K-12 community school system, several colleges, a cultural center that included art and historical museums, and a large community auditorium. In 1950, the city was awarded with an "All American City" designation by the National Civic League, which is given to communities demonstrating community-wide cooperation that accomplishes noteworthy objectives. Leadership (and funding) for many of the city's most successful community groups was commonly drawn from GM, the UAW, and the Mott Foundation.

Established in 1926, the Mott Foundation was meant to be a vehicle for the philanthropy of C. S. Mott, one of the founding members of General Motors. Mott served on the board of directors of GM and was elected as Flint's mayor three times. As the foundation expanded, it lent support to many local developments. Starting in the 1930s, it led the development of Flint's community school system, which later became a nationwide model for making schools an active and involved part of the local community. The Mott Foundation has long been an engine for new initiatives and growth in Flint, as well as Genesee County as a whole.[4]

Decline of Flint, GM, and the UAW

As even a casual observer can easily see today, Flint was unable to sustain these booming times. However, the city's decline was not swift but gradual and began without huge fanfare, a major disaster, or some kind of earth-shattering collapse. The city's growth and decline has always been intimately connected to the growth and decline of General Motors.

The first moves that can be connected to the decline of the city may have been seen as less threatening because they were not as obvious as those that would follow. As early as the 1940s, GM began to move some operations to the suburbs and rural areas surrounding the city, even as the corporation was expanding.[5] There were eight new GM industrial complexes built in the Flint metropolitan area between 1940 and 1960, but none were within in city limits.[6] Therefore, even before GM began closing its urban factories—what many look to as the decision that started real decline in the city—Flint was losing both tax base and income base within its own boundaries, since it was unable to annex the surrounding territory.

The signals of decline that are much more familiar began in the 1970s and 1980s, as foreign competition began cutting into the American automobile market. With this, the people of Flint began to face a recurring series of auto plant layoffs. These layoffs were only the harbinger of things to come, but at the time they simply seemed to be the usual cycle of layoffs and rehires that had long been part of the automobile manufacturing industry. For that reason, many expected that the good times would return as they had before, and failed to take appropriate action to deal with the decline associated with long-term restructuring of the auto industry.

The layoffs of the 1970s and 1980s turned into plant closures, among them some of the oldest plants in the GM system, dating back to the earliest days of the corporation. One of the largest closings, which also created the biggest impact, was the Buick factory, which had become known as "Buick City." It had almost a 100-year history in the city; it began as a manufacturing plant in 1908 and was closed in 1999, though a few parts kept functioning for about a decade longer. At one time Buick City had been the largest manufacturing plant in the world, before Henry Ford's Rouge plant in Dearborn was built, and comprised some 28 separate buildings.

A major Chevrolet production factory located along the Flint River (popularly called "Chevy in the Hole"), which was opened in 1913, closed in 2004 after a series of gradual steps and scale-backs. Similarly, the AC Spark Plug plant (which would later become part of the large supplier Delphi) finally closed in 2013, and, like many of the plants that closed in the city, was demolished shortly afterward. In the end, the long series of plant closings reduced GM employment in Flint and Genesee County from a peak of about 80,000 in the late 1970s to only about 8,000 in 2016.

Flint's long-term economic decline beginning in the late 20th century was made even worse as the city and the state of Michigan suffered through the Great Recession of the early 2000s. Most economic and social indicators had worsened by 2005, and while some recovery occurred by 2015, the city and its surrounding areas continued to struggle. Average wage growth continued to be low, the manufacturing sector continued to shed jobs, and home prices declined over 50 percent between 2007 and 2012.[7]

The decline in GM jobs and in the city of Flint was paralleled by a decline in UAW local and national membership. Nationally, in 1979, the United Auto Workers had about 1.5 million members. By 2015, even though recent gains in membership have occurred outside of automobile manufacturing, national membership totals still totaled only slightly more than 400,000.[8] The decline in the UAW's local Flint membership—several of Flint's largest locals have closed or been merged with others—was not simply a loss of jobs and income for those who had been the backbone of Flint's middle class. It also weakened one of the mainstays of the leadership for much of the Flint community. For decades the UAW played a role in recruiting and providing leaders for school boards, city councils, and other local leadership positions. The members of the UAW were a dependable source of volunteers for many community projects, from community cleanups to blood drives. With the decline of the UAW's membership, that leadership is not totally gone, but it has been substantially diminished along with its impact on the community.

As might be expected, the city of Flint's population took a steep dive after the plant closings. At its peak, Flint had 196,000 residents in 1960. According to the U.S. Census, the city's population was barely over 100,000 in 2010 and is estimated to have fallen to about 98,000 in 2015 (further declines have almost certainly taken place since the water crisis). The mid-2010s mark the first time the city had fallen below 100,000 in population since the 1920s. Slipping below the 100,000 mark was significant, not just as a signal of the decline the city has experienced but for what it might do to respond to challenges it faces. Falling under the 100,000 level made it more difficult for the city to qualify for larger state and federal grants that could supplement funding for key services. Moreover, state revenue sharing will be lower and more akin to that received by small cities and townships.[9] Evidence of this already exists—Flint received about $22 million in revenue sharing in 1998 and saw it shrink to $10 million in 2014.[10]

Also fueling the decline of the city was a trend that has affected almost every large northern U.S. city—a shift to the suburbs. In 1940, 70 percent of Genesee County's population lived within the city of Flint. By 2013, only 25 percent did. The shift was caused not only by the fact that nearly all of the new GM plants were built outside the city but also that in the 1970s, a large mall development—the Genesee Valley Mall—was built in Flint Township, located outside of the city. That development triggered a significant move of retail business out of the Flint downtown area to a suburban location in the 1980s.

As automobile manufacturing plants closed and the population declined, so did the city's tax base. The taxable value of city property, valued at $1.5 billion in 2001, declined by half, to $750 million by 2015. Personal income in Flint stood at nearly $3.5 billion in 1996; by 2013 it had fallen to $400 million.¹¹ Similarly, property tax revenues were about $12 million in 2006 and only about $5 million by 2014. During this time Flint had one of the highest millage rates in Genesee County. Between 2008 and 2014, Genesee County faced a dramatic drop in residential property values, which had declined by 26 percent. Even if property values should rise, Proposal A and the Headlee Amendment limit the rate of tax revenue increase (see chapters 3 and 13).

Most of the elements of Flint's decline were typical for many industrialized Rustbelt cities that have faced deindustrialization in recent decades. One difference was that Flint was so heavily dependent on one industry and just one company—General Motors. There is a parallel in Flint's experiences to the entire state in the dependence, for so long, on one economic sector—the auto industry (see chapters 1 and 4). The fact that the city had been through so many downturns with the automotive business cycle led to a sense of false complacency when the plants began to shut down but unexpectedly did not reopen later. That complacency, tied to the financial problems with a rapidly downsizing city, led Flint to a series of financial problems, and finally to a succession of state-mandated emergency managers.

Responses to Flint's Challenges

Local leaders in the Flint area have sought to deal with the city's and region's decline over many years and in many different ways. In the 1980s, local leaders and businesses attempted to make Flint a tourist center by funding and building AutoWorld—an indoor theme park and automobile museum. AutoWorld closed about six months after it opened, but sporadically opened off and on (e.g., on weekends), until it permanently closed in 1994. The University of Michigan–Flint has become a major anchor for Flint's downtown area (including building on the former AutoWorld site). In 2010, an economic development study of Genesee County noted several areas of potential growth, including agribusiness, advanced manufacturing, and the role that local colleges and universities' (e.g., the University of Michigan–Flint, Kettering University, and a local campus of Michigan State University) research and development can have on Flint's growth.¹² Among those strategies, the city also considered adopting an "Eds and Meds" economic development strategy, in which education and health care industry investments in the downtown area would be a special focus.¹³

However, the city has continued to struggle over the years. As a result of Flint's declining population and loss of tax base and revenues, the city faced a number of years of budget deficits and ultimately a financial crisis. As one response to Flint's challenges, Michigan governor John Engler placed Flint under the direction of its first emergency manager, Ed Kurtz, between 2002 and 2004. There was a break from EM control after Kurtz left office, but there were a series of EM appointments between 2011 and 2015.[14] With several different EMs in place after 2002, and different mayors with limited powers elected during this time—Don Williamson (2003), who resigned in 2009; Dayne Walling (2009); and Karen Weaver (2015)—it was not always clear who in Flint had the authority and power to make decisions.

It is also worth noting that over the years Michigan's emergency manager law has undergone significant changes (see chapter 3). An early version—Public Act 72—was commonly referred to as the Emergency Financial Manager Act, and it centered on trying to address the financial problems of a local government. Public Act 72 was replaced by Public Act 4 in 2011; of significance here is that the new law gave greater and more expansive powers to the emergency managers. After a public referendum repealed Public Act 4 in 2012, the Legislature replaced it with Public Act 436—the Local Financial Stability and Choice Act—which included an appropriation of money, making it immune from repeal by referendum. Public Act 436 was quite similar to Public Act 4 in the sense that it gave very broad powers to an emergency manager, including the power to modify contracts, change city personnel, and supervise city budgets. While other chapters in this volume have discussed the impact and role of EMs in Michigan, arguably the most pointed effects of the emergency manager laws have been felt in Flint. Indeed, the extraordinary powers of an EM were at the center of the decisions that led up to the Flint water crisis.[15]

The Flint Water Crisis

The Flint water crisis is a culmination of problems created because of Flint's long history of economic decline, and a number of decisions attempting to respond to the challenges created by the city's overall decline. These decisions were made at all levels of government and by a number of elected and appointed officials over a period of several years. At the time many of the decisions may have seemed reasonable, but each laid the groundwork for the water crisis in Flint. Contamination in the city's water system cannot be understood by only examining Flint's history of decline. Rather, the role of the state-appointed emergency managers (in both Flint and Detroit), and the sometimes-contentious relations between officials in state government agencies and representatives from Flint are also critical.

A Brief Chronology of the Water Crisis[16]

In part because of the financial stress experienced by the city of Flint, in March 2013 the Flint City Council voted (7 to 1) to join a new water system, called the Karegnondi Water Authority. The city's emergency manager, Ed Kurtz, did not want to make this decision alone, which required a formal vote by the city council. A major reason for the switch was that it was projected to help save millions of dollars for the city over the subsequent 25 years. Water from this system would deliver water directly from Lake Huron rather than from the city of Detroit's system that was operated by the Detroit Water and Sewerage Department (DWSD; the name has since changed to the Great Lakes Water Authority). The emergency manager ratified the Flint council's decision, and State Treasurer Andy Dillon approved the switch as well. The move to the new water authority would take three years—until 2016 (which later was pushed back to 2020). At the time, the City of Detroit and the DWSD were operating under their own emergency manager—and Detroit did not want to lose its biggest customer.[17] Upon hearing of Flint's decision, DWSD informed Flint that it would stop selling water to the city as of April 2014. Consequently, Flint was forced to find a temporary source of water. A few months after Flint's decision to switch to a new water authority, in June 2013, Kurtz made the decision to use the Flint River as the source of Flint's water supply, until the Karegnondi water supply was operational.

In April 2014, Flint lost Detroit's water supply per DWSD's decision to terminate the city's contract. As Flint's Department of Public Works prepared to make the shift to Flint River water, some questions were raised about the need for corrosion controls because of the nature of the new source of water. The Michigan Department of Environmental Quality (MDEQ) assured the city that the corrosion controls were not necessary. A local Flint water supervisor responded to the MDEQ, saying that the city was not ready to handle the switch to the Flint River, but MDEQ never responded to this concern. On April 25, 2014, city employees and local officials made a ceremonial toast with water from the new Flint water supply as they pushed the button that shifted the city's water source to the Flint River. Within weeks, many residents began to complain about discolored, odd-tasting, and bad smelling water.

By mid-summer 2014, several areas of the city were given "boil water" advisories after fecal coliform was discovered in water on the west side of the city. Later that year, General Motors refused to use city water at its engine plant facility, saying it was too corrosive to use for manufacturing purposes.

In January 2015, the city notified citizens that because of elevated levels of total trihalomethanes that the city was in violation of the Safe Water Drinking Act. The MDEQ continued to reassure the public that the water was safe, but the official state office building in Flint had begun to use bottled water and two water fountains at the University of Michigan–Flint showed high levels of lead. Even with this, Emergency Manager Jerry Ambrose declined an opportunity to reconnect Flint to the Detroit water system. In February, a federal Environmental Protection Agency employee—Miguel Del Toral—warned of high lead levels in Flint's water. As complaints began to mount, the Flint City Council voted to end its use of Flint River water in March 2015, but Ambrose overruled that decision.

E-mails later released by Governor Rick Snyder's office indicated that the state was becoming increasingly aware of the problems with Flint's water by early-to-mid 2015, but neither the MDEQ nor the EPA took action to notify the public. Around this same time, residents continued to raise questions about lead and other contaminants in the water and a lack of corrosion controls. In July 2015, the MDEQ stated that there was no lead problem with Flint's water in response to a published report by the American Civil Liberties Union about the possibility of lead in the water. At this time, the EPA began to pressure MDEQ to start corrosion controls.

In September 2015, Virginia Tech University civil engineering professor Dr. Marc Edwards and his team began testing Flint water, where they found lead levels above the federal guidelines. The MDEQ responded by arguing that the lead levels were at acceptable levels. In September 2015, Hurley Hospital's Dr. Mona Hanna-Attisha announced in a press conference that she found elevated lead levels in children she had tested. The next day, the city issued a public health advisory about the increased lead levels in Flint water. Local political leaders demanded a public response from the director of the MDEQ, Dan Wyant. By the end of September, Governor Snyder and Wyant began to communicate about the issue, as shown by e-mails released by the governor.

By October 2015, the State of Michigan officially announced that there was a problem with Flint's drinking water. Governor Snyder also announced that Flint would reconnect to the Detroit water system. In November 2015, Dr. Karen Weaver was elected mayor of Flint after defeating the incumbent, Mayor Dayne Walling. The Flint water crisis was understandably a major campaign issue. Near the end of 2015, Mayor Weaver declared a state of emergency in the city and appealed to the federal government for help. In addition, MDEQ director Dan Wyant and the department's communications director, Brad Wurfel, both resigned.

In January 2016, a possible link between the discovery of a number of new cases of Legionnaires' disease in the Flint area and the water crisis was suspected after 12 deaths in Genesee County. In mid-January 2016, President Barack Obama signed an emergency declaration for Flint in response to a request by Governor Snyder. Shortly afterward, Susan Hedman, the EPA official who headed the office that oversees the region that includes Flint, resigned. In addition, the head of the Office of Municipal Drinking Water in the MDEQ, Liane Shekter Smith, was fired. In March, an investigative body convened by Governor Snyder—the Flint Water Advisory Task Force—issued its report. It found the state—especially the MDEQ—primarily responsible for the water crisis, although it regarded the crisis as the result of the failure of government at all levels. At a later congressional hearing, Governor Snyder testified that the emergency manager system failed during the water crisis.

Later in 2016, Attorney General Bill Schuette filed charges against several MDEQ and City of Flint water employees. By September 2016, Virginia Tech professor Marc Edwards and the EPA reported that Flint's water was "dramatically better," but still recommended city residents use water filters. The city's plan to replace lead pipes with copper pipes, through the "Fast Start" program, began to make some progress in 2016, but efforts were often thwarted due to inaccurate records about pipe locations and a complicated bidding process for selecting contractors.[18]

In December 2016, Michigan Attorney General Bill Schuette brought new felony charges against two of Flint's emergency managers, Darnell Early and Gerald Ambrose, along with two city employees. The charges involved misuse of funds as part of the water crisis. In early 2017, a $722 million class action lawsuit, on behalf of over 1,700 Flint residents, was filed against the EPA for its role in the water crisis. Also in early 2017, the MDEQ reported that Flint lead levels had fallen enough to be considered safe, although residents were still advised to continue using filters as water supply pipes continued to be replaced. By February 2017, delays in upgrading the Flint water plant were expected to postpone the city's use of the Karegnondi pipeline to as late as 2020.

Response to the Water Crisis

Not surprisingly, the problems created by the responses to Flint's financial woes in turn created the need for further responses to remedy the earlier failed decisions. There were many groups and organizations that produced responses to and recommendations about the Flint water crisis on all levels. Perhaps the best single summary of those actions and responses arose from the final report of the Flint Water Advisory Task Force, published in March 2016. The Task Force—a group composed of five members with expertise in public policy, public utilities, environmental protection, public health, and health care—was appointed by Governor Snyder and given the duty of reviewing the causes of and cures for the Flint water crisis. They were also charged with making recommendations to prevent future problems in Flint or any other municipality. While the Task Force found serious problems with and made recommendations for local, state, and national levels of government, they laid most of the blame on the doorstep of the Michigan state government. As noted early in the Task Force report:

> The Flint water crisis is a story of governmental failure, intransigence, unpreparedness, delay, inaction and environmental injustice. The Michigan Department of Environmental Quality (MDEQ) failed in its fundamental responsibility to effectively enforce drinking water regulations. The Michigan Department of Health and Human Services (MDHHS) failed to adequately and promptly act to protect public health. Both agencies, but principally the MDEQ, stubbornly worked to discredit and dismiss others' attempts to bring the issues of unsafe water, lead contamination, and increased cases of Legionellosis (Legionnaires' disease) to light. With the City of Flint under emergency management, the Flint Water Department rushed unprepared into fulltime operation of the Flint Water Treatment Plant, drawing water from a highly corrosive source without the use of corrosion control.[19]

The report listed a number of key findings for several departments on both the state and the local level. For example, it found that the MDEQ bore primary responsibility for the contamination of the water in Flint, that it misapplied the federal Lead and Copper Rule (LCR), and that it waited months before bringing in experts to assist with the problem. It also failed to move quickly to examine whether Flint's water was a factor in the increase in Legionellosis cases in the area. In addition, the MDHHS was criticized for a failure to analyze the data on childhood lead in a timely manner. The report also found that the MDHHS failed to coordinate effectively with the MDEQ and inform the public of their findings.

The Task Force also reported that the governor's office relied on incorrect information supplied by the MDEQ and the MDHHS. It noted that the governor ignored complaints and concerns from others for too long, and only began to deal with the problem when the MDEQ and the MDHHS finally recognized the problem. Suggestions that Flint should switch back to the Detroit water system were also set aside (although the city eventually did switch back), because of the concerns over cost. The report said that the governor's office made a mistake in relying on only one or two staffers in one or two departments.

However, the Task Force found that it was Flint's emergency managers who made the set of real decisions to make the switch to Flint River water. Even though there were city council votes on the issue, the decision-making power remained in the hands of the emergency manager because of the state law noted above. The report found that the emergency manager lacked the knowledge to deal with the water crisis, since the EM's expertise was in financial management rather than water policy. Since emergency managers' main goal was to reduce costs to balance the budget, most were reluctant to spend any extra monies on what was reported to be, at first, a minor water issue.

Similarly, the report found that Flint's Department of Public Works was not prepared to run the water treatment plant when the water source was shifted to the Flint River. It found that the city had failed to invest in and upgrade its water system over the years, and that the technologies available at the Flint Water Treatment Plant were inadequate for the problems that occurred with the shift to river water. It further pointed out that the Flint Department of Public Works received inadequate guidance from the MDEQ. Finally, the emergency manager system made it more difficult for residents to be informed of the decisions made during the shift to the Flint River water. The Genesee County Health Department also was criticized for its failure to effectively coordinate information with the MDHHS and city government. In particular, it failed to follow up quickly and effectively when elevated blood levels of lead were found in children, and when increased rates of Legionellosis were discovered.

The EPA was faulted for its failure to effectively exercise its authority in enforcing the LCR. The Task Force also found that the EPA failed to insist on proper corrosion control for the Flint River water, and relied too much on the MDEQ for its information. Other reports charged that the EPA held back on a plan to investigate Flint's cases of Legionnaires' disease, while the state worked out a plan to inform the public.

Despite the failure of government officials at all levels to adequately respond to the crisis, a number of individuals and Flint activists helped bring about awareness of the problem and forced action to deal with the crisis. Dr. Mona Hanna-Attisha, a pediatrician at Flint's Hurley Hospital, first began to notice the rising lead in blood tests she did with Flint's children. After seeing that some levels of lead had doubled in blood samples following the move to Flint River water, she pressed for corrective action from governmental officials, often facing harsh criticism and pressure from hospital officials and others. Another major contribution was made by Marc Edwards, the Virginia Tech engineering professor and expert on public water supplies, who led the research that confirmed the rising lead levels in Flint water. His expertise made him one of the most effective critics of the MDEQ and the EPA. At the federal level, EPA employee Miguel Del Toral was the first to demand that the MDEQ use proper corrosion control to avoid having the lead leach into Flint's water from the system of pipes under the city. Two local Flint mothers also became leading voices on behalf of Flint's residents and children. Lee-Anne Walters, a Flint mother of four, noticed the physical effects of the leaded water on her children and demanded that the EPA and MDEQ take action. Another local activist and Flint mother, Melissa Mays, founder of the nonprofit advocacy group Water You Fighting For?, saw the effects of the Flint water crisis on her family and emerged as one of the major voices of protest and activism as the crisis developed.

In addition to the individuals who led the efforts, a number of citizen groups—some formal, others informal—brought pressure on elected officials and bureaucrats to respond to the water crisis. Two groups in particular led the effort. In the spring of 2015, the Democracy Defense League, which has been primarily formed to oppose the emergency manager in Flint, joined with Water You Fighting For?. The two groups formed the Coalition for Clean Water and were instrumental in bringing Professor Edwards to the city to conduct further tests on the water. The same groups also protested at many public meetings and were among the first to assist in distributing test kits to residents. The Flint Water Advisory Task Force Report specifically noted the positive role that local citizens and activists played in the crisis:

> The Flint water crisis is also a story, however, of something that did work: the critical role played by engaged Flint citizens, by individuals both inside and outside of government who had the expertise and willingness to question and challenge government leadership, and by members of a free press who used the tools that enable investigative journalism. Without their courage and persistence, this crisis likely never would have been brought to light and mitigation efforts never begun.[20]

In addition to citizen activist groups, one of the strongest responses to the water crisis came from private foundations, most notably the C. S. Mott Foundation, that, as noted above, has a long history in the development of Flint. The Mott Foundation provided leadership that brought a number of other foundations together to aid in the crisis. While pledging up to $100 million over five years, the Mott Foundation was joined by the FlintNOW Foundation, the W. K. Kellogg Foundation, the Kresge Foundation, the Carnegie Corporation, the Ford Foundation, the Hagerman Foundation, the Robert Wood Johnson Foundation, the Ruth Mott Foundation, and the Skillman Foundation in bringing resources to help address the crisis and aid the residents of Flint.[21] All collaborated on a variety of programs and projects to deal not only with the immediate impact of the water crisis but the long-term effects on the health and welfare of those living in Flint.

State-Local Government Relations in the Flint Water Crisis

The Flint water crisis is a case study that can be understood better when analyzing the crisis through the four themes of this book, including the final theme of *state-local government relations*. In the case of the Flint water crisis, the nature of state and local relations was largely a story of how the various levels of government *failed* to work together. However, the responsibility for Flint's water crisis also could be claimed by some part of all levels of government—federal, state and local. Certainly the EPA had the first responsibility for implementation of the relevant federal laws, particularly the Safe Drinking Water Act and the Lead and Copper Rule. At the state level, the duty to enforce these rules was generally delegated to the MDEQ. In turn, the actual delivery of the clean water was the responsibility of the Flint Water Treatment Plant and the city government. However, as noted above, during the events that led up to the Flint water crisis, the city was under the direction of a series of emergency managers, whose main job was to cut expenses and balance the city's budget. The story of this crisis has rightfully put the emergency manager law under scrutiny, not only because of the impact on Flint and its residents but because emergency managers have been widely used in Michigan when responding to fiscal challenges.

In the end, all levels of government failed. They failed to enforce the existing laws and rules, they failed to effectively communicate and work with each other. Each level blamed the others for its failure and often tried to discredit those who raised questions about the water issue. While the relations between state and local governments were often contentious, tense, and partisan, some cooperation did develop over time.

Perhaps the best example of this tension is reflected in the changing relations between Flint's mayor, Karen Weaver, and Governor Snyder. When first elected, Mayor Weaver made several overtures to Governor Snyder and he seemed to respond. Flint needed the state's financial help for much of the expected expense in rebuilding the water system in Flint. However, it did not take long for the initial relationship to turn frosty. In the spring of 2016, Mayor Weaver failed to inform the governor of the city's intent to file a lawsuit against the MDEQ. For his part, the governor (and other Republicans in the Legislature) did not appreciate the fact that the mayor was committed to support Hillary Clinton in the 2016 presidential election and made Flint's problems a national issue at the Democratic National Convention. In turn, Mayor Weaver was often left out when the governor developed and announced plans for Flint. For example, she was not part of the development of the governor's 75-point plan for Flint,[22] and was not invited to the initial presentation of the Flint Water Advisory Task Force report. Out of necessity, both sides made moves to heal the breach, but much division remained.[23]

The tension between state and local governments was exacerbated by a series of threatened lawsuits, both civil and criminal, between the two levels of government. By early 2017, Michigan Attorney General Bill Schuette had brought criminal charges against 13 individuals, with the possibility of more in the future. Flint threatened its own suit against the state, and the ACLU also threatened a suit on behalf of private citizens as well.

State Legislative Action in Response to Flint's Challenges

The state Legislature also faced similar conflict and divisions, but was able to reach an agreement to offer assistance to Flint. In October 2016 the Joint Committee on Flint Public Health Emergency released a report recommending several changes. The special committee was composed of six members of the Legislature including four Republicans and two Democrats. Members representing various areas of Michigan in both the state House and state Senate were appointed to the Committee, including Democratic senator Jim Ananich from Flint. The committee chair, Jim Stamas (R–Midland), noted at the outset of the report, "Our primary task was not to find fault or place blame, but rather to identify the means to bring positive change to the people of Michigan and particularly those in Flint."[24] Nonetheless, the committee concluded, in part:

The Flint water crisis spurred nationwide inquiries and calls for positive change. Unlike environmental crises that result from a natural disaster, what happened in Flint in 2014–2015 is the result of human errors and poor decisions made over the course of months by officials and employees at the local, state, and federal levels. This series of bad decisions compounded a growing problem that ultimately proved disastrous.[25]

In addition, the committee made a series of recommendations for overhauling state government in response to the Flint crisis. Importantly, a focus of the recommendations was on Michigan's emergency manager law. The committee recommended replacing the current structure (i.e., one emergency manager) with a three-person panel that would include a financial expert, a local government operations expert, and a local ombudsman. The report also recommended prohibiting an emergency manager from changing a drinking water system in the future; prohibiting cost from being a primary factor in dealing with issues of public health or safety; and making emergency managers liable when they cause harm through gross negligence or misconduct.[26]

Other recommendations were focused on Flint specifically. These included creating a "Flint Toxic Exposure Registry" that would track all children and adults exposed to lead as a result of the crisis, and generating economic development in Flint (including making the city a promise zone like that in Kalamazoo to promote affordable postsecondary education). Other proposals would apply statewide, such as helping residents and communities replace lead water service lines; increasing screening for lead poisoning in public schools; transferring responsibility for safe drinking water from the MDEQ to the MDHHS; increasing Michigan's lead and copper standards beyond current federal requirements; and others.[27]

While the committee did produce a report containing the recommendations above along with many others, the agreement did not come easily. Both Chairman Stamas and Senator Ananich found both agreement and disagreement with the report. Ananich, who also served as Senate minority leader at the time, remarked that the "challenge for this Legislature now is whether we can get results on some of these reforms." He continued,

> I've said all along we need to change the state's emergency manager law and this misguided culture. We need to make public health the top priority when it comes to decision-making, and we need to have long-term solutions for the people in Flint. This isn't exactly how I

would have drafted every item, but there is an opportunity to make some important changes—and now we need to act on them.[28]

Chairman Stamas issued his own statement noting that not all members agreed with all of the proposals included in the report. But he maintained, "My goal has always been to bring positive change to our state and specifically to the families of Flint who have been adversely affected by the water crisis in their community. I do not expect us all to agree on each proposal, but I do expect the work of this committee to generate further legislative action."[29]

In June 2016 the state Legislature, with some partisan division, passed an appropriation of $165 million for the Flint water crisis. In September, the federal government stepped in to offer additional funds. After some partisan disagreement about the proper vehicle for federal aid (amid other negotiations), the Congress approved $170 million for Flint when the U.S. House of Representatives passed this as part of a water projects bill.[30] In the end, the divisions and conflicts between the state and local (and federal) governments reflect a real commitment to deal with a genuine crisis.

Conclusion

In the end, the story of Flint's water crisis was not just a story of one city's tainted pipes. Rather, the story of the Flint water crisis reveals a history of decline and attempts to respond to the many challenges that have confronted similar cities in the United States that have also struggled through the process of deindustrialization that has led to economic decline. There have been many attempts to rebuild the city and formulate effective economic development strategies, but changes in the economy have continued to leave Flint behind. Short-term attempts to fix Flint's long-term problems have not been successful. Some, like the imposition of emergency managers who in turn made decisions for the city, created their own problems through unintended consequences.

The state government in Michigan had a significant hand in the crisis as well. In an effort to save money at the state level, a number of state-funded local programs were cut and a major reduction in revenue sharing money to cities occurred. Flint, like so many former manufacturing centers, experienced a drop in revenues due to population loss and a decrease in property values. At the same time, the city saw increased need and demand for local government services from an increasingly poorer population. The most recent response to challenges in Flint came in the form of state-appointed emergency managers, who contributed to the water crisis with a single-minded goal of reducing local government expenditures and balancing the budget, with less concern about the possible health and safety implications of those decisions to cut expenditures. Finally, agencies in the state government simply dismissed many of the calls for action made by local residents and officials. State-local relations need to improve not only to find a sustainable solution to the water crisis but also to help Flint find a path to economic recovery and growth. In the end, among the most effective responses to the challenges of the Flint water crisis were nongovernmental individuals and average citizens. Their dedication and perseverance raised awareness of the problem and forced governments to finally respond to the crisis.

WEB RESOURCES

AECOM engineering consultants' *Final Report: Flint and Genesee County Comprehensive Economic Development Strategy* (http://www.gc4me.com/business/docs/AECOM_Genesee_County_Final_Full_Report_3_22_2010_1_.pdf) was commissioned by Genesee County and the City of Flint to analyze the region's economic challenges and propose strategies for recovery and growth.

The *City of Flint* webpage (www.cityofflint.com) provides regular updates on the water crisis and steps being taken to improve water quality.

The State of Michigan, Office of Governor Rick Snyder, Flint Water Advisory Task Force, *Final Report,* March 2016 (https://www.michigan.gov/documents/snyder/FWATF_FINAL_REPORT_21March2016_517805_7.pdf) provides an analysis of the causes of the water crisis and make recommendations for future state and local government action.

Water You Fighting For? (www.wateryoufightingfor.com) is a nonprofit advocacy group of citizens organized around water quality in Flint.

NOTES

1. Edwin O. Wood, *History of Genesee County, Michigan, Her People, Industries and Institutions,* chapter 13 (Indianapolis: Federal Publishing Company, 1916); accessed November 21, 2016, https://archive.org/details/historyofgenesee00wood

2. Vivian M. Baulch, and Patricia Zacharias, "Rearview Mirror: The Historic 1936–37 Flint Auto Plant Strikes," *Detroit News,* June 23, 1997.

3. Ron Fonger, "Flint's Population Falls below 100,000 for First Time since the 1920s," *MLive.com,* May 22, 2014; accessed October 22, 2016, www.mlive.com/news/flint/index.ssf/2014/05/flints_population_falls_below.html

4. The Mott Foundation: Annual Report 2015, accessed Nov. 2, 2016, https://www.mott.org/

5. Andrew Highsmith, *Demolition Means Progress: Flint, Michigan and the Fate of the American Metropolis* (Chicago: University of Chicago Press, 2015).

6. Ibid.

7. Ted Roelofs, "Billions More Lost, but Property Value Drop Slowing," *Bridge Magazine*, April 2, 2013; accessed November 21, 2016, http://bridgemi.com/2013/04/billions-more-lost-but-property-value-drop-slowing/

8. "UAW Membership Tops 400,000 for First Time since '08," *USA Today*, March 31, 2015; accessed October 22, 2016, www.usatoday.com/story/money/cars/2015/03/31/uaw-membership

9. Fonger, "Flint's Population Falls below 100,000 for First Time since the 1920s."

10. Eric Scorsone et al. "Flint Fiscal Playbook: An Assessment of the Emergency Manager Years (2011–2015)"; accessed November 20, 2016, http://msue.anr.msu.edu/resources/flint_fiscal_playbook_an_assessment_of_the_emergency_manager_years_2011_201

11. Ibid., 8.

12. AECOM, "Final Report: Flint & Genesee County Comprehensive Economic Development Strategy (CEDS)," March 1, 2010; accessed November 21, 2016, http://www.gc4me.com/business/docs/AECOM_Genesee_County_Final_Full_Report_3_22_2010_1_.pdf

13. Steve Carmody, "Flint Is Looking for the Right Prescription to Cure Its Downtown Woes," Michigan Radio, August 25, 2013; accessed November 21, 2016, http://michiganradio.org/post/flint-looking-right-prescription-cure-its-downtowns-woes

14. Dominic Adams, "A Timeline of State Control over Flint," *MLive.com*, September 11, 2013; accessed November 21, 2016, http://www.mlive.com/news/flint/index.ssf/2013/09/a_look_at_michael_browns_tenur.html

15. It is also worth noting that the rapidly changing leadership of the city and local officials' lack of power, has led to a decline in voter participation. Some of the mayoral and city council elections that took place under EMs produced a voter turnout of just a little over 10 percent.

16. Some excellent analysis and reporting by journalists and many others across the region have generated a number of timelines related to the water crisis. For more detail than can be provided here, see Flint Water Advisory Task Force—Final Report, especially pages 16–21 (https://www.michigan.gov/documents/snyder/FWATF_FINAL_REPORT_21March2016_517805_7.pdf); and *MLive.com*, "Timeline of Flint Water Crisis since Gov. Snyder Took Office"; accessed November 20, 2016, http://www.mlive.com/news/index.ssf/2016/05/timeline_of_the_flint_water_cr.html

17. John Counts, "Flint Water Crisis Got Its Start as a Money-Saving Move in Department of Treasury," *MLive.com*, May 3, 2016; accessed November 21, 2016, http://www.mlive.com/news/index.ssf/2016/05/flint_water_crisis_got_its_sta.html

18. Initially begun with much media attention, the first phase of the program aimed to replace Flint's lead pipes quickly. After seven months only 33 of the 11,300 lead and galvanized steel pipes in the city had been replaced. The progress was slowed by a lack of accurate records about the pipes and a higher than expected cost for the project. By late in the summer of 2016, however, the second phase of the

program was under way and the pipes at more than 200 homes had been replaced. By November 2016 the third phase was initiated with plans to replace the pipes in about 800 homes by the end of that year. For more details, see Chad Livengood, "Flint's 'Fast Start' Plan Replaces Few Faulty Pipelines," *Detroit News*, August 4, 2016; accessed November 4, 2016, http://www.detroitnews.com/story/news/local/michigan/2016/08/04/flints-fast-start-plan-replaces-faulty-pipelines/88050832/

19. Flint Water Advisory Task Force—Final Report, 1.
20. Ibid.
21. Mott Foundation: Annual Report 2015.
22. For more details, see State of Michigan, "Goals to Strengthen Flint"; accessed November 20, 2016, http://www.michigan.gov/documents/snyder/Goals-ToStrengthenFlint_FinalMarch_20_2016_517484_7.pdf; Roberto Acosta, "Gov. Snyder 75-Point Plan for Flint Water Crisis Draws Mixed Reviews," *MLive.com*, March 21, 2016; accessed November 20, 2016, http://www.mlive.com/news/flint/index.ssf/2016/03/state_plans_for_flint_water_cr.html; and Jonathan Oosting, "Snyder Unveils Sweeping Flint Plan," *Detroit News*, March 21, 2016; accessed November 20, 2016, http://www.detroitnews.com/story/news/michigan/flint-water-crisis/2016/03/21/snyder-flint-action-plan/82067424/
23. Zoe Clark and Rick Pluta, "The Complicated Relationship between Gov. Snyder and Flint Mayor Karen Weaver," Michigan Public Radio, April 4, 2016; accessed November 2, 2016, http://michiganradio.org/post/complicated-relationship-between-gov-snyder-and-flint-mayor-karen-weaver
24. Quoted in Paul Egan, "Flint Report: Fix Law on Emergency Managers," *Detroit Free Press*, October 19, 2016; accessed November 20, 2016, http://www.freep.com/story/news/local/michigan/flint-water-crisis/2016/10/19/flint-water-committee-sweeping-changes/92405150/
25. Joint Select Committee on the Flint Water Public Health Emergency, "Report of the Joint Select Committee on the Flint Water Emergency," Michigan Legislature; accessed November 20, 2016, http://media.mlive.com/news_impact/other/Report%20of%20the%20Joint%20Select%20Committee.pdf
26. Ron Fonger, "Flint Water Crisis Proposals Could Overhaul Michigan Emergency Manager System," *MLive.com*, October 19, 2016; accessed November 20, 2016, http://www.mlive.com/news/index.ssf/2016/10/michigan_legislatures_report_c.html; Egan, "Flint report: Fix law on emergency managers."
27. Egan, "Flint Report: Fix Law on Emergency Managers."
28. Quoted in Fonger, "Flint Water Crisis Proposals."
29. Ibid.
30. Mike DeBonis, "Congress Acts to Avert Government Shutdown after Striking Deal on Flint Aid," *Washington Post*, September 28, 2016; accessed November 20, 2016, https://www.washingtonpost.com/news/powerpost/wp/2016/09/28/house-leaders-reach-deal-on-flint-aid-potentially-averting-shutdown/

16 ✦ Conclusion

JOHN S. KLEMANSKI AND DAVID A. DULIO

This examination of Michigan's government, politics, and policy has offered an in-depth analysis of the state's foundational elements, the structure and organization of state and local government, the state's major political actors and processes, and some of the policy outcomes resulting from governmental action. The use of four related themes throughout this volume—*historical context, decline, responses to challenges,* and *state-local government relations*—has provided a useful and consistent framework for each chapter of the book to explore its topics. These themes can help readers better understand specific events and allow for an opportunity to perform an analysis that goes beyond a specific action or time period.

For example, the Flint water crisis became a national and international news story in 2016, which touched not only state and local governments, but came to involve hearings in the U.S. Congress and even a presentation to the United Nations. The Flint water crisis brings together each of this book's four themes in a powerful way. Understanding the water crisis requires an understanding of the city's history. Flint's history is about early growth but also a long economic decline—intimately tied to the fortunes of General Motors. The city had grown throughout the first half of the 20th century, but after World War II, GM first began to leave the city and by the end of the century had largely abandoned Flint. GM's departure greatly impacted Flint and its people (see chapter 15). In fact, the departure of GM led to Michael Moore's film, *Roger and Me*, which chronicled the downsizing of GM facilities in the Flint area and its effects on the city. In 1987, *Money* magazine placed Flint last out of the 300 top places to live in America. In more recent years, Flint has continued to make lists of the "worst places to live" in the United States, largely due to high crime rates, a poor school system, high levels of unemployment, high poverty rates, and deteriorating housing values.[1]

As part of the decline, Flint's city government faced an all-too-common story in older industrial cities in the United States—declining revenues that accompany a declining population, business disinvestment, and a declining tax base. However, at the same time, significant demand for services by those who remained in the city continued. The city government's many financial challenges ultimately led to appointment of an emergency manager by Governor John Engler in 2002. After a break from EM control, several other EMs were appointed between 2011 and 2015.

Even before the Flint water crisis, the issue of a state-appointed emergency manager with extensive decision-making powers had been a controversial one. In effect, an EM renders local elected officials essentially powerless; critics claim that this destroys the democratically elected governments in the areas where EMs are placed. A long-standing emergency manager law (Public Act 72 of 1990) had been in place for over 20 years, but a new law giving EMs even more power (Public Act 4 of 2011) caused such a backlash that the law was put on the ballot as a referendum in 2012. Public Act 4 was repealed by the voters in 2012, but a next-generation EM law (Public Act 436 of 2012) was quickly passed by the Michigan Legislature and signed by Governor Rick Snyder late in 2012.

Partisans on both sides tried to blame the other side for the problems surrounding Flint's water crisis. Some Republicans blamed the federal Environmental Protection Agency and local Flint officials. At the same time, some Democrats blamed Governor Snyder for his appointments to the Michigan Departments of Environmental Quality and Health and Human Services. He was also blamed for failing to act quickly and in a more transparent way, and for the appointed emergency managers in both Flint and Detroit. Also, Detroit was blamed by some for Flint's split from Detroit's water system in the first place as a cost-saving measure for Flint.

But Flint's story is useful also because it underscores a common occurrence related to one theme of this book. Several discussions related to the *responses to challenges* theme involved a story in which the policy response to a challenge itself became a problem. The history of Michigan's public policies is full of attempts to fix a problem, only to have that policy fix become a problem later on. For example, the appointment of an emergency manager was a response to Flint's budget challenges. In attempting to respond to the many budget challenges that the city faced, emergency managers and city officials sought out a cheaper alternative to the increasing costs of participating in the Detroit water system.

Themes of the Book

Historical Context

Each of the book's chapters traces some piece of the historical context surrounding its central topic. For instance, the importance of history can be vividly seen in the chapter devoted to Michigan's Constitution (chapter 2). The evolution of the state's organization and structure of government seen in its four different constitutions sheds considerable light on the increasing complexity of the state as it became a leader in the national economy and grew in population and in the diversity of that population. Chapter 2 also illustrates how the constitutional changes have altered the organization and structure of government, various political processes (including the election of nonpartisan state judges), and the addition of direct democracy provisions in the 1908 Constitution during the height of the Progressive Era. The related discussion on ballot proposals in Michigan (chapter 11) notes how complicated the Michigan Constitution has become due to the lack of a major revision and the relatively large number of constitutional amendments that have been approved by voters since 1963. One could speculate that there will be increased demands for a constitutional convention when the question is next placed on the ballot in 2026, since by then it will have been 63 years since ratification of the most recent Constitution in 1963.

The history of Michigan's court system (chapter 8) also reflects the formal and legal changes that occurred as the state grew in population and complexity. Michigan's courts grew and became more specialized in their respective jurisdictions, but the chapter also notes a more recent decrease in the number of judges as the state sought to decrease spending on its court system.

The historical development of political parties in Michigan (chapter 9) has been important for Michigan politics but also for national politics. Michigan saw an evolution of parties throughout the 1800s, with the emergence of the Democratic Party, then later the Republican Party in the 1850s. Indeed, Jackson, Michigan, professes to have hosted the first meeting of Republicans in 1854. The chapter notes that the history of the two major political parties in Michigan during the modern era has been one of competitiveness generally, although Republicans have tended to dominate state offices since 2010.

History also has helped us understand the rise of cities in Michigan, both urban areas (chapter 4) and small towns and rural areas (chapter 5). The history of industrial cities such as Detroit and Flint reveal a spectacular growth in population and wealth due to the automobile industry, especially during the first half of the 20th century. The history of changes in local governments involves provisions such as home rule, which have given more autonomy to smaller governments that were granted home rule in the 20th century.

Decline

In addition to charting the rise of the state's population and its cities, history also traces the steady decline of these cities. For instance, Michigan's population has not grown as fast as that of other states and even declined between 2000 and 2010; population decline has also played a part in the stories of many Michigan cities and towns (see chapters 1, 4, 5, and 15). This has had major implications for the state beyond those discussed in some of the book's chapters (e.g., declining revenues in chapter 13); for instance, Michigan has lost several congressional seats since the 1970s, one potential result of which is a decreased level of power in the nation's capital.

Of course, the chapter focused on urban governments in Michigan (chapter 4) highlights the theme of decline, especially for the city of Detroit. Several cities (e.g., Detroit, Flint, and Pontiac) had emergency managers placed in them by the governor in order to avoid bankruptcy and turn around their continual budget deficits. Detroit was one of the wealthiest cities in the United States in the early 20th century, but became one of the poorest by 2000. Detroit's decline—in population, business investment, number of jobs, and in household income, as well as other areas—ultimately led to the declaration of bankruptcy by the city government in 2013. Detroit's experience became a cautionary tale about industrialized cities that failed to respond to the many changes in the knowledge-based global economy. However, larger cities in Michigan were not the only areas that faced decline; smaller population communities also faced several challenges related to decline (see chapter 5). In part, small towns and rural areas in the state have witnessed the exodus of their younger adults, who leave their smaller community for job prospects in larger metropolitan areas of the state—or even outside of Michigan entirely.

Economic and urban decline has been intimately tied to the changing fortunes of the automobile industry in the state. Economic decline was such a powerful force that many people left the state at the beginning of the 21st century in order to find jobs in other states. However, not all decline has been economic in nature. It has even extended to the state Legislature (chapter 7). Term limits for elected state officials provides an example of declining power of state legislators compared to the executive branch and to lobbyists. This is also evident in the discussion of state ballot proposals (chapter 11), because term limits were established by a constitutional amendment approved by Michigan voters in a 1992 ballot question. In addition, state ballot proposals have played other roles in responding to decline. For example, there has been a steady number of attempts to place policy questions directly on the ballot over the past 30 years. This suggests at least a potential decline in the power of the traditional policy-making process involving the governor and the state Legislature.

In addition, the state's budget and fiscal policies (chapter 13) have sometimes forced the state to pick winners and losers in the allocation of state funds. Changes in revenue sharing to local governments, for example, have greatly affected the ability of those governments to provide services to their residents. Economic development policy (chapter 14) also reveals an ongoing attempt by the state to respond to declines in business investment in the state, through policies that attempt to recruit new businesses to the state, but also retain those businesses still operating in Michigan.

Responses to Challenges

The third theme of this book has been how the state has responded to various challenges it has faced over the years. As noted, many of these challenges are related to the state's long economic and population decline, but all states must face challenges that could take a political, economic, technical, or social form. Indeed, any challenge that could potentially be addressed through public policy could be a candidate for a policy response.

Larger Michigan cities (chapter 4) have arguably had the most to overcome given the many challenges they have faced over time. As early as the 1950s and 1960s, large cities in Michigan—and in the United States—often faced problems of poverty, unemployment, high crime rates, and economic decline. Early federal programs such as urban renewal attempted to respond to these challenges, but more recent state-level strategies in Michigan cities have included economic development and security programs that intend to decrease crime and economic decline. Some of the cities that were in the worst shape also had EMs imposed on them by the state; the intent was to fix long-term fiscal crises in these cities. In addition, the introduction of functional regionalism, which hopes to solve the problem of political and racial fragmentation in metropolitan areas, was another kind of policy response in areas that were in financial hardship.

A central actor in Michigan's responses to challenges has been the governor (see chapter 6), given that the person in that office often plays an agenda-setting role for state policy and takes leadership responsibilities in attempting to curb economic downturns in the state. Michigan suffered substantially from the Great Recession in the 2000s, but the state's reliance on the automobile industry, beginning in the early 20th century, also meant that its fortunes rose and fell with the auto industry's typical business cycle. In the 1990s, Governor John Engler supported tax cuts for businesses and individuals, reduced welfare rolls, saw the state's unemployment rate fall by the end of the decade, and increased the state's rainy day fund.

During her administration, Governor Jennifer Granholm and the state Legislature attempted to support businesses by championing tax credits for automobile manufacturers in the state. One of the strategies the state encouraged was diversification of the state's economy, especially in high-tech industries and filmmaking. She also pushed for funding the "Cool Cities" initiative, which attempted to attract young and innovative entrepreneurs to selected Michigan cities.

After his election in 2010, Governor Snyder, along with the state Legislature, passed new legislation providing for EMs to be placed in cities in fiscal crisis and nearing bankruptcy. These EMs (see chapters 3, 4, 6, and 15) were given broad powers to cancel city services, renegotiate labor union contracts, and lay off city employees. While earlier governors also had appointed EMs under the old laws, a new law giving even more powers to the EMs was passed. The new law was controversial, and it led to a voter referendum ballot proposal where voters rejected the new law (see chapter 11). However, the Legislature passed and the governor signed a new law after the referendum; the result of this evolution of the law saw EMs retain many of the same broad powers.

The Michigan Legislature's passage of a "right to work" law (see chapter 7) is another example of a policy response to a challenge—and the challenge was largely one of economic decline in the state. Right to work legislation frees workers from being required to join a labor union. Supporters argue the legislation sends a message to business and employers that Michigan is a "business friendly" state—a stark difference from the state's reputation as a heavily unionized state with high wages. Critics, however, are skeptical of the legislation's effectiveness. Regardless of one's opinion of the law, this legislation can be considered a policy response to a challenge facing the state.

Moreover, each of the policy chapters in the volume has provided a number of examples of policy responses to challenges. For example, state education policy (see chapter 12) has changed several times in the recent past in response to either the financial problems of a school district or poor student performance. Most recently, the state has debated how to respond to a previous policy that was itself an attempt to fix public education. Since public education is an important state-level policy area, considerable interest and attention to reforming schools has been of major interest to the governor and the state Legislature. A number of other education-related reforms have been instituted in Michigan to respond to challenges, such as Proposal A in the 1990s, which, among other goals, attempted to equalize funding across public school districts in the state. Still, Michigan continues to struggle to fund public schools and to deliver instruction, especially to students in school districts located in the state's larger cities.

Over time, Michigan has made a number of attempts to reform tax policy in order to encourage business investments in the state, as well as several attempts to close the budget deficit gap—by increasing taxes and fees or by reducing spending in selected areas (see chapter 13). The agreement to expand Medicaid in Michigan, especially with a Republican governor and a Legislature with majorities of Republicans in both chambers, made Michigan somewhat unusual compared to other state governments led by Republicans who were generally very hostile to the expanded Medicaid provisions that came with the Affordable Care Act (also known as Obamacare).

Michigan's economic development policy (see chapter 14) is an obvious and direct arena wherein the state has attempted to respond to economic challenges. States need a tax base and revenue stream that will allow it to provide necessary services, but also a tax policy that attracts businesses and residents to the state. Economic development policies generally take two forms in most states. One, a state can enact policies that attempt to recruit new businesses into the state from another location. Or two, a state can implement policies that seek to retain businesses currently located in the state, with the hope that they will remain.

One of the lessons to be drawn from the responses to challenges theme is that the policy responses that were designed to fix a particular problem sometimes caused their own set of problems. For example, Governor Granholm's attempt to keep businesses in Michigan through long-term tax credits caused a major problem when it was discovered in 2015 that the state would be obligated to pay out billions of dollars over the next 20 years to businesses that were eligible for the tax credits.[2] This constituted a major hit to the state's budget, which will present its own set of challenges for at least two decades.

Governor Snyder's appointment of emergency managers to Flint, and the subsequent Flint water crisis, is another example of a response to a challenge that created its own set of problems. It is perhaps now the most notorious example of a policy that attempted to fix problems but created its own problems that the state will be forced to deal with for decades to come—and in this case, massive problems that caught the attention of people around the world.

State-Local Government Relations

The relationship between a state and its local governments is a multifaceted one. State-local relations touch on legal, economic and fiscal, administrative, and political dimensions. The legal and constitutional relationship between Michigan's state government and its localities is summarized in the state's Constitution (see chapter 2) and various state statutes enacted by the state Legislature (see chapter 7) and governor (see chapter 6). More fundamentally, this relationship is formed through elections (see chapter 10), as that process is what shapes the makeup of government by deciding which candidates will hold elected office at the state and local level for those offices' prescribed terms.

The various dimensions of state-local relations come together in a discussion of intergovernmental relations (see chapter 3). Important for the state aspect of state-local relations, there are both horizontal (i.e., state-to-state interactions) and vertical (i.e., federal-state as well as state-local) dimensions to intergovernmental relations. However, when focusing on a particular state, most of the important interactions are between the state government and its local governments. One of the most important of these dimensions centers on finance. As in other policy areas, over time there have been a number of changes to policies centered on state and local finance, including such changes as revenue sharing, state funding for roads, and policies such as Proposal A, which increased the state sales tax while decreasing the property tax base that funded public schools (see chapters 3 and 13). Also prevalent have been various changes in funding K-12 and higher education in the state, including an examination of the School Aid Fund and the addition of performance budgeting for higher education institutions in Michigan (see chapter 12).

Michigan is a diverse state, not only in its population and politics but also in its mix of local governments. There are fundamental differences in the relationship between the state and large cities (see chapter 4) and the relationship between the state and smaller communities (see chapter 5). State government and local government officials have not always had a great relationship, but in more recent times the crisis of Detroit's bankruptcy brought at least some cooperation between Lansing and Detroit (see chapters 4 and 6). The smaller communities often fought a slightly different battle, where issues of home rule autonomy and state aid to localities have been issues (see chapter 5). However, these issues also center on legal and finance questions, which are often the same concerns that larger cities in Michigan have.

The relationship that Michigan's governors (see chapter 6) have had with the state's cities—especially Detroit—is a mixed one, which includes some surprises. In the 1970s, Republican governor William Milliken and Detroit mayor Coleman Young[3] had a positive working relationship. In some respects, this surprising mutual cooperation and support could not be sustained after Democratic governor Jim Blanchard (1983–91) took office. However, that relationship changed as both Governor Blanchard and Mayor Young left their offices in the early 1990s, to be replaced by Republican governor John Engler and Detroit mayor Dennis Archer, respectively.[4] Mayor Archer took a more cooperative and conciliatory approach to dealing with the city's surrounding suburbs, but the governor's partial takeover of Detroit Public Schools in 1999 was a sore point for many city of Detroit supporters. Somewhat surprising is that partisan politics has not always been able to predict state-local relations. For example, in 2009, it was governor Jennifer Granholm—a Democrat—who first appointed an EM to manage the Detroit Public Schools.

Sound economic development policy requires at least some cooperation between state and local governments. After all, business investment in a state is actually an investment in selected localities. As such, both state and local governments tend to offer their own version of incentives to business, including cheap or cleared land ready for development; improved infrastructure designed to serve a large business operation (e.g., roads, sewers, and power); state and local tax deductions or tax credits; and payments or support to train employees. State public policy support for economic development on behalf of its cities has come in the form of enabling legislation for downtown development authorities, tax increment financing authorities, renaissance zones, among other statutes, which have allowed Michigan local governments to create economic development districts that offer incentives not available outside of those designated districts (see chapter 14).

Final Thoughts

Government, politics, and policy in a state like Michigan are a complex system of actors, processes, and results. There are multiple players who interact with different structures of government (e.g., the Legislature, the executive branch bureaucracy), and political dynamics (e.g., election campaigns, lobbying efforts). Moreover, there are multiple levels of interaction in our federalist system where governments at the federal, state, and local levels all have a role. Certainly everyone in Michigan desires a vibrant economy, a strong educational system, and a government that can solve problems without dysfunction. How these are achieved, however, has become the big question, and this is where many of the challenges are found in the particular democratic system in which American politics operates. The confluence of elected officials, political parties, interest groups, and the public does not always yield optimal results. It is not for a lack of effort, however. All too often, as this book has noted, the solution to one problem may create another once-unforeseen problem in the future.

The state of Michigan has seen a number of important program and policy changes since the late 1970s. From Proposal A to EMs and from the Headlee Amendment to changes in revenue sharing, these policies have emerged from a complex interaction of many different actors in Michigan politics. The lesson in this is that when considering what takes place in Michigan government, politics, and policy, it is wise to consider the many different actors and dynamics that are present and may have some influence in nearly all policy decisions.

One of the major themes of this volume has been the long-term economic decline experienced in Michigan, especially in the state's large cities such as Detroit and Flint. Consequently, other types of decline have been felt in nearly all corners of the state, whether they be economic, budgetary, or in terms of population. It is obvious that Detroit's bankruptcy and Flint's water crisis continued to shine a light on the plight of those cities and their attempts to recover.

However, it should be noted that not all the news in Michigan is bad. While some responses to challenges faced by the state have resulted in other problems, some have, in fact, produced positive results. There will be disagreements over the imposition of an EM in Detroit and the decision to enter bankruptcy. However, postbankruptcy, Detroit is showing signs of a rebound with greater private investment and a more stable fiscal situation. In 2017, *U.S. News and World Report* ranked Detroit 89th out of 100 in its "Best Places to Live" ranking, ahead of cities such as Miami, Memphis, and New Orleans. Grand Rapids appeared even higher on that list, ranking as the 19th best place to live.[5] There are other positive indicators as well. For instance, the business-focused news outlet CNBC rated Michigan as the 7th best state in which to conduct business in 2016.[6] Michigan jumped 15 spots between 2015 and 2016, making it the year's "most improved" state in the ranking. Even more striking is that in 2008, when Michigan was in the grips of the "lost decade," the same ranking had Michigan 40th.[7] While rising to 7th in this ranking by CNBC is a very positive sign, there is still more work to do to create the economically vibrant and successful state residents desire.

Other recent trends also show promise for the state and its future. As illustrated in figures 1.2 through 1.4 in chapter 1, some macro-level indicators are moving in a positive direction. The year-to-year change in gross domestic product has returned to levels last seen at the turn of the 21st century, rather than showing either very small growth or even negative growth. In addition, the number of manufacturing jobs grew after the declines of the Great Recession, while overall unemployment fell during the same time, approaching levels not seen since the mid-1990s.

Michigan has been forced to face serious problems since the end of World War II, many of which directly affect its government, politics, and policy. But there are certainly some bright spots that offer reason for some optimism. It is our hope that future editions of this book can turn away from decline as a theme and instead introduce recovery, growth, and vitality.

WEB RESOURCES

American Black Journal, with host Stephen Henderson, covers issues largely related to Detroit and Michigan's urban areas; it is aired on Detroit Public Television, but can also be accessed online at www.dptv.org

The Ballenger Report (www.theballengerreport.com) provides news, commentary, and podcasts from Bill Ballenger, a longtime observer of Michigan politics and government.

Capitol Report is a public television program broadcast by WCMU; this program covers issues of Michigan government, politics, and policy; the episodes also can be accessed online at video.wcmu.org/show/capitol-report/

Inside Michigan Politics is a weekly newsletter of Michigan state politics and policy, which also can be accessed at www.insidemichiganpolitics.com/

MiWeek, with host Christy McDonald, covers a wide range of issues related to Michigan politics. It is carried by Detroit Public Television, but can also be accessed via the web at www.dptv.org

MLive is an online news source that provides news stories about events occurring in, and affecting, the state of Michigan. *MLive* has operating arrangements with a number of local news sources in various parts of the state, so that there is relatively wide coverage across the state; it can be accessed at www.mlive.com

Off the Record, a weekly public TV program hosted by Tim Skubick, covers state politics and policy each week. WKAR also provides online video of each show at video.wkar.org/show/record

Stateside, with host Cynthia Canty, is a public radio program, but it also streams stories on the web about Michigan politics, government, and public policy issues at michiganradio.org

NOTES

1. Area Vibes, "Top 10 Worst Cities, Worst Places to Live 2013"; accessed November 5, 2016, http://www.areavibes.com/library/top-10-worst-cities-to-live-2013/

2. Chad Livengood, "Michigan Business Tax Credit Liability to Soar to $9.4 B," *Detroit News*, February 19, 2015; accessed November 5, 2016, http://www.detroitnews.com/story/news/politics/michigan/2015/02/18/michigan-business-tax-credit-liability/23614611/

3. Detroit elects its mayors on a nonpartisan ballot (i.e., there are no party affiliations listed). However, Coleman Young, and every other Detroit mayor since the early 1960s, has been a Democrat. Young was a member of the Democratic National Committee, the main Democratic Party organization at the national level.

4. Dennis Archer's Democratic Party connections are also clear as he served as president of the National Conference of Democratic Mayors during his time in office.

5. Brian Manzullo, "Grand Rapids Cracks Top 20 on U.S. News' 'Best Places to Live,'" *Detroit Free Press*, February 7, 2017; accessed February 12, 2017, http://www.freep.com/story/news/local/michigan/2017/02/07/grand-rapids-us-news-best-places-to-live/97600286/

6. CNBC, "America's Top States for Business 2016"; accessed February 4, 2017, http://www.cnbc.com/2016/07/12/americas-top-states-for-business-2016-the-list-and-ranking.html. CNBC's ranking incorporates multiple indicators including measures for factors such as the economy of the state, cost of living, and infrastructure. More details on these measures are available from CNBC.

7. CNBC, "America's Top States for Business 2008"; accessed March 8, 2016, http://www.cnbc.com/americas-top-states-for-business-2008/

Contributors

Joyce Baugh is Professor of Political Science and Public Administration at Central Michigan University where she teaches courses in constitutional law, civil rights and liberties, judicial process, and the civil rights movement. Dr. Baugh is the author of numerous articles, book chapters, and books, including *The Detroit School Busing Case: Milliken v. Bradley and the Controversy over Desegregation* (University Press of Kansas).

Mitch Bean is the former Director of the Michigan House Fiscal Agency, a nonpartisan agency within the Michigan House of Representatives. As part of this role over his 17 years of service, he was one of three voting members of the Michigan Consensus Revenue Estimating Conference which, by law, determines the official economic and revenue forecast that serves as the basis for the state budget. Prior to his appointment as Agency Director, Mitch was the Chief Economist for the Michigan House of Representatives. He has extensive experience in forecasting Michigan's tax revenue, and has produced numerous publications on related topics. In addition, he has been a regular participant in discussions at the Midwest Economic Roundtable, Federal Reserve Bank of Chicago. Mitch is currently a principal at Great Lakes Economic Consulting.

Mark R. Beougher an adjunct professor at Western Michigan University where he teaches courses on judicial politics and serves as coach of the mock trial team. His principal areas of research include immigration courts, administrative law judges, and state and federal courts. He is a practicing attorney who represents indigent defendants in Kalamazoo County.

Timothy Bledsoe is a former member of the Michigan House of Representatives and is currently Professor of Political Science at Wayne State University. He is the author of *Careers in City Politics: The Case for Urban*

Democracy and coauthor of *Urban Reform and Its Consequences: A Study in Representation*. His articles appear in the *American Political Science Review*, the *American Journal of Political Science, American Politics Quarterly, Urban Affairs Review, Policy Studies Journal*, and other journals in the discipline. He teaches courses that include the Legislative Process, State and Local Government, and Urban Politics.

Douglas Carr is Associate Professor of Political Science at Oakland University where he teaches courses that include Government and the Economy, Public Budgeting, and American Public Policy. His research centers on issues related to education policy and environmental policy with a specific focus on the Clean Air Act. He also provided testimony before the Michigan House Appropriations Subcommittee on Higher Education in 2012 on the issue of performance funding measures in higher education.

John A. Clark is Professor and Chair of the Political Science Department at Western Michigan University. He teaches courses on topics such as legislative politics, political behavior, political parties, and elections. His research is in the areas of political parties, elections, and southern politics and has been published by journals and presses including *Political Research Quarterly, Polity, American Politics Research*, the University of Arkansas Press, and Oxford University Press.

David A. Dulio is Professor and Chair of the Political Science Department at Oakland University where he teaches courses on topics including campaigns and elections, Congress, political parties, and interest groups. He has published nine books, including *Campaigns from the Ground Up* (2015), *Cases in Congressional Campaigns: Riding the Wave* (2011), and *For Better or Worse? How Professional Political Consultants Are Changing Elections in the United States* (2004).

Thomas J. Greitens is Associate Professor of Political Science and Public Administration and Director of the Public Administration Program at Central Michigan University. His research centers on several aspects of e-government as well as aspects of local government, program assessment, and public management. He teaches courses including State and Local Government, Administration and Policy in American State Government, Managing Modern Local Government, Public Budgeting and Finance, and many others.

Mark S. Hurwitz is Professor of Political Science at Western Michigan University. He currently is on leave from his faculty position while he serves as Program Officer for the Law and Social Sciences Program at the National Science Foundation. His research, which focuses on judicial politics in state and federal courts, and judicial selection and diversity, has been published in journals including *American Political Science Review*, *Journal of Politics*, *Judicature*, *Justice System Journal*, *Law & Policy*, *Political Research Quarterly*, and *State Politics & Policy Quarterly*, among others. Hurwitz is co-principal investigator on a grant from the National Institute of Justice to fund the WMU Cooley Law School Innocence Project. He is former editor-in-chief of *Justice System Journal*, and he teaches courses in the areas of judicial process and behavior, civil liberties, and constitutional law.

Richard Jelier is Professor of Public Administration and Director of the School of Public, Nonprofit and Health Administration at Grand Valley State University. His research is in planning, economic development, and urban and community affairs. He has published work in the *International Journal of Economic Development*, the *Journal of Public Affairs Education*, *Urban Education*, and the *Urban Review*. He also coauthored *Sustaining Michigan: Metropolitan Policies and Strategies* and *State of Michigan Cities*. He teaches courses in Metropolitan Politics and Administration, Economic and Community Development, Community Analysis, Comparative and International Administration, and Local Politics.

John S. Klemanski is Professor of Political Science at Oakland University. He has published research on Michigan politics and policy in *Economic Development Quarterly*, *Judicature*, *American Review of Politics*, *Michigan Academician*, *Urban Affairs Review*, and *Journal of Urban Affairs*. He also has coauthored Michigan-related books, including *Campaigns from the Ground Up* (2015) and *Power and City Governance* (1999).

Kevin G. Lorentz II is a doctoral student at Wayne State University, specializing in American politics. His research interests include the influence of polarization on the judicial branch, constitutional theory, and term limits.

Robert J. Mahu is a doctoral candidate in the Political Science Department at Wayne State University and a research assistant in the Center for Urban Studies. His research interests include performance measurement and interstate variation in policy implementation. He has coauthored articles and book chapters on economic development, disproportionality monitoring, Detroit politics, and state legislators' representation orientations.

Paul Rozycki has taught in the Political Science Department at Mott Community College since 1969. Prior to that he taught political science at Ball State University. On a regular basis he has been the "Political Pundit" for ABC TV12 as well as NBC 25 in Flint. He had also been a weekly political commentator on a local radio program and is a columnist for the *East Village Magazine* in Flint. He is also the author of *Politics and Government in Michigan* (with Jim Hanley) and the history of Mott Community College "A Clearer Image: The 75 Year History of Mott Community College."

Mitchel A. Sollenberger is Associate Professor of Political Science and Associate Provost for Undergraduate Programs and Integrative Learning at the University of Michigan–Dearborn. He teaches courses including the American Presidency, the American Judicial Process, American Constitutional Law, and others. His recent research has focused on issues involving the presidency, the executive branch, and executive privilege, and has included *The President's Czars: Undermining Congress and the Constitution*, and *The President Shall Nominate: How Congress Trumps Executive Power*.

J. Cherie Strachan is currently Co-Director of the Civic Engagement Division, and Professor of Political Science at Central Michigan University. She is the author of *High-Tech Grassroots: The Professionalization of Local Elections*, as well as numerous articles and book chapters. She teaches courses including Civil Society and Politics, Political Behavior, Women in American Politics, and many others.

James M. Strickland is a doctoral candidate at the University of Michigan–Ann Arbor. His research and teaching interests include lobbying, legislatures, and American state politics.

Dale Thomson is Associate Professor of Political Science at the University of Michigan–Dearborn where he teaches courses including Political Environment of Public Policy, Policy Analysis and Development, Michigan Government, Politics and Policy, Strategic Planning and Needs Assessment, and others. His research centers on areas such as local government management, neighborhood revitalization and community development, and urban policy and politics.

Lyke Thompson is Director of the Center for Urban Studies and Professor of Political Science at Wayne State University. Among other issues, he has studied interlocal arrangements among cities in southeastern Michigan, collaboration arrangements in local and state government, and spatial mismatch of jobs and residential locations. He teaches courses in program evaluation, urban administration, Detroit politics, and Michigan politics.

Logan T. Woods is a doctoral student in the Political Science Department at the University of Michigan–Ann Arbor. His broad fields of interest are American politics and research methods. Specifically, his research and teaching interests include voter roll-off, voter turnout, representation, and political psychology.

❖ Index

Note: Page numbers in italics indicate a reference to a table or figure.

Affordable Care Act (ACA) [2010], 53, 59, 60, 236, 300, 306, 370
AFL-CIO, 161, 320
African Americans
  emergency management law impact on, 93
  in Michigan urban areas, 8, 39, 83–84, 85–86, *87*, 88, 93
  and 2012 and 2016 elections, 240, *240*
  and "urban renewal" efforts, 85–86
  and voting rights, 33, 36–37, 224
agriculture industry, 17, 113, 241, 316, 319, 328, 331, 337, 349
Ambrose, Gerald (Jerry), 352, 353
American Recovery and Reinvestment Act (ARRA) [2009], 54, 55–56, 300
Ananich, Jim, 358, 359–60
Ann Arbor, MI, 82, 97n14, 106, 187–88, 233, *327*
annexation, urban growth and, 78, 79–80, 90, 105, 108
Anspach, Charles L., 41
Anuzis, Saul, 180
appellate courts. *See* court system, Michigan; Supreme Court, Michigan
Archer, Dennis, 88–89, 372, 375n4
authorities, multijurisdictional, 93–95, *95*, 166, 183, 308, 333, 372
automobile industry

  bailout of, 56–58, 136, 236–37, 335, 341n56
  and Big Three market share decline, 294, *295*, 313
  in Detroit, 1, 5, 6–7, 80, 84–85, 91, 367–68
  in Flint, 18, 344–49, 364, 367–68
  and intergovernmental relations, 56–58
  in Lansing, 18, 80
  and labor unions, 14, 15–16
  and manufacturing job loss, 9, 10, *11*, 19, 84, 136, 294–95, 313, 320–21
  and Michigan job growth, 294–95, *296*
  in Pontiac, 18
  UAW and, 14, 15, 16, 58, 320, *327*, 344–46, 347–48
  See also Chrysler; Ford Motor Company; General Motors (GM)

Baker v. Carr (1962), 117n14
Ballard, Charles, 322, 328
Ballenger, Bill, 257
ballot proposals
  and ballot access, 250–57, *251*, 263
  and constitutional amendments, 47–48, 247–49, *247*, 250, 254–57, *255*, 262
  and court intervention, 183, 185, 249, 252, 256, 263

383

ballot proposals (*continued*)
  and direct democracy, 13, 246, 247, 261–62, 263
  financing campaigns for, 258–60
  historical use of, 248–50, *253*, 263
  and referendums, 13, 48, 223, 247, *247*, *251*, 257–58
  and state-local government relations, 260–62, 263
  and statutory initiatives, 13, 246, *247*, 247, 250–254, *251*, *253*, 258, 262–63
Beeler, Jaye, 331
Benton Harbor, MI, 93, 184, 261, 286, 319
Berman, Maxine, 157
"Big Three." *See* Chrysler; Ford Motor Company; General Motors (GM)
Bing, Dave, 92
Bishop, Michael, 137
Blanchard, James, *135*, 234, 235, 316, 323, 372
"blue economy," 14, 17, 113, 337
Bolger, Jase, 138, 164
Bolt v. City of Lansing (1998), 299–300
Brown v. Board of Education (1954), 273
budget process, state, 296–99, 312, 315n2
Buick Motor Company, 344, 347
Bush, George W., 53, 57, 58, 136, 237

Calley, Brian, 226
campaign finance laws, 136, 181–82, 214, 217n10, 227–28
Carnegie Corporation, 357
Cavanagh, Jerome, 88
Charles Stewart Mott Foundation, 346, 357
charter schools, 16, 72, 281–84, 285, 288–89, 308
Charter Township Act (1947), 105–6, 108
charter townships, 80, *101*, 105–6, 108, 109, 111
Chrysler, 18, 19, 56–58, 84, 91, 136, 293, 294, 335
Chrysler, Walter, 320

circuit and district (trial) courts, 171–74, *172*
CIT (Corporate Income Tax), 302
Citizens United v. Federal Election Commission (2010), 181
civil service system, state, 39, 47, 126, 131, 248
Clinton, Hilary, 237, 238, 239, 241, 358
community colleges, 273–74, 276–77, 278, 281–82, 337–38
Consensus Review Estimating Conference (CREC), 296–98, 312, 315n2
constitutional amendments, 47–48, 247–49, *247*, 250, 254–57, *255*, 262
Constitution, Michigan. *See* Michigan Constitution
Constitution, U.S., 8, 37, 52, 59, 188, 209, 224, 225, 229, 230
Cotter, Kevin, 156–57
council-manager system of government, 82, 97n14
county government
  and elections, 225
  in local government organization, 45, 82–83, 100, *101*, 102, 103, 104–5, 117n14
  and multijurisdictional authorities, 94
  and political party organization, 204–6, 218n22
  in state court system, 33–34, 36, 173, 174
  and state tax policy, 109
Court of Appeals, Michigan, 171–72, *172*, 174–75, 182–83, 184, 188–89
court system, Michigan
  and judicial campaigns, 181–82
  judicial independence versus accountability in, 170–71, 181, 182, 185–89
  judicial selection and retention in, 175–82, 186–87, 189, 191n18
  in Michigan Constitution, 33–34, 36, 45, 104, 191n18
  and state-federal relations, 58–60

state-local relations and, 182–83, 184–85, 366
structure of, 171–75, *172*
See also Supreme Court, Michigan
Cox, Mike, 60
Croswell, Charles, 136

Davis, Alton, 180
Dearborn, MI, 82, 83, 347
Declaration of Rights, Michigan Constitution, 33, 43, 151
The Deindustrialization of America (Bluestone; Harrison), 321
Del Toral, Miguel, 352, 356
Democratic Party, Michigan
  and party control, 35, 38, 39–40, 41, 42, 197–99, 215, 366
  and fundraising, 206–7
  and ideological position, 202–4, *203*, 215
  in Michigan electoral history, 134–36, *135*, 199, 202, 206–7, 208, 234–38, 239, 241
  and party identification among voters, 200–202, *201*, 215, 239, 241–42
  and party organization, 204–6, 218n22
  and redistricting, 229–30
Detroit, MI
  auto industry in, 1, 5, 6–7, 80, 84–85, 91, 367–68
  bankruptcy of, 2, 5–8, 65–66, 89, 92, 123, 138, 286, 333, 335–36, 367, 373
  challenges facing, 5, 8, 10–11, 85–88, 90, 92, 94, 99n47
  and Detroit Public Schools, 16, 72–73, 285, 286, 289, 372
  economic decline in, 2, 5–7, 62–63, 65, 84–85, 88–89, 321
  economic development strategies in, 91–92
  emergency management of, 2, 7, 8, 64, 65–66, 92–93, 343, 350, 365
  and Michigan urban expansion, 78, 79–80, 81, 83, 90, 97n2

leadership in, 88–89
political structure in, 81, 82, 97n10, 375n3
racial issues in, 8, 83–84, 85–88, *87*
residential diversity in, 83–84, 86
and state-local relations, 7, 65–66
Detroit Public Schools, 16, 72–73, 285, 286, 289, 372
Detroit Public Schools Community District, 284, 286, 289
Detroit Water and Sewerage Department (DWSD), 2–3, 66, 351, 352
DeVos, Richard "Dick," 228, 258–59
Dillon, Andy, 137, 155, 223, 351
Dillon's Rule, 81, 97n11, 111–12
direct democracy, 13, 39, 152, 223, 242n1, 246, 247, 256, 257, 261–62, 263, 366. *See also* recall elections; referendums; statutory initiatives
district courts. *See* circuit and district (trial) courts
Dodge Brothers, 320
Dolan, Matthew, 24n, 340n24
Duggan, Mike, 6, 93, 233, 336
Dunbar, Willis, 34, 37
Durant, William C., 320, 344

Early, Darnell, 353
economic development policy
  "blue economy in," 14, 17, 113, 337
  in context of federal economic development, 316–19
  and economic diversification efforts, 316, 320, 330, 337–38
  emergency manager law and, 333–34
  and growth industries, 10, 14, 17–18, 100, 113, 303, 328, 330, 331, 332, 337
  in historical context, 319–20
  human infrastructure investments and, 337–38
  infrastructure in, 328–29, 337
  and job growth, 294–96, *296*, 337
  public-private partnership in, 318
  and reduced revenue sharing, 334–35

economic development policy (*continued*)
  and state economic decline, 317, 320–25, 327–33
  state-local relations and, 216, 316, 317, 333–37
  and strategies to address economic challenges, 91–92, 316, 320, 323–25, 327–33, 337
  and tax policy, 317, 321–22, 325, 327–28, 333–34
economic indicators, Michigan, 9–12, *10–13*, 14, 374
Economic Vitality Incentive Program (EVIP), 112, 335
Educational Achievement Authority (EAA), 72–73
Education, Michigan Department of, 56, 128, 270, 272–73, 331
Education, State Board of, 46, 128, *128*, 133, 208, 225, 270, 331
education policy
  and academic performance accountability, 270–71, 272, 273, 278, 279, 280–84, 288–89
  and charter schools, 16, 72, 281–84, 285, 288–89, 308
  decentralized nature of, 269, 270, 273
  federal role in, 272–73, 274–75
  and K-12 funding, 45, 72–73, 269, 274–76, 275, 283, 284–87, 288–89, 297, 302–5
  and K-12 governance structure, 270–73, *271*
  in Michigan Constitution, 42, 45–46, 47, 49, 269
  Michigan Department of Education and, 56, 128, 270, 272–73, 331
  and responses to fiscal crises, 278–79, 283–87, 288–89
  standardized testing and, 270–71
  State Board of Education and, 46, 128, *128*, 133, 208, 225, 270, 331
  See also higher education policy; school districts
Edwards, Mark, 352, 353, 356

Egan, Paul, 146n, 192n, 265n, 266n, 341n, 363n
Eisenger, Peter, 318, 321, 330
election law, state, 136, 204–5, 222, 223–25, 228
elections
  and exit polls, 245n45
  in historical context, 234–36, *235*
  and judicial selection, 175, 176–82, 185–86, 189
  and legislative elections, 152, 153–55, 167n5, 167–68n9, 223, 271
  as nonpartisan, 39, 45, 82, 177, 179, 181, 222–23, 225, 248, 366, 375n3
  and primaries, 39, 41, 93–94, 154–55, 207–8, 217n10, 222, 225–27, 228, 231, 232, 236
  and recall elections, 13, 39, 48, 126, 152, 155, 223, 246, 271
  and redistricting, 154–55, 166, 229–31, 243n19
  rules governing, 208, 225–31
  state-local relations and, 221–22, 223–25
  and state party conventions, 179, 204, 205, 206, 208, 222, 225–26
  types of, 222–23
  and voter turnout, 177, 231–34, *232*, 362n15
  See also ballot proposals
Elementary and Secondary Education Act (ESEA) [1965], 272–73
emergency management as response to fiscal crises
  Detroit and, 2, 7, 8, 64, 65–66, 92–93, 343, 350, 365
  Flint and, 2–3, 4–5, 66, 67, 93, 184, 261, 334, 343–44, 349–50, 353, 360–61, 362n15, 365
  state-local relations and, 2, 7–8, 62, 64–65, 92–93, 183, 184, 261–62, 286–87, 333–34, 365
emergency management (EM) law, 2, 7–8, 64–65, 92–93, 184, 259, 261–62, 316, 333–34, 350, 365
Engler, John
  elections of, 134–35, *135*, 136

emergency management appointments by, 350, 365, 372
Michigan Supreme Court appointments and, 180
and responses to economic challenges, 9, 310, 316, 323–25, 350, 365, 369, 372
and veto power, 129, 130
Environmental Protection Agency (EPA), 3, 4–5, 59, 67, 139, 352, 353, 355, 356–57, 365
Environmental Quality (MDEQ), Michigan Department of
budget cuts to, 331
Flint water crisis and, 3, 4–5, 67, 139–40, 351–53, 354–56, 357, 358, 359, 365
governor-appointed leadership of, *128*
EPA. *See* Environmental Protection Agency (EPA)
Erie Canal, 18, 30, 32, 78–79, 103, 319
Every Student Succeeds Act (ESSA) [2015], 269, 272, 273
executive branch, Michigan
budget responsibilities of, 129–30, 296–97, 299
elected offices of, 36, 44, 125, 133, 225
and intergovernmental relationships, 58–59, 60–61, 372–73
in Michigan Constitution, 33, 34, 36, 44, 46, 125–33, 134, 144n25, 296–97
legislative oversight of, 133–34, 141, 152, 153, 167n8
and reorganization authority of the governor, 126–27, 143n18
structure of, 127–28, *128*, 130–32
and term limits, 123, 134–35, 230, 244n37, 250
See also governor, Michigan office of

Family Educational Rights and Privacy Act (FERPA), 273
federalism. *See* intergovernmental relationships, federalism and

Fino, Susan, 33, 35, 39, 40
fiscal policy
and budget process, 296–99, 312, 315n2
economic development and, 317, 321–22, 325, 327–28, 333–34
and education funding, 45, 72–73, 269, 274–76, 275, 283, 284–87, 288–89, 297, 302–6, 313
and federal funding for Medicaid, 55, 56, 58, 300, 306, 370
and federal revenue sources, 299, 300, *301*, 305, 306
global economic competition and, 313–14
Michigan economy and, 293, 294–96, *295*
and revenue sharing, 110–11, 116, 293–94, 308–10, 313, 334–35, 348
and short- and long-term state debt, 306–8
and state-local relations, 61–62, 333–35
and state revenue growth trends, 303–5
and state revenue sources, 239, 256, 276, 293, 297–98, 299–304, *301*, 305, 307, 310–13, *312*
and state spending trends, 305–6
supply-side approach to, 313, 317–18, 321–22, 324
and tax expenditures, 10, 23, 293, 303, 313
See also Headlee Amendment (1978); Proposal A (1994)
Flint City Council, 2–3, 351, 352
Flint, MI
auto industry in, 4, 18, 344–49, 364–65, 367–68
challenges facing, 4, 85, 87, 89, 348, 364–65
emergency management in, 2–3, 4–5, 66, 67, 93, 184, 261, 334, 343–44, 349–50, 353, 360–61, 362n15, 365
growth and decline of, 4–5, 80, 90–91, 97n7, 321, 343, 344–50, *345*, 360–61, 364–65

Flint, MI (*continued*)
  state-local relationships and, 66–67, 334, 348
  See also Flint water crisis
FlintNOW Foundation, 357
Flint Water Advisory Task Force, 2, 5, 66, 67, 139, 140, 353, 354
Flint water crisis
  chronology of, 351–53
  citizen and foundation response to, 355–57, 361
  decisions leading to, 66–67, 93, 97n9, 139, 140, 184, 343–44, 350, 351–52
  Detroit water system and, 3, 5, 139, 351, 352, 354, 355, 365
  EPA and, 3, 4–5, 139, 352, 353, 355, 356, 357, 365
  "Fast Start" plan to replace lead pipes in, 353, 362–63n18
  federal government response to, 4, 139, 353, 360, 364
  Flint Department of Public Works and, 5, 67, 351, 355, 357
  Flint emergency management structure and, 4–5, 139, 352, 353, 354, 355, 357, 359–61, 365
  Flint River as water source in, 3–4, 66–67, 93, 97n9, 139, 140, 184–85, 351, 352, 355–56
  Flint Water Advisory Task Force report on, 2, 5, 66, 67, 139, 140, 353, 354–56
  in historical context, 2–4, 343, 344–50, 364–65
  and Legionnaires' disease, 4, 66, 67, 353, 354, 355
  MDEQ and, 3, 4–5, 67, 139–40, 351–53, 354–56, 357, 358, 359, 365
  Michigan court system and, 184–85
  Michigan Health and Human Services Department and, 4–5, 67, 354–55, 359, 365
  political partisanship in, 4–5, 358
  Rick Snyder and, 2, 3, 4–5, 66, 67, 139–41, 184–85, 336–37, 352, 353, 354–55, 358, 365, 370–371
  state-local relations and, 66–67, 139–40, 141, 152, 333, 334, 336–37, 343–44, 357–61
Florida, Richard, 113, 114, 324
Fonger, Ron, 361n, 363n
Ford, Henry, 320, 347
Ford Foundation, 6, 357
Ford Motor Company, 18, 56, 57, 84, 293, 320, 347
Fuller, George, 34

"Gateway Amendment," 40–41
GDP, Michigan, 9, *10*, 11, 12, 53, 320, 335, 374
"general law" townships, 105, 108
General Motors (GM)
  and auto industry bailout, 56–58, 136, 335, 341n56
  in Detroit, 85, 91
  in Flint, 4, 344–49, 364–65
  structured bankruptcy of, 294
Genesee County, 345–46, 347, 348–49, 353
Genesee County Health Department (GCHD), 5, 66–67, 355
gerrymandered districts. *See* redistricting
GF/GP (General Fund/General Purpose) revenue, 297, 303–4, 305, 307
Gilbert, Dan, 91
GM. *See* General Motors (GM)
Gore, Al, 243n9
governor, Michigan office of
  appointment powers of, 130–32, 153, 167n8, 179, 180
  budgetary powers of, 129–30, 148–49, 298
  and budget process, 296–99
  checks on power of, 133–34, 141, 153
  Constitutional evolution of, 125–27, 129, 131–32
  executive branch reorganizational authority of, 126–27, 143nn18, 20

and executive branch staff and departments, 127–28, *128*, 130–32
executive orders power of, 132–33, 299
executive privilege and, 132, 133, 140
formal and personal powers of, 127–33, 141, 144nn24, 25, 148–49, 153, 167n8, 179, 180, 298
and gubernatorial elections, 134–36, *135*, 234
legislative process and, 162
and term limits, 123, 134, 244n37, 250, 263
veto power of, 129
See also governors individually by name
Grand Rapids, MI
appellate court in, 174
economic development in, 324, 332, 333, 338, 373
early economic growth in, 18, 79, 80
government structure in, 82, 97n14
population diversity in, 83
race issues in, 86, 98nn24, 28
and reduced state revenue sharing, 334–35
regional transportation authority in, 94
and 2016 presidential election, 237, 238
Granholm, Jennifer
auto industry bailout and, 57, 58
budget disputes and, 130, 137
"Cool Cities" initiative of, 114, 324–25, 340n29, 369
elections of, 134–35, *135*, 228, 234
emergency manager appointments by, 4, 372
Michigan Supreme Court appointment by, 180
and responses to economic challenges, 4, 9–10, 114, 316, 323, 324–25, 331, 369, 370, 372
SmartZones program of, 325, 326–27

and state attorney general challenge to federal authority, 60
state economic decline during tenure of, 21
Gray, Kathy 146n
Gray, Virginia, 210, 213
Great Depression, 79, 316, 320
Great Lakes Water Authority (GLWA), 2, 94, 95, *95*, 99n48, 351
Great Recession
American Reinvestment and Recovery Act and, 54, 55–56, 300
auto industry and, 136, 294–95
and impact on local governments, 49, 70–71, *71*, 89, 112, 136–37, 302
intergovernmental relations and, 53–54, 62, 63
Michigan economy and, 9–13, *10–13*, 14, 21, 53–54, 136–37, 277, 294–95, 296, 347, 369, 374
Greimel, Tim, 141, 164
Gribbs, Roman, 88
Groesbeck, Alexander, 126

Hagerman Foundation, 357
Hamilton, Alexander, 316
Hanna-Attisha, Mona, 352, 355–56
Hannah, John, 41
Hathaway, Diane, 187
Headlee Amendment (1978)
local government impact of, 71–72, 89, 293, 309–10, 349
state-local government relations and, 22, 260–61
tax revenue limits of, 26n38, 46, 47, 49, 70, 89, 111, 255, 260–61, 293, 302, 309–10, 349
Health and Human Services (MDHHS), Michigan Department of, 4–5, 67, 128, *128*, 269, 354, 359, 365
Hedman, Susan, 353
Help America Vote Act (2002), 224
Henderson, Stephen, 374

higher education policy
  community colleges and, 273–74, 276–77, 278, 281–82, 237–38
  decentralized structure of, 273–74
  performance budgeting in, 287–88, 289, 371
  and state funding, 276–77, 277, 287–88, 289, 297, 305–6, 313, 325, 371
Holbrook, Thomas, 233
home rule
  constitutional provision for, 45
  emergency management law interference with, 92–93, 316
  local autonomy granted by, 78, 316, 367, 372
  local governments and, 22, 38, 39, 45, 78, 79, 81, 82, 97n2, 97n13, 104–5, 106, 107, 109, 111–12, 149, 372
Home Rule City Act (1909), 104, 105
House of Representatives, Michigan, 154, 156–58, 159, 161–63, 250
House of Representatives, U.S., 20–21, 20, 31, 32, 154, 204, 226, 229–30, 360
Hubbard, Orville, 88
Hull, William, 124
Hunter, Tupac, 138
"hybrid" democracy, 175, 179, 246, 257, 261–62, 263

Ilitch, Mike, 91
initiatives, ballot. *See* ballot proposals
interest groups and lobbyists
  courting of legislators by, 163
  for-profit versus nonprofit interests of, 211
  increase in, 209–11, *210*, 213–14
  laws governing, 209, 211–13, 214, 218n31, 219n42, 220n56
  legislative term limits and, 157, 158, 159–60, 215, 220nn55–56, 255, 263, 367–68
  policy-making influence of, 197, 208–9, 211, 213–14, 215, 216, 220n55
  and political action committees (PACs), 153–54

spending on, 214, 215
state-local relations and, 197
intergovernmental relations, federalism and
  and Republican leadership, 73
  recent patterns of, 53
  and state-federal relations and federal funding, 53–56, *54, 55*, 56–58, 74
  and state-federal relations and the courts, 58–60

Jackson, Andrew, 30–31, 32, 176
Jacksonian democracy, 30–31, 35, 36, 81, 125
Jackson, MI, 79, 85, 90–91, 198, 234, 366
Jefferson, Thomas, 78, 81, 102
Johnson, Gary, 199–200
Johnson, Lyndon, 235, 272
Joint Committee on Flint Public Health Emergency, 358–60
judicial branch. *See* court system, Michigan; Supreme Court, Michigan

Kalamazoo, MI, 79, 85, 100, 332, 359
Karegnondi Water Authority (KWA), 2–3, 66, 93, 94, *95*, 99n48, 351, 353
Karn, Dan E., 41
Kelley, Frank, 212
Kellogg, W. K., 319
Kelly, Marilyn, 181
Kelly, Mary Beth, 180
Kilpatrick, Kwame, 49, 82, 89, 92
Kincaid v. City of Flint (2015), 184
Kingdon, John, 278
Kobrak, Peter, 235–36
Kresge Foundation, 6, 357
Kuhnke, Carol, 188–89
Kurtz, Ed, 350, 351

labor unions. *See* unions; UAW (United Auto Workers)
Land Ordinance of 1785: 78–79

Lansing, MI
  auto industry and, 18, 80
  constitutional conventions in, 35, 38, 41–42
  and Lansing Regional SmartZone, 326
  local government in, 82, 94, 97n14
  as state government center, 137, 148, 149, 163, 164, 174, 209–11, 213–16
Larsen, Joan, 132
Lawler, Emily, 147n, 193n, 244n
Legislature, Michigan
  and constitutional amendments via legislative referral, 247–48, 247, 256–57, 255
  and elections and recalls, 126, 152, 153–55, 167n5, 167–68n9, 168n13, 223, 246
  executive branch oversight by, 133–34, 141, 152, 153, 167n8
  historical evolution of, 148–49, 167n1
  in legislative process, 161–63
  in Michigan Constitution, 148–49, 152, 167n1
  organization and structure of, 44, 148, 149–52, 153, 156, 167n8
  political party leadership in, 160–61
  powers and responsibilities of, 151–53, 168n13
  redistricting and, 154–55, 166, 229–31, 243n19
  and state budget process, 296–99
  and state-local government relations, 155, 166
  and term limits, 13, 15, 134, 141–42, 149–50, 155–63, 166, 168n19, 215, 230, 243n21, 250, 255, 263, 367–68
  work schedule of, 163
  See also interest groups and lobbyists
Leonard, Tom, 157
Livengood, Chad, 76n, 149n, 243n, 363n, 375n
"Lobby Act" (1978), 213

lobbyists. *See* interest groups and lobbyists
Local Financial Stability and Choice Act (PA436) [2012], 7, 47, 49, 62, 65, 92, 256–57, 261, 286, 334, 350, 365
Local Government and School District Fiscal Accountability Act (PA 4) [2011], 64–65, 261, 334
Local Government Fiscal Responsibility Act (PA 72) [1990], 64
local governments
  and elections, 98n16, 223, 225
  and functional regionalism, 93–95
  Great Recession impact on, 49, 70–71, 71, 89, 112, 136–37, 302
  in historical context, 78–84, 96, 97nn2, 10, 102–6, 117n14
  and home rule, 22, 38, 39, 45, 78, 79, 81, 97nn2, 13, 104–5, 106, 107, 109, 111–12, 149, 372
  in Michigan Constitution, 36, 38, 39, 42, 45–46, 47, 48–49, 97n12, 104, 105, 106, 309–11
  and multijurisdictional authorities, 93–95, *95*, 99n46, 166, 183, 308, 333, 372
  organizational structure of, 45, 75–76n13, 81–83, 97nnn10, 11, 14, 100, *101*, 102, 103, 104–8, *108*, 117n14, 308
  personal property taxes and, 68, 69–70, 110, 262
  revenue raising restrictions on, 109–10, 111, 309–10
  and revenue sharing, 90, 101, 109, 110–11, 112, 115–16, 293–94, 308–11, 313, 334–35, 348
  in rural areas and small towns, 101, 102–9, 109–12, 113–16
  and special district governments, 100, *101*, 308
  state fiscal policy impact on, 63–67, 293–94, 313
  and state-local government relations, 61–67, 67–73, 101–2, 111, 116, 182–83, 184–85

local governments (*continued*)
and urban areas, 78, 79, 81–82, 97nn10, 11, 14, 98n16
See also Headlee Amendment (1978); municipalities; Proposal A (1994); school districts; townships; villages
"lost decade," Michigan's, 14, 21, 136, 277, 296, 374
Lowery, David, 210, 213
Luke, Peter, 146n
Lyon, Lucius, 31–32

Macomb County, 15, 17, 71, 83, 90, 99n46, 233, 238, 239, 241
Maguire, Thomas, 330
Mahtesian, Charles, 321
majority-minority government, 184, 192n73
Management and Budget Act (1984), 296–97
manufacturing jobs, 9, 10, 11–12, *11*, 19, 83, 85–86, 321, 333, 374. *See also* automobile industry
Martin, Tim, 146n, 169n
Mason, Stevens T., 30, 31, 32
Mastin, Phil, 155, 223
May, George, 34, 37
Mays, Melissa, 356
mayor-council system of government, 81, 82
MBT (Michigan Business Tax), 302, 303, 311
McCotter, Thaddeus, 226
McDaniel, Ronna Romney, 244–45n39
McDonald, Christy, 374
MDEQ. *See* Environmental Quality (MDEQ), Michigan Department of
MDHHS. *See* Health and Human Services (MDHHS), Michigan Department of
Medicaid, federal funding for, 55, 56, 58, 300, 306, 370
Meekhof, Arlan, 157
Michigan Campaign Finance Act (1976), 136

Michigan Constitution
—of 1835: 29, 30–34, 35, 36, 37, 42, 43, 81, 103, 117n12, 124–25, 148, 167n1
—of 1850: 29, 35–38, 43, 104, 125–26, 148, 152, 178
—of 1908: 29, 38–40, 41, 43, 45, 81, 104, 105, 126, 130, 248, 366
—of 1963:
Declaration of Rights in, 43
education in, 45–46, 49, 269
elections and voting rights in, 43, 48, 168n13, 229
executive branch in, 33, 34, 36, 44, 46, 125–33, 134, 144n25, 296–97
judicial branch in, 45
key provisions of, 42–48
legislative branch in, 44, 149, 151–52, 153, 156, 167n8, 168n13
local government in, 45, 48–49, 82–83, 106, 109–10
and methods for amending and revising, 47–48, 49, 247–48
and 1961 constitutional convention, 41–42
taxation and finance in, 44, 46–47, 49, 297–98, 306–10, 312, 315n2
See also Headlee Amendment (1978); Proposal A (1994); term limits
Michigan Economic Growth Authority, 302–3, 330
Michigan Educational Assessment Program (MEAP), 270
Michigan Education Association (MEA), 15, 16, 161
Michigan Election Law Act (1954), 116, 224
Michigan Judicial Tenure Commission (MJTC), 186–87
Michigan Medical Marijuana Act (2008), 183, 185, 254
Michigan Municipal League, 97n13, 309, 335
Michigan Renaissance Zone Act (1997), 324
Michigan Student Test of Educational Progress (M-STEP), 270

Michigan Transportation Fund (MTF), 297, 303, 304
Milliken, William, 88, 129, 135, *135*, 137, 249, 372
Mondale, Walter, 15, 235
Moore, Michael, 4, 364
Moroun, Manuel, 258–59, 329
Mott, C. S., 346
municipalities
  and "edge cities," 90
  emergency management law and, 7–8, 64
  and fiscal stress, 62–64, 67–68, 69, 76n15
  home rule and, 104, 105, 106, 107, 109, 111–12, 149
  in local government organization, *101*, 107
  and municipal courts, 36
  state power over, 111–12
  and state revenue sharing, 90
Muskegon, MI, 80, 85

NAFTA (North American Free Trade Agreement), 15, 238, 240
National Voter Registration Act (1993), 13, 224
Nisbet, Stephen S., 42
Nixon, Richard, 53, 140
No Child Left Behind (NCLB) Act (2001), 269, 272, 273
Northwest Ordinance of 1787: 30, 32, 33, 102–3, 108, 124

Obama, Barack
  and auto industry bailout, 57, 58, 237
  and Flint water crisis, 139, 353
  and state challenges to federal authority, 59, 60
  in 2008 and 2012 elections, 236, 239, 241
  See also Affordable Care Act (ACA) [2010]; American Recovery and Reinvestment Act (ARRA) [2009]
"Obamacare." *See* Affordable Care Act (ACA) [2010]
Obergefell v. Hodges (2015), 249, 256

Olds, R. E., 320
Oosting, Jonathan, 24n, 144n, 145n, 146n, 147n, 193n, 220n, 340n, 341n, 363n
Orr, Kevyn, 7, 92–93, 123, 138, 336
Osborn, Chase, 130

partisan v. nonpartisan elections, 176–77, *178–79*
Patient Protection and Affordable Care Act. *See* Affordable Care Act (ACA) [2010]
personal property tax (PPT), 68, 69, 262
Pingree, Hazen, 81
Pluta, Rick, 26n, 363n
political action committees (PACs), 153–54, 161, 181, 218n31, 227
political parties
  and fundraising, 206–7
  and legislative party leadership, 160–61
  in Michigan political history, 197–200, 215, 366
  and minor political parties, 199–200, 217n10, 217n12
  organizational structures of, 204–7, 218n22
  and partisan elections, 176–77
  and partisanship, 202–4, *203*, 215
  and party identification among voters, 200–202, *201*, 215, 239, 241–42
  and primary elections, 207–8, 217n10
  "tripartite" model of, 200–205, 217n13
  See also Democratic Party, Michigan; Republican Party, Michigan
Pollock, James K., 41
Pontiac, MI
  auto industry in, 18
  economic decline in, 1, 10–11, 85, 87, 286, 321, 337, 367
  emergency management in, 93, 184, 261, 367
  redevelopment efforts in, 91

Post, C.W., 319
poverty rates, Michigan, 4, 14, 85, 98n21, 364–65
presidential election outcomes, 2012 and 2016: 15, 199–200, 202, 234–35, 237–41, *240*
Proposal A (1994)
 as constitutional amendment through legislative referral, 46, 47, 255, 256–57
 property tax revenue limits of, 49, 70–72, *71*, 77n36, 255, 275–76, 284, 293, 302, 309, 310–11, 349, 371
 and public education funding, 47, 49, 275–76, 284, 302, 310–11, 370, 371
 and state-local relations, 371
public education. *See* education policy
public employee unions, 15, 16, 138

racial segregation, 83–84, 85–86, 88–89, 273
Reagan Democrats, 15, 241
Reagan, Ronald, 15, 53, 235
recall elections, 13, 39, 48, 126, 152, 155, 223, 246, 271
redistricting, 154–55, 166, 229–31, 243n19
referendums, 13, 48, 223, 247, *247*, 251, 257–58
Republican Party, Michigan
 election party rules and, 226–27
 fiscal policy and, 300, 370
 and fundraising, 206–7
 and ideological position, 202–4, *203*
 and intergovernmental relations, 60, 74
 in Michigan electoral history, 134–36, *135*, 180, 207, 229, 234–36, *235*
 in Michigan political history, 38, 39–40, 41–42, 81–82, 198–99, 215, 226–27, 366
 and partisanship in Flint water crisis, 365

 and party identification among voters, 201–2, *201*, 215, 218n22
 and party organization, 204–6
 and party polarization, 202, 215
 and redistricting, 229–30
 and state challenges to federal authority, 60, 74
 in 2010 elections, 180, 229
 in 2012 and 2016 elections, 199, 202, 206, 207, 236–41
 in 2014 elections, 207
"right-to-work" (RTW) legislation, 15, 16, 159, 163–66, 183, 261–62, 327, 369
Roger and Me (film), 4, 364
Romney, George, 41, 135, 136, 235, 236
Romney, G. Scott, 244–45n39
Romney, Mitt, 236–37, 239, 240–41, *240*
Romney, Ronna, 244–45n39
Roosevelt, Theodore, 39, 81, 199
Ruth Mott Foundation, 357

SAF. *See* School Aid Fund (SAF)
Saginaw, MI, 82, 85, 87, 90, 97n14
Sault Ste. Marie (Soo) Canal, 80, 319
SBT (Single Business Tax), 302, 311
Schauer, Mark, 228
School Aid Fund (SAF), 276, 297, 302, 303, 304, 305
school districts
 constitutional provisions affecting, 42, 45–46, 47, 48–49
 and elections, 225
 emergency management of, 64, 183, 184, 286–87, 289
 enrollment trends in, 284–86, 288
 and funding-related ballot proposals, 263
 federal funding to, 56, 274–75
 Headlee Amendment and, 260, 261
 and intermediate school districts, 271–72, 276, 281–82, 287, 308
 local funding to, 275–76, *275*
 organizational structure of, 270–73, *271*

and Proposal A, 47, 62, 72, 256–57, 261, 275–76, 370
and school choice, 280–83, 284–85, 288–89
state authority over, 269, 270, 283–84, 288–89
state funding to, 62, 69, 72, 260, 274–75, 275, 276, 281, 285–86, 288, 308, 370
and state-local government relations, 62, 183, 184, 370
See also education policy
Schuette, Bill, 60, 133, 141, 353, 358
Scott, Paul, 155, 223
Senate, Michigan, 154, 156, 157, 161–63, 250
Senate, U.S., 57, 131
Serotkin, David, 155, 223
Service Employees International Union, 15
Sigler, Kim, 136, 209, 235
Skillman Foundation, 357
Skubick, Tim, 147n, 243n, 374
SmartZones program, 325, 326–27
Smidt, Corwin, 245n47
Smith, Jacob, 344
Smith, Liane Shekter, 353
Snyder, Rick
  Affordable Care Act and, 300
  Detroit bankruptcy and, 6, 7, 65, 123, 138
  and economic development policy, 323, 334, 335
  elections of, 134–35, 135, 136, 180, 234
  and emergency management, 65, 92, 123, 138, 183, 184–85, 334, 365, 369
  and fiscal policy, 43, 90, 130, 132–33, 137–38, 141, 214, 301, 304, 305, 334, 335
  Flint water crisis and, 2, 3, 4–5, 66, 67, 139–41, 184–85, 336–37, 352, 353, 354–55, 358, 365, 370–71
  Health and Human Services department created by, 128
  state courts and, 132, 184–85, 189

probusiness philosophy of, 189, 236
  Republican Legislature relationship with, 137–38
  and responses to economic decline, 20, 21, 165, 175, 183, 316, 325, 327, 328–29, 330, 331, 335
  right-to-work legislation signed by, 163–66, 183, 261–62, 327
special district governments, 100, *101*, 308
SpeechNOW.org v. FEC (2010), 181
Stamas, Jim, 358, 359, 360
Stanley, Woodrow, 89
State Boundary Commission, 79–80
State Court Administrative Office (SCAO), 175
statehood, Michigan, 29, 30–32, 33, 117n12, 124–25
state party conventions, 179, 204, 205, 206, 208, 222, 225–26
State Transportation Commission, 307–8
statutory initiatives, 13, 246, 247, 247, 250–254, 251, 253, 258, 262–63
Stryker, Jon, 258–59
superPACs, 181–82, 227–28
Supreme Court, Michigan
  in *Bolt v. City of Lansing*, 299–300
  and election campaign spending, 181–82
  in court organizational structure, 45, 171–72, 172, 174–75
  and judicial selection and retention, 33, 36, 125, 178, 179–82, 187, 208, 222, 225–26
  in *Kincaid v. City of Flint*, 184–85
  partisanship of, 154, 179, 180, 181
  redistricting and, 154, 229
  and state-local government relations, 184–85
  and state responses to economic decline, 182–83
  in *Ter Beek v. City of Wyoming*, 185
  and Weaver controversy, 179–81
Supreme Court, U.S., 86, 117n14, 136, 181, 243n19, 249, 252, 256, 273

Swainson, John, 212, 235
Switalski, Jon, 164

TARP (Troubled Asset Relief Program), 57
Taubman, Al, 258–59
tax policy. *See* fiscal policy, state
Ter Beek v. City of Wyoming (2014), 185
term limits
  via constitutional amendment, 215, 250, 255, *255*, 262
  executive branch and, 123, 134–35, 230, 244n37, 250, 263
  legislative impact of, 156–61, 210–11, 220n55, 230–31, 255, 263, 367–68
  for legislators, 13, 15, 134, 141–42, 149–50, 155–63, 166, 168n19, 215, 222nn55, 56, 230–31, 243n21, 250, 255, 367–68
Tisch Independent Citizens Party, 200
"Toledo Strip" dispute, statehood and, 30, 31, 33, 117, 125
tourism industry, 10, 18, 100, 113, 328, 330, 331, 332, 337
townships
  and charter versus general law townships, 80, *101*, 105–6, 108, 109, 111
  and citizen participation, 114, 115
  functional regionalism and, 94
  in historical context, 78–80, 97n2, 102–6, 117n14
  and local elections, 98n16, 223, 225
  in local government structure, 45, 75–76n13, 100, *101*, 106, 107–8, *108*, 116, 308
  and state-local government relations, 73
  state revenue sharing to, 110–11, 116, 308, 348
  and survey townships, 102, 103, 104–5, *108*
TPP (Trans-Pacific Partnership), 238, 240
transportation authorities, regional, 94, 95

trial courts. *See* circuit and district (trial) courts
Trump, Donald, 15, 199, 202, 228, 234, 237–38, 239–41, *240*

UAW (United Auto Workers), 14, 15, 16, 58, 320, 327, 344–46, 347–48
unemployment, 4–5, 8, 9, 10–11, *12*, *12*, 14, 294–96, 320, 322, 337, 364–65, 369, 374
unions, 14, 15–16, 84–85, 164, 165. *See also* AFL-CIO; UAW (United Auto Workers)
universities, state. *See* higher education policy
urban areas, Michigan
  African Americans in, 39, 83–84, 85–86, *87*, 93
  government responses to challenges facing, 91–95, 96
  in historical context, 78–84, 96, 97n2, 97n10
  industrial growth in, 80, 97n7
  leadership in, 88–89
  and perceptions of public safety, 87–88
  population and spatial growth of, 78, 79–80, 90–91, 105, 108
  public services expansion in, 80–81, 97n9
  racial issues in, 85–87, *87*, 98n24
  residential diversity in, 83–84
  structural fiscal crises in, 89–90
  "urban renewal" in, 85–86, 91, 368
  See also local governments
Urban Cooperation Act (1967), 94, 99n46

villages
  and home rule, 38, 39, 97n12, 104–5, 106, 107, 109, 111
  in local government organization, 75–76n13, *101*, 107, 108, *108*
  and state economic decline, 322, 336
  and state-local government relations, 73, 111, 116

state revenue sharing to, 110, 308, 335
taxation powers of, 309–10
Viviano, David, 132
voter registration laws, 13, 231–32
voter turnout, 177, 231–34, 232, 362n15
voting rights, 33, 36–37, 38–39, 43, 224, 231–32

Wade, Joshua, 187–88
Wagoner, Rick, 335
Walling, Dayne, 350, 352
Walsh, John, 138
Walters, Lee-Anne, 356
Wayne County, MI, 64, 83, 90, 99n36, 99n46, 104, 238, 249–50, 287

Weaver, Elizabeth, 179–80
Weaver, Karen, 350, 352, 358
Weinschenk, Aaron, 233
Williams, G. Mennen, 129, 135, 136, 234
Williamson, Don, 89, 350
W. K. Kellogg Foundation, 42, 357
Wong, Ulysses, 188
Woodward, Augustus, 124
World War II, 79, 84, 105, 317, 320, 364, 374
Wurfel, Brad, 139, 352
Wyant, Dan, 4, 139, 352

Young, Coleman, 88–89, 372, 375n3

Zaniewski, Ann, 77n